PHYLLIS SMITH

Bozeman
and the
Gallatin Valley

a history

TWODOT

HELENA, MONTANA

Howie Selke
Alaska Ho 1998

A · TWODOT · BOOK

© 1996 by Phyllis Smith

TwoDot is an imprint of Falcon Press® Publishing Co., Inc.

Printed in Canada.

Library of Congress Cataloging-in-Publication Data
Smith, Phyllis.
      Bozeman and the Gallatin Valley : a history / by Phyllis Smith.
          p.   cm.
      ISBN 1-56044-540-8 (softcover)
      1. Gallatin Valley (Wyo. and Mont.)—History.   2. Bozeman (Mont.)—
History.   I. Title.
F737.G2S65   1996
978.6'662—dc21   96-36881
                                                                          CIP

You can order extra copies of this book and get information and prices for other TwoDot books by writing to Falcon Press, P.O. Box 1718, Helena, MT 59624, or by calling 1-800-582-2665. Also, please ask for a free copy of our current catalog listing all Falcon Press books. Our e-mail address is: falconbk@ix.netcom.com.

To Merrill G. Burlingame,

who helped generations of those curious

about Montana history

with kindness and congeniality

CONTENTS

ACKNOWLEDGMENTS

Our ability to record history is dependent first upon those who long ago kept diaries and journals, or wrote letters back home: Lady Isabelle Randall's observations on the brief but colorful British presence in the Gallatin Valley; Charles D. Loughrey's diaries detailing his day-to-day struggles to make a living here and his desire to become a good photographer; Joseph Kenney's and his brother-in-law Thomas Rhoten's letters back to Iowa, which reflected their difficulties in securing work in the region; Emily Meredith's notes to her family in Minnesota; the journals of William White Alderson and Walter Cooper; Davis Willson's reports to the *Montana Post*.

I also am indebted to the massive notes and research papers of historian Merrill G. Burlingame, the stories of Malcolm Story, Polly Renne, and Marguerite Pruitt Fulker. I listened with pleasure to Laurence Christie, Ray Atteberry, Phyllis Wolcott, Charles Crouse, William Merrick, Ray and Shirlie White, Lou Ann and Vernon Westlake, Gene Brooks, Grace Bates, Phill Forbes, Don Nell, Esther Nelson, Helen E. Fechter, Eleanor Buzalsky, Don Langohr, Jr., Mary Kay Peck, Mary Jane DiSanti, William Fairhurst, and Dorothy Eck.

Librarians are the greatest boon to the historical writer: Marge David, Deborah Nash, Elaine Peterson, and Kim Alan Scott from the Merrill G. Burlingame Special Collections at the Renne Library, Montana State University; Dave Walter at the Montana Historical Society; and the research librarians at the Bozeman Public Library are all due thanks.

Fellow writers Jenna Caplette and Stan West listened to rough first drafts every two weeks for two years. Dennis Seibel, Ursula Smith, and Linda Peavy encouraged me to continue with the project. My husband Gene Smith is a master in finding inconsistencies in geography, knocking out split infinitives, and adjusting comma fault. The photographs in the book are from the archives of the Gallatin County Historical Society, unless otherwise noted. Photographer Richard Harrison shares my love of old black and white images and made copy prints for this work. I am also indebted to Rick Newby, Erin Turner, and Noelle Sullivan for their professional support and cordiality. My gratitude goes to all of them. ▨

chapter

O N E

Sometimes out of the corner of my eye I see an earlier Gallatin Valley. Looking up at the irregular gray cliffs that line the Madison River at the county's western edge, I catch a glimpse of mounted Blackfeet horsemen silently studying the valley for sign of game or some of their many enemies. I turn back to watch Captain Meriwether Lewis scramble up a bluff overlooking the three forks of the Missouri River to determine which stream his expedition should follow on its way west to the Pacific. I imagine a naked John Colter on the run from his pursuers, his feet bloody from prickly pear cacti.

Coming down the Bridger Canyon road on a moonlit night, I fancy I hear sleigh bells and laughter from an earlier excursion through the mountains. I find ovens for coking coal in the mountains east of the valley. I see the tall timbers of the coal washers that once stood above them. I hear the accented voices of Eastern European miners as they come off their shifts, joking and calling to one another.

Driving near Gallatin Gateway, I watch the 1909 electric car arriving at the Salesville station; long-skirted women with magnificently flowered hats step down from the train after a day of shopping in Bozeman. In downtown Bozeman itself, I walk down Main Street, taking care not to stumble as I look up to the tops of the older buildings, where

Alonzo Dwight cuts hay at Springhill.

remnants of old facades bear dates and names of pioneer merchants.

This is the story of those who traveled through or, later, settled in the Gallatin Valley region in successive migrations for perhaps as far back as thirty thousand years. Some visits were fleeting: certain groups came to hunt, then moved on; others came to take away what was valuable; travelers crossed the valley on their way to other places. Some families established camps and settlements as if they meant to stay.

The Blackfeet looked upon this valley as one of their prime hunting grounds and were not happy

*Miners pose for a 1904 portrait in front of the North Western Improvement Coal Company
coal washer on Trail Creek Road near the little settlement at Storrs.*

with those they regarded as intruders entering the area—Crow, Flathead, or Shoshone hunters, European explorers, adventurers, fur trappers, American settlers. The Blackfeet vigorously fought to keep these interlopers out of what they regarded as their territory. The resulting bloody skirmishes belied the often-stated description of the region as a "valley of the flowers," peaceful and idyllic.

After Lewis and Clark traversed the area, however, the Blackfeet found it more and more difficult to police the territory. Soon, fur trappers and adventurers cautiously moved through the area, with a watchful eye for Blackfeet sign. Catholic priests, European noblemen, artists, and curious naturalists followed.

Discovery of gold southwest of the Gallatin Valley in the mid-1860s led to serious settlement a few years later by farmers, ranchers, blacksmiths, and merchants, all eager to start a new life on the high plains and just as eager to supply the booming gold camps with agricultural produce and mining supplies. Add to this cultural mix men on the run from military service during the Civil War, both northerner and southerner, Democrat and Republican, Mason and Catholic, law-abiding and outlaw. They were soon followed by railroad men, Indian fighters from the military, bankers, coal miners, barley malters, pea canners, lumbermen, and the ever-present real estate promoters.

The new businessmen and farmers, hoping to attract capital and sales for their various enterprises, produced pamphlets proclaiming the Gallatin Valley "The Egypt of America." Speculator John Bozeman predicted it would become the "Garden of Montana."[1] Often quoted is the story of traveler Colonel Robert G. Ingersoll who, upon reaching the crest of Bozeman Pass where he saw fields of brilliant green and gold, asked his stagecoach driver, "What is that, sir?"

"That is the Gallatin Valley," answered the

Interurban Car No. 10 is about to roll out of the Salesville Depot, 1909. Apollo "Paul" Busch is the conductor.

Four Bozeman ladies all dressed up for a special occasion.

Ten women from the Huffine and Brock families enjoy an outing.

Bozeman's Sangerfest members mug for the camera. BOTTOM ROW, LEFT TO RIGHT: *William Nuber, Herman Relle, William C. Glawe, Augustus Henke, H. Rice.* MIDDLE ROW: *Fred Happel, Charles Papke, Wilhelm Stuve, John G. Fechter.* BACK: *first-Henry Lehrkind; last-Joe Feltsheim.*

Bozeman Free Silver Kids' Band, 1890s. STANDING, LEFT TO RIGHT: *Harry H. Howard, Will Simons, O. Perry Chisholm, Jr., Charles Morris, Carl Spieth, Robert Chisholm, Claude Dairs, Louis H. Howard, director.*
SITTING: *Edwin E. Howard, Walter Story, T. Byron Story*

driver, proudly.

"Ah," mused Ingersoll, "it is a dimple on the fair cheek of Nature."[2]

As in other parts of Montana and the West, some people came to prey on others; to rob, exploit, and destroy what they regarded as their private colony; to get rich, and then get out. Some new settlers flourished and some did not, driven away by unexpected frigid winters, lack of water, changes in fashion, collapse of markets, and adjustments in technology. Many who thought they were here to stay were forced to leave for opportunities elsewhere. The beaver men never intended to stay. Would-be gold-seekers from the States came "to see the elephant," a then-common expression meaning "to see the world and gain experience of its sin and glitter, generally at some cost to the investigator."[3] Satisfied or not, they went back home to farm again.

Early Blackfeet visitors did not have such choices; they died in tragic numbers from successive smallpox epidemics.

Most Chinese laborers stayed in the valley just long enough to build the railroad; as elsewhere in the West, they were strongly encouraged to leave once the job was completed. British horse breeders came to raise thoroughbreds but did not reckon with the violent winter of 1886-1887; they left, leaving little trace of their residence. Men from England, Wales, and Eastern Europe came to mine coal; few stayed after the mines closed. Just after the turn of the last century, families looking for cheap farming land tried tilling unclaimed parcels with meager soil and water resources; they, too, were forced to leave the area. John Wesley Powell, early director of the U.S. Geological Survey, predicted this would happen, but few listened to his warning.

Third grade youngsters on their best behavior at Bozeman's Longfellow School, c1905.

5

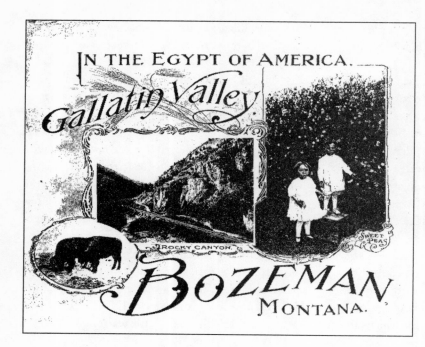

Pamphlet advertising the charms of the Gallatin Valley, 1905.

Families from the Netherlands moved in to grow barley for malters near the new little town of Manhattan; they settled together in a tightly knit society that flourishes today. Adding to the cultural mix, a small but exuberant German community formed in Bozeman in the 1880s and 1890s; they became saloon-keepers, brewers, and merchants; their love of robust songs led to the formation of bands, choral groups, and a symphony orchestra.

Settling in a remote area off any previously beaten western track, Bozeman and Gallatin Valley residents hustled to make a living, grabbing at any opportunity that would assure them a stable economy. They welcomed federal money with the establishment of military Fort Ellis and Yellowstone National Park. They fought for a railroad line through the valley, and sold goods to nearby Indian reservations and military forts. They tried for the brass ring of a state capital but settled for a land-grant college instead.

New migrations in the late twentieth century caused the Gallatin Valley and surrounding region to grow in population while much of the state, especially its eastern counties, lost people. Many of these newcomers brought their businesses with them by way of computers. Or they became fishing and hunting guides, leaving a hectic way of life behind. Some found other ways to serve an expanding tourist industry. Others did not reckon with the weather or the limited job market, and drifted out of the Gallatin Valley soon after they arrived.

In our valley today, the ubiquitous real estate developer is still on hand, building homes for the retired or second residences for those who can afford respite from urban life elsewhere. Some promoters, for reasons best left to themselves, call the Gallatin Valley the future "Athens of America" or "Aspen of Montana." Others regard the area as their private colony and are viewed by older residents with disdain and distrust that is similar to that expressed by the Blackfeet in an earlier day. 🔳

chapter

T W O

One hundred million years ago, the Gallatin Valley was part of a flat plain covered by an immense but shallow inland sea that periodically rose and fell. Dinosaurs fed upon its tropical vegetation, which decayed and compressed in such quantities that coal deposits formed at the eastern edge of the valley. Fossil trilobites (the animal lifeform with the first well-defined backbone), estimated to be 550 million years old, can be found in the arid Horseshoe Hills north of the valley. Other fossil imprints of ancient sea life lie in Bridger Canyon.

At the time of mountain building, some sixty million years ago, immense areas of molten rock began to push upwards, breaking through the level sea plain, gradually forming some of the peaks evident today. This thrust moved from south to north, tilting the Gallatin Valley to the north and west. The volcanic dust and the glacial activity that followed left behind a rich, slightly askew alluvial fan of soil, twenty-four miles long and from five to fifteen miles wide, with an average elevation of 4,700 feet. This rich valley floor comprises about thirty percent of the land within present Gallatin County boundaries.

To the west, the valley is separated from the narrow, longer Madison Valley by horizontal ancient lakebeds. Beyond the Madison Valley, farther west,

lies the Jefferson Valley, separated by low benchlands. West of the county line, the Tobacco Root Mountains loom. These were named for a plant native to the area used by impoverished miners there as a substitute for tobacco.

As the Missouri River flows north, away from the Gallatin Valley, it twists and bends past sparsely grassed hills that take their name from the river's Horseshoe Bend—the Horseshoe Hills.[1] These arid, south-facing lands do not support the lush forests of the nearby Gallatins; rather, small, widely spaced bushes struggle for survival.

The rest of the county is a jumbled near-circle of mountains, called by the Shoshone people To yabe-shockup, or "mountainous country." The disordered peaks, thrust up and scattered as by some giant force, rise between the more aligned Rocky Mountain Front near Glacier National Park and the Middle Rockies of Wyoming and Colorado. The Bridger Range lies northeast of the valley, its twenty-five miles of peaks tilted to the east—Baldy, Bridger, Sacajawea, Hardscrabble, Ross—forming a mosaic of fault blocks. Its forested ridges lead to rounded and bare peaks resembling the backs of running Indian ponies. Mountain man Jim Bridger spent some of his later years guiding westering settlers through these mountains.

South of the Bridgers and directly east of

The Horseshoe Hills roll north of the valley.

Rivers and mountains of the Gallatin area.

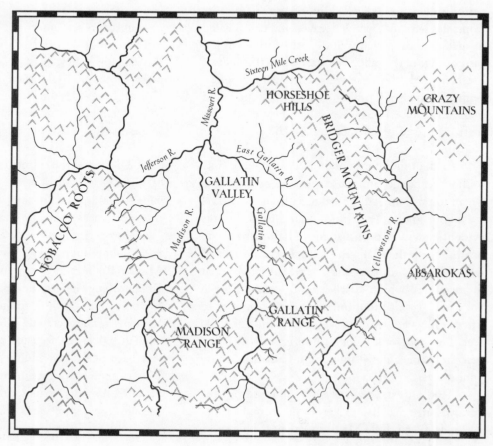

The Spanish Peaks rise south of the Gallatin Valley.
ALBERT SCHLECHTEN PHOTO.

Bozeman is the 5,760-foot mountain saddle now called Bozeman Hill or Bozeman Pass, earlier called Yellowstone Pass. Modern travelers do not cross this place with bare bloody feet as did John Colter on the run from the Blackfeet, but winter storms still make Bozeman Pass a treacherous crossing.

To the southeast, rolling hills forested with Douglas-fir and Colorado juniper give rise to the Gallatin Range; Hyalite Peak and Mount Blackmore stand watch over the valley. More peaks continue a swing along the southern edge of the valley to the deep cut of Gallatin Canyon. West of the canyon, a series of irregular benchlands leads to the Madison Range, tilted to the southwest and highlighted by the higher and more rugged Spanish Peaks: Wilson Peak is 10,700 feet high; Gallatin Peak rises to 11,015 feet above sea level. How the peaks came to be called "Spanish" gives rise to an image of early prospectors traveling north from Spanish-held lands in the Southwest, looking for gold, a romantic but unsubstantiated folktale. The true origin of the name is still unknown. To the south, Lone Mountain oversees all at 11,166 feet.

Three rivers dominate the area, although many smaller streams race down from the surrounding mountains. The Gallatin River was named for a man who never saw it. When the Lewis and Clark Corps

Albert Gallatin, Secretary of the Treasury under President Thomas Jefferson, never visited the valley named to honor him by explorers Lewis and Clark.
COURTESY LIBRARY OF CONGRESS.

9

of Discovery arrived at the three forks of the Missouri River in the summer of 1805, the captains decided that the smaller but more swift of the three rivers, the eastern tine of the fork, should be named for Albert Gallatin, then Secretary of the U.S. Treasury. (Others had named this stream earlier; for example, the Shoshone called the river Cut-tuh-o-gwa, or "swift water.")

The broader and somewhat slower stream, forming the center tine of the fork, they named for Secretary of State James Madison. The even larger river to the west, which runs inside the present county line for a short distance, they named for the man who sent them on their way west, President Thomas Jefferson. The names for these rivers have survived, but many of the creeks, mountains, and hills that the explorers christened have since been renamed by others. For example, Howard's Creek, named by the captains for expedition member Thomas P. Howard, is now Sixteenmile Creek. The leaders named one Jefferson River tributary the "Philosopyhe River"; it is now known as Willow Creek.[2]

The climate of this country has been characterized as semi-arid, an extension of Great Plains weather patterns, at times intensely cold and at times intensely hot. This, in practical terms, means

Thomas Jefferson planned for an expedition to explore the West long before he became president.
OIL PORTRAIT (1791) BY JAMES WILLSON PEALE, COURTESY INDEPENDENCE NATIONAL HISTORICAL PARK.

Headwaters of the Missouri River. A. E. MATHEWS LITHOGRAPH.

In 1908, the East Gallatin was filled with beaver dams. ALBERT SCHLECHTEN PHOTO.

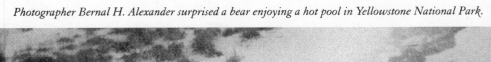

Photographer Bernal H. Alexander surprised a bear enjoying a hot pool in Yellowstone National Park.

that local farmers and stockmen have never known whether or not it is going to rain. In the eastern part of the valley, eighteen inches of rain or snow might fall in a season, most of the rain in May and June. The Three Forks area to the west, however, usually receives far less annual precipitation, often as little as ten inches. On the average, one hundred days per year are frost-free. The native grasses are shorter and more sparse to the west, but ranchmen, to their surprise, have found them to be most nutritious for stock. Concludes historian Thomas R. Wessel, "All who have lived in the plains area and felt its hostility and occasional benevolence develop a wary affection for its ruggedness and a respect for those who struggled to release its bounty."[3]

Historian Hiram Chittenden painted a dismal picture of the Three Forks region when he wrote in 1902 that the area had always been "limited" and the soil "sterile on account of the alkali washed down from the higher sections . . . it seems as if nature had ordained that this meeting place of the sources of the world's longest river should remain unchanged by the hand of man." Chittenden further suggested that perhaps the area was forever doomed because it was the "immemorial fighting ground of hostile tribes." But, he concluded, the streams there produced "the best trapping ground on the continent."[4]

Some Montana winters are open and mild. The resulting lack of moisture gives the dryland farmer special meaning to the term "semi-arid." A good many Gallatin Valley winters, however, are long and fierce. A sudden chinook wind can eat up heavy snows within days, even hours. During most years, the captured spring runoff from mountain streams provides water for irrigation and domestic use during the usual rainless summers. When winter snowpack is meager, water becomes scarce. Geologist John Wesley Powell was right when he warned high plains residents that the conventional water distribution methods employed in the eastern part of the United States would not be useful in the West.[5]

Today, thousands of years after the retreat of the last glaciers, long after the disappearance of the dinosaur, the mastodon, and the woolly mammoth, visitors from all parts of the globe thrill at the sight of elk grazing, pronghorns or deer feeding, grizzly or black bears hunting for huckleberries, or mountain goats and bighorn sheep standing like statues along the high reaches of the mountains. If tourists are lucky, they may glimpse a mountain lion on the prowl. Though the valley is not within an established bird flyway, birders may watch a golden eagle drift lazily above on an air current, or observe a group of pelicans wheeling in unison, their black-tipped wings sharp in the sun, or listen to the chattering magpies scolding anyone or anything that displeases them. Anglers from around the world come to match wits with this region's wild trout. Other outdoors enthusiasts come to ski, bike, climb, or hike.

After a spring rain, the pungent smell of sage (a plant important to western Indians) is strong. The valley is lined with a variety of grasses, wild bergamot or horsemint, salsify, sticky geranium, balsamroot, lupines, yellow-blossomed potentilla, and, along the streams, cottonwood, willow, chokecherry, service-berry, and dogwood. Before irrigation ditches, silver sagebrush, bluebunch fescues, and wheat grasses were evident here. Despite fears that her British husband was going broke with his horse-breeding experiment, Lady Isabelle Randall was enchanted with the wildflowers that sprang up from the valley's apparent arid and lifeless ground. The area, she wrote, was "covered with flowers; pink and white ox-eyed daisies in tiny round bunches, growing quite close to the ground . . . yellow flowers called prickly pear, really a sort of cactus, small pansies, lenten lilies, and many others. The air is literally scented with them all."[6]

Indeed, Lady Randall might well have agreed with the characterization of this area as the "valley of the flowers." The Blackfeet saw the valley in a harsher light, naming the area "the place of the thorns," an interesting twist of observation.[7]

chapter

T H R E E

The first migration through the Gallatin Valley may have occurred more than thirty thousand years ago after small groups of hunters from Asia tentatively crossed a fifty-six-mile-long land bridge to this hemisphere, now underwater as the Bering Strait. As these early travelers tracked mastodon, caribou, mammoth, and giant bison with wide-spreading horns, they may have watched small horses and camels traveling in the opposite direction to Asia. They passed along grassy corridors through towering glaciers and filtered slowly down the eastern face of the Rockies along what is sometimes called the Old North Trail. They seldom went into the mountains to hunt because the remaining glaciers blocked their passage. They avoided the high plains as well because they felt vulnerable without forest cover.

This migration may well have ranged east to the Atlantic seaboard and south to Tierra del Fuego, the southern tip of South America. Anthropologist H. M. Wormington warned, however, against seeing too much in

glib statements pertaining to migration into the New World [which] often convey an impression of masses of people moving swiftly across the Strait and marching briskly down the continent in search of a pleasanter climate or in pursuit of

animals that were rushing south. This is probably far different from the true picture. People dependent on hunting and food gathering cannot move together in large numbers. Furthermore, to the primitive the unknown and the unseen are strange and terrifying, and primitive man does not willingly depart from known familiar things to face the unknown.[1]

About twelve thousand years ago, more small groups of hunters ventured across the land bridge, assured of plentiful game and clear water during the summer months, even though glaciers were still building and moving in the surrounding mountains.

The weather patterns of the Gallatin Valley gradually changed about five thousand years ago, however, resulting in a desertlike region. Large game animals no longer flourished in the area. Existing plants and trees died out to be replaced by those that required less water. This drought persisted for at least two thousand years. From the southwest ventured people who were used to such conditions. They foraged for plants and snared such small animals that survived the dry period.

When the Gallatin Valley again returned to a more moderate climate some four thousand years ago, the land adjusted as well. Some of the big game animals returned, and with them came people who

13

lived as hunters, not as foragers and cultivators.

Below the bluffs along the Madison River, opposite the mouth of Cherry Creek, these early people left behind evidence of a village—some one hundred circles of boulders scattered up and down the benchland, marking temporary lodges. Later collectors picked up points, chips, pieces of knives of basalt, and, more rarely, jasper and obsidian, at this site. Other early camps ring the valley as well, most notably in Kelly Canyon in the Bridgers.

A bluff on the west side of the Madison River, high on a hill, features a ceremonial site, an arrangement of rocks, seventeen feet long, forming an effigy with bent upright arms and a prominent phallus. Some anthropologists suggest that the stones were placed there some six hundred years ago to memorialize the spot where an esteemed warrior fell. Others say it is a stone representation of Napi,

a mischievous Blackfeet god, though this is more unlikely since the Blackfeet were not in the area until the late 1700s. Such effigy figures are scarce, but can be found elsewhere on the northern plains as far east as Minnesota. Archaeologist Carling Malouf said the Madison River effigy "is one of the finest in existence."[2]

For possibly four thousand years or more, these early Gallatin Valley people utilized the steep cliffs generally associated with high plains country to force grazing bison to run to their death over the drop. Many of these buffalo jumps, or *pishkuns*, a Blackfeet term, have been studied (as well as pillaged) in Montana, southern Canada, and as far east as the Dakotas. One of the largest of these archaeological meccas is the Madison Buffalo Jump, seven miles south of Logan, facing west to the Madison River.

Lest we assume that bison, sleek and fat from

On May 30, 1956, the stones outlining some one hundred lodge sites on the west side of the Madison River received a whitewash by a group of archeological enthusiasts from the Montana Institute of the Arts. A few days later, historian Merrill G. Burlingame packed his camera into Louis True's biplane and off they flew to photograph the boulders from the air.

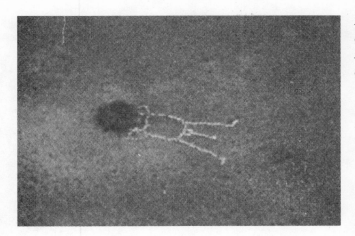

A stone effigy stretches seventeen feet atop a high hill overlooking the west side of the Madison River, one of several such arrangements found on the northern plains of the United States and southern Canada.

eating summer grasses, obligingly jumped off the cliffs along the Madison to provide meat for the winter, we should understand that this method of providing food, clothing, and tools was complicated and totally absorbed the energies of everyone in the hunters' band. Indian groups trained specialists to direct religious ceremonies held before the drive. Fleet runners located bison herds grazing as far away as twenty-five or thirty miles. Others had the job of exciting the bison, forcing them to thunder toward a narrow stone-lined path ending at the cliff. Some of these drovers hid under bison robes near the stone

Before they acquired the horse, which enabled them to ride after their game on the plains, Indians used the Madison Buffalo Jump to trap bison.

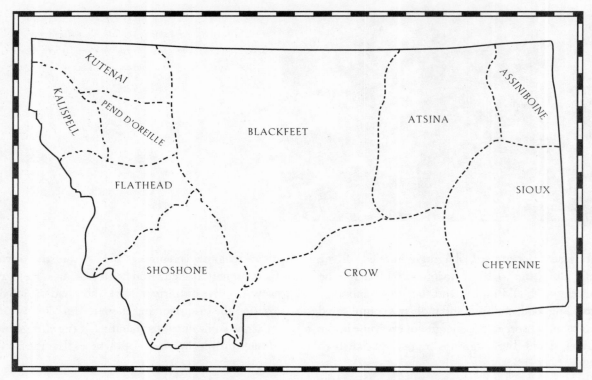

Indian groups in Montana at the time of the Lewis and Clark Expedition.

driveways, then leaped up and further frightened the running beasts on their way to a cliff-bottom death.

The first precipice at the Madison Jump is thirty feet down, followed by a rolling drop of another two hundred feet. Those few animals still alive after suffering the ordeal of the drop died by bow-and-arrow down below. Postmortem workers, usually women, skinned and prepared the animals for winter meals. Left behind at the base of the Madison cliffs were knives, scrapers, small points, animal bones, flakes, and chips, waiting for the modern anthropologist (or vandal). Taking historic materials from the Logan site is illegal today.

It seems certain that many early groups of people, both foragers and hunters, regularly traveled through the Gallatin Valley in search of food. These early parties moved across the flatlands along well-worn natural highways. At the time of European settlement, these pathways still gave evidence of the earlier traffic. Peter Koch observed a well-defined trail from the Three Forks area leading to the Gallatin Canyon. From that trail, he wrote, another "traverses the valley in an easterly course, striking

almost a bee line for the Bozeman pass and across to the great bend of the Yellowstone. It crosses the streams by the best fords, ascends and descends table-lands and mountains by the most favorable ridges and ravines. Across stony bottoms it is barely discernible, but conspicuous and deeply worn on the loose, porous soil of the prairie."[3]

By the time of the Lewis and Clark expedition in 1805, however, most of the travelers had been in or near the Gallatin Valley a relatively short time. The pressures of English and French activity to the north and American expansion from the east forced, in turn, the movement of Indian groups south and west. In addition, Spanish settlement in the distant southwest pushed native peoples north.

There is some indication that Kiowa bands from the south roamed here for a time, only to be forced back again by other hunters. Groups of plateau Indians, including the Flathead (Salish), Nez Perce, Kutenai, and Pend Oreille, came from the northwest in the 1500s and 1600s to visit the valley in search of game, staying for a time in the Three Forks area.

From the east, around 1620, ventured Crow

hunters, a Siouan group, who, after splitting from the more eastern Hidatsa, regarded their former Sioux kinsmen as enemies. They called themselves Absaroke, or the "children of the large-beaked bird." Often friendly to incoming whites, some Crow men would later scout for U.S. military groups moving west.

Occasionally the Tukudika, or Tukuarika, a timid people who lived in the Yellowstone Park area, slipped into the valley to hunt. The proper name for these former Yellowstone residents is seldom used because the group has been tagged with the somewhat denigrating name, "Sheepeaters." At about the same time, the related Shoshone, also called Snakes, moved out of the mountains to the west and roamed the valley and beyond in search of bison. At some point, they saw the "elk dog" or horse for the first time in a neighboring encampment of Ute people. The Shoshones stole a few horses to try their hand at riding them. The Utes had stolen them from tribes farther to the southwest, who had taken them from the Spanish. The horse culture probably

Crow lodge. RICHARD THROSSEL PHOTO. COURTESY ANNETTE EVANS.

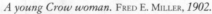

A young Crow woman. FRED E. MILLER, *1902.*

spread into Canada and to other Plains Indian groups in much the same way.

The enduring custom of stealing horses was incomprehensible to later white settlers, who believed that stealing a horse was a heinous crime, punishable by instant hanging. But, as Wallace Stegner observes in his book *Wolf Willow,* "Plains Indians generally regarded the theft of a horse from someone outside the tribe the way Americans regard the theft of home base."[4]

As more Plains people acquired the horse and gained the skill to hunt from its back, they also acquired a new confidence and pride. As they felt good about themselves, they became more belligerent toward one another. Shoshone hunters and warriors forced the Flathead and other plateau tribes to return to the western mountains; Shoshone horsemen controlled use of the Gallatin Valley until the arrival of an even more fierce adversary.

Although no clear-cut legend describing early Blackfeet movement has passed down to modern tribal members, the Algonquin ancestors of the Blackfeet probably migrated west from Canadian

A summer shelter for wandering Sheepeater Indians, this wickiup was in a sheltered stand of trees above Gallatin Canyon.
HELEN E. FECHTER PHOTO, 1956.

forests north of the Great Lakes region. By the 1720s, however, three Blackfeet groups were moving about in western Canada, each with a separate social organization: the Kainah or Blood, the Siksika, and the Pikuni or Piegan (a name meaning "poorly made robes"). Ten years later, Piegan hunters ventured south into the Montana area.

As Blackfeet groups moved south, Shoshone hunters retreated west and south to the mountains, preferring to keep out of the Blackfeet's range. The Flathead, Nez Perce, Kutenai, and Pend Oreille still visited the valley from time to time in search of game, making certain that they, too, were not trapped by a Blackfeet hunting party. Much later, from the north, Assiniboine and Cree occasionally came south to look for bison, keeping watch for Blackfeet sign. The Atsina, or Gros Ventre of the Prairie, hunted

near the three forks in the company of the Blackfeet; these friends also fought together against both Indian and European incursion. (Gros Ventre, which means "Big Bellies" in French, is a misnomer; historians Michael Malone, Richard Roeder, and William Lang have noted these men "had ordinary stomachs."[5]) The Crow also continued to hunt in the valley, on the lookout for the notorious Blackfeet.

Members of the Blackfeet Nation became particularly adept in the management of horses; within an amazingly short period of time, they were regarded as expert horsemen. Life on the plains was never the same again. No longer did hunting groups hug the eastern face of the Rockies or seek shelter in forested areas to the east. A life on the high plains near the buffalo was possible now. With the addition of guns acquired from French and British

Blackfeet move through a storm. ROLAND REED PHOTO, 1911. COURTESY ANNETTE EVANS.

adventurers to the north, the Northern Plains Indians, Blackfeet warriors especially, were formidable.

In 1650, before they acquired the horse, Indian peoples roaming the high plains numbered an estimated 50,000; by 1780, with bison more readily available as a source of food, the Indian population soared to 100,000. The Blackfeet tribes themselves rose to 15,000, becoming the most numerous of the Great Plains people despite the first serious outbreak of smallpox in 1780 (a "gift" from Europeans to the north). Although the Blackfeet were dominant in Montana by 1800, the various Indian tribes moving here and there formed, as Malone, Roeder, and Lang described it, the "eye of a cultural hurricane," hunting and fighting across the land.[6]

When Meriwether Lewis and William Clark made their preparations for the Corps of Discovery, they knew little of the Indians on horseback they would soon encounter. But Indian groups, in and out of the Gallatin Valley, knew quite a bit about the approach of the white explorers. The legends of many western tribes describe the eventual coming of a non-Indian people who would subdue and destroy them. Indian travelers from the north and east told western friends of the approach of pale-skinned adventurers. Historian Walter Fleming summed up in a few words Indian sentiment with regard to a European invasion: "We knew you were coming."[7]

chapter

F O U R

Although some Indian groups continued to favor the Gallatin Valley as prime ground for hunting and fighting, others claimed the area, along with most lands west of the Mississippi River. Few of these early landlords came to visit the property, however.

In 1682, France assumed ownership of the region up to the Continental Divide (though the French were not certain just where the divide was) and called the land Louisiana in honor of King Louis XIV. Sometime before 1742, a French fur trader with the imposing name of Pierre Gaultier de Varennes, Sieur de la Verendryé, who operated a post north of Lake Winnipeg, explored the northern Louisiana area, getting as far as what are now the Dakotas. Age and ill health forced him to return home before he had learned much. He sent his sons François and Louis-Joseph back south from Canada in 1742;

20

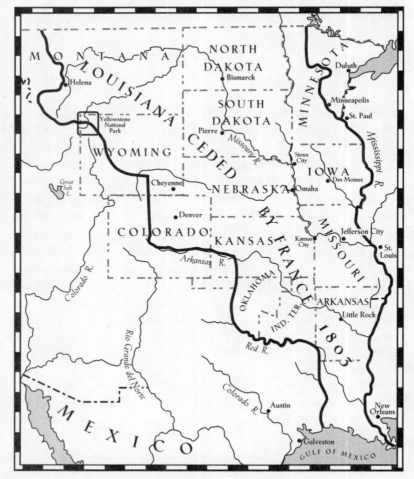

Louisiana Purchase, 1803.

Meriwether Lewis, 1774-1809.
OIL PORTRAIT (1807) BY CHARLES WILLSON PEALE,
COURTESY INDEPENDENCE NATIONAL
HISTORICAL PARK.

they may have wandered through the Black Hills or possibly got a look at what is now eastern Montana. The romantic notion that the Verendryé brothers ascended the Missouri River to its source persists, but there is no evidence they visited the Gallatin Valley.

Twenty years later, in 1763, France ceded Louisiana to Spain, which claimed the land for thirty-seven years as a buffer between British activity in Canada and Spanish settlements in the Southwest. Then, in October 1800, agents for Napoleon took back Louisiana under the terms of the Treaty of San Ildefonso.

Adventurers may have traveled about the territory during these years. No known diary or record gives evidence of any Frenchman or Spaniard moving about the Gallatin Valley before 1800.

Perhaps a few fur traders from the northeast ventured to the area, but seldom did any of these early wanderers commit their observations to paper or map—perhaps because, as historian Robert Athearn said, they were "an uncommunicative lot and had no precise information about what they had seen."[1]

Despite French ownership of vast Louisiana, Thomas Jefferson, even before he became president in 1801, quietly began to plan for an American expedition to the Far West. As president, he secured $2,500 from Congress to finance an overland trip of exploration to the Pacific Ocean, although he did not advertise the appropriation widely. At the same time, Jefferson sent diplomatic feelers to Paris for a possible $2 million land purchase of the Florida region and the land surrounding New Orleans.

William Clark, 1770-1838.
OIL PORTRAIT (1810) BY CHARLES WILLSON PEALE,
COURTESY INDEPENDENCE NATIONAL
HISTORICAL PARK.

Neither Jefferson nor his associates dreamed that Napoleon would be open to American purchase of Louisiana itself for $15 million. The French leader had suffered sufficient military losses in the New World to determine that he could not explore or exploit Louisiana for French benefit. The real estate deal was struck on April 30, 1803, but it was not until July that President Jefferson learned that "his representatives had bought not only a city, but a whole wilderness empire. . . . In retrospect, it was a transaction of daring proportions and of considerable significance. At the stroke of a pen, about one third of modern America was attached to the young nation . . ."[2] Thus, the United States bought "the world's largest pasture, considerable mineral rights, one major and several minor rivers—all in good working order—and the best-known desert in the

Western Hemisphere."[3]

Jefferson appointed his personal secretary, Virginian Meriwether Lewis, to lead what the president called a Corps of Discovery to explore the newly acquired territory and seek the elusive Northwest Passage to the Pacific Ocean. At Lewis's suggestion, the president then named as co-leader William Clark, another Virginian, whose older brother George Rogers Clark had been a hero in the Revolutionary War. The twenty-nine-year-old Lewis received a captain's rank; thirty-three-year-old Clark became a second lieutenant with a promise that he too would become a captain. A cantankerous U.S. Congress and an equally cantankerous War Department balked at making Clark's higher rank official. Nevertheless, the two men regarded one another as military equals, as did the party of twenty-six regular army men. Clark's black slave York, two French voyageurs, interpreter George Drouillard (sometimes written Drewyer), and Lewis's dog, a Newfoundland named Seaman, completed the group.[4] Members of the Corps, who had been carefully selected by Lewis, were "good hunters, stout, healthy unmarried men, accustomed to the woods and capable of bearing bodily fatigue in a pretty considerable degree."[5]

The two leaders complemented one another, both in their different personalities and the skills they brought to the enterprise. Lewis was lean; Clark was heavyset. Both were tall men, over six feet, and in good physical condition, although Clark was plagued by occasional digestive complaints. Lewis was better educated; Clark learned from the school of experience. Lewis needed long periods of solitude and was inclined to be introspective. He was somewhat formal, even a bit pompous with the men, although he could be charming enough at the Washington soirées Jefferson asked him to attend. Red-haired Clark was a hearty open fellow, genial with the men.

Lewis was meticulous and precise; Clark was expansive and imaginative (witness his prowess as a master misspeller). Lewis planned the route; Clark drew the maps to show where they had been. Lewis collected plants and animals, made extensive notes on their appearance, and packed them away so that the president could study them later in Washington. Clark collected medicines and doctored the men when needed, although most remained healthy. (The expedition lost only one man, Charles Floyd, who probably died of a ruptured appendix as the group neared the present site of Sioux City, Iowa.) It was appropriate that Clark was in charge of such potions as Dr. Benjamin Rush's Thunderbolt pills because he often doctored himself for one ailment or another. Lewis was temperamental; Clark was sanguine and more comfortable in negotiations with Indian groups. Lewis usually went ahead, investigating the choice of route. Clark often stayed with the boats and saw to their maintenance.

Toward the last of May 1804, after a winter of drill, the assembling of equipment, and the packing of a fifty-foot-long keelboat and two pirogues, the group left Saint Louis to ascend the Missouri, as William Clark reported in his creative spelling,

"under a jentle brease."[6] After hauling the keelboat and pirogues upstream for a grueling distance of sixteen hundred miles, the group arrived in late October at the Mandan villages twenty miles north of present-day Bismarck, North Dakota. There they stopped for the winter.

During their cold weather stay, Lewis and Clark found out what they could about the journey ahead. They learned of a great falls upstream and of the three forks, sources of the Missouri. They also learned of a large tributary that their informants told them was called "the river which scolds all others," and wondered whether this waterway might give passage to the Pacific Ocean.

They discovered that Clark's servant York greatly interested the Indian groups they encountered, since none had seen a man with black skin before. Indian women rubbed his arms and cheeks, tried to peer down his trousers, and pressed him for sexual services to such an extent that he often complained of fatigue.

The captains hired a French interpreter, Toussaint Charbonneau, who brought along his wife Sacagawea, a young woman who had been forcibly taken from her Shoshone band by the Hidatsa (Minataree) some years before. Sacagawea's baby boy, Jean Baptiste, was two months old. Charbonneau turned out to possess less skills than the leaders had hoped, but Sacagawea recognized landmarks and provided information about possible routes when the party reached the Three Forks area. Before they set off again on April 7, 1805, from the Mandan villages, the captains sent the keelboat back to Saint Louis, along with two men expelled for disciplinary reasons.

Now the party traveled in the two pirogues, an additional six canoes, or on foot beside the river. They passed the "river which scolds all others," but not before Lewis determined that the swollen stream, now called the Milk River, was not the miracle passageway to the Pacific, despite contrary advice from the men. The meticulous Lewis studied the creekbeds of both the Milk and the Missouri, observing that the Missouri had more stones that might be seen in a waterway that had its source in the mountains.

By the time the expedition arrived at the Great Falls on July 9, its members had seen their first elk,

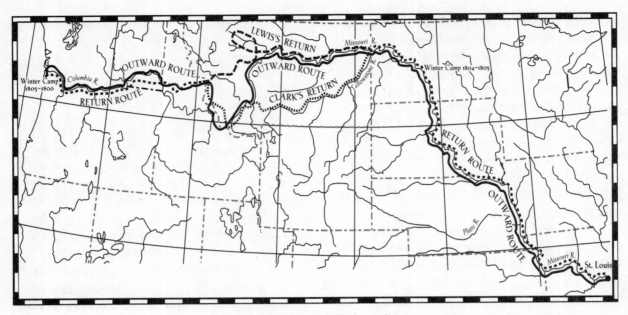

Route of the Lewis and Clark expedition.

bison, and grizzly bear. They had been bitten by their first western "musquetores." (The pesky mosquito was spelled nineteen different ways in William Clark's journals.) Lewis, no champion speller himself, reported the "musquetoes extreemly troublesome to me today nor is a large knat less troublesome, which dose not sting, but attacks the eye in swarms and compells us to brush them off or have our eyes filled with them."[7] They also had learned the backbreaking job of portaging their goods around rapids and through increasingly swift streams with numerous channels. They were surprised at the height and spread of the mountains, some still covered with late-summer snow.

On July 22, Lewis wrote: "The Indian woman recognizes the country and assures us that this is the river on which her relations live, and that the three forks are at no great distance. this peice of information has cheered the sperits of the party who now begin to console themselves with the anticipation of shortly seeing the head of the missouri yet unknown to the civlzed world."[8] Sacagawea recognized the chalky cliffs where her people gathered white powder to paint their faces and their horses. Lewis and Clark hoped they would soon meet her relatives, or any Shoshone band with sufficient horses to trade for the overland trip to the Snake River and along the Columbia drainage to

the Pacific Ocean. Lewis ordered "canoes to hoist their small flags in order that should the indians see us they might discover that we are not Indians, nor their enemies . . ."[9]

William Clark reached the Three Forks first. He went ahead with Robert Frazier, brothers Joseph and Reuben Fields, and Charbonneau, arriving at the forks of the Missouri on July 25. The men's feet were in terrible shape from stepping on the thorns of prickly pear cactus. Despite their discomfort, Clark reported in his journal that it had been "a fine morning":

> we proceeded on a fiew miles to the three forks of the Missouri those three forks are nearly of a Size, the North fork [Jefferson] appears to have the most water and must be Considered as the one best calculated for us to assend Middle fork [Madison] is quit as large about 90 yds wide. The South fork [Gallatin] is about 70 yds wide & falls in about 400 yards below the midle fork those forks appear to be very rapid & Contain Some timber in their bottoms which is verry extincive.[10]

He took note of burned areas to the north: "the Indians have latterly Set the Praries on fire, the Cause I can't account for." He spied the track of one lone horse, also the sign of many elk, beaver, and otter.[11]

After a breakfast of venison, Clark left a note for Lewis and took his party up what he called the north fork of the Missouri. He left two men whose feet were the most painful (one was Charbonneau) and climbed to the top of a mountain, but found no Indian sign. On the way down, hot and thirsty, he drank from a cold spring and, almost immediately, he reported later, became ill. Even so, the tough captain hiked cross-country from the Jefferson to the Madison. At some point, the hapless Charbonneau fell into some water and Clark was obliged to fish him out.

Lewis and the others arrived at the Three Forks two days later, July 27. Always the naturalist, Lewis noted the intense blue color of the broken limestone cliffs and a number of bighorn sheep. As he reached the mouth of what he called the southeast fork, the Gallatin, he wrote in his journal:

> . . . the country opens suddonly to extensive and beatifull plains and meadows which appear to be surrounded in every direction with distant and lofty mountains; supposing this to be the three forks of the Missouri I halted the party on the Lard. shore for breakfast. and walked up the S.E. fork about a mile and ascended the point of a high limestone clift from whence I commanded a most perfect view of the neighbouring country. From this point I could see the S.E. fork about 7 miles. it is rapid and about 70 Yards wide. throughout the distance I saw it, it passes through a smoth extensive green meadow of fine grass . . .[12]

In order to give the men a rest and to wait for Clark's return to the spot where he had left the note, Lewis halted the party. While the company aired and dried their goods, Lewis made notes of the probable latitude and longitude of the area.

Sure enough, Clark returned, but with a high fever. He took to a brush shelter with chills. Lewis suggested a dosage of Dr. Rush's Thunderbolt pills. Taking advantage of Clark's indisposition, the men made new moccasins, shirts, and leggings from deerskin, and tended to their aching feet.

On Sunday, July 28, Lewis and the ailing Clark made some decisions. Lewis wrote:

> Both Capt. C. and myself corrisponded in opinion with rispect to the impropriety of calling either of these streams the Missouri and accordingly agreed to name them after the President of the United States and the Secretaries of the Treasury and state having previously named one river in honour of the Secretaries of War and Navy. In pursuance of this resolution we called the S.W. fork, that we meant to ascend, Jefferson's River in honor of that illustrious personage Thomas Jefferson, the author of our enterprise, the Middle fork we called Madison's River in honor of James Madison, and the S.E. Fork we called Gallitin's River in honor of Albert Gallitin. the two first are 90 yards wide and the last is 70 yards, all of them run with great valocity and thow out large bodies of water. Gallitin's River is reather more rapid than either of the others, is not quite as deep but from all appearances may be navigated to a considerable distance. Capt. C. who came down Madison's river yesterday and has also seen Jefferson's some distance thinks Madison's reather the most rapid, but it is not as much so by any means as Gallitin's. the beds of all these streams are formed of smooth pebble and gravel, and their waters perfectly transparent; in short, they are three noble streams. there is timber enough here to support an establishment, provided it be erected with brick or stone either of which would be much cheaper than wood as all the materials for such a work are immediately at the spot.[13]

Lewis also noted in his journal that

> Our present Camp is precisely on the spot that the Snake Indians were encamped at the time the Minnetares of the Knife R. first came in sight of them five years since, from hence they retreated about three miles up Jeffersons river and concealed themselves in the woods, the Minnetares pursued, attacked them, killed 4 men 4 women a number of boys, and mad prisoners of all the females and four boys, Sah-cah-gar-we-ah or Indian woman was one of the female prisoners taken at that time; tho' I cannot discover that she shews any immotion of sorrow in recollecting this event, or of joy in being restored to her native country; if she has enough to eat and a few trinkets to wear I believe she would be perfectly content anywhere."[14]

By Monday, July 29, Clark had recovered, and

he and Lewis agreed that the Jefferson River was surely the way to the mountains where the expedition might meet Sacagawea's people, the Shoshone, and secure horses for the overland trip to the Columbia Basin. They traveled up the Jefferson for a week but, by August 8, Lewis determined that to follow the waterway farther would not be productive. He left Clark to nurse his now-ulcerated feet and, taking Drouillard, Shields, and McNeal, climbed the Beaverhead Mountains to cross the Continental Divide at Lemhi Pass. Here they saw some Indians, but they slipped away from the explorer and disappeared.

Finally, the four men were able to convince a small band of Indians through sign that they should go with the party to the place where Clark and the rest of the expedition were camped. They would receive gifts, they would see with their own eyes a man with black skin, and they would be reunited with a woman from their band. With utmost caution they came, following their chief Cameahwait. Sacagawea, upon seeing members of the band approach, "began to dance and show every mark of the most extravagant joy, turning . . . and pointing to several Indians . . . sucking her fingers at the same time to indicate they were of her native tribe."[15] When she recognized chief Cameahwait as her brother, she "ran and embraced him, throwing over him her blanket and weeping profusely. The chief was himself moved, though not in the same degree."[16] The man to whom Sacagawea was promised in her infancy was part of the chief's band and, although he claimed she was his wife by right, he did not want her since she had had a child by another.

The expedition traded for Shoshone horses and "proceeded on," as both Lewis and Clark said repeatedly in their journals, to travel over Lolo Pass and then downstream to the Pacific Ocean before winter set in, an arduous and sometimes frightening trek. Thomas Jefferson's Corps of Discovery had completed the first half of one of the most amazing expeditions in the New World, lauded and studied two hundred years later.

The party started back toward the States on March 23, 1806. William Clark was the only captain to return to the Gallatin Valley the following summer. Meriwether Lewis took his group through the Missoula Valley and east toward the Great Falls of the Missouri, bound for the mouth of the Yellowstone. Sergeant Nathaniel Pryor was charged with bringing horses through the mountains to the Three Forks. Clark, Sergeant John Ordway, and a few other men took a wild canoe ride down the still-swollen Jefferson River, traveling ninety-seven miles the first day, quite a different experience from the arduous pulling of canoes upstream the year before. On Sunday, July 12, all met at the Three Forks, including Pryor and the horses, and the group was again divided.

Ordway and ten of the men were to follow Lewis down the Missouri, a relatively pleasant canoe ride, except for the "musquetoes." Clark was left with York, Sergeant Pryor and eight privates, Charbonneau, Sacagawea, the now-eighteen-month-old Jean Baptiste, forty-nine horses, and one colt.

The group was bound for what many called the Roche Jaune or Yellowstone River. To spare the sore feet of the horses, the party camped the first night, July 12, a mere four miles from the three forks, at a spot near the present town of Logan. The next day, as the relaxed group ambled east across the Gallatin Valley, they saw elk, deer, beaver, antelope, wolves, and otter on the bottomlands. Overhead, they watched wheeling eagles, hawks, crows, and wild geese. After considering a more northerly route leading east, Clark said in his journal that he deferred to the judgment of another: "The indian woman who has been of great Service to me as a pilot through this country recommends a gap in the mountains more south which I shall cross."[17]

Clark's party had some difficulty crossing the Gallatin River in several places as they moved east, due to swift currents and beaver dams. The leader wrote that he saw old sign of buffalo but none of the animals themselves. "The Indian woman informs me that a fiew years ago Buffalow was very plenty in those plains & vallies quit as high as the head of Jeffersons river, but fiew of them ever come into those vallys of late years." Further, "the Shoshones . . . are fearfull of passing in-to the plains."[18] Perhaps the Blackfeet had something to do with that.

On the evening of July 14, Clark's group camped on high ground at the mouth of Kelly Canyon at the east end of the Gallatin Valley. After breakfast on Tuesday, July 15, the party broke camp and followed an old buffalo road, then crossed Jackson Creek and went over what is now Bozeman Pass. They arrived at the Yellowstone River near the site of present-day Livingston in the early afternoon.

They then continued down the Yellowstone to its junction with the Missouri, where they joined the rest of the party in mid-August. Indians along the way celebrated the expedition's leaving the country by stealing a good number of its horses, much to Sergeant Pryor's embarrassment. All seemed anxious to return to Saint Louis. As they said good-bye to Charbonneau and Sacagawea, Clark vowed to the couple that he would educate their son Jean Baptiste (Clark called him "Pomp") when he was grown. Years later, he remembered his promise.

chapter

F I V E

During the winter of 1806-1807,
only a few months after Lewis and Clark left the
area on their way back home, a mysterious trader
ventured up the Missouri River to the three forks.
Little is known about French-Canadian Charles
Courtin, who slipped into the region and established
a crude shack there.[1] Canadian trader David
Thompson of Montreal may have sent him up the
Missouri to quietly investigate the area recently
visited by the Corps of Discovery. Perhaps another
trading firm sent him; possibly he came on his own.

Joseph Dickson and Forrest Hancock, trappers
from Illinois, had met Courtin wintering with the
Teton Sioux the season before, 1805-1806, and said
so to Lewis and Clark when they met later on the
Missouri.[2] Acting Governor of Louisiana, Frederick
Bates enclosed a letter from Courtin with one of
his own to Henry Dearborn of the U.S. War
Department, dated August 2, 1807, adding, "Of
Courtin I know nothing; it is said that he is
respectable."[3]

Respectable or not, Courtin did not stay long
at his Three Forks fort, doubtless driven out by the
Blackfeet. Probably the would-be post broke up
during the next spring runoff. The adventurer moved
west to the Clark Fork where he established a real
trading post, operating it until February 1810, when
he was killed by a Blackfeet war party. British traders
called the Clark Fork itself Courtine's Creek in his
memory until the 1820s.[4]

The men who had accompanied Lewis and
Clark had every intention to return to the States,
but one of them didn't make it for six years. John
Colter got as far as the villages of the Mandan when
he became possessed with a driving curiosity that
led him back to the Yellowstone and Three Forks
areas, again and again, a virtual Ulysses of the
Rockies.

Private Colter, like his leaders, was a native
Virginian, born to a farm family. He was probably
in his early thirties, older than most of the men,
shy, almost taciturn, but "wore an open, ingenuous
and pleasing countenance of the Daniel Boone
stamp."[5] Colter had traveled west to Kentucky when
he learned about the forthcoming expedition. He
stood five feet ten inches, was of robust constitution,
and, like other Lewis and Clark men, was willing
to take extraordinary risks. Colter, it would turn out,
was almost foolhardy.

As the returning party neared the Mandan
villages in August 1806, the men met Joseph Dickson
and Forrest Hancock, the trappers who had talked
to Charles Courtin the winter before. Colter was
immediately taken by the plans of the two
adventurers and asked permission to leave the Corps
of Discovery to return upstream with them. Lewis

28

Some representative trappers.

and Clark granted his request and wished him well. Colter trapped with Dickson and Hancock, probably along the Yellowstone River and its tributaries, until the spring of 1807, when he parted company with them and traveled back downstream along the Yellowstone and Missouri Rivers to the mouth of the Platte.

There he met Manuel Lisa, an enterprising trader originally from New Orleans, who was either greatly admired or violently despised by those who worked with him, described variously as wily, avaricious, keen of mind, or ambitious. Lisa had formed the Saint Louis Missouri Fur Company and was anxious to employ men who knew the reaches of the Upper Missouri. He enticed Colter to return west again with other former Lewis and Clark men George Drouillard, John Potts, and Peter Wiser, who were already members of his party. Also included in the group were a number of trapping adventurers more rough-mannered than most, which did not bother the single-minded Lisa.

He wanted to move closer to the sources of furs and therefore decided to establish a trading post up the Yellowstone at the mouth of the Bighorn River, located one hundred miles west of present-day Miles City, Montana. The party reached the site by October 1807, and the men built a crude log cabin before winter set in. Lisa named the post Fort Raymond after his son Remon, but most came to call it Manuel's Fort. Now the trader needed fur peltries from both Indian and European trappers. Lisa determined that John Colter was the man to contact Indian groups to the west, to encourage them to come to Manuel's Fort with their goods.

Colter set out in midwinter, alone, a thirty-pound pack strapped to his back, to wander through parts of the present Wyoming and Yellowstone National Park areas, a trek of more than five hundred miles. He stood before stinking eruptions from mud baths. When he described them later to skeptical listeners, they laughed at his hallucinations and called them "Colter's Hell." Colter also watched glistening water displays from many geysers and traveled valleys filled with steam from hot springs. Those who heard his descriptions of these wonders did not believe him and scorned him with condescending jokes.

After he recovered from his arduous journey, Colter again left Manuel's Fort to hike west to the Three Forks area. This time Lisa wanted the trapper to meet with the Blackfeet to encourage them to trade with his men at the fort. On his way through the Gallatin Valley, Colter fell in with a large party of Crow who were traveling in the same direction. As the group moved leisurely down the lower Gallatin River, an equally large number of Blackfeet suddenly attacked. Since there was no place to hide, Colter fought the Blackfeet within Crow ranks, who were enthusiastically joined by Flathead warriors. Wounded in the leg, Colter crawled into a nearby thicket for safety. "He . . . loaded and fired while sitting on the ground."[6] As they retreated, the Blackfeet took note of the white man fighting with the Crow and memorized his appearance. Colter hobbled back to Fort Raymond to begin his convalescence.

Anxious to trap beaver, Colter stubbornly planned yet another excursion to the Three Forks area with John Potts. They arrived in the region by July 25, 1808, each with his own canoe and traps. The two moved about the Jefferson drainage at night, choosing tributaries in which to set their traps. When they did venture out in their canoes in broad daylight, they heard what Potts thought was the noise of a large bison herd nearby. Colter said no, it sounded to him like many horsemen approaching. Potts jokingly called Colter a coward, but it turned out Colter was right.

Quickly, Potts and Colter were surrounded by five or six hundred grim Blackfeet on the east side of the creek. Both men slipped their traps in the water. Come ashore, the horsemen beckoned. Potts gave the Blackfeet a sign that he would not do so and was immediately pierced by an arrow. He leveled his gun and shot one of the men on shore. A volley of arrows felled him in his canoe. He then was hauled to shore and chopped to pieces.

The Blackfeet next pulled Colter out of his canoe, marched him to land, "stripped him entirely naked, and began to consult on the manner in which

he should be put to death."[7] Colter could not be certain if his captors recognized him from the previous battle with the Crow, but they appeared to want to kill him in some slow, special way. It would be a shame to merely riddle his body with arrows, they seemed to think. Why not a race?

They asked Colter by sign if he were a fast runner. He could understand a few Blackfeet words and replied that, no, he was an extremely poor runner. The chief led the naked Colter some four hundred yards from the main party, wished him well in this sporting event, and made the motions to start running. The scene was described by John Bradbury in the language of an earlier day: "At that instant the horrid war whoop sounded in the ears of poor Colter, who, urged with the hope of preserving life, ran with a speed at which he was himself surprised."[8]

He ran from the creek to the Jefferson River, a distance of some six miles. His feet became bloody almost immediately from the spines of prickly pear cactus. Halfway to the Jefferson, Colter turned to see how close the runners were behind him. Some had turned back, leaving a scattered group, except for one man who was obviously the best sprinter of the band. He carried a spear and, Colter judged, ran about one hundred yards behind him.

Blood dripped from Colter's nose, covering his bare chest, as he moved ahead. Surely, he was close to the Jefferson. Sounds of the Blackfeet runner grew louder and louder. Now he was not more than twenty yards behind.

Suddenly, Colter stopped and turned to face the man with the spear. Whether the Indian was shocked to see a bloody Colter, or whether he was surprised at his stopping, the man tripped and fell, his spear shattering. Colter grabbed the remainder of the spear, plunged it into the fallen runner, grabbed his blanket, and sped off again toward the river. He ran toward a cover of cottonwood trees, dived into the cold water, and hid under a pile of driftwood, which had lodged against a small island during the last spring runoff.

All day he heard searching sounds directly above his hiding place. By nightfall, all was quiet. He cautiously crawled out from under the driftwood, swam to the eastern shore, climbed on land, and continued his naked or near-naked trek across the Madison River and the Gallatin Valley to the pass leading to the Yellowstone River. There he moved into the snowy brush above, fearing that the Blackfeet might catch him in the open. It was at least seven days before an emaciated, bleeding John Colter arrived at Manuel's Fort, after a three-hundred-mile ordeal.

Needless to say, a story of such epic proportions has been told in many ways. Some sources state Potts was felled by gunfire, not arrows. Some say Colter hid inside an abandoned beaver lodge in the Jefferson River. Colter had the Blackfeet runner's blanket, or he did not. Some say he ran to the Madison River. Whatever the details, it was an amazing race.

How Colter was disposed to return to the Three Forks area the following winter is almost beyond belief. He stubbornly claimed it was to retrieve the beaver traps that he and Potts dropped in the creek where they were accosted by the Blackfeet. He camped near the Gallatin on his way to the Jefferson. Confident that no Blackfeet would be around during such bad weather, he warmed himself before a small campfire. He was wrong. According to Thomas James, to whom Colter told the story later, the trapper heard noises nearby, not the usual night sounds.[9] He leaped over the fire to take cover. Gunshots rang out and he hid until he could again make his lonely way by night over the high mountains and back to Manuel's Fort where he rested, dreaming, perhaps, of the final leg of his journey home to Saint Louis.

Sources disagree as to the exact timing of these adventures, but Colter's biographer Burton Harris says: "Colter's three encounters with the Blackfeet apparently all took place during the summer, fall, and winter of 1808, thus making that the most eventful year of his life."[10]

But John Colter would have one more adventure in the Gallatin Valley. Trader Manuel Lisa had suffered severe financial reverses; moreover, a number of lawsuits against his business made the speculator nervous. He returned to Saint Louis, leaving partners Colonel Pierre Menard and Andrew Henry in charge of the next foray into the Three Forks area. In late winter, the Menard-Henry party of thirty-two French and American trappers left Manuel's Fort with now-veteran John Colter as principal guide.

When they reached the pass to the Gallatin Valley, a heavy snow made passage difficult. Colter lost the trail for a time. When the sun came out, the snow severely blinded most of the men. Later, expedition member Thomas James recalled that "hot tears trickled from the swollen eyes nearly blistering the cheeks, and the eyeballs seemed bursting from our heads."[11] Not being able to see well added to their apprehension as they approached the Gallatin Valley. They sensed Indians nearby but could do nothing to protect themselves. The usually intrepid Colter was nervous as well.

By the time the party descended into the Gallatin Valley, their swollen eyes were on the mend. Colter pointed out to James and others the cliff he had scaled in the night during his epic run. The group passed the battlefield where Colter fought with the Crow and Flathead in the rout of the Blackfeet, a field strewn with whitened skulls and bones. "The recitation of his experiences in that region let Colter give vent to his nervousness, and served to keep all members of the expedition on the alert."[12] According to Thomas James, "an undefinable fear crept over all."[13]

The melancholy party reached the Three Forks area on April 3, 1810. There, about two miles up the Jefferson fork, they built a double-walled, ten-foot-high stockade of cottonwood logs set three feet deep, about three hundred feet square.[14] Colonel Menard sent a party of eighteen men, including Colter, forty miles up the Jefferson to trap for beaver. Nearer the fort, a group of Gros Ventre attacked and killed trappers James Cheek, Hull, and Ayers. Later, the bodies of Rucker and Fleehart were found upstream, their furs gone. Eventually, the skins surfaced in Canadian trading posts.

All seemed quiet as Colter returned to the new fort near the Three Forks; he saw no Indian sign. When he entered the stockade, the horrid news stunned him. James reported that Colter threw his hat on the ground, crying, "If God will only forgive me this time and let me off I will leave the country day after tomorrow and be damned if I ever come into it again."[15]

On April 21, Pierre Menard wrote to his brother-in-law Pierre Chouteau and quickly prepared a brief note to his wife, handing them both to the departing Colter. Said Menard to Chouteau,

"Unless we can have peace with these [word unclear] . . . or unless they can be destroyed, it is idle to think of maintaining an establishment at this point."[16] Even though Colter's small party of three was obviously leaving the area, they encountered more Blackfeet from whom they hid as they traveled. Their whirlwind river trip downstream to Saint Louis took just thirty days.

Meanwhile, the greatly mutilated body of George Drouillard, the able translator for the Lewis and Clark expedition, was found up the Jefferson River. That was enough for Colonel Menard. He ordered Andrew Henry and nine men to stay behind and properly close the fort at Three Forks while he marched the rest of the party over the pass to the Yellowstone River. By the middle of July, Menard was safely back in Saint Louis. Henry and his men pulled out in September and moved quickly up the Madison and over the mountains to a tributary of the Snake River, now known as Henry's Fork. Whether the men knocked down the fort at Three Forks behind them or the Blackfeet did them that favor is not known.

Years of heavy snows and runoff swept away the cottonwood logs and camp items left in a hurry. Early Gallatin Valley settler Peter Koch saw the fort entrenchments and some weathered debris in 1864. An anvil, left behind by the would-be traders, remained on the site for more than fifty years. In 1867, Gallatin City blacksmith James Aplin picked it up and used it in his shop for a time. Aplin gave it to Carl Hopping, who used the anvil at the hapless Copper City mining camp nearby. (The anvil is now on display at the Headwaters Heritage Museum in Three Forks.)

For years after the beaver men abandoned trapping at the headwaters of the Missouri River, both fur traders and companies kept the site in mind as an out-of-reach goal. The Blackfeet and their enemies had the country to themselves again, at least for a while.

When John Colter arrived in Saint Louis, he barely recognized the community he had left six years before. He was devastated to learn that his former leader Meriwether Lewis had died on the Natchez Trace, either by his own hand or by foul play. He paid a visit to William Clark and probably discussed his solitary amble through Wyoming and the Yellowstone area during the winter of 1808. Clark may have used some of Colter's descriptions on a map he was preparing.

Colter settled down to farm near Dundee, Franklin County, Missouri, married a young woman named Sally, and sired a son named Hiram. John Bradbury tried to induce Colter to return to the Missouri with his party, but the new farmer declined. Soon after, however, this robust mountain man with seemingly limitless good health became jaundiced and died in November 1813 at age thirty-eight. Was it hepatitis as alleged, or was Colter bored to death with farming and the quiet life? ▨

chapter

S I X

Despite the reluctance, even inability, of most fur trappers and adventurers to set down on paper their impressions of the Gallatin Valley, no doubt they saw what historian Hiram Chittenden described:

> Along the lower courses of the Gallatin and its principal tributary, the East Fork, is one of the most extensive and beautiful mountain valleys in the West. It is the vacant bed of an ancient lake, surrounded by a cordon of mountains which are flecked here and there with patches of snow and are clothed in the varying hues of the atmosphere. . . . The valley is upwards of thirty miles long, with a remarkably even topography and a bountiful supply of water . . . It was the scene of great activity during the entire period of the fur trade and yielded untold wealth to the coffers of the traders.[1]

Perhaps Chittenden overstated the extent of the fur trade at the three forks. During the height of the beaver-pelt trade, the Gallatin Valley lay between the areas heavily traveled by both mountain man and fur trader. To the north, British adventurers still moved about, eager to take advantage of American preoccupation with the War of 1812. To the south, "Western Wyoming and the adjacent regions of Idaho and Colorado became the pivot of the trade, and so remained for two decades."[2]

Although the beaver men regarded taking major risks as a normal part of life during this period, many of them avoided the three forks area, not wanting to fall at the hands of the Blackfeet, a fate they felt was almost certain if they ventured into the Gallatin Valley. We have to assume their personal assessments of danger, for we have only scant written records, since the trappers "were men of the rifle and the knife, not of the pen."[3] The experiences of those few parties that did cross the valley only heightened the uneasiness of the others. These events "came too often for the success of Manuel Lisa," the businessman who had made the first push into the upper Missouri to exploit new beaver fields, and his "enterprise proved a failure."[4]

By 1822, the wartime slump in markets seemed to be over; business prospects looked healthier than they had for some years. Consumers again shopped for luxury clothing made or trimmed with beaver fur. In Saint Louis, Joshua Pilcher took over the Missouri Fur Company (Manuel Lisa had died two years before), revitalizing the firm with the Three Forks on his mind. One Saint Louis paper proclaimed that the Three Forks region contained "a wealth of furs not surpassed by the mines of Peru."[5]

About the same time that Pilcher was reorganizing the Missouri Fur Company, General William H. Ashley placed a notice in the *Missouri Gazette and Public Advertizer* on February 13, 1822, stating his intention "to engage one hundred men, to ascend the river Missouri to its source, there to be employed for one, two, or three years." Ashley was a desperate man; he had no desire to go into fur country himself, but he was, alas, $100,000 in debt. In 1821, he met Andrew Henry, the man who was forced to retreat from the Blackfeet eleven years earlier; Ashley became convinced that he had found the right leader for an expedition to the sources of the Missouri, enabling him to avoid going into Blackfeet country himself.

Among those who answered Ashley's ad were young men who would one day become legends as American mountain men and fur traders: New Yorker Jedediah Strong Smith was just twenty-three; William Sublette was also twenty-three; his brother Milton Sublette was twenty-one; Irishman Tom Fitzpatrick was twenty-five; Virginian Jim Bridger was a mere eighteen; David E. Jackson was an "old" man in his mid-thirties.

Andrew Henry began his push up the Missouri River on Wednesday, April 3, 1822. By early fall, he and his men arrived at the mouth of the Yellowstone River, where they intended to leave the stream and travel cross-country to the Three Forks area. The Assiniboine put a damper on Henry's plans by stealing more than forty horses from the expedition, so the party stayed put for the winter. Meanwhile, Ashley's second boat, the *Enterprize*, started up the Missouri on May 8. But before the vessel reached the site of present-day Kansas City, it hit a snag in the river and broke up. The *Enterprize* and its stores were lost, but no one drowned. A nervous Ashley, his eye on Joshua Pilcher and Missouri Fur Company preparations, outfitted a third boat, moved upstream from Saint Louis in late June with Ashley himself as captain, picking up survivors from the *Enterprize* wreck on the way.

By October 1, all of Ashley's men had made it to the mouth of the Yellowstone. A relieved Ashley went back to Saint Louis to mount yet another expedition for the following season. Pilcher's group, headed by veterans Robert Jones and Michael Immel, on their way to Manuel Lisa's old fort at the mouth of the Bighorn River, waved to the Ashley men as they passed by the mouth of the Yellowstone. While waiting out the winter, the Pilcher and Ashley parties, as well as others, dreamed of spring and the riches from furs just ahead in the Gallatin Valley.

When the weather opened in spring 1823, Jones and Immel, with one hundred and eighty adventurers, were first to get to the Three Forks area, trapping with good success. The Blackfeet they met seemed friendly enough. But when the men broke camp at the end of May and started on their way back through the present Bozeman Pass to the Yellowstone River, the Blackfeet were no longer friendly. The Indians had followed the decamped trappers, and near Pryor Creek killed seven of the party, including Jones and Immel, taking $15,000 worth of furs with them to sell in Canada. Back in Saint Louis, Joshua Pilcher mourned his loss, saying "the flower of my business is gone; my mountaineers have been defeated, and the chiefs of the party both slain."[6]

An early group of Ashley men, led by Andrew Henry, came up the Missouri that same spring but were similarly pushed back by the Blackfeet, just above present-day Great Falls; four trappers were killed. Moreover, the two fur giants were not the only companies suffering losses. As Don Berry concludes in *A Majority of Scoundrels*, "Within a two-week period every major trapping party on the upper river had been assaulted—and worse, overwhelmingly defeated—by the Indians."[7] General Ashley reluctantly gave up his dream of a fort at the Three Forks. Most of the beaver men turned to fur-trapping opportunities elsewhere.

Even though the Blackfeet controlled access to the Gallatin Valley for the next fourteen years, a few travelers were able to enter and leave, with or without profit. Evidently, the British were not ready to give up on the Missouri River source country. In 1824, the eccentric but tough Canadian Peter Skene Ogden led a large party into the Three Forks area from the northwest, knowingly trespassing on American territory, with orders from the Hudson's Bay Company to evaluate business possibilities there. Destined for a career in either the ministry or the law, Ogden sought a more adventurous life in his midteens, first as a trading clerk and then as a trapper. Despite his large force of men, guns, and

Jim Bridger, c1866. C. M. Ismert drawing, courtesy Kansas State Historical Society, Topeka, Kansas.

horses, the Blackfeet attacked near the three forks, and Ogden was forced to retreat to the Salmon River. The Gallatin Valley lay quiet again.

Five years later, in 1829, a party led by older and seasoned Jedediah Smith, Tom Fitzpatrick, and William Sublette crossed the valley, from west to east, on its way to the Yellowstone River. The Blackfeet had not given up; they harassed the trappers all the way. Smith, a tall, spare, clean-shaven man with a limited sense of humor, always carried with him a Wesleyan hymnal, Matthew Henry's *Commentaries*, Rollins's *Ancient History*, and his Bible. He studied scriptures whenever he was at rest. Unlike most trappers, he did not use tobacco and

seldom took a drink. The men called him "Mr. Smith." Since his first trip with General Ashley seven years before, this "true knight errant"[8] had crossed the Sierra Nevada into California, walked to Oregon, and had traveled along the Santa Fe trail in the Southwest. In two more years, he would die on that trail along the Cimarron River at the hands of the Comanche.

Tall and bony Tom Fitzpatrick was now called "Broken Hand" because an exploding gun had maimed his hand; except for the Blackfeet, he ordinarily got along well with Indian groups. William Sublette, older brother of Milton, Andrew, Pinckney, and Solomon Sublette, had just turned

35

thirty. He stood six feet two inches, his sandy hair contrasting with strong blue eyes. Joe Meek, a brash youngster of nineteen from a patrician Virginia family, was with them for a time, but he got separated from the main party and was chased out of the area by the Blackfeet. A hungry and cold Meek made his way to the Yellowstone River and eventually rejoined the main party.

After the 1830 rendezvous along the Wind River in Wyoming, Sublette, Fitzpatrick, and Jim Bridger led a Rocky Mountain Fur Company party of two hundred men to the Three Forks area; by March 1831, they had trapped a creditable number of beaver. Probably because of the large size of the expedition, the Blackfeet left them alone. In the fall of 1832, the party returned to the Three Forks with fifty men and their traps. This time, the Blackfeet monitored their activities at a distance but did not attack.

Perhaps the Indians had their eyes on another group following Fitzpatrick and Bridger. William Henry Vanderburgh was carrying out orders from the American Fur Company; his party was to spy on the Rocky Mountain Fur Company and to determine the sites of their trapping operations. On October 14, the Blackfeet decided enough was enough; on a tributary of the Jefferson River, they attacked the American Fur Company, killed Vanderburgh, and chopped off his arms. At some point, Fitzpatrick and Bridger joined the fight; Bridger took two arrows in his back. His companions pulled out one arrow, but a three-inch segment from the other remained in Bridger's back until the 1835 rendezvous on the Green River, when Dr. Marcus Whitman removed it.

Others thought about trapping in the Gallatin Valley and, in fact, planned for it, but the closer they got to Three Forks beaver country, the more they were inclined to change course and veer south through Wyoming and over to Idaho for their trapping activities. Although the "valley of the flowers" was rich in furs, the aggressive Blackfeet made it seem more of a "place of thorns" to the frustrated beaver men.

In 1840, western mountain men held their last rendezvous on the Green River in Wyoming. With the development of woolen and cotton mills in the northeastern states and England, customers chose the new fabrics rather than beaver fur for their clothing. Although some beaver trapping continued, most of the mountain men retired with their families to towns either in the Saint Louis area or in settlements in the Far West. Some entered politics. Jim Bridger took a Shoshone wife and turned to guiding pioneer groups moving west; he would visit the Gallatin Valley again and again. The short but romantic era of the mountain man had come to an end. ▦

chapter

S E V E N

In the 1830s, a new type of traveler journeyed up the Missouri, and even as far as the Gallatin Valley. Steamboats regularly moved upriver from Saint Louis, eventually as far as Fort Benton, carrying a clientele different from the hardy mountaineer. In 1832, the first steamboat, the *Yellowstone,* arrived at Fort Union at the mouth of the Yellowstone River with artist George Catlin aboard, on the lookout for new Indian faces to paint. Others came by boat or across country, anxious to see the western frontier.

Prussian naturalist Friederich Paul Wilhelm, Prince of Wurttemberg, combed the West for plant and animal specimens ranging from wildflowers to wood ticks. The prince was not a dilettante. He had studied zoology and botany, eventually earning three doctorates. On his way west for the first time in 1823, he stopped in Saint Louis to visit William Clark, then superintendent of Indian Affairs, and received permission to travel up the Missouri into Indian country. Clark must have trusted Prince Paul, since he later allowed him to take Sacagawea's son Jean Baptiste back with him to Wurttemberg for his education.

On his second journey to the West in May 1830, the prince visited Fort Union. He continued up the Missouri to the Gallatin Valley, carefully studying whatever "ran, flew, slithered, crawled, or

blossomed."[1] He also made copious notes on his impressions of the Sioux, Blackfeet, and Assiniboine. The prince was fascinated by the jackrabbit and its winter change to white fur. He thrilled at flights of the Canada goose, but suggested the bird was misnamed because he saw them flying throughout the American West. He studied the prairie rattlesnake, describing its behavior in great detail. He saw similarities between the Great Plains of the United States and the grasslands of South America, where he previously had visited.

Prince Paul and his men crossed the Gallatin Valley to its eastern pass and returned to the Missouri River by way of the Yellowstone. Father Pierre-Jean DeSmet described the prince, whom he met years later. He "is a man of an intellectuality far beyond ordinary comprehension. . . . But his weak point is impulsiveness. His courage is so boundless that it often approaches downright madness itself."[2] Unfortunately, the prince died before he could organize his written words and specimens; an alleged manuscript detailing his experiences in southwest Montana has never been found. (A World War II bombing raid over Stuttgart destroyed the rest of his writings.)

Other naturalist travelers to Montana included a flamboyant prince who called himself the Baron of Brausenburg. Prince Maxmilian of Neuweid,

Pencil sketch of Missouri headwaters. A. E. MATHEWS.

dressed in a white slouch hat, tattered black velvet coat, and greasy trousers, ascended the Missouri to the Great Falls. Since the noted artist Karl Bodmer came with Maxmilian, it is unfortunate that the party did not continue up the Missouri to the three forks; Bodmer might have painted a Gallatin Valley scene. Ten years later, in 1843, naturalist James J. Audubon considered a trip to the valley, but the sixty-year-old painter of birds decided he did not want to risk a meeting with the Blackfeet. He concluded his western travels just beyond Fort Union.

That same year, another German naturalist, Charles Andreas Geyer, dared to visit the Gallatin Valley after he had explored Wyoming. Because he did not want to travel alone, he joined forces with a group of Jesuit missionaries on their way to Saint Mary's Mission in the Bitterroot Valley. Perhaps the early attention to the West by these German naturalists explains the intense and sustained popularity in Germany of anything characterized as "western": Indians, clothing, jewelry, novels.

In 1840, a rotund, gray-haired Belgian Jesuit made the first of his many trips across southwest Montana. Pierre-Jean DeSmet, an energetic thirty-nine-year-old "Black Robe," rode or walked the West, despite his 210-pound weight. Although he was not trained as a naturalist, DeSmet observed with sharp precision and wrote about all that he passed (Indian, plant, animal) in sharp contrast to the tall, spare, laconic mountain men of earlier years. On his first visit, he came down the Jefferson River with an American Fur Company party, camped in the Three Forks area, and crossed the Gallatin Valley on his way to the Yellowstone River. The priest's sharp eyes had observed color in Alder Gulch but, because DeSmet believed that man's frenzy for gold contributed to his almost certain ruin, he did not speak of what he saw for the next twenty years.

Father DeSmet was both horrified and fascinated by the grizzly bear, one of which he examined closely when hunters killed it and brought it into camp. It had paws thirteen inches long, he noted; its claws measured seven inches.[3] In 1841, in response to repeated requests by the Flathead for religious instruction, he founded Saint Mary's Mission in the Bitterroot Valley, the first permanent white settlement in the Montana area. He crossed the Gallatin Valley again that year, and on many other occasions, on his way to Saint Louis or to Europe to raise money for his religious projects. The Black Robe continued his western walks until 1870.

In 1844, English naturalist Joseph Burke followed the Germans and Belgian priest into the valley but stayed a little longer. He approached the area from the west, in an unseasonably cold and damp journey. Burke lost most of his equipment and his specimens, and the mosquitoes lived up to their reputation in the Lewis and Clark notes. "I am stung out of all patience by the Moschettos."[4] Burke was enchanted with his first view of a columbine, never having seen such a flower before.

On July 23, Burke's party descended into the Three Forks area from the west, moving down the Missouri to Sixteenmile Creek, then crossed the mountains to the Yellowstone River. They returned

Pierre-Jean DeSmet, wearing decoration of the Order of Leopold, presented by the King of Belgium. COURTESY MONTANA HISTORICAL SOCIETY, HELENA.

by way of Bozeman Pass to the valley again, hiking west and south to the future Raynolds Pass. Burke noted in his journal a phenomenon he heard about but did not see: nearby boiling springs. "One of them, I am told, throws the water to the height of one hundred feet."[5] So the naturalist wrote of what he did not see, the same thing that, thirty-seven years earlier, John Colter probably watched but did not describe in writing.

In 1837, the steamboat *St. Peters* brought something other than passengers and goods upstream, something that was to end the domination of the powerful Blackfeet. By the time Bernard Pratte, Jr., captain of the *St. Peters*, called at Fort Pierre, South Dakota, several of his crew members and passengers were seriously ill, and some were dying. He surely knew his boat harbored the deadly reason: smallpox. He could have returned downriver; he could have put the vessel under quarantine. He decided, however, that the business of transporting goods and passengers should proceed on schedule.

The *St. Peters* moved upstream to the Mandan villages and Fort Clark, North Dakota, arriving on

June 15. More and more people on board sickened and died; those who fled the boat in terror spread the disease throughout the area. Within a short time, fifteen hundred to two thousand Mandan Indians died of the disease, leaving few survivors. Still Captain Pratte continued his deadly journey up the Missouri to its destination at Fort Union. A keelboat, on its way to the fort, backed up the Missouri River in order to avoid contamination, an unsuccessful strategy; Pratte carried the disease to Fort McKenzie, six miles above the mouth of the Marias River. There Major Alexander Culbertson, twenty-six Indian women, and one other man became ill. All but Major Culbertson died.

Culbertson, temporarily distracted with his own convalescence that summer, finally noted that he had not seen Blackfeet families for some weeks; Fort McKenzie seemed an "eerie human vacuum."[6] The major traveled upstream to the Three Forks area to discover the reason for their absence. There he found

a silent, stinking village. Hundreds of rotting corpses were strewn about.... It was like another Assyrian host that the Angel of Death had overwhelmed in a night. Two old women, too feeble to travel, were the sole living occupants of the village. All who had not died on the spot had fled in small bands here and there, frantic to escape the pestilence which pursued them at every turn, seizing its victims on the prairie, in the valley, among the mountains, dotting the country with their corrupting bodies, till thousands had perished.[7]

Doubtless, those who thought they were healthy had raced from village to village, spreading contagion as they went. Jim Bridger was traveling along the Madison River with Osborne Russell the following year when he spied a desolate tepee; peering inside, he stepped back in horror when he saw nine swollen Blackfeet bodies. As the trappers went along, they saw more empty lodges and many more sick and dying people.

By the winter of 1839-1840, smallpox had infected the Pawnee, Osage, Kiowa, and Choctaw, and then moved to the Comanche and Apache in the Southwest. When the siege was over, an estimated seventeen thousand Plains Indians had

39

died, including many of those Lewis and Clark had met: the Mandan, Arikara, Minataree, Sioux, Assiniboine, and Blackfeet. Smallpox struck again five years later, in 1845. More Indians died from smallpox than from all military engagements between tribal groups or between Indian and European.

Dr. Edward Jenner's vaccine against smallpox had been available in the States since 1798. Explorers Lewis and Clark had brought some of the protective medicine with them on their expedition. Trader Joshua Pilcher did vaccinate some three thousand Indians living below Fort Pierre in 1838, but the effort was made too late. Moreover, most Indians resisted the vaccine as yet another white trick to exterminate them. Healthy Crow warriors, believing that their Blackfeet enemies were weak enough to conquer, moved into their camps, and caught the "Red Death" instead.

Some historians suggest that someone, perhaps a disgruntled traveler denied passage, threw infected blankets on the steamboat *St. Peters*. Or was it men eager to settle the fate of the Indian without military engagement? The continued introduction of liquor, the spread of venereal disease and smallpox, and, later, the systematic slaughter of the buffalo signaled the end of freedom for the Indians, who had always lived where and how they chose. ▣

chapter

EIGHT

By 1850, "All America seemed to be on the move."[1] Settlers looking for rich land traveled to the West Coast by way of Cape Horn, the Santa Fe Trail, and the California and Oregon Trails. Mormons streamed to the Utah area. A few steamboats ascended the Missouri River as far as Fort Benton. The winds of an approaching civil war raked across the land. Some of the financial institutions in the East failed in the Panic of 1857, leaving many with few prospects. All was busy and restless, but not the Gallatin Valley. It lay beyond the reaches of the developing routes to the West, relatively peaceful and undisturbed.

In 1853, a West Point man avidly read the journals of Lewis and Clark and anything else he could find that would acquaint him with the land lying between the Continental Divide and Puget Sound, a territory about which he knew little. President Franklin Pierce had just appointed Major Isaac Ingalls Stevens governor of the new Washington Territory, which had been created out of the northern part of Oregon Territory. Stevens had to learn quickly. He was to survey a possible road or rail line stretching west from Saint Paul, Minnesota, crossing Indian country and going on to the Pacific coast, a distance of two thousand miles. Not only was he to deal with the various tribes living within Washington territorial boundaries, but he also was ordered to conduct peace negotiations with

Indian groups along the entire survey route. Stevens was to suggest to the Indians that they must pursue the agricultural life of the white man in order to survive. The notion did not interest people who lived by the horse and the buffalo.

The governor engaged as guide Alexander Culbertson, the man who had recovered from smallpox sixteen years before. The rest of the Stevens survey was a grand operation, supported by a $40,000 congressional appropriation. It included a military escort, packers, voyageurs, scientists, a mapmaker, artist John M. Stanley, geologist Elwood Evans, a meteorologist, and surgeon/naturalist George Suckley. Stevens received an additional $6,000 appropriation to distribute gifts to those Indians with whom he would discuss the advantages of white life.

The Assiniboine told the new governor that a railroad, or any kind of road, cutting through lands guaranteed them by the Horse Creek (Laramie) Treaty of 1851 would destroy the buffalo and their way of life. Governor Stevens listened politely, distributed gifts, and assured all that the father in Washington would not harm them. Farther on, Stevens met at the mouth of the Judith River with the Gros Ventre, Blackfeet, and Flathead, who generally expressed the same views as had the Assiniboine. The governor listened politely, distributed more gifts, and went on his way.

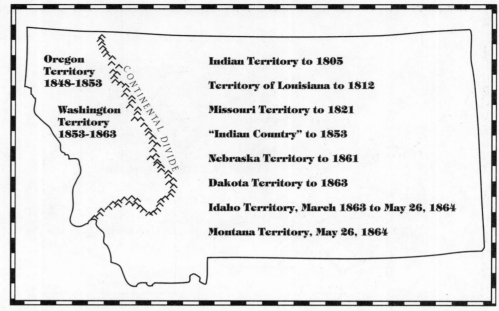

Montana before it became a Territory.

Oregon Territory 1848-1853

Washington Territory 1853-1863

CONTINENTAL DIVIDE

Indian Territory to 1805

Territory of Louisiana to 1812

Missouri Territory to 1821

"Indian Country" to 1853

Nebraska Territory to 1861

Dakota Territory to 1863

Idaho Territory, March 1863 to May 26, 1864

Montana Territory, May 26, 1864

When the various meetings had been concluded, a new treaty was proclaimed and forced upon the Indians. The Gallatin Valley, which had been promised to the Blackfeet by the terms of the Laramie Treaty signed four years before, was now regarded by Stevens and the 1855 treaty signers as open territory. The headwaters of the Missouri and the Gallatin Valley were to be "common Indian hunting grounds for ninety-nine years, where all nations of Indians may enjoy equal and uninterrupted privileges of hunting, fishing and gathering fruit, grazing animals, curing meat and dressing robes."[2]

Governor Stevens kept Lieutenant John Mullan busy for the next several years building what came to be called the Mullan Road, stretching east 624 miles from Walla Walla, Washington Territory, up the Coeur d'Alene River in Idaho, into the western Montana area along the present Clark Fork and Little Blackfoot Rivers. The road builder reached Fort Benton on August 1, 1860. Even though the Gallatin Valley lay well to the south of the Mullan route, it would soon feel the effects of the cross-country road and waken from its pastoral slumbers to bustle with activity as the Stevens party completed its mission.

In 1859, the U.S. War Department authorized the sum of $60,000 to fund a military expedition under the command of Captain William F.

Raynolds; he was charged to explore the possibility of new routes from the central plains to the Idaho mines. The captain was to investigate the habits of Indians living along each route, the topography and navigability of streams in the region, and the mineral and agricultural resources of the area. Would a more direct trail be feasible between Fort Laramie and the Yellowstone? Was there was a better way to travel between Fort Laramie, along the base of the Bighorn Mountains, and on to Fort Benton to join the Mullan Road under construction? And could there be a more direct route between the sources of the Wind River to the sources of the Missouri?

Captain Raynolds hired Ferdinand Vandeveer Hayden, former schoolteacher and doctor, now geologist, to accompany the group; in twelve years, Hayden would return to the area as head of his own expedition. Jim Bridger, fur trapper turned guide, now known as "Old Gabe," joined the Raynolds party, which left Saint Louis in June to ascend the Missouri by steamboat to Fort Pierre in the present South Dakota. There the expedition disembarked to cross overland to the divide between the headwaters of the Little Missouri and Little Powder Rivers to enter the Yellowstone basin. As they entered the region, Raynolds noted in his journal,

Three large [buffalo] bulls charged down upon us at one point in the march, to the great alarm of one of the escort, who dropped his gun, and,

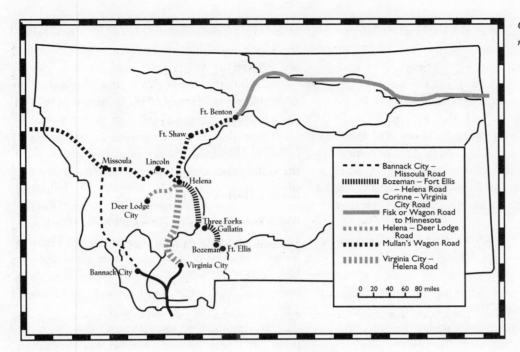

Chart showing various roads in area.

raising his hands, exclaimed, in all the accents of mortal terror, "Elephants! elephants! my God! I did not know there were elephants in this country."[3]

Raynolds traveled down the Little Powder River to the Powder River through desolate territory he characterized as "unfit for the white man."[4] His party turned west, crossing Pumpkin Creek to the mouth of the Tongue River, then south to follow the Bighorn River, continuing east of the Bighorn Mountains. They wintered on the North Platte River. In the spring, Raynolds divided the party and sent Lieutenant Henry F. Maynadier down the Bighorn and then across the Shoshone and Clark's Fork of the Yellowstone River to the Yellowstone Valley. The lieutenant's group then moved up the Shields River, crossing the mountains to Flathead Pass on July 1. Maynadier wrote later:

we entered the pass by a well defined road with evident marks of recent passage of a large bank of Indians. . . . The pass followed the winding of a small stream, and gradually ascended by its crooked course until it was lost in a dark narrow canyon. Then turning abruptly the trail led up a very steep hill through a dense pine forest, and in about a half mile the divide was reached, notwithstanding this was higher than the limit of snow, the surrounding peaks towered loftily

above us; the white snow glistening above us through the pine trees, and the wind keeping up a monotonous roar, as it swayed the myriads of pine boughs to its course. A halt was called on the summit to allow all hands to breathe, and to prepare for the decent, which bade fair to be worse than the ascent. I was surprised to find the mosquitos very troublesome at this elevation, and while I was eating a piece of snow in one hand, the other was kept busy brushing them away. The decent was very steep and rocky, and there were many places where the mules had great difficulty in keeping on their feet. At one point, near the bottom, the gorge opened and presented a charming view of the broad plain in which the three forks of the Missouri unite, and soon after we came to a beautiful mountain stream which provided an easy road into a fine valley, where we camped on the ground of some deserted Indian lodges, which promised a plentiful supply of wood.[5]

The following day, Maynadier and his party "passed over rolling hills well covered with grass, but on crossing the stream down which we were traveling we came upon a miry plain so full of sloughs that the animals could not travel." The men recrossed the stream, moving toward the Three Forks area. There they stopped to wait for Raynolds and his group.

43

Raynolds's goal was the exploration of the Wind River and Yellowstone headwaters, for he had heard stories about weird land formations and spouting waters in the region. Jim Bridger told the captain it would be difficult, if not impossible, to bring such a party through the area. Frustrated, Raynolds turned west, arriving at the site of present-day Jackson, Wyoming. The expedition then turned north across the pass that now bears Raynolds's name to the Madison River and downstream to the three forks where they joined Maynadier on the last day of June 1860.

From there, Raynolds traveled to Fort Benton, pausing to look over John Mullan's work on the ambitious road through the Montana area. Maynadier again split off from the main party, recrossed the Gallatin Valley, and descended the Yellowstone to Fort Union where he rejoined Raynolds and the main expedition. They all went down the Missouri by steamboat back to Saint Louis after a difficult trip with not much to show for it except Raynolds's extensive notes for a future map of the area. His report was not published until 1868, years after many westering families had already made decisions as to which route they would follow.

* * *

The gold flecks in southwestern Montana streams did not remain Father DeSmet's secret for long. The fever that comes with the notion that one can pick up pieces of glittering rock and get rich affected restless men across the nation in the late 1840s; they gravitated toward California in 1849 and Colorado a decade later. They left their wives and children behind, often with no support, and traveled west with a shovel, a pick, and an ax. If they did not bring any equipment, someone was on hand to sell gold-seeking items to them. Few had any information about how to tell which type of rock held gold deposits, how to build a placer chute, and how much work it would take to extract gold and other minerals.

Stories of gold in Montana had been circulating since the early 1850s. No one knows for certain who first found pay dirt in southwestern Montana. But in 1852, François "Benetsee" Finlay, just back from the California mines, discovered color on a little creek that bore his name for a few years, a tributary of the Hell Gate River, located near the present Drummond, Montana. (Benetsee Creek was later

called Gold Creek, and the Hell Gate is now called the Clark Fork.) For whatever reason, Finlay did not develop his find.

Considering the highly competitive nature of most gold prospectors and their intense need to nose out each new rumor of color in the creeks, it is surprising that five years passed before brothers James and Granville Stuart, on their way east from the California camps, saw gold shining at another spot on Benetsee-Gold Creek in 1857. The following year, the Stuart brothers, with Rezin "Reece" Anderson, staked their claims on Gold Creek, one hundred and fifty miles northwest of the Gallatin Valley. Those who found gold were never able to keep secrets. Fifty men suddenly appeared to stake their claims beside the Stuart party along the creek. The Montana gold rush was on.

During the next several years, others with the fever left Colorado and Orofino, Idaho, to rush north for yet another chance to go home rich. A group of sixteen men from Colorado were part of the original gold-seeking group from Georgia led

John Bozeman. He left Georgia, came to the Colorado gold fields with the "Green Russell crowd," then drifted north to investigate the Idaho mines.

by Green Russell in 1860. They came to Gold Creek on June 24, 1862, upon the recommendation of Thomas Stuart, whose older brothers James and Granville reported to him that the new mines were worth looking into. Among them was a tall, ruggedly handsome twenty-seven-year-old man from Pickens County, Georgia: John M. Bozeman. Maryland native Thomas W. Cover, equally handsome but not as rugged, also came up from Colorado to investigate the mines; he, too, would play an important role in the development of the Gallatin Valley.

Road-builder John Mullan, now a captain, stopped to examine the new mines along Gold Creek and the little camp nearby called Pioneer, fully aware that his efforts at providing a route close at hand were bringing would-be financiers into the area daily. (Idaho became an official territory on March 3, 1863, and included all of the present Montana; thus, the new mines in the future Montana area were also called the Idaho mines.)

When John White found good placer gold in July 1862 on Grasshopper Creek (Lewis and Clark called it Willard's Creek) near the Beaverhead Valley, the resulting stampede of one thousand men into the area spilled into the Gallatin Valley as well. The prospectors came by steamboat up the Missouri, or followed the Mullan Road east from Washington Territory, or left Orofino in the Idaho area—all in a hurry to gain the ultimate strike. With the establishment of a new camp called Bannack City (named after the nearby Bannock Indians but spelled differently), miners fanned out to file their claims.

During the spring of 1863, James Stuart led a prospecting party to study some of the tributaries of the Yellowstone River to determine whether gold could be extracted in paying quantities from any of the streams, but a group of determined Crow, defending lands guaranteed to them by treaty, forced the prospecting party south to the Oregon Trail. Six men, split off from the main Stuart expedition, were also pushed to retreat by a Crow war party; disconsolate, they tramped west across the Gallatin Valley, then up the Madison Valley, heading for the safety of Bannack City. Bill Fairweather and Mike Sweeney were from New Brunswick; Harry Rodgers hailed from Newfoundland; Henry Edgar had come from Scotland; Barney Hughes was from Ireland; Tom Cover was the only American in the party. Just over the Madison-Jefferson divide, they camped along a lonely little creek overgrown with alder

Miners stop their work to pose for the camera in Alder Gulch. Joshua C. Crissman, *1872.*

45

bushes. There the men found what would become the greatest gold field in southwestern Montana. Henry Edgar named the place Alder Gulch.

By the end of 1863, the gulch was no longer quiet and lonely. Some six thousand people crowded the area. The difficulty in naming the new camp there reflected the strong feelings of miners loyal to either the Confederate or Union forces fighting back in the States. Southerners wanted to name the fledgling town "Varina," in honor of the wife of Jefferson Davis. But a Connecticut doctor, Giles Gaylord Bissell, casually selected as a new judge, said he would be damned if he would sign official papers that way and wrote "Virginia" on the Idaho Territory document which named the settlement. Virginia City it became.

Some of the would-be argonauts passed through the Gallatin Valley on their way to the new mining camps, and a few looked over the area with other than gold-seeking eyes. Those who had farmed back in the States noted the rich soil. Someone would have to grow the potatoes, the grains, and other produce to feed the busy miners frantically digging along Alder Creek from dawn to dusk, they thought. Why, this valley could become the granary of Montana! Few realized at that time that growing crops on the high plains was a different kind of agriculture than they had practiced in the East. Those who had been merchants back home began to see the possibilities of selling all manner of supplies to the Virginia City men.

Perhaps some of the westering adventurers had the opportunity to read Chicago newsman John Lyle Campbell's advice to newcomers in his book *Idaho: Six Months in the New Gold Diggings: The Emigrant's Guide Overland*. He described the Three Forks area and the Gallatin Valley in glowing terms: "The valley at the Three Forks, as also the valleys along the streams as they recede from the Junction, are spacious and yield a spontaneous growth of herbage, upon which cattle fatten during the winter."[6] In fact, Campbell wrote, Mormon leader Brigham Young had considered the advantages of establishing a colony at the western edge of the region. As news of the gold strikes reached Salt Lake City, however, Young realized that the gold camps would be a source of conflict with the Mormon way of life.

Future Helena lawyer Cornelius Hedges later described some of the newcomers who were decidedly un-Mormon.

Unlike other states settled before or after the civil war, the war-times during which Montana was settled brought together some of the worst elements of both warring sections of the country, deserters from both camps, seeking a cover in the wilderness beyond the reach of the civil or military arm of government, where they could shoot off their mouths or guns with comparative impunity.[7]

Perhaps fearing that he was too strong in his condemnation, he softened

Advertisements from newspapers of the day.

his remarks by saying, "It would be rank injustice to assert that a majority or a large portion of the early settlers of Montana were desperadoes, seeking a field for unrestricted crime."

John Campbell recommended a number of ways a westering family could prepare for the trip to the gold camps. He noted that a team of oxen is preferable to that of horses or mules. They are cheaper to purchase, easier to feed, don't wander about, and less apt to be stolen by Indians. A simple wagon would be easier to sell at the mines; fancy rigs are seldom used there. "No party," Campbell warned, "should leave the Missouri river next spring for Idaho without a supply sufficient to LAST THEM NINE MONTHS."

> The emigrant may ask, why cumber our wagons with such an amount when we shall be but sixty or seventy days on the route? But remember, you are not going to an agricultural country, or at least one developed, but are going to a very new section where produce is scarce and high and has to be freighted several hundred miles...[8]

Why spend thirty dollars for one hundred pounds of flour when you could bring it with you?

Tethering a milk cow to your wagon would be a wise investment, Campbell advised. The milk could be used inside the tent when bad weather prevents cooking outside. Beware of scurvy, he warned. Those who bring along dried or canned fruit, tinned butter, and eggs packed in oats are usually healthier than those who subsist on flour and meat. Best buy a cast-iron stove for twenty-five dollars than bring in the sheet-metal variety, which wears out and is worthless at the mines. A cast-iron stove can be sold at journey's end for one to two hundred dollars—a tidy profit. Two woolen blankets, three pairs of sturdy boots, three changes of durable clothes and a rubber coat will suffice. You probably won't need to use a firearm on the trip to the mines, observed Campbell, but traveling without a gun would be foolhardy. A pony, while not completely necessary, is useful to herd stock, chase buffalo, or flee when encountering a grizzly.

Under the heading "The Reality," Campbell gave counsel that probably was seldom heeded:

> Have a good reason for breaking the old moorings before looking for better ones, and when you start on a trip of this kind, do not cherish the idea that

it is to be but a holiday excursion, soon to be over, when you will tumble into some rich gulch, only to come forth laden with stores of gold.

> To succeed in any new field of labor, great industry and perseverance is required, and the emigrant to Idaho will secure his fortune only through hardship, privation, endurance and great industry. Let well enough alone when you are comfortably situated, and do not believe every story that goes the rounds . . . .

> Persons who have good homes and means of livelihood, should not be induced by extravagant stories, however true they may be, to emigrate to a far-off country after a phantom fortune. Neither should any man who is so indisposed to labor as to have always failed at home to obtain an honest living, ever think of succeeding in a mining country, however rich it may be.[9]

Honest or avaricious, foolish or thrifty, newcomers crowded the new Idaho mines. On the way, would-be promoters studied the advantages of the Gallatin Valley, mentally subdividing the land and toting up the riches to be made. For these men, a fever for gold was just that and seldom paid off. They believed that those who supplied the growing camps had a better chance for financial success. They figured their advantage in freighting from the Gallatin Valley, a distance of sixty miles, much closer to the mines than Walla Walla in Washington Territory or Salt Lake City, four hundred miles away.

Moreover, they were here first. As yet, they had little competition. What an opportunity! They would have to hustle. No matter the guarantees to Indian groups in the 1851 Horse Creek Treaty near Laramie. No matter the 1855 Stevens Treaty with the Blackfeet guaranteeing the Gallatin Valley as a hostility-free zone open to all Indian groups.

By January 1862, the Homestead Act was in place—a piece of legislation that President Abraham Lincoln reputedly predicted "will do something for the little fellow."[10] Ten dollars paid the filing fee on one hundred and sixty acres, but those "little fellows" who had served in the Confederate army were not eligible, at least not until 1866. Despite this restriction, both Union and Confederate families started west, hoping to leave the Civil War and their financial problems behind.

Sometime in November 1862, a small number of speculators from Missouri stood on the west bank of the combined Jefferson-Madison River, just above the mouth of the Gallatin. They had already looked over real estate possibilities in Bannack City. But here, at the three forks, what a spot to plat a town and sell lots! The climate seemed mild, a variety of game could sustain them, and, most important, they could see what the Mormons had already determined: the grass looked good for raising livestock. They would sell hay, meat, and, eventually agricultural produce to the miners over the western ridge.

Before the promoters had a chance to stake out their new townsite, which they called Gallatin City, Frank J. Dunbar and his brother Thomas had finished building an eighteen by twenty-foot cabin, the first residence in the valley. Constructed of undressed cottonwood logs, their home would eventually serve as hotel and meeting place as well.

By December 30, twenty-five settlers had left the noise and confusion of Bannack and Virginia City to relocate to Gallatin City. They signed the

"Articles of Association of the Gallatin Town Company," and helped to plat their new home town. A. K. Stanton built the first cabin within the town site. Since the winter was open, the Missouri speculators started to build sixty cabins to house the newcomers they expected in the spring. A flour mill had first priority even though no land surrounding Gallatin City had yet been plowed or seeded. Several residents started digging a crude canal from the Madison River to a grist mill under construction.

What grand plans these pilgrims had. They saw a large church with a mammoth steeple overlooking the settlement. There would be a fairgrounds with a racetrack and, nearby, a university campus. At the river's edge, they would construct a wharf, ready to welcome new Gallatin City residents stepping down from steamboats moving upstream from Fort Benton. Steamboats? What were they thinking of? Were these Missouri men that ignorant of the geography downstream? Did they not know of "a slight obstruction below in the shape of a tremendous falls?"[11] Or were they counting on the portage around the falls of lighter boats presently

W. H. Everson's map of the second Gallatin City, c1881. Note that the fort near the three forks, near top center, is called Fort Henry, after Andrew Henry, whose party left the area for the present Idaho to escape the attentions of the Blackfeet.

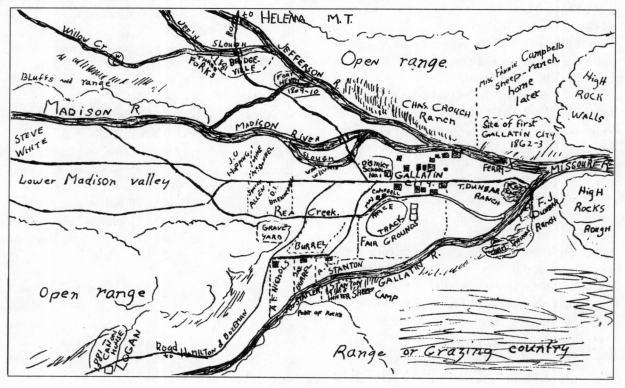

What Frank Dunbar's ranch looked like after 1900.

being manufactured in Saint Louis?

Emily and Frederick A. Meredith also came away from Bannack City to look over the new settlement. Mrs. Meredith wrote home to Minnesota: "There are fifty or sixty log houses in Gallatin but most of them at the present are unoccupied. . . . many persons believe that it will be the San Francisco of a Northern Eldorado." However, it soon became evident to the Merediths and others that Gallatin City "was not one of the cities toward which people gravitate."[12] The couple left the area after five weeks' residence and eventually settled in another part of the valley.

Those who stayed felt that, given the need for supplies by the Alder Gulch men, it was simply a matter of time. Gallatin City would become a real town with unlimited opportunities. After all, it was now the seat of Jefferson County under Idaho Territory jurisdiction. Some of those who stayed filed claims on land surrounding the settlement, hoping that future crops and fattening livestock would change their prospects. They dismantled a few of the new Gallatin City cabins—their roofs had yet to be built— and freighted them out to their

ranches. Some were "left for the nightly carnival of bats and owls," reported traveler Edward B. Neally as he surveyed the settlement.[13] Young John Bozeman filed homestead claim No. 60 early in February 1863, a parcel along the river near Gallatin City, but did not stay to begin plowing.

Undaunted by the settlement's slow start, James Gallagher (sometimes spelled Gallaher), Samuel Weir, and O. D. Loutzenhiser built a barge to operate as a ferry across the Jefferson; they soon discovered, however, that a ferry business could operate only during periods of high water. On February 9, 1865, the new Montana Territorial Legislature chartered the Gallatin Ferry Company, capitalized by Gallagher, J. W. S. Wilson, and G. W. Hill. The men charged five dollars for the crossing of any vehicle, one dollar each for men on horseback, and twenty-five cents per stock animal or pedestrian. Those who found the fees too rich took their chances by crossing without benefit of ferry.

By 1865, W. D. Fredericks had completed the flour mill started three years before, ready to receive the first harvest; he sold the mill to George D.

By the time this photo was taken, the Gallatin City Hotel had seen livelier days.

Thomas, who hoped that his Thomas Mill would prosper in the years to come.

John Lyle Campbell, the man who wrote advice to emigrants, published a modest pamphlet about Gallatin City prospects and took it to the editors of the new *Montana Post* in Virginia City. Evidently, the editors found the news of a flourishing metropolis along the Gallatin hilarious:

Not wishing to say by any means this is a paper town. Oh, No! . . . We don't know the town company but presume when they laid out the city, it was like the fellow that set the hen on 100 eggs, he wanted to see her spread herself. Whether Gallatin will be able to sow her 'oats' remains to be seen but things certainly at the present are in a bad condition, let it be recorded.[14]

Sometime during the summer of 1864, a few of the town's original organizers again stood on the riverbank, shading their eyes to look across to the eastern side. Gallatin City was not booming. Was it a spring flood that discouraged the men? Was the newly established stage stop on the other side a consideration? Did the farmland look richer across the way? Perhaps we have made a mistake, they thought. Let us move the settlement across the river. They moved what they could to the east bank and started a second Gallatin City on the tongue of land between the Jefferson-Madison and Gallatin Rivers. ▨

chapter

N I N E

During the winter of 1862-1863, John Bozeman decided he was not meant to be a gold miner. He had had no luck at the Bannack City diggings and lost his enthusiasm for such a venture when he saw that mining for gold was a grubby business, much like the farming life he left behind in Pickens County, Georgia. As he watched tired men standing in cold stream water, hour after hour, he decided that the prospecting life was not for him. As his friend George Irwin said later, "Mr. Bozeman's restless activity and love of adventure prevented his possible contentment in any mining camp."[1]

The former southern farmer and would-be financier had also left behind to fend for themselves his wife Lorinda Cathrine and three young daughters: Melinda Jane, Lila, and Martha. At fourteen, Bozeman had learned firsthand of the lure of far-off places when his father William left the family for the California gold fields, never to return.

The younger Bozeman stood six feet two. He was all bone and muscle at two hundred pounds. His light brown hair, carefully trimmed sandy mustache, flashing brown eyes, and fair cheeks often flushed with red, together with his phenomenal strength, served to attract the ladies. His friend W. J. Davies philosophized on Bozeman's attractiveness to women: "Woman is a sweet, frail, clinging vine and she always gets desperately in love with that kind of man. . . . But you have never known an effeminate, chicken-hearted dude being loved and respected by a noble woman."[2]

Men liked him too, sensing undeveloped qualities of leadership. Good friend and fellow Georgian William S. McKinzie said, "he was a free, open-hearted man, of a speculative tendency, investing in everything. He was a natural speculative genius. He was game to the back-bone. . . . He was always good natured. I never saw him angry."[3] George Irwin said, "He was genial, kindly and as innocent as a child in the ways of the world. . . . He had no conception of fear, and no matter how sudden a call was made on him day or night, he would come up with a rifle in his hand. He never knew what fatigue was."[4] W. J. Davies remembered Bozeman's special sense of humor—he told funny stories—and "was a more interesting companion than I had expected."[5] He added, "His sense of honor in some directions was terribly sensitive, while in other directions his conscience was very elastic. He never posed as a saint, but it would have been a very dangerous experiment to call him a liar."[6]

Unlike many westering men, Bozeman was meticulous in his dress, choosing the black beaver-cloth cutaway coat and striped dress trousers favored by gamblers. He preferred the black single-slouch hat; he never tucked his trousers into his boots as many pioneer men did, but wore them smooth and unwrinkled over his footwear. (A painting of Bozeman by Edgar Samuel Paxson shows him with

John M. Bozeman at twenty-five. Bozeman left his wife Cathrine and three daughters to come to the West to search for gold, as had his father before him.

A care-worn Cathrine Bozeman, c1890s.

heavy whiskers, wearing a gaudy fringed buckskin suit. Of that canvas, Bozeman's friend William McKinzie said later, it is "a good likeness of Liver-eating Johnson . . . Bozeman never wore such a suit and did not wear a beard."[7] Perhaps Bozeman wore fringed buckskins a time or two to enhance his role as a wagon train recruiter.) When he gambled, which he enjoyed a great deal, he wore his cutaway coat. "Bozeman had no use for money except to bet with, and the most congenial place on earth to him was the saloon, with a few boon companions at a table playing a game of draw."[8]

The restless Bozeman met a kindred soul during the winter of 1862-1863. John M. Jacobs, a tough, red-bearded Italian, had left his Flathead wife and family in the Deer Lodge Valley. Bozeman learned that his new friend had been leading parties throughout the Northwest since the early 1850s. Jacobs's reputation as a guide was sound despite his bad temper and tendency to fight and bicker with

others. With him was his eleven-year-old daughter Emma, who bore the brunt of his ill humor with frequent cuffings and beatings.

Both men sensed the opportunity to develop a shorter route from the States to the Idaho mines at Bannack and Virginia City. In the spring of 1863, John Jacobs, Emma Jacobs, and John Bozeman left Bannack City, traveled to the Three Forks area, crossed the Gallatin Valley, and moved through the eastern pass to the Yellowstone River, taking the same route that William Clark had traveled fifty-seven years before. Ignoring the fact that they were entering lands reserved by treaty to the Crow, Sioux, and Cheyenne, they sought a shorter route and planned to pick up a westering wagon train at Council Bluffs or some spot in Wyoming. This would be the first of a number of attempts, as W. J. Davies said later, to "swallow up all the tenderfeet that would reach the territory from the East, with their golden fleeces to be taken care of."[9]

The two men and the little girl skirted a Crow war party on the Yellowstone River near the mouth of the Bighorn River. At about the same time, James Stuart and his men, who had fled from the Crow south to the Oregon Trail, were returning north. On May 11, 1863, Stuart spotted the small party and tried to warn them of possible misadventure ahead. Bozeman and Jacobs did not trust the intentions of the advancing men and ducked into a ravine, moving briskly along. Stuart said later, "We found we could not overtake them until their horses tired out, and it would not pay to run ours down to see three fools. We found a fry-pan and a pack of cards on their trail."[10]

The two would-be trailblazers ran into serious trouble two days later when a band of eighty Indians on horseback stopped them, stripped them of their goods, "traded" their fine horses for three nags, and beat Emma Jacobs for being in the company of white men. Her father had managed to hide one rifle but he had little ammunition.

The forlorn little group, tired and famished, continued on to the North Platte River, near present-day Glenrock, Wyoming, to rest and recruit the first party to travel the short way to the Idaho mines. They were convinced that by leaving the North Platte and the Oregon Trail near the present Douglas, Wyoming, a wagon train could travel northwest, cross the Powder and Tongue Rivers, continue on to the Bighorn and the Yellowstone through Crow country, and move through the pass at the eastern edge of the Gallatin Valley to reach Virginia City. Such a route offered good grass, a saving of an estimated eight hundred miles and six weeks' time on the trail. Jacobs and Bozeman felt the cutoff was good for them too; it left them with no competition for the collection of wagon fees. At that point, Bozeman may have traveled on to Council Bluffs to find those with golden fleeces.

By July 1863, Bozeman, Jacobs, Emma, and guide Rafael Gallegos stood with forty-six wagons and eighty-nine people, ready to push off from the North Platte to the Bozeman-Jacobs cutoff. They got as far as what is now Buffalo, Wyoming, when they looked up to see a "long, dark, sinuous line on the slope of a distant ridge."[11] It was a formidable party of one hundred and fifty Sioux and a lesser number of Cheyenne.

As the Indians approached, Bozeman told his charges not to worry: he could see women and children traveling with the men; they would not attack. The Sioux signed to the whites, This is our land; you may not pass. The wagon group stalled for a few days, sending out horsemen to discover if other trains were nearby, or whether a military escort was possible. While they waited, some of the women in camp sought to ease the tension by offering food to the Indians. Bozeman warned them not to make the gesture. The women saw no harm in it and went ahead; the resulting fighting and confusion among the tribesmen made them realize that the recruiter knew his business. (The offering of food to Indians would figure in events along another trail four years later.)

Bozeman had told the families to travel light, but he did not count on "one attractive female pilgrim [who] jettisoned a husband . . . this troublesome wren was charitably disposed towards any number of the males on the Bozeman train, whether or not such males were otherwise bound in holy wedlock."[12] In order to avoid trouble, Bozeman played a captain's role and joined in matrimony the young wren to a unmarried male named Beaumont "who, according to some of the matrons, should long since have been in wedlock's bonds . . . Bozeman kindly consented to mitigate the scandal by tying the nuptial knot, one bright evening at the head of the corral."[13]

After learning that no other wagon train was in the area and that no military party would escort them through Indian land guaranteed by treaty, the train chose to return to the longer but safer Oregon Trail, and then on to the mines. John Jacobs went with them as far as the Platte, arguing along the way with most of the party; he and Emma went on to Denver for the winter to recruit a new wagon train. (This was the last year of Emma's life; she died during the winter of 1864-1865 and was buried along the Helena-Virginia City road near the site of the future silver camp of Clancy.)

A few men of the wagon train did not want to give up on the new trail. Bozeman, George Irwin, Mike J. Knoch, and seven other brave—or foolhardy—men packed their horses and rode hard and fast across Wind River country and down the Clark's Fork to the Yellowstone, traveling at night, arriving safely in Bannack City.[14] Grateful to Bozeman for a successful journey, George Irwin suggested that the pass into the Gallatin Valley be named after their leader and the name "Bozeman Pass" stuck. Despite the failure of the first attempt, both Jacobs and Bozeman now felt that future wagons could and would make a successful trip along the cutoff. They would be back on the North Platte in the spring of 1864.

Down through the years, the Bozeman Trail was variously called Montana Road, the Bozeman-Jacobs Cutoff, the Reno Road, the Carrington Road, the Yellowstone Road, the Bonanza Trail, the Virginia City Road, the Powder River Road to Montana, the Big Horn Road, and the Bozeman Road.[15] Writer Grace Stone Coates believed the trail, whatever it was called, was "doomed before it was opened."[16] The Crow, Sioux, and Cheyenne,

defending their treaty lands, saw to it that this was true.

For a few short years, the Bozeman Road became such a popular route for westering families that the federal government established three forts along the way for their protection: earlier Fort Connor on the Powder River became a refurbished Fort Reno in 1866; Fort Phil Kearny, the largest of the three, was established that same year on Clear Creek, east of the Bighorn Mountains, a choice Indian hunting ground; Fort C. F. Smith was built where the Bozeman Trail crossed the Bighorn River. These posts were fortified at the same time other government officials were in the field assuring the Sioux that such development would not happen. Two years later, at the Fort Laramie Treaty of 1868, both military and Indian forces agreed that the Bozeman route was illegal and the road closed.

* * *

The Bozeman Trail.

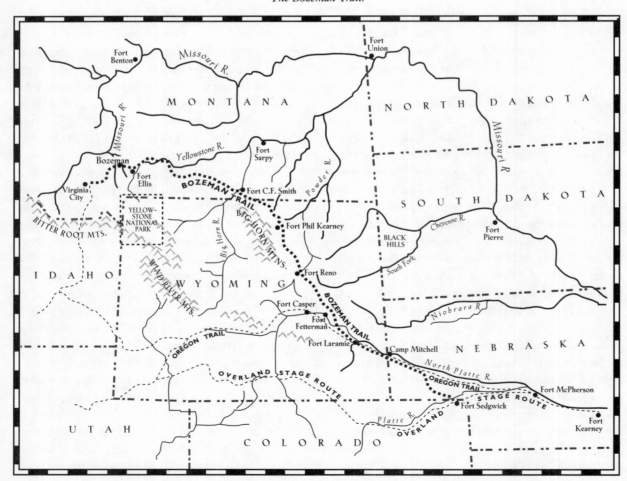

BOZEMAN.

Daniel Elliott Rouse, who had a passion for platting new towns. ETCHING FROM MICHAEL LEESON, *HISTORY OF MONTANA*, 1885.

Elliott Rouse had a passion for moving. Before he stood with the Missourians on the site of what they hoped would be a bustling Gallatin City in 1862, he had farmed in Michigan, had left for New York, and had farmed again in Michigan, then in Minnesota, Wisconsin, and Iowa. He had gone west to Colorado, but soon left to see the elephant in California. On the way, he was sidetracked to Idaho. The news of the strikes at Bannack City lured him even farther north.

Rouse also had a passion for platting settlements. He platted streets for a town near the Red River in Minnesota and helped with the platting of the Gallatin City site. Years later, he would plat an ill-fated venture in the Yellowstone Valley called Rouse's Point. He considered the possibilities of farming and mining, and even learned about the life of road agents (roadway robbers, sometimes called banditti). He stayed with five such men in a Deer Lodge Valley cabin, leaving with haste when he realized they were about to rob and kill him.

Rouse's younger brother Elisha was along on some of his travels but usually stayed behind to harvest the crops that Elliott planted and left. Their father had deserted the family for the California gold fields and never returned, a familiar family pattern at that time. Even though Elliott had settled land near the three forks in 1863 with the intention to farm, he was freighting salt from Salt Lake to Virginia City when he met John Bozeman during the winter of 1863-1864.

Although not as addictive a wanderer as Elliott Rouse, Pennsylvanian William Johnston Beall also had traveled a bit himself before he came to the Gallatin Valley. He lived in Kansas for a time, went to Fort Laramie, Wyoming, then back to Kansas. He tried Denver, Salt Lake City, and then the mining life at Virginia City. The quiet, unobtrusive Beall also settled on Three Forks land and started to raise potatoes. The industrious farmer would use his training as an architect in a few years. Beall was selling potatoes in Virginia City when he and Rouse first talked with John Bozeman.

William J. Beall built some of the first buildings in Bozeman. ETCHING FROM MICHAEL LEESON, *HISTORY OF MONTANA*, 1885.

WILLIAM J. BEALL
BOZEMAN.

55

MRS. ROSA V. BEALL
BOZEMAN.

Early settler Rosa V. Beall wrote many articles on early Bozeman. ETCHING FROM MICHAEL LEESON, *HISTORY OF MONTANA,* 1885.

The three men learned they were of like mind. Perhaps Bozeman initiated the plan, saying he would go east to get the people. Rouse and Beall would leave their ranches and lay out a town at the eastern end of the Gallatin Valley. Despite its swampy character, they agreed this site was a better location for commerce than the faltering Gallatin City; furthermore, the eastern location was surrounded by richer farmland. Bozeman was a man of his word; by the spring of 1964 he had made a financial arrangement with the Missouri and Rocky Mountain Wagon Road and Telegraph Company—a group of Virginia City speculators—and was on his way east to find a wagon train whose leaders were venturesome enough to travel the cutoff he and Jacobs had scouted the summer before.

Jim Bridger had the same idea; he picked up a wagon train west of the present Casper, Wyoming, on May 20; leaving the Platte and traveling northwest, he kept west of the Bighorn Mountains until he reached the Yellowstone River. Perhaps he

was conservative and wanted to avoid Indian treaty lands. He moved northwest again, following the Shields River. On July 6, he brought the wagons through the present Bridger Canyon and down into the Gallatin Valley.

John Jacobs also assembled a wagon train, following more or less Bridger's route west of the Bighorns, reaching Bozeman Pass and the Gallatin Valley a few days later. He was closely followed by the Townsend train, whose passengers included Rosa Barker Van Vlierden, her husband, and two little girls. The young mother spent the first three months in the new settlement of Bozeman living in a wagon box. At night, howling wolves circled the makeshift home, scratching at the door, terrifying Rosa and the girls. Soon after, her marriage to A. H. Van Vlierden broke up; he took the girls and went back to the States. Rosa would marry again in 1868, this time to William Beall.

Interestingly, Bridger and Jacobs, the two experienced mountain men, led their trains west of the Bighorns, avoiding much of the Indian treaty land, while newcomer Bozeman led his pilgrims from the Platte on June 18 east of the Bighorns through Indian territory, then followed the Yellowstone and headed over the pass which now bore his name to the Gallatin Valley. His party arrived around the first of August; Bozeman continued with some of his wagon people to Virginia City, making a quick return to check on the progress of Rouse and Beall. The two men had sketched out a site for the new town. Beall stayed in a small tent they set up to protect their new claims while Rouse hurried back across the valley to their ranches for food and other supplies.

On the morning of July 14, while Bozeman's party was crossing Indian territory, the Reverend William White Alderson and his brother John came into the valley, having traveled with the Bridger wagon train on its tiresome, ten-week journey west. A native of Yorkshire, Alderson had worked in the lead mines at fourteen. As an adult, he had studied to be a lay preacher, marrying Frances Weatherby and fathering four children; his family was waiting in Wisconsin for the right time to come west. The minister was particularly shocked at the behavior of some of his fellow travelers—"drunkeness and profanity was very prevalent," he wrote—and he

W. W. Alderson

BOZEMAN.

William W. Alderson, a man with many interests—
churchman, newspaper publisher, dairy operator,
Indian agent, town promoter.
ETCHING FROM MICHAEL LEESON, *HISTORY OF MONTANA,* 1885.

welcomed the chance to leave their company.[17] In later years, he remembered his first view of the valley:

Not a fence pole nor a log house was then in sight to designate the future city of Bozeman. After looking around, however, for a few moments, we noticed a small wedge tent constructed out of a wagon cover and after a little careful inspection we found a lonesome occupant in person of W. J. Beall.[18]

Beall enthusiastically described to the minister and his brother the proposed platting of the townsite. Four streets would run north and south and four would run east and west to complete the grid. Beall had already chosen his homestead just northwest of the present Main Street and Bozeman Avenue; Rouse opted for a similar parcel to the northeast of the same corner. As promised, they staked out a claim for John Bozeman on the south side of Main Street. The speculators were hauling

logs down from the mountains for their own cabins plus one for Bozeman, to be ready upon his return. Take some land for yourself, invited Beall.

Alderson noted in his diary entry for July 15:

Here the valley and stream looked so pleasant and inviting that we concluded to lay over and look around. . . . The grass was tall everywhere, and as it was just heading out, the valley looked like an immense field of grain waving gracefully before the gentle breeze. . . . Weather delightful.[19]

He later added, "We had come, of course, like all the other vast army of 'pilgrims,' prepared to dig gold and make a fortune in a year or two. But the fever was gradually abating as we had already met several parties return disappointed and disgusted from Alder Gulch."[20] Alderson decided to settle on a little hill one mile south of Main Street on what would become Central Avenue (South Willson); he intended to establish a dairy. He would also continue with his ministry, buy a successful newspaper, help with establishing schools, and act as Indian agent. Brother John would move to help found the town of Coulson, near Billings.

Another pilgrim who came with a wagon train that summer did not fare as well as the Reverend Alderson. Franklin Luther Kirkaldie made his tentative way through life under a dark cloud of depression, doomed to fail at whatever he tried. He had been a marble cutter in Vermont, but had to give up the job because the dust hurt his lungs. He moved west to farm in Joliet, Illinois, but did poorly. He moved on to Des Moines, Iowa, to try again. Now he was a family man, married to Elizabeth Risley, father to Fanny, Bub, and twins Nellie and William. Kirkaldie listened to stories of the riches to be had further west at the Idaho mines. In despair, he sent his family back to Joliet to live with Elizabeth's mother, even though mother and daughter did not get along. Frank Kirkaldie was thirty-six years old; he feared that he could never adequately support his family. He made plans to join a wagon train.

Kirkaldie was already broke when he started west in May 1864, forced to work as a hired hand along the way. His letters to his family were both hopeful for a better life and forlorn as he recounted each failure to Elizabeth.

They say that there is only that one gulch by Virginia City that pays anything, that there is twenty men to every day's work there is to do and more flocking in all the time and i have not the least doubt that people who are going there nearly destitute of money or provisions will suffer the coming winter.[21]

Writer Dorothy Johnson concluded that "Virginia City was no place for Frank Kirkaldie. He was a farmer, not a miner."[22] He backtracked to the Gallatin Valley, settled near the present site of Central Park, started to build a cabin for his family, and broke prairie for his first crops. His cabin had no window. He didn't understand the need for irrigation in a semi-arid land. No matter. His first crops froze anyway.

The grass looked greener in young Helena where Kirkaldie speculated on gold mine shares in Nelson's Gulch nearby. He lost his money except for the price of two oxen which he drove back to the Gallatin Valley to work his land. They died. He planted again. The grasshoppers came and destroyed the crop. He told Elizabeth he was thinking of growing strawberries. He was desperately homesick. He worried about his son's crooked legs. Would they ever straighten so that William could walk normally? He tried farming in Diamond City. Then Helena again.

It would be 1868 before Kirkaldie would see Elizabeth and the children at the railroad station at Corinne, Utah. He was forty years old with few prospects. He was neither the first nor the last pilgrim to discover that Montana was not all he had hoped for.

As the Bozeman wagon train came through the pass on August 1, the travelers saw a number of tents and the outlines of the first cabins under construction. Most parties hurried along to Virginia City. Some, however, stayed in the valley to evaluate agricultural and business opportunities. Once they had made their decision, they wasted no time. On August 9, the Upper East Gallatin Association formed. Reverend Alderson was named secretary of

the twelve-man real estate group. His minutes for that day read:

> East Gallatin, Montana,
> August 9, 1864.

At a meeting held by settlers of Upper East Gallatin at Jacobs Crossing on Tuesday, August 9, 1864, John M. Bozeman was elected chairman and W. W. Alderson, secretary. The chairman stated the object of the meeting to be to form a claim association for the purpose of making laws, etc., in relation to farming claims, and for mutual protection. On motion of W. W. Alderson, it was Resolved, First: that the town and district be called Bozeman. Resolved, Second: that the boundary of the district shall be as follows: Commencing at the northeast corner of Kimball's claims, thence east to the base of the mountains, to the Gallatin River, thence down said river to a point due west of said Kimball's claim, thence east to the place of beginning. Resolved, Third: that after any settler stakes out and records a claim he must be an actual resident thereof within ten days thereafter in order to hold said claim. On motion J. M. Bozeman elected recorder, and the sum of one dollar made the fee for recording such a claim.[23]

Admittedly, the association's boundary lines were vague, a description typical, however, of town companies throughout the West. (The Surveyor General would complete an official survey in 1867.) The following day, Bozeman recorded seven claims; James E. Burtsch was the first to lay down his dollar.

Earlier that summer, a few people called the new settlement "Jacobs Crossing." Now it was "Bozeman." At a September 14 association meeting, however, Burtsch moved to change the name to "Montana City." Perhaps he did not favor naming a town after a man from the South, or perhaps he did not like that particular man, a fortune hunter at best. Whatever his reasons, "After a vigorous discussion," according to secretary Alderson, "the motion was put and was lost."[24] Bozeman it stayed.

chapter

T E N

During the year's flurry of incoming settlers and cabin construction at the western end of the Gallatin Valley, activities of a more violent nature occurred near the gold mines to the west. Not all of the new residents engaged in the relatively peaceful pursuits of establishing farms, ranches, sawmills, grist mills, and general stores. As the more fortunate miners collected gold in small pouches and sought to move their new riches to banks outside the territory, men described by historians Michael P. Malone and Richard Roeder as "cutthroats, thieves, and fast-buck artists,"[1] arrived to take their goods away from them. Fellow historian Merrill G. Burlingame described the new arrivals as "Draft dodgers, drifters, gamblers, saloonkeepers, and one of the largest collections of thieves and murderers ever to infest a community."[2] Road agents moved in from the Idaho mines to the south or hurried along from Nevada and California, scenting the spoor of freshly dug gold.

Most notable of the men accused of being such road agents was the handsome and charming Henry Plummer. Plummer was personable enough to be elected sheriff of Bannack City in May 1863, despite whispers as to his previous activities as head of a large but silent group of robbers and murderers operating first in California, then in Nevada and Idaho. It was not long before Plummer's authority extended to Virginia City. His position gave him solid information regarding the movement of gold and, the story goes, he quietly passed on this knowledge to his reassembled band of road agents, who ambushed, robbed, and killed.

Legal redress was four hundred miles away in the more settled portions of Idaho Territory. True, there was a sheriff—but his name was Plummer. Moreover, justice was slow to develop in the gold camps because the residents did not yet know one another. And, where gold was concerned, they did not trust anyone.

To head off growing suspicion and rumors, Sheriff Plummer gave elaborate dinner parties for local "society," which included Wilbur Fisk Sanders and his uncle Sidney Edgerton, then chief justice of Idaho Territory. Thanksgiving 1863 at the Plummer cabin was notable for turkey imported from Salt Lake City, for which the host paid forty dollars in gold.

For almost a year, the road agents had a clear field; they killed more than one hundred souls and made away with gold pouches, watches, jewelry, and other valuables brought in from the States. Their take amounted to more than $250,000 of gold and other valuables.

The network of criminals began to unravel on December 21, 1863, when George Ives, a first

The hurdy-gurdy house, Virginia City, Montana. Etching from Albert D. Richardson, *Beyond the Mississippi*, 1867.

lieutenant in the secret Plummer organization, was found guilty of murder and sentenced to hang by a miners' court in Nevada City. Ives was hanged quickly the next day to avoid certain rescue by some of his friends. To insure the success of the hanging, future Bozeman grain merchant Nelson Story kicked the box from under Ives, who stood waiting on the gallows.

Two days later, a number of more-or-less law-abiding territorial residents formed a Committee of Vigilance, modeled after California's earlier extra-legal and unnamed enforcers. Some of these men had met earlier at the Bannack City funeral of William H. Bell, coming together for the last rites of a fellow Mason. Although they did not know one another well as yet, the bond of Masonic membership forged a tentative trust. Cornelius Hedges was to say later, "While it was by no means true that every Vigilante was a Mason, it might be said without serious deviation from the exact fact that every Mason in those days was a Vigilante."[3]

A number of Bozeman's future business leaders were participants in the Committee of Vigilance. Most were northerners. The accused road agents came from both the North and the South. Sheriff

Plummer, understandably enough, called the Committee of Vigilance a "dark-lantern association."[4] Some of his associates called them "The Stranglers." The road agents called themselves "The Innocents."

None of the three major histories of the vigilantes named the participants. *Banditti of the Rocky Mountains and the Vigilance Committee in Idaho* was published in March 1865. John Lyle Campbell, the Chicago reporter who wrote about Gallatin City, may have been the author, although he is not listed. Thomas J. Dimsdale, editor of the *Montana Post*, brought out his version of what happened, *The Vigilantes of Montana*, the following year; it was the first book published in Montana. Nathaniel P. Langford did not publish *Vigilante Days and Ways* until 1890. Later, less reticent sources list attorney and politician Wilbur Fisk Sanders, Sheriff Plummer's dinner partner of five weeks before, as organizer of the extra-legal group.

Sanders's uncle Sidney Edgerton, serving on the Territorial Court of Idaho, was soon to become the first territorial governor of Montana; he knew about the Committee's activities and quietly encouraged it. Livery stable proprietor James

Nathaniel P. Langford, engineer, civil servant, writer, and first superintendent of Yellowstone National Park.
F. JAY HAYNES PHOTO.

Williams was "executive officer," or enforcer. History writer Dorothy Johnson noted that Charles Beehrer remembered that "Jim Williams didn't fetch anybody in. He hung them where he found them."[5]

Apparently, Virginia City mayor Paris S. Pfouts was president of the Vigilance Committee. John S. Lott was treasurer; Nathaniel P. Langford, sometime collector of Internal Revenue and (later) the first superintendent of Yellowstone National Park, was sympathetic to the Committee's goal, but was not in the area at the time. John X. Beidler, who later became a more-or-less legal law enforcer, joined the group. Beehrer, also known as "Charlie the Brewer," and Neil Howie, who replaced Henry Plummer as sheriff of Madison County, were members. Nelson Story joined the group, as did future Bozeman hotelkeeper and sheriff John C. Guy. Samuel T. Hauser, James Stuart, and George

Gohn were named. Tom Cover was also associated with the vigilante movement, which may have led to his undoing years later. John Bozeman also attended meetings, but was not in the immediate territory when the vigilantes became active.

The secret group drew up bylaws, swore to uphold certain standards of behavior, and divided into local committees to study the robbery patterns of road agents operating in their immediate area. Once organized, the vigilantes moved quickly. In one month's time they hanged twenty-one suspects, leaving with each dead man a note with the mysterious numbers "3-11-77" or "3-7-77." Some say the numbers referred to the dimensions of a grave— three feet across, seven feet long, and seventy-seven inches deep. Others allege that the notes were a warning to other road agents: you have three hours, seven minutes, and seventy-seven seconds to leave

ETCHING FROM JEROME PELTIER, ED., *BANDITTI OF THE ROCKY MOUNTAINS AND VIGILANCE COMMITTEE IN IDAHO*, 1964.

EXECUTION OF PLUMMER, STINSON AND RAY, AT BANNOCK.

the territory. Still others state that each vigilante member had a code number, and 3-7-77 was one of these.

First to meet his death by rope on January 4, 1864 was G. W. Brown, supposed secretary of the Plummer organization. Before a terrified Erastus "Red" Yeager was hanged, he named names—which made the vigilantes' job easier. The flamboyant Sheriff Plummer was taken by the enforcers on January 10 and, despite his reputation for entertaining the finest, was strung up immediately. One by one, Plummer's men were located and hanged, usually left aloft for a time as an example. Quiet William Beall, soon to become a Bozeman resident, stood guard with a shotgun at most of the hangings to deter anyone who thought to stop the proceedings.

The more agile of the road agents fled to Deer Lodge or left the territory altogether, too frightened to return. At least one slipped into the Gallatin Valley to hide, after he was encouraged to run by his friends in the vigilante group. Twenty-four-year-

old William "Bill" Hunter was said to have spied for the Plummer gang, passing on information as to which miner had made a lucky strike and what route he would take to secure his new riches. Dressed in an old Army overcoat and "foxed" trousers, decorated with leather strips, Hunter fled Virginia City and struggled over the mountains in waist-deep snow, crossing the Madison River.

Begging from settlers along the way, he reached the Gallatin Valley. Living outside became impossible when a winter storm moved in, so the near-frozen Hunter sought shelter in Wesley P. Emery and Dennis Riordan's cabin, twenty miles upstream from the Three Forks, near the present town of Manhattan. The cabin was empty and Hunter made himself at home, wrapping his frozen feet in blankets. With a knife, he trimmed off his distinctive mustache. When the owners arrived home, Hunter told them he was wanted but that he was innocent. As soon as his frozen feet recovered, he would be on his way to Fort Benton.

Emery and Riordan were not about to turn

Perhaps this hanging tree was similar to the one where Bill Hunter met his end. A.E. MATHEWS ETCHING.

Hunter out in the bitter cold; besides, they knew him and liked him. Hunter hobbled on swollen feet to a corner of the hut, wrapped himself in heavy blankets to cover up his clothes and Colt revolver, and fell asleep, snoring noisily.

In Virginia City, Jim Williams sent A. B. Davis, John S. Lott, John S. Bagg, and Richard S. McLaren and a few others to find Hunter. By midnight, they had tracked him to the cabin and questioned the owners as to the identity of the heavy snorer. No one claimed to know him. Through the night, the vigilantes took turns on watch, their guns drawn. At morning's first light, the leader of the tracking party strode to the corner and pulled away the blankets to see the Army overcoat and the foxed pants. "Hello, Bill. Wake up. I want to talk to you," he said.[6]

Hunter rose unsteadily from his blankets

protesting his innocence. The men took him from the cabin, telling him that he would be fairly tried in Virginia City. They then put Hunter on a horse while one of the men walked in the snow—a sure sign that he would not reach Virginia City alive. As the party reached the west bank of Camp Creek, they came to a very large cottonwood with a strong branch. There would be no trial; he was about to die.

He pleaded with the vigilantes to give him a decent burial. "You know we can't do that, Bill, the ground is frozen solid," they said. They pinned a note to his overcoat: "Bill Hunter, executed to satisfy the strict requirements of justice," and strung him up. In this way the vigilantes hanged the last member of the Plummer gang in the Gallatin Valley on the morning of February 3, 1864, and left him there, swinging in the winter storm. ▣

chapter

ELEVEN

Although relieved that many road agents faced hanging or exile, the settlers realized that law enforcement with real courts and a government closer to hand was essential. Evidently President Abraham Lincoln agreed. On May 26, 1864, he signed into law a bill creating Montana Territory. Congressman James M. Ashley, Ohio, suggested the name "Montana," from the Latin, meaning "mountainous." "Montana" had been kicking around for some time, having already been offered when Colorado became a territory, then again for Idaho. The name had become "a sort of illegitimate waif."[1]

Some of Ashley's congressional colleagues disliked a word from a dead language to name the new territory. Why not "Jefferson Territory?" "Douglas Territory?" How about "Shoshone Territory?" The congressmen discarded the Indian name when they learned it meant "snake." Ashley's "Montana" won out. (Later, President Ulysses S. Grant appointed Ashley territorial governor, a job he apparently botched, since, some months later, Grant removed him.) Idaho Territory officials weren't that worried about the names; they lusted after the mines and the new ranches to the north, then mourned the potential riches they felt were stolen from them.

On June 22, Sidney Edgerton became Montana's first territorial governor. He chose Bannack City as a temporary capital. The first legislature met there on December 12, 1864, a few months after the town of Bozeman was established, and spent most of its first deliberations fighting— Republicans with Democrats, Union men with Confederate men. They demanded to know when, as befitting a new territory, would money be forthcoming from Washington? Edgerton's tenure was neither popular nor long; his strong bias against transplanted Southerners led to further dissension, and he left office and the territory after eight months.

When the Territorial Legislature met on February 2, 1865, the representatives stopped fighting long enough to create nine counties: Gallatin County extended east to include the present Park and Sweet Grass Counties. Governor Edgerton named Gallatin County's first commissioners: dairyman Philip Thorpe, rancher Al F. Nichols, and physician D. H. Ketchum. The new commissioners were charged with conducting the affairs of remote Big Horn County as well, which included more than the eastern third of the territory, largely populated by Indians (from whom Edgerton did not wish to select commissioners). The two land parcels totaled eighty thousand square miles, one of the largest county jurisdictions in the United States.

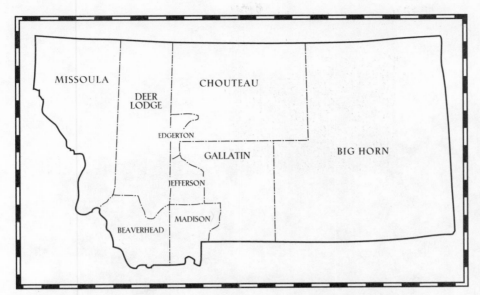

Montana Territory counties, 1865.

In 1865, the territorial capital moved to Virginia City. The Gallatin County seat remained at the now-incorporated Gallatin City. The commissioners appointed W. M. Wright as county clerk, J. B. Campbell as treasurer, and miller George Thomas as assessor. C. D. Loutzenheiser, builder of the ferry at Gallatin City, became county sheriff. All were sworn in by Probate Judge Thomas Dunbar, the man who built the first house in the area. The commissioners agreed to meet at the home of J. B. Campbell.

In fall 1865, elections were held, with thirty-four men voting. Thomas Cover became county clerk, John S. Mendenhall was the new sheriff, P. W. McAdow was treasurer, Stephen Allen became superintendent of the county's few schools, Frederick M. Meredith was elected surveyor, J. H. Shober was district attorney, and John M. Bozeman became the county's probate judge. George Thomas remained assessor. Shortly thereafter, Thomas Cover resigned to go back east for a wife, and W. M. Wright took his place as county clerk. The appointed commissioners were re-elected and remained in place.

The *Montana Post* predicted a busy year for the new Montana: "Look out for spring immigration. By a private letter we hear that 2,300 teams are ready to start from Omaha with the first good weather."[2] As settlers who had already arrived moved about the Gallatin Valley, they noted the differences from mile to mile in the quality of the

soil, availability of water, plant life, and climate. Little was familiar on the plains. The seasons didn't progress in a regular order here. When spring came back East, it was there to stay; here spring could be followed by heavy snow and frost. Summer's heat could be interrupted by frost as well. "It rained, but all at once, and then not for months at a time. It was hot and parched, and it was cold with blizzards seemingly intent on leveling every intrusion on the open spaces." Hail was not unknown back East, of course, but this hail "was like carrying all your money in a bucket, and then you fall and the wind blows it all away."[3] Farmers everywhere complained about the weather, but Montana storms were especially discouraging.

Even the usually optimistic Reverend Alderson was dispirited in 1865. On April 20, he entered an uncharacteristic note in his diary:

It is winter here yet. Thawing a little during day. Bare spots here and there, but many frequent showers of snow and such hard freezing at nights that it is becoming really discouraging to a person expecting to make money by farming here. Instead of a mild climate as it appeared and as it was reported to be when we came last summer, it is, in fact, nearly a perpetual winter. I have given up the idea of making a permanent home here and am debating the question with myself whether it will even be best to bring my family here at all.[4]

Three men seem proud of their just-finished log cabin.

However, he added, "we must try it for one season."

The native plants here were unfamiliar, some lush, others dwarfed and stunted. The new residents thought they had left grasshopper plagues behind in the Midwest and East; in 1869, however, the hungry insects appeared here, clouding the sky.

In addition to the settlers' limited experience with farming on high plains, seed was scarce and so were farming tools. Goods had to come on steamboats chugging up the Missouri River to Fort Benton, along the Overland Trail, from Walla Walla in Washington Territory, or from Salt Lake City, four hundred miles away. Reverend Alderson was forced to order seed in Utah for his first wheat crop. He got potato starts locally, however, by trading horses to Elliott Rouse. If he had not had the two hundred and fifty dollars' worth of horseflesh to trade, Alderson would have paid from twenty to

forty cents per pound for the starts.

The new Montanans ignored for a time what other westerners had learned from the first gold strikes in California in 1849: that the right to divert water in a semi-arid region is not necessarily tied to a land parcel; moreover, a water right could be considered a separate commodity acquired by those who used it first.

On January 11, 1865, in an attempt to copy the water law of the East, the Territorial Legislature voted to base water use on the Doctrine of Riparian Rights, assuming that the water flowing by each homestead would be used by that land owner in equal amounts. They assumed that "Every proprietor of lands on the banks of a river has naturally an equal right to the use of the water which flows in the stream adjacent to his lands, as it was wont to run . . . without diminution or alteration."[5]

As historian Robert G. Dunbar states, the

Doctrine of Riparian Rights was

ill suited to the agricultural needs of Montana.... There is ... more land in Montana than there is water to irrigate it. In many valleys, if there were an equal division of the stream among the water-users, there would not be enough water for each user to farm an economical unit.[6]

Although some farmers and ranchers in the Gallatin Valley did divert water for their use from streams flowing by their land, others used water brought to their property by means of irrigation ditches. In time, this early use of water was adjudicated as a separate property right by courts relying on the Doctrine of Prior Appropriation—first in time, first in right.

The sixth Territorial Legislature repealed parts of the earlier water law based on riparian rights stating that "in all controversies respecting the rights to water ... the same shall be determined by the date of appropriation."[7] The Montana Supreme Court issued a similar declaration in 1870, as had the U.S. Congress four years earlier, but state law still had on the books conflicting water rights, based on either riparian or prior appropriation. As Dunbar concludes, "Montana seemed to have a foot in both camps."[8] For the next fifty years, confusion over the right to divert water and a satisfactory method to record that right resulted in acrimonious fights between Gallatin Valley users and with the state.

* * *

Ever the promoter, John Bozeman outlined in the *Montana Post* the steps prospective farmers in the Gallatin Valley were taking:

The valley is being fast settled up with farmers, many of whom came to Montana as a better class of miners and after a while quitting their original pursuits secured 160 acres of land on which they stick a stake giving the date, the name of their claim, they then build their cabins and go to work in true farmer fashion.[9]

Perhaps Bozeman was a bit pompous about farmers and their superior character; however, the agricultural migration and settlement had begun.

Families grouped about the settlement called Willow Creek in 1863 and 1864. The little creek which ran through the camp had been called the Philosophy River by Lewis and Clark, but was now called the more prosaic Willow Creek. Settlers lived in tents while they built the first cabins. The Tinsley brothers, Joseph and William B., arrived from Missouri, determined to raise crops for the miners at Virginia City. Michigan farmer James Ritchie staked out his Michigan Ranch, where he would grow vegetables. Henry and George Geddes came from California, bringing a string of horses to breed. Levi Maxwell brought in the area's first threshing machine. Blacksmith Marshall C. Coursein and wife Sarah O'Green would eventually build a stately, three-story, seven-gabled frame home at Willow Creek, freighting the lumber from Helena. Jean Baptiste, sometimes known as "Mexican John," came with an early wagon train to homestead, raising horses and cattle. Wellington A. Fredericks built the area's first flour mill in 1873. A. J. Woodward opened the first hotel.

Willow Creek became the site of one of the first church missions in the area. Larned B. Stateler, a Southern Methodist minister (the Methodist Church had split from the main church over the question of slavery) who had come with Jim Bridger's wagon train in 1864, so enjoyed meeting his new neighbors at a Christmas Eve social that he decided to found a circuit mission. For thirty years, Reverend Stateler traveled throughout the area on horseback, conducting services as far away as Virginia City. He built the Stateler Chapel in 1873.

Within a few years of settlement, Willow Creek children attended school; Sally Leeper was their first teacher. Until the Willow Creek Post Office opened in 1867, residents picked up their mail at the Sturgis Ranch.

Another cluster of buildings formed in 1866 around a stage stop, later called Canyon House. The resulting settlement would eventually be called Logan, named for early resident Odelia Logan and her army husband, who died at the Battle of the Little Bighorn. A general store there would be owned and managed by L. C. Bevier; Jess Parrish would open his meat market; O. W. Gilhooley would run the grocery; and Toy Wing would preside over a restaurant. Other businesses included seven saloons, Flynn's Hotel, Byron McCollum's livery,

The Downing Hotel in Willow Creek.

The Marshall C. Coursein house in Willow Creek.

and P. T. Moorse's blacksmith shop. Logan children attended first and second grades at Gallatin City School; in a few years, the later grades would be added to form Logan School.

The character of Logan would radically change in 1883 with the decision of the Northern Pacific Railroad to center its siding operations there with a roundhouse, water tank, section house, coal dock, sand house, and homes for company officials. The Logan Depot was an elegant affair with a slate roof and marble floors; at one end of the depot was the Beanery, a cafe patronized by farmers and ranchers when they came to town.

In 1861, a family of ten Cornish children in Scales Mound, Illinois, had to decide whether to stay in the Midwest or to join others moving west to the gold fields in Bannack and Virginia City. Their parents, William and Margaret Ann White, had died from pneumonia within a few months of one another. The girls elected to stay in Illinois and tend to their youngest brother, eight-year-old Stephen. Thomas, James, John, and William White (with his wife and daughter) came west with the understanding that they would return for Stephen when he was older. William and Thomas opened a butcher shop in Virginia City in 1864; John and James ranched in the Lower Madison Valley near Gallatin City; thirteen-year-old Stephen joined the family there in 1866. Although the lure of a possible gold strike remained strong, eventually all of the brothers except Thomas ranched in or near the Gallatin Valley, William in Bridger Canyon, James west of Bozeman, John near the present Manhattan, and Stephen on Middle Creek.

As the fortunes of Gallatin City declined, another settlement nearby began to take shape. It shifted location from time to time and changed its name but eventually was called Three Forks. James Thompson Shedd (sometimes spelled "Shed"), a Scottish immigrant who had a passion for building bridges, arrived from South Carolina with his wood cutting tools. Setting up a sawmill, he cut down cottonwoods nearby and constructed two bridges across the Madison River, bypassing Gallatin City by two miles and thus providing a shorter way to get from the Gallatin Valley to Virginia City and the mines. The site became known as Bridgetown, Bridgeville, and Old Town.

By 1871, Shedd had completed seven toll bridges, two of which were covered, an unusual sight

The Logan Depot, an elegant building. It was torn down in the 1970s.

The settlement at Shedd's Bridge, an early stage stop on the way to Virginia City.

in the West. Soon, numerous Shedd relatives arrived from South Carolina with a string of thirteen horses and a mare. They helped the senior Shedd to build even more bridges and engaged in a variety of other business ventures. While her husband built bridges, Mrs. Shedd collected gold dust as toll and presided over a hostelry variously called Madison House, Shedd's Madison Bridge House, and Bridge House. Described as an "elegant stop," the hotel supplied "a good assortment of liquors, wines, and cigars" at the bar.[10]

By 1880, Shedd had sold his bridge complex to Asher Ware Paul and Michael Hanley and moved to Trail Creek to build another sawmill to accommodate the growing coal industry. Bridgeville burned in 1881; Paul and Hanley quickly rebuilt and expanded to serve travelers going west to the mines.

By 1865, a settlement called Hamilton surrounded another stage stop one mile south and east of the present town of Manhattan. It would soon boast of a post office established in 1868 by Daniel Small, a school, a blacksmith, several residences, and a two-story general store built by Elkanah Morse and managed by Elijah Dumphy. By 1872, it was known as John Potter's general store; Good Templars lodge meetings and dances were held on the second floor, attended by lonely farmers and ranchers, eager for a bit of social life. There was no saloon in Hamilton, unusual for a western town. Hamilton, including Potter's building, would move to a new location closer to the railroad in 1883 and be renamed Moreland by a group of aspiring British horse breeders. The town would become Manhattan in 1891.

When Charles Leon Anxionnaz and his wife Marie Angelique settled south of Hamilton in 1864, he soon realized that Americans would never learn to spell his French name. The following year, he appealed to the Montana Territorial Legislature and had his name legally changed to Anceney. The energetic immigrants increased their holdings around their ranch, called Meadow Brook, to fourteen hundred acres.

THREE FORKS HOTEL, PAUL AND HANLEY, PROP'S, THREE FORKS, GALLATIN Co, MONT.

Shedd's Madison Bridge House became the elegant Three Forks Hotel, Asher Paul and Michael Hanley, Proprietors. ETCHING FROM MICHAEL LEESON, HISTORY OF MONTANA, 1885.

STORE of JOHN POTTER, HAMILTON, GALLATIN CO.

John Potter's stage stop and general store became the center for the settlement at Hamilton (Manhattan). ETCHING FROM MICHAEL LEESON, HISTORY OF MONTANA, 1885.

The Anceneys excelled at tackling oversize projects that might daunt residents with more modest goals. Their barn was the largest in the county, their three-story brick residence a showplace. The Anceneys had trailed a number of shorthorn cattle from Idaho, hoping to add purebreds from Kentucky to improve the breed. In order to raise extra money for more cattle, Anceney freighted goods to nearby towns. This meant that Marie Angelique and eleven-year-old Charles II managed the ranch. With the freighting money, Anceney also bought Percherons; at one point, twenty-four hundred horses grazed on Meadow Brook land.

A staunch Republican, Anceney found time

A busy day at the Alonzo Dwight Ranch, Springhill.

to serve as Gallatin County Commissioner. The taking on of a partner, Helena tycoon Thomas Cruse, and the winter of 1886-1887 led Anceney to bankruptcy; both events soured the operation. The harsh winter killed much of the purebred livestock and "partner" Cruse somehow engineered foreclosure on Meadow Brook. By July 1893, Anceney was left with five dollars; his son had seventy-five cents in his pockets. The Anceneys would surface again in a different part of the Gallatin Valley with a new bank loan and renewed dreams for the largest ranch in the county.

Mormons John and Mary Reese, originally from Wales, settled at the north end of the valley near Courts, a small settlement named for mail carrier P. O. Courts, eventually renamed Reese Creek. The Reese women had earned a bit of money doing laundry as the family moved about the mining camps. Daughter Jane fell in love with Missourian John Wells. Her father was so upset at her falling in love with a Southerner that he forbade the marriage. The rest of the family was more sympathetic and helped the couple to elope; later, John Reese became

reconciled to the couple. In time, Reese Creek supported a general store, a blacksmithy, a church, a school, and a cheese factory.

To the southeast of the Reese Creek settlement, fourteen miles north of Bozeman, a large spring tumbles down from the Bridgers. This attracted a number of newcomers who realized the stream, called Spring Creek or Mill Creek, could be harnessed for a variety of projects requiring water power. On the valley floor below, simple cabins sprouted near what is now called Springhill. When Melvin Ross, Sr., arrived in 1863, he took one look at the 9,007-foot mountain towering above the new settlement, climbed to its peak carrying an American flag, and planted it at the summit, enthusiastically naming it Ross Peak. As Mill Creek flowed down to the settlement, its name changed to Ross Creek. The Rosses were one of several Mormon families to move into the valley. Determined to separate from the Salt Lake community, they called themselves Josephites.

Springhill resident Lewis M. Howell joined forces with Henry Monforton to be the first businessmen to use Ross Creek water. They established the Mountain Dew Distillery and made whiskey, a product in great demand in the mining camps. Eager farmers sold their rye crop to the men, although not everyone approved. When in full operation, 350 to 500 gallons of Mountain Dew whiskey sat stacked and ready for freighting to the mines or to Bozeman. Indian customers slipped down from the north to buy the liquor. John Bogert remembered his first "dose of Howell's Springhill Mountain Dew . . . 'Twas made of Gallatin White— and white as water and twice as pure, it made me feel like a red-hot furnace blown up by an electric light."[11] In 1869, Howell sold out to Monforton and established another distillery downstream.

Using Ross Creek water as power, Howell and Isaac Benham built a sawmill in 1864, which was later acquired through foreclosure on a $2,012 debt by an imposing fifty-year-old immigrant from Norway—Annie Ryen. Long dresses did not impede Miss Ryen as she logged in the area with a team of oxen. Arthur Truman established his lumber business in 1869, buying from Howell and Benham, and then from Ryen. Nearby, Tom Crane established a blacksmith shop "with an ingenious contrivance by which to keep the forge going in the shape of a blowing machine propelled by water."[12] He added a shingle factory to his operation in 1872. Ruben Foster ran a planing mill powered by Ross Creek water.

Merritt, John, and Oscar Penwell came from Alder Gulch in 1865 to look over the Springhill area. Originally from Indiana, Merritt had prospected for gold for two years near Virginia City; he established a bakery near Alder Gulch which proved to be profitable. Both Merritt and Oscar homesteaded on land a few miles northwest of Springhill; brother John went on to Kansas to become a wheat farmer. Merritt and Oscar Penwell completed a two-mile irrigation ditch from the East Gallatin River to their wheat fields. Looking to the mountain streams coming down from the Bridgers, they realized that a flour mill to process their wheat could be powered by Ross Creek water. Two years later, customers could buy finished flour at the Penwells' Union Flour mill.

Eventually the brothers improved the water power to the flour mill by constructing a giant flume

Annie Ryen was an astute businesswoman who started several successful ventures.

from Mill Creek. With the resulting increase in production, the Union Mill supplied flour to military posts as well as to local customers. Oscar took over management of the mill while Merritt concentrated upon growing wheat. Down through the years, the Union mill changed hands and its name a number of times. Because of her ability to loan money to those who could not repay her, Annie Ryen acquired the business by foreclosure. She sent for her nephew Martin to manage it. In 1930, Bozeman merchant Eugene Graf leased the mill. The following November, he lost it when the old building burned to the ground.

Miller George D. Thomas would establish another flour mill in Springhill in 1878, three miles downstream from the Union mill. Since he already had milling machinery located at Gallatin City, where he operated the Thomas Mill, he hauled some of it to his new location. The resulting Empire Mill offered three brands of finished flours: Lily the White, Rose, and Belle of Montana, named after his daughters. Flour sacks imprinted with these

73

The flour mill at Springhill with remodeled flume, c1903. Ross Peak is in background.

A harvesting crew takes a break.

brand names often appeared on local wash lines in the form of diapers, underwear, and dish towels.

Also downstream from the Union Flour Mill, a furniture factory was established, using water power from Ross Creek. The Sash and Door Factory produced carved beds and other fine household items. Across the road from the factory, residents built a little log cabin and used it as a dance hall. It has since been replaced by the Springhill Pavilion, which stands there today.

For a number of years, Henry Crouse came in and out of Montana Territory. He prospected in Bannack and Alder Gulch in 1864 with no success; disappointed, he went home to Illinois. Two years later, he came out again, walking most of the way; he tried prospecting once more but earned his livelihood by freighting supplies from Salt Lake. This time he stayed three years, homesteading in Springhill; he planted apple trees and wheat fields,

irrigating with water from Ross Creek. He then went back to Illinois to begin a seven-year courtship of Anna Millhouse; they were married in 1877. When the newlyweds boarded the steamboat *Osceola* in Saint Louis, en route to the Gallatin Valley again, they had among their baggage a one-hundred-pound school bell which Anna's brothers insisted she bring with her to call for help should she need protection. For years, she rang the bell to call Henry from the fields.

Andrew L. Corbly settled in a nearby canyon which today bears his name, setting out four hundred apple tress and planting potatoes. He and other settlers tramped the nearby mountains looking for profitable mining sites. Bachelor Jim Bamber spent his days digging holes in the Bridgers, hoping to strike gold; he was personable, it is said, but he seldom bathed, and never found the treasure he sought.[13]

An early saw outfit near Springhill. Owner William P. Schrink is fourth from left.

Frenchwoman Madame Mouche—her real name was Elizabeth Guyrand—worked as a cook for rancher Charles Anceney and lived near Corbly Gulch. Soon after she arrived, her husband died and her daughter ran away to her beloved Paris to join the Folies. With her son Marcus, Madame Mouche maintained a home filled with antiques, surrounded by beautiful flower gardens. No one could turn down her delicate pastries. Evidently Madame Mouche contracted gold fever; she could often be found in the Bridgers digging for precious ore, dressed in a black skirt with voluminous pockets, which held her personal papers and all of her money.

Until 1872, Springhill children went to school in nearby homes, barns, and even the furniture factory. A log schoolhouse was built that year near the by-then-defunct distillery to house all eight grades taught by one teacher. During recess, the teacher had to rout out some of her pupils who were fascinated with the inner workings of the rusting distilling equipment. In 1880, classes were held in a former residence. Eight years later, Springhill School opened and still operates today.

Church services were also held in schoolrooms until 1907, when the Reverend Davis Willson helped to dedicate a little white church located on an acre donated by Henry Crouse. The parents of the Springhill Church Sunday School bought a threshing machine for the use of local farmers and ranchers. Incorporated as the S.S.T.M.C., the Sunday School Threshing Machine Company rented the thresher six days a week at low rates to encourage both farmer and machine to rest on Sunday.

On July 14, 1864, John W. and Lavine Nelson, with their four boys, left the Hensley wagon train

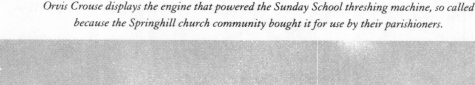

Orvis Crouse displays the engine that powered the Sunday School threshing machine, so called because the Springhill church community bought it for use by their parishioners.

to settle on the West Gallatin River near a site that would become Old Central Park. Evidently, the Nelsons stopped just in time, because Lavine Nelson delivered a baby boy on July 27 in a small lean-to draped with blankets. The parents named their fifth son William Gallatin Nelson, later called "Pike." (Three years later, Lavine Nelson delivered another son; they named him Frank, later called "Doc," who grew up to be one of artist Charles M. Russell's favorite models, featured in his famous painting, *Bronc to Breakfast.*)

C. P. Blakeley, the man who would later petition the Territorial Legislature to designate his Farmington Ranch as the county seat, homesteaded across the river from the Nelsons. Both families won permission in 1868 to build a toll bridge. They named the site Central Park. Two years later, in 1870, Vardiman A. Cockrell bought the toll bridge and added a two-story home and inn for those traveling across the valley by stage. Cockrell was appointed postmaster in 1871.

In the early 1880s, Cockrell sold the entire development to William Fly. After a fire at the inn, Fly improved and enlarged the property to house more guests. In 1884, he became postmaster and called his settlement "Fly's Bridges." H. C. Cockrell, brother to Vardiman, settled nearby, raising livestock and operating a creamery. When postmaster Fly died in 1887, H. C. took over the job and moved the post office to his ranch, calling it "Creamery." Later, he renamed it "Central Park," thus adding to the confusion of names for the same place. When the Northern Pacific ran its line near the "new" Central Park, most of the buildings from the "old" Central Park, three miles south, were moved closer to the railroad.

The Zachariah Sales family, who had come to the valley with a wagon train along the Bozeman Trail in 1865, formed another agricultural nucleus with new neighbors near what is now Gallatin Gateway. Sales had come from England to the United States, settling in Jennie, Wisconsin, for

William Fly residence and toll station at Central Park. ETCHING FROM MICHAEL LEESON, *HISTORY OF MONTANA*, 1885.

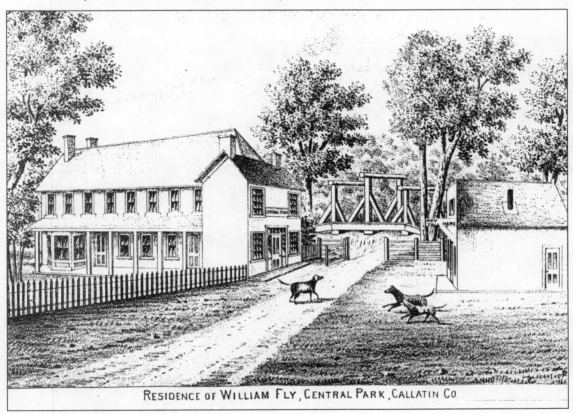

RESIDENCE OF WILLIAM FLY, CENTRAL PARK, GALLATIN CO.

Early Salesville. CHARLES KINSEY PHOTO.

Salesville schoolchildren mug for the camera.

some years. He had established a lumber business there, rafting logs down the Mississippi River to Saint Louis; thus, it was natural for Sales to operate a sawmill at the gateway to the Gallatin Canyon. As Sales was joined by other members of his family from Wisconsin, he expanded the business to establish logging camps in Gallatin Canyon at Hell Roaring Creek, Greek Creek, and Taylor Fork, floating logs down the rocky Gallatin River during spring high water to Salesville.

The little gateway community was first called Slabtown, then Salesville in 1883 after the senior Sales, who did not stay around to watch it grow; "too many people," he grumbled, and moved to remote Flathead land near Murray, Montana. John J. Tomlinson, who had been running a sawmill in the Yellowstone Valley, bought out the Sales interest in 1887 (he had owned it once before) and continued the business. He also platted Salesville, predicting a sharp rise in its fortunes.

*　*　*

By 1864 and 1865, the valley's first crops were coming in. Reverend Alderson's first potato crop matured just before the harsh snows of 1865 fell. He and his brother knew there would be a demand for spuds in the mining camps but wondered how to get them there. They decided that prospects in the new gold diggings near Diamond City, sixty miles east of Helena, would prove to be the best. Diamond City was the result of the discovery of gold in a nearby gulch opened by four Confederate soldiers and named, appropriately enough, Confederate Gulch. Diamond City had the reputation of being a place for wealthy but wild and tough miners, and would boom to five thousand residents in three years. The Alderson brothers wanted to see it.

They had no sacks—an expensive item—and nothing to cover their wagons loaded with potatoes. Off they started toward the gold camp, a ten-day trip; they were almost immediately hit with a bitter winter storm. They used their bedrolls to cover their produce. As they traveled north, crossing Sixteenmile Creek and beyond, temperatures remained well below zero, not a good prospect for their haul. They passed one unfortunate rancher who had loads of potatoes frozen solid. On December 1, they arrived in Diamond City and, within a few minutes, sold their entire load, including thirty-six

pounds of butter, for $554.80 in gold dust. Even those who brought frozen potatoes to the camp were able to sell them, though at a discount.

Welshman John J. Thomas of Springhill, with his son David Davis, brought in one bushel of seed from Salt Lake City and harvested fifty bushels of wheat on his Springhill farm later in 1864. By the fall of 1865, Gallatin Valley farmers had harvested twenty thousand bushels; two years later, three hundred thousand bushels went to market.

In order to insure that farmers could harvest their first wheat crops, Bozeman flour mill owners Tom Cover and the McAdow brothers got together five hundred dollars to buy a threshing machine, which came first by steamboat to Fort Benton and then was freighted overland to the valley. Local farmers paid twenty-five cents per bushel to use the machine and brought their finished grain to the flour mill in Bozeman, the first to begin operations in Montana Territory. To the west, the Fredericks Mill in Gallatin City, under construction since 1864, opened for business in 1866.

Following the example of the Penwell brothers, others added more irrigation ditches from the East and West Gallatin Rivers or their tributaries within a few years, crisscrossing the valley to water new crops of wheat, potatoes, and other vegetables and grains. As John Bozeman had predicted, the Gallatin Valley had become the "Garden of Montana."

Livestock dotted the fertile valley; settlers brought in horses, cattle, dairy cows, sheep, and swine, a few at a time. It was feared that sheep might not flourish in such a mountain valley but the first flocks grew healthy and multiplied. By 1881, more sheep grazed on Montana lands than cattle.

When Nelson Story left Alder Gulch early in 1866, the former Athens, Ohio, man had accumulated twenty thousand dollars, more than enough to underwrite an ambitious cattle drive. Having spent two seasons in Alder Gulch, the budding business tycoon, still in his late twenties, could see that beef would bring a lot of money in the gold camps. Story traveled to Fort Worth, Texas, where he bought a thousand Longhorns at ten dollars a head. Story's crew of twenty-seven men drove them north to Kansas, where farmers stopped the drive, claiming they did not want their farms trampled by hundreds of cattle.

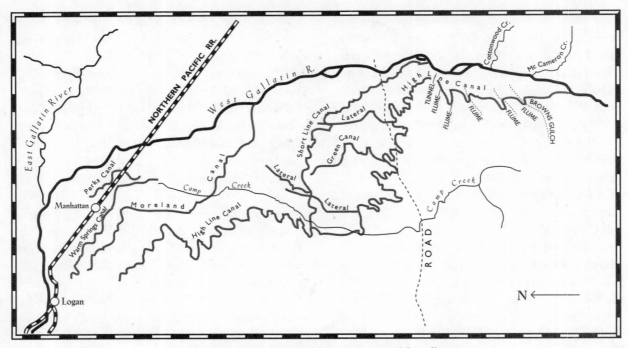

Irrigation canals crisscross the western part of the valley.

BOZEMAN.

*Nelson Story trailed cattle from Texas to the Yellowstone
Valley in 1866. Businessman, promoter, and benefactor,
he was never dull and always controversial.*

ETCHING FROM MICHAEL LEESON, *HISTORY OF MONTANA*, 1885.

80

Undismayed, Story decided to bypass the farmland, stocking up with groceries at Fort Leavenworth and buying a new Remington rapid-fire breechloader for each man. From Fort Leavenworth, the cattle moved leisurely north with no trouble until they approached Fort Reno, Wyoming, on the Bozeman Trail. There they were met by a large party of Sioux. Since the cattle train was now traveling through Indian treaty land, the Sioux ran off some of the cattle and wounded two of Story's men.

Leaving the wounded to recover at the fort, Story recaptured most of the stolen cattle and trailed the herd toward Fort Phil Kearny. There he met with fort commander Colonel Henry B. Carrington, who told Story he could go no further on the Bozeman Trail with a mere twenty-five men; forty armed guards were required. Even though it was late in the season, the cattle man would have to stay put until another train came along the trail. Additionally, Carrington ordered Story to corral his cattle three miles from the Fort. Why so far away? asked Story. Animals from the fort need the closer grass, replied the colonel.

Story built two corrals to contain his stock and waited about one week to see if the colonel would change his mind about allowing him to continue.

When he did not hear from Carrington, Story changed his own mind. Late one night, after a near-unanimous vote of the men, he moved his cattle on their way. George Gow was the only cowboy to object to the move and Story put him on "wagon-arrest" for the rest of the trip. Traveling at night seemed to be the safest way to avoid Indian interference; they rested by day, aiming their Remington rifles on the few Indians that came their way. When the party got to Fort C. F. Smith, the danger of Indian theft or attack lessened.

Early in December, Nelson Story moved more than six hundred cattle up the Yellowstone River to the Upper Yellowstone Valley (sometimes called Paradise Valley), where he established a ranch. The trip had taken four months, "probably the longest continuous overland drive every made north from Texas."[14] The ranch site was an ideal spot from which to supply neighboring mining towns and military posts with beef. Nelson Story's financial eye was bright and far-seeing, however; ranching was only one of many ways he hoped to make money.

Dairies began operations throughout the Gallatin Valley, with Reverend Alderson a leader in that endeavor; soon, his herd grew to twenty-two cows. When Gallatin City hosted the first county fair in 1866, County Commissioner Philip Thorpe amazed visitors with his decorative display of two hundred pounds of butter. Four years later, dairyman Alderson took first prize at a fair in Helena for his cheese and butter.

In 1867, at the eastern end of the valley, Colonel James D. Chesnut, along with two blacksmiths and two dogs, did some wandering. Chesnut was looking for coal deposits, as he had in California, Kansas, and Colorado. The former New Yorker had led an eventful life before coming to Montana. At the age of eighteen, he had booked passage on a steamer bound for California; it exploded, killing one hundred passengers. Chesnut escaped. Later, he joined the notorious Independence Brigade, a band of mercenaries led by William Walker. The brigade invaded western Mexico; Walker declared himself President of Southern California.

After further misadventures in Mexican provinces, Chesnut decided he had had enough and returned to San Francisco to board a steamer bound for New York. This time the passenger launch to the ship sank; thirty-eight drowned, but Chesnut swam to shore and later boarded the steamer. Just before the Civil War, Chesnut was involved in the Kansas border wars and was arrested and jailed for high treason. By war's end, however, he had risen to the rank of colonel in the Union Army and had commanded Indian and black units.

In Bozeman, Chesnut—short, stocky, with a distinguished Van Dyke beard—settled down to preside over a log cabin saloon called Chesnut's Corner. It was a businessmen's retreat with reading and club rooms where men retired to discuss Republican issues and local business ventures. The colonel eventually built an elegant two-story saloon on the southwest corner of Main Street and Bozeman Avenue, sometimes known as "Chesnut's Folly" because some felt he had put too much capital into the venture. The businessmen moved their retreat, called the Board Room, to the second floor

Colonel James D. Chesnut found coal deposits east of the Gallatin Valley.

The area's first coke oven was built by William Williams in 1882 near Cokedale.

of the new saloon where Chesnut maintained a bar that was "the finest to be found in Montana."[15]

Naturally, the colonel heated the establishment with coal when he opened his first mines. He had located coal deposits east of the valley in the Bozeman Pass area. Coal was to Chesnut as the building of bridges was to James Shedd. He was the butt of many jokes because of his interest in mining coal; many thought it an impractical business despite the growing shortage of wood as heating fuel. But within a number of years, settlements near Bozeman Pass—Storrs, Maxey, Timberline, Cokedale, Hoffman, Trail Creek, and Chestnut (The U.S. Post Office added another "t" to the town's name)—bustled with small trains, giant wooden washers, and smoking coke ovens. A few businessmen, including Colonel Chesnut, grew prosperous on what was first dismissed as nonsense and then touted as "black diamonds." Eventually, Chesnut moved to Rocky Canyon to operate a hotel near Chestnut-with-a-t.

As in other parts of the West, homesteading appealed to single women as well as single men. Margaret Maccumber was the first woman to file for a homestead in Montana Territory; she paid the ten dollar fee on September 8, 1870, for parcel No.

299, land just southwest of Bozeman, adjoining the homestead of her son-in-law Matthew Bird. Since she did not like the idea of living by herself, the Birds built two cabins along their common property line, with connecting doors.

Years later, Bertha Crouse, daughter of Springhill residents Henry and Anna Crouse, was also attracted to a homestead of her own. She filed on a parcel near Three Forks sometime after 1900, proving up by living in a one-room cabin at least part of the year. Despite her intense fear of rattlesnakes, she walked her land, armed with a shotgun. Bertha's brother Walter homesteaded next to her and may have done the heaviest farm work for her. When Bertha married Sven Carlson in 1915, the couple concentrated their farming on Springhill land. She sold her Three Forks homestead in 1940 for $2.50 per acre.

In May 1867, Surveyor General Solomon Meredith of the Territorial Land Office wandered about southwestern Montana, looking for the proper place to establish an Initial Point. He took Walter deLacy and Benjamin F. Marsh with him on his travels; deLacy would become noted for his beautiful maps. The closest existing Initial Points were near Boise, Idaho, to the west, and in the Black Hills, to the east. A Principal Meridian and Principal Parallel stretching out from an Initial Point would permit more precisely defined townships and sections, which would make those who claimed homestead land more secure with clarification of their boundaries. Meredith finally chose a spot four-and-one-half miles south and one mile west of the community of Willow Creek; he placed an official marker on an eight-hundred-foot-high hill.

Some newcomers did not prosper in the Gallatin Valley. Twenty-four-year-old Joseph Kenney had left his wife Susan and several children in Iowa to make his fortune in the West. He said good-bye to farm life and "Mr. Lincoln's infernal Negro war"[16] in June 1864, traveling to Montana Territory with his brother George, his brother-in-law Tom Rhoten, and several other young men to find gold and the good life, as well as to avoid conscription into the Union army. Kenney held strong views on political questions, expressing himself vividly in letters back home to Susan, describing one of their neighbors as that "abolitionist son of a bitch"[17] who supported the "cruel, unrighteous war."[18]

He wrote his wife that Montana was not a place she would find agreeable, at least not at that time. It was lonely and desolate, he said, with few women to talk to. He asked for pictures of the children and copies of the Chicago papers. A child had been born since he left home; Kenney told Susan that, since it was a girl, she could name it.

A year would pass before he got any word from home—no letters, no photos, no newspapers. He and the men he had come west with fanned out, looking for opportunities. They fancied themselves miners, but visits to Virginia City proved unrewarding. Some traveled up and down the Yellowstone River looking for work. Kenney and Rhoten lived in Diamond City for a time, building cabins for those too busy looking for gold. They always gravitated back to the Gallatin Valley, however; nothing much happened here, according to Kenney, but it looked a little like Iowa if you didn't count the mountains.

The men worked for Henry Monforton now and then and saw the first crops come in. Kenney wrote home: "the crops are magnificent and the dullest times I ever saw in any country."[19] For the next four years, Kenney and his friends continued their attempts to strike it rich with little result. Kenney told Susan he was coming home in the spring, maybe at the end of the summer, surely this fall, or maybe next spring after the winter storms.

Finally, the men decided that they had had enough. They no longer had to worry about military service—the war was over and President Lincoln was dead. The men who would be miners admitted that they were, indeed, born and bred farmers. They had seen the elephant and looked forward to home.

They found an available mackinaw boat on the Yellowstone and made their plans for a quick downstream trip home. Brother George Kenney decided to go back by a different route. A friend who decided to stay in Montana wrote the Iowa families that this time the others were coming home, for sure.

Sometime during the fall of 1868, the Virginia City *Weekly Montana Democrat* printed a brief story about five young men traveling down the Yellowstone by mackinaw who were killed by the Sioux. The article named Jeff Whittington, M. Crow, Mason Medley, Tom Rhoten, and Joseph Kenney.

chapter

TWELVE

Most wagon trains from the Bozeman Trail came down into the Gallatin Valley, rumbling past what looked like a desolate outpost at the base of the pass. They saw a few settlers building cabins and stores, but their eyes looked farther west. Single men rushed by to see if any gold was left at Bannack and Virginia City. Others were moving fast, too, anxious to leave the Civil War and conscription behind. Families had their eyes on the rich farmland to the west. By the fall of 1864, however, Bozeman City began to look like a settlement.

New arrivals John Stafford and W. S. Rice saw the need for a hotel and quickly put together a tiny one-and-a-half-story structure at the northwest corner of Main Street and Bozeman Avenue to accommodate those who didn't want to live in a tent and could afford not to. Rice soon found he was not meant to be an innkeeper. He left for Diamond City almost immediately to try his hand at the new gold diggings there.

On Christmas Eve, 1864, before the hotel room partitions were up, a "grand ball" was held at the Stafford building to celebrate the founding of the new community. As was usual with "first" western dances, the men lined up to dance with the few women in the settlement. Romance bloomed for hotelkeeper Stafford and Sallie Smith, who were

married two weeks later on January 11 by Reverend Alderson.

Stafford later sold out to Caleb D. Fitz, who, in turn, passed the little building on to J. J. Parham, who had brought forty thousand dollars' worth of merchandise from the States. It was not long before the newly formed Masonic Lodge No. 6, A.F. & A.M., used the building's upstairs for meetings; membership in Lodge No. 6 was more or less restricted to those men or their sons with Confederate ties. The Masons bought the building in 1866 for five hundred dollars, renting the first floor to the Empire Corral and then to Osborn's Drug Store.

Before the winter of 1864's first snow, six or seven log cabins defined the new settlement. William Beall finished his first home on the site of the present Carnegie Library building; Elliott Rouse built a small cabin on John Bozeman's claim, located on the south side of Main Street, east of Bozeman Avenue, then put up another cabin for himself, on the north side of Main, east of Bozeman Avenue. French-Canadian John Richard, Jr. (also spelled Reshawe or Richau), guide for the Townsend wagon train along the Bozeman Trail, moved into another new home. Mexican immigrant Joe Merraville and his Sioux wife built a double log cabin on the southwest corner of the present Bozeman Avenue

John Stafford and W. S. Rice constructed this one-and-a-half-story hotel on the northwest corner of East Main Street and Bozeman Avenue during the late summer of 1864. The Masons purchased the building in 1866, which was later used as Willson & Rich's general store, then as Osborn's Drug Store.

FIRST HOUSE BUILT IN BOZEMAN 1864
BY ROUSE & BEALL

Bozeman's first cabin. ETCHING FROM MICHAEL LEESON, *HISTORY OF MONTANA*, 1885.

Joe Merraville built this double log cabin, later used as a school. ETCHING FROM MICHAEL LEESON, *HISTORY OF MONTANA*, 1885.

85

Early Main Street, facing west, in the late 1860s. Note wooden bridge over Bozeman Creek, lower left.

and Mendenhall Street, which would later be used as a school.

Caleb Fitz and his son Payne lived in the back room of their new general store at 130 East Main. And Frederick F. Fridley invited everyone to inspect his Main Street cabin, which boasted a floor covered with real wood planks. His wife America would be pleased when she arrived.

John S. "Jack" Mendenhall opened Bozeman's first saloon, which also featured canned peaches and sundries, at 27 East Main. When Dr. Achilles Lamme arrived, he decided not to practice medicine; instead, he joined forces with Springhill man Lewis M. Howell to open another general store; later he became partners with Mendenhall. After trying the Stafford building location, J. J. Parham moved to a new spot but soon sold out to Charles Rich and Loren W. Tuller in 1866. Rich and Tuller had first brought their goods to the Penwell Ranch, operating from a tent, but moved the merchandise into Bozeman while they were waiting for their third partner to arrive—General Lester S. Willson.

The former New Yorker had enlisted in the Union army in 1861 as a private; three years later,

he was a brevet brigadier. General Willson heard his friend Horace Greeley exhorting men to come west; he did, despite Greeley's apparent change of mind, for he told Willson he was a damned fool to settle in Montana Territory. Tuller sold out to the general when he arrived in April 1867.

With encouragement and help from John Bozeman, Perry W. McAdow and Tom Cover started to build a grist and flour mill north of town on October 1. When they opened for business in the fall of 1865, one thousand wagons had come along the Bozeman Trail.

During the summer of 1865, word spread through the settlement of a buildup of Sioux warriors east of Bozeman Pass. Rumors said the Indians were preparing to descend upon the valley pioneers. Rosa Beall remembered midnight knocks on the door of her cabin: "Get up and go to town, the Sioux Indians are just over the divide, and they have killed Colonel Kimball and another man, and are coming at daybreak to attack the settlers."[1] Women and children were herded to the former Stafford hotel for safety for a few days while men marched over the pass to fight. Despite stories of Sioux on the

Main Street lined with wood frame buildings in the late 1860s. (The 1865 date may not be correct).
Brick will not be used as a building material until another five years have passed.

Loaded mule trains on muddy Bozeman streets. Note the new trees along the boardwalk.

Wagons line muddy Main Street, c1867.

*Bozeman's first flour mill was a simple structure north of town, built to take advantage of water power nearby.
The mill opened for business in the fall of 1865.* Etching from Michael Leeson, History of Montana, 1885.

GALLATIN MILL P.W. McADOW & BRO PROPRIETORS, BOZEMAN GALLATIN, CO. MONT.

march, the men could not find them.

More hotels were constructed. George Washington A. Frazier, who fled Georgia in 1865, and his wife Elmyra enlisted the help of John Bozeman in 1866 to build a hotel. The building would eventually display the town's first commercial sign "ever swung to the breeze": CITY HOTEL.[2] Elmyra's maiden name was Bozeman but neither she nor John could determine if they were related. The Fraziers reserved rooms upstairs, one for Bozeman and one for his friend William McKinzie; the men took their meals at the hotel and could come and go as they pleased. The Fraziers would build a new hotel in 1871 called Frazier House on East Main Street and Bozeman Avenue.

John C. Guy, sometime sheriff and former resident of Gallatin City, built the two-story Guy House in 1868 on the northwest corner of Main Street and Black Avenue. Guy House quickly became the social center of town. Bozeman bachelors were marrying, one by one, and brought their brides to live at Guy House while proper accommodations could be finished. Sarah Jane Bessey Tracy remembered her first meal at the hotel on June 5, 1869:

When supper was served . . . Mrs. [Sophia] Guy insisted that I take a seat by her at the table. Every stool around the two long tables was occupied— Mrs. Guy, Mrs. [Ellen Trent] Story and I being the only ladies. It did look somewhat like curiosity . . . and Mr. Guy told me later he had seventy-five extras for dinner. I wonder if they thought Mr. Tracy's investment was a good one—I was then just a young girl of seventeen.[3]

Nelson Story and his new wife Ellen also stayed at Guy House, awaiting completion of their first home on the southwest corner of Main Street and Tracy Avenue.

Within a few days, Sarah Jane Tracy regarded herself a veteran as she welcomed General Lester Willson's new wife. Emma Weeks Willson did not have to meet Bozeman's male population all at once; the general took her to their new home at 224 Main Street. When her piano arrived—the first in town— she took up her old habit of singing a bit in the afternoons; one by one, lonely bachelors and wandering Indians stopped to listen to Emma Willson's remarkable voice. (In the 1880s, the Storys would build a showy mansion on West Main Street,

Two-story Guy House on the northwest corner of Main Street and Black Avenue welcomed newly arrived settlers'
wives while their residences were being completed. Note the saplings with protective fencing.

300 block, and the Willsons would move to their 504 South Willson Avenue home in 1886.)

Walter Cooper did not travel back to the States to fetch his bride; he brought Miriam Skeels in to Guy House from Jefferson County. Samuel Ruffner shyly told everyone he was going to Salt Lake City for supplies; he brought back Mrs. Ruffner as well. Eventually Leander M. Black bought Guy House, changing its name to the Northern Pacific Hotel, in anticipation of the railroad coming west.

Another hotel, the Metropolitan, one of the settlement's first brick structures, opened its doors in 1867 on the northeast corner of Bozeman Avenue and Main Street. Its second story opened on a balcony built over the wooden sidewalk; there residents passed the time, watching wagon and mule trains plod through Main Street mud. The Metropolitan was later called the Grand LaClede, but it never enjoyed the social prestige of Guy House.

Spieth & Krug Bozeman Brewery. Left to right: unidentified men and 3-Jim Latta, Sr.; 4-Jim Latta, Jr.; 5-A. Pierstorff; 6-F. Roy; 7-Joe LaBree; 10-Jim Gee.

Samuel E. Lewis traveled to many places before he decided on Bozeman in 1868. A black native of Haiti, Lewis spent several years traveling in Europe, then investigated gold camps in California, Oregon, and Idaho where he earned his living as a barber. He cut hair in Elk Creek, Radersburg, and Helena as well. After he arrived in Bozeman, he built the Lewis Block on the south side of East Main Street, which housed a number of businesses, including his barber shop and bath house. The genial Lewis participated in Bozeman civic affairs, often singing at public events, accompanying himself with a harp, banjo, or guitar. His son took up the guitar and accompanied his father on these occasions. Lewis built twin houses at 209 and 211 South Tracy Avenue and a residence for his family at 308 South Bozeman Avenue.

When his half-sister Edmonia was sixteen in 1859, Lewis encouraged the talented girl to apply to Oberlin, one of the few American colleges that would accept a black woman. After Oberlin, Lewis sent Edmonia abroad to study art in Florence, where she became a noted sculptor. When Lewis died in 1886, one hundred mourners attended his funeral; Mayor Frank L. Benepe gave the eulogy.

A few other American black families also sought refuge in the West from an uncertain future during the Civil War years. Richard and Mary McDonald left their home in Saint Joseph, Missouri, in 1864, and traveled by covered wagon with their three children to the new Montana Territory. They bought land near Sourdough Creek on what is now 308 South Tracy and built a cabin. The family fished the creek for summer meals; in

Successful barber and builder Samuel Lewis owned a number of private and commercial structures in town. (Templar Avenue is the present Tracy Avenue.) ETCHING FROM MICHAEL LEESON, *HISTORY OF MONTANA*, 1885.

winter, the children enjoyed skating on the frozen stream. McDonald began freighting goods from Bozeman to Virginia City; by 1872, he was affluent enough to build a two-story home around the original cabin.

Years later, Melinda M. Rich described her first impressions of the settlement:

Back of everything else is a confused picture in which are mule trains, and ox trains, emigrant wagons and cowboys with bucking horses, and the welcome arrival of the stage coach that brought to us the letters which told us of all the dear ones left behind in the old home. Not infrequently numbers of Indians would camp near town, coming every day to the dwellings, standing outside the houses with noses flattened against the window panes. At times whole tribes passed through, the chiefs in advance often dismounting to visit the stores. Squaws and papooses followed mounted upon all sorts and sizes of horses, which were otherwise laden with pots and kettles and other articles belonging to the household, with lodge poles trailing behind. The sounds of murderous pistol shots were often heard at midnight or in the early morning hours. Then followed the measured tread of men's feet as they bore some dead or wounded body away from the midnight revel. The deadly thing that usually instigated the murders and the angry shouts and curses which so often rang out upon the midnight air, was sold in low board houses.[4]

The "deadly thing," of course, was liquor, which Melinda Rich, a founding member of the local Women's Christian Temperance Union (WCTU), abhorred.

What Melinda Rich heard as bumps in the night quite possibly were men dragging drunks or other hapless law-breakers to the edge of town. It was customary in many western communities for a judge to fine the miscreant or banish him from the territory; there was no need for a jail building. O. D. Loutzenheiser, the county's first sheriff,

Members of the International Order of Odd Fellows line the street before the J. W. Tilton building and a photograph gallery.

Melinda Rich, who heard ominous noises at night in early Bozeman.

operated out of his home near Gallatin City, but as the population shifted to the eastern end of the county, law enforcement officers moved to the Bozeman area.

By February 1869, the need for a jail became evident. The county commissioners asked Sheriff John C. Guy to raise subscriptions for a building. Most families contributed ten dollars; the more affluent gave fifty. This simple method of establishing a "bond issue" resulted in the collection of $487.50. A simple log cabin was constructed on the south side of East Mendenhall Street, just one-half block from its intersection with Bozeman Avenue. Sophia Guy, who already cooked for the guests at Guy House, added more meals for whoever found himself locked up after a weekend of boisterous revelry.

On one occasion, residents, tired of waiting for the court to decide two cases, resorted to vigilante justice and hanged the alleged wrongdoers without benefit of judge or trial. Sixty-three-year-old gold

prospector Z. A. Triplett found himself in jail in October 1872, after a drunken night during which he fatally stabbed John Gempler in the stomach, the result of a long-standing feud. The *Bozeman Avant Courier* reported that Triplett was a normal sort, "generally free of quarrels and showing an absence of a vicious nature, but has not always been excusable in his conduct."[5]

There Triplett stayed until January 1873, when he was joined by John W. St. Clair, otherwise known as "Steamboat Bill," "who had been living on the proceeds of Chinese depravity," a journalistic euphemism implying "pimp."[6] Alleged to have killed a number of young Chinese women, St. Clair was awaiting a hearing scheduled for the afternoon of February 1. The night before, after insuring that the sheriff and the judge were detained elsewhere, a number of "outraged citizens" pulled the unfortunate Triplett and St. Clair from the log jail, marched them four blocks away to a slaughterhouse, and hanged them from a meat dressing rack. Five years would pass before a vigilante-proof jail was installed in the basement of a new brick courthouse.

On New Year's Eve, 1869, Horatio Nelson Maguire issued the first Gallatin Valley newspaper, the *Montana Pick and Plow*. Maguire had been with the *Montana Post* and believed that the growing fortunes of Bozeman and the valley would support a local weekly newspaper. He told his new readers to expect an issue every Friday afternoon. Subscriptions would cost eight dollars per year or one could pay by the month. He stated firmly that all orders for the paper "without distinction of persons must be accompanied by the money. Bear this in mind. Orders will be disregarded if not accompanied by the cash."[7] Maguire also reminded his subscribers that "We are, it is well known, Democratic in our political faith."[8]

What news made the first issue? Mrs. Joseph J. Davidson died that week, an exemplary wife and mother. Peter Daily was recovering from a number of stab wounds; how he got them was not stated. Two couples had recently wed. Maguire editorialized, "May their pathway through life be strewn with flowers, and their good example be followed by many others we wot of, now treading the rugged and thorny path of single life."[9]

Editor Maguire described a Christmas Eve

The meat dressing rack holding the bodies of Z. A. Triplett and John W. St. Clair, hanged January 31, 1873.
JOSHUA C. CRISSMAN PHOTO.

ball, a benefit for the *Montana Pick and Plow*, which raised seven hundred dollars. One hundred and fifty couples had danced the night away at the Bozeman City Social Club, breaking at midnight to hear Maguire speak at great length about the glories of pioneer life. Supper included an oyster stew, and then dancing began again. No more speeches.

Dr. Achilles Lamme, representative in the Territorial Legislature, was sponsoring a bill to change the water law from riparian use to "first in time, first in right," and editor Maguire approved, saying it was high time. Evidently, Dr. Lamme did not have the votes, because the law would not be changed for several years.

And the ads:

Despite fifteen hundred subscribers, the *Montana Pick and Plow* lasted only eighteen months.

By September 13, 1871, Joseph Wright had leased Maguire's now-quiet plant, which businessman Leander Black had bought, to put out the first issue of the *Bozeman Avant Courier*. Anticipating that residents would wonder about its curious name, editor Wright told his new readers that it meant "before the railroad . . . that great Northern Pacific, now with unparalleled celerity coming over plains and mountains, through canyons and across rivers, to our Territory."[11] The title *Avant Courier* may be pretentious, he wrote, but was an accurate description of the wonderful events yet to take place in this "beautiful valley, in which it is our privilege to live . . ."[12] Wright remained editor for five years. When he became ill, he turned over management of the *Avant Courier* to his assistant Joseph Allen.

A man already known for a variety of financial interests, the Reverend Alderson bought the *Avant Courier* in 1877, with the help of Lester Willson and Achilles Lamme, continued it as a weekly, but vowed that, this time, the paper would speak to Bozeman with a Republican voice. His son Matt took an active role in producing the paper, as did his daughter Lina Alderson Houston, who eventually wrote one of the first histories of the area, *Early History of Gallatin County, Montana*.

Another weekly had a short run beginning on November 13, 1874; the *Bozeman Times* was published by J. V. Bogert and M. M. Black, followed by Henry C. and Ralph Wilkinson. Before it was absorbed by the *Avant Courier* in 1878, this little paper would scoop all others in the United States by publishing the first account of the battle at the Little Bighorn.

* * *

Before William Alderson became a newsman, he devoted himself to the establishment of a religious community in Bozeman—a difficult business. Church organization developed slowly in the West, observes historian Edward Laird Mills. Miners and adventurers were usually single with little interest in religious activities. Women were the dominant force in church organization; since farming was essentially a family operation, "religious progress must depend in large measure upon the development of agriculture."[13]

On June 4, 1865, the Reverend Alderson gave the valley's first sermon at the Merritt and Oscar Penwell ranch in the valley. He sadly reported to his diary, "Rode down to Penwells and preached from the words, 'This man recently sinned.' Not many out." Two weeks later, a much happier note: "25-30 out. Good time."[14]

The following summer, Alderson started a Sunday school, which met at the former Stafford and Rice Hotel, now owned by the Masons. On August 8, 1866, he helped the Reverend A. M. Hough found a local Methodist Episcopal organization, similar to that being established at the western end of the county by missionary Stateler in Willow Creek, except the Bozeman church did not use "South" in its title.

Although Alderson had not completed his cabin for Frances and the four children, he found time to start a fund for a first church building. John Bozeman gave twenty-five dollars; the more affluent Tom Cover gave one hundred dollars. In the fall of 1866, William Beall contracted to build a little frame church near the southwest corner of Main Street and Templar (now Tracy) Avenue, the first frame construction in town. Reverend Alderson preached in the new building on July 28, 1867. Worshippers tried to ignore the hardness of the crude slab benches. In order to raise $2,500 for construction costs, the Methodists rented the building to the Territorial Supreme Court when it met in town, but the church sexton had to cover the planed-wood floor with dirt and sawdust to protect it from the tobacco juice expectorated by the litigants.

THE FIRST CHURCH

Bozeman's first church. ETCHING FROM MICHAEL LEESON, *HISTORY OF MONTANA*, 1885.

Since no other religious building was constructed until 1874, Presbyterians, Episcopalians, Baptists, Catholics, and non-denominational families worshipped in the little church until it was moved north of Main Street to become a drug store. By that time, an elegant brick United Methodist Church was finished in 1873 at the northwest corner of Central (now Willson) Avenue and Olive Street. The church bell, imported from Saint Louis at a cost of one hundred dollars, not only called worshippers to services, but also pealed on Independence Day and other holidays. It told lagging schoolchildren to get to their classes; it notified citizens that fire had broken out in town. Another Methodist Church South organized in 1866 with its quarters on Ingersoll (North Church) Street.

On May 23, 1867, a romantic young New Yorker who had never been west of Niagara Falls left the East to become Episcopal bishop of Montana, Utah, and Idaho Territories. Daniel Sylvester Tuttle spent fourteen years and traveled forty thousand miles to cover this immense religious jurisdiction. His later memoirs are filled with accounts of Indians, robbers, and murderers, as well as his admiration for the vigilantes—a regular western penny dreadful. In order to protect himself from this assortment of dangers, real and imagined, he went out to the country to practice his shooting skills by aiming at wandering hapless curlews. Tuttle preached for the first time in Virginia City on July 21, 1867; one year later, he led a Bozeman congregation in prayer at the little wooden Methodist Church. The bishop established his headquarters in Salt Lake City but visited Bozeman every summer.

The first Episcopal priest to live in Bozeman, the Reverend Thomas E. Dickey, finished a halfway-constructed Good Templars Hall located on the northwest corner of Olive Street and Tracy Avenue, site of a future stone structure built in 1890. He called the log cabin Saint James Mission. Dickey also preached twenty miles away at the general store in Hamilton (Manhattan).

* * *

At the time of first settlement, only a handful of children ran about, free to play without formal lessons. When cabins were completed and merchandise placed on the shelves of general stores, parents had the time to think of educating their children.

Bozeman's first teacher, Samuel Anderson, had been living earlier in Virginia City but decided, in 1865, that quieter Bozeman was more to his liking. He had come across the plains from Virginia with businessman J. J. Parham and worked for him in the store. His first scholars were Benjamin, Edwin, and Rosa Fridley, Jay Jay McArthur, Frank Merraville, and another child whose name is lost to history. Classes were held in the back room of Caleb Fitz's new store; each family paid Anderson tuition; he took his meals with the Fridleys.

In the spring of 1866, the school population more than doubled with small Aldersons, Fraziers, and Davises. Teacher Anderson had moved on; a new instructor was needed. Florence Royce had just come into the valley with a wagon train from Janesville, Wisconsin, and was induced to stay to teach. The school moved to the McArthur cabin, on the southeast corner of Main Street and Black Avenue, until the term ended in October. In December, Miss Royce attended a double wedding and elegant ball at Rea's in Gallatin City and was so entranced with life in that community, she decided to stay there to teach fourteen pupils. At the end of term, Miss Royce departed for California. (It was not unusual in the West for teachers to stay a term or two only before moving on.)

On January 3, 1867, Davis Willson, General Lester Willson's brother, became the first Bozeman teacher to be paid with public funds. He taught eight boys and two girls in the double cabin of the Joe Merravilles. Tubercular Willson had come to Bozeman on a stretcher, also weak from a bout with scarlet fever; the invalid would fully recuperate in three months' time, but his mother back in Albany, New York, still worried about him. General Willson wrote home: "I presume you cannot help feeling bad because Davis don't write. . . . I think he has at last come down to the realities of life, has left off some of his poetry and the writing of sonnets to the moon."[15] Teaching was not to be Davis's only vocation; eventually, he became a correspondent to the *Montana Post*, a Bozeman ticket agent, and a minister in Springhill.

Willson was followed by Sarah Sanford, who

went home to Illinois after her term. Mr. King followed Miss Sanford but did not stay long. During an altercation with some of the male scholars, King was brained with a slate, his head forced through the frame. In November 1868, Mr. Kemster took over the education of Bozeman pupils; now, they met in the recently completed Methodist Episcopal Church. At the same time, Reverend Alderson and other residents hauled logs into town for a real school on what would become West Olive Street. William Beall was on hand to construct the schoolhouse for five hundred dollars. Mr. Green followed Mr. Kemster, and Wesley Brown followed Mr. Green. No record exists of any more thrown slates.

Whatever the state of public education, on June 2, 1872, a private school for young Christian scholars, the Bozeman Academy, opened in the Good Templars Hall, guided by minister Lyman B. Crittenden and taught by his daughter Mary Gertrude. First nine students appeared for private training, then thirteen. When twenty-one pupils enrolled, it became impossible to remain at that location. The following year, Miss Crittenden restricted the school to sixteen female pupils, having moved to a smaller facility at Babcock Street and Bozeman Avenue.

In 1874, the Crittendens decided to establish a girls' boarding school in the valley. They chose the former Culver Ranch property, near the present Manhattan, the showplace of the county, and renamed it the Gallatin Valley Female Seminary. Father and daughter offered "a substantial and polite education in connection with the influence of a Christian family and a happy home"[16] to young women aged nine to seventeen years. A polite education included instruction in reading, writing, arithmetic, spelling, history, geography, grammar, drawing, botany, astronomy, algebra, and philosophy. The young ladies were taught to sew and play the piano. Instruction in other instruments or French and German was available at an extra charge. Tuition for boarding students was twenty dollars per month. Day students paid four dollars per month.

The Crittendens had planned for a dozen boarders but taught, instead, more than twenty pupils. Since the Culver place could not accommodate the growing number of girls, the seminary moved to the Drew house in 1875, located southeast of Manhattan. Ella Aylsworth was hired as second teacher when enrollments reached thirty-five. The seminary continued to attract private students for the next three years until Miss Crittenden closed the school because of her forthcoming marriage to Edward M. Davidson. By that time, more than two hundred Gallatin Valley young women had been graduated from the Female Seminary.

During the summer of 1872, "Professor" J. L. Vernon came from Denver to teach the public school in Bozeman. At the close of his term the following February, the Good Templars sponsored a benefit to establish a school library, which raised $244.80. The parents gave the money to Vernon to buy library books. Alas, he left town, and the $244.80 went with him. Vernon would surface again in a year or two, but not as a teacher.

By 1867, residents in the Gallatin Valley did not have to travel to Bozeman for most of their goods. Merchants opened stores across the valley in Three Forks; some sold their wares from tents, anxious to do business before store buildings could be finished.

Those farmers who realized eastern agricultural practices did not work in the semi-arid West and who adapted to a land less favored by abundant rain, did well. Some, however, clung to the old ways and suffered crop failure, cursing the weather. Ranchers looked forward to the birth of colts, lambs, and calves to increase their livestock, but they would learn that pilgrim cattle and sheep, imported from outside the territory, often did not have the constitution to withstand harsh Montana winters.

More cabins appeared on the land, both in town and on recently filed homesteads. Resident children now attended small schools in the settlements, makeshift at first. Post offices opened, sawmills were busy, creameries sold fresh products, and flour mills turned grist into white flour. Those who could not adapt to the new life—such as Frank Kirkaldie and Joseph Kenney—moved on. For others, the Gallatin Valley was too tame, and they left to explore such places as Diamond City or city life in San Francisco. For many of those who stayed, the richness of the valley promised good times ahead. ▨

97

chapter

T H I R T E E N

John Bozeman was still casting about, searching for his niche in the growing settlement. He farmed a bit, got in a few fights, gambled a lot, dreamed up business schemes, and was out of town for long periods of time. He may have visited friends among neighboring Indian tribes. He went to church now and again and applied for membership in Masonic Lodge No. 6.

One of his more notable fights occurred at Nelson Story's general store. Democrat Bozeman made an insulting remark about Republican F. F. Fridley's politics and blows followed. Bozeman's friend William McKinzie watched the fisticuffs for a bit, then lifted some scales to help the Democratic side. Storekeeper Story hoisted an ax handle to stop McKinzie. Someone ran to find America Fridley, who came to the store and stopped what she thought was a silly altercation.

Bozeman did not mention his fights when he wrote home in the summer of 1866:

Bozeman City, Montana
July 11, 1866
Dear Mother:

Once more I imbrace an opportunity of wrighting you a phew lines to let you know that I am yet on the land and among the living. I have not had any word from there but twice since I left the

The last known portrait of John Bozeman by a photographer named McLachlan.

States. Cathrine wrote me. I got the letter about three months ago for the first time since I left home and she spoke of you living on the William Parting land and that was all she said about you. I wrote and wrote to you all time and again but never could hear from any of you . . . .

I have made some money in this country a nough eavin to make any man a fortune but I have spent a good deal in speculating of one kind and a nother. I am farming now though I have followed mining and speculating the most of my time in this country and was up and down rich and poor several times. I have a good start now again and I can not see what will hinder me from making all the money I want in 2 or 3 years more. I stade in Colorado till the spring of 62 then came to this country and this is a good country and for farming it can not be beet and this is the most healthy country I ever saw.

I have never bin sick a minute in this country except when I had the measles two years ago. I would like to see you all mity well but it is out of the question at present. I want you and all the inquiring friend to here from and wright to me as soon as possible then I will give you the particulars of this country. Tell Cathrine I would like to pay her and the children a visit but I do not know when I can as my Business is in this country and I cannot leave it very well and I am getting well weaned off from the States and any way the Emigration is heavy to this country this season and times are good as could be expected. Dear Mother Brother and Sisters I am well at present and doing well and I hope these phew lines will find you all the same. I want you to all to write me and give all the news so I must close nothing more at present But I remain your affectionate Sone and Brother.

J. M. Bozeman

For fear money is scarse I will send a little greenbacks for you and Cathrine equal.[1]

Five months later, Bozeman wrote again to his family:

Bozeman City, M. Terr.
December 4, 1866

Dear Mother & Brother & Sisters,

I received your loving letter the other day, which gave me much pleasure to here that you were well, but it was very mortifying to me to hear that times are so hard there. . . .

I am getting along well in this country. I want you to write me where you are, and how you are getting along, and also how Cathrine and the children are getting along. I will be pleased to hear from all of you often and I will pay you a visit in a year or two, but do not expect me to come there to live any more. I have made a great amount of money in this country but have had some bad luck and spent a great deal. I am comfortably situated yet and can make a good living. I will send you some photographs for you and Cathrine and the children and my brothers and sisters. I will close for the present by saying I am quite well and hope these few lines will find you all in the same health, there is one thing I forgot to speak of, I am glad that all of you are trying to get to that good place, where trouble will be no more, I attend church frequently but I don't do as I ought to do, or as I would wish to do. We are building a nice church and school house in this town, and I hope God will be more glorified in this country in the future than in the past, as society is getting pretty well organized in this country.

I am partnership with a man by the name of Frazier in a Hotel and some groceries, he has a family of a wife and 3 children all at home, I very much like. His wife name was Bozeman before she was married. I don't know whether we are any relation or not so nothing more at present, but remain your affectionate Son until death.

J. M. Bozeman, to his loving Mother and inquiring friends.

P. S. I will send you a piece of chiney money as it will be an odity in that country. There is people in this country from all parts of the world.

Sometime during this period, Rosa Van Vlierden was wakened in the middle of the night by a nervous Bozeman, who told her that a woman was having a baby in his cabin; he begged her to come and help with the delivery. All went well but Mrs. Van Vlierden reported that she saw neither mother nor baby after the birth.[2]

In spite of the general enthusiasm for a fresh start in the West, the year 1867 brought dark uncertainty about permanent white settlement in the Gallatin Valley. Rumor after frightening rumor spread from homestead to town. Residents passed the word that large numbers of Crow warriors would move from the Yellowstone River through Bozeman Pass to swoop down into the Gallatin Valley to force them out. Another rumor: Chief Red Cloud and the Sioux had massed on the Platte River, waiting for the greening of spring grass to push toward Montana and the Gallatin Valley. If three or four Indian raiders stole a few horses from an outlying rancher, the number of Indians and horses was magnified with each retelling.

Believing that members of the Crow, Blackfeet, and Sioux tribes were about to go on a rampage, either tribe by tribe or all together, two thousand Gallatin Valley men cleaned and oiled their guns, ready to fight the Indians. Meetings held in Bozeman to consider the Indian problem often ended in near hysteria. The settlers demanded help from the federal government and became angry when they realized that President Ulysses S. Grant and the military did not believe the Gallatin Valley was in danger from Indian attack. The Cover-McAdow Flour Mill, so valuable to the valley's food supply, operated from within a hastily built stockade. The *Montana Post* reported on February 9 that Gallatin Valley residents faced "imminent danger" and called for "an organization for mutual protection and defense."[3] On March 23, Reverend Alderson wrote in his journal, "Quite an Indian scare at Bozeman and throughout the valley on account of recent raids."[4]

Acting Territorial Governor Thomas Francis Meagher did not try to quell these fears; instead, he seemed to enjoy his role of beleaguered general threatened by Indians from every direction. Meagher thrived on controversy and excitement. Born to a rich Irish family—his father was a Member of Parliament—Meagher got into trouble as an Irish revolutionary before he finished his schooling. After his activities against the British crown came to light, he was convicted of treason in 1848 and sent to Van

Known as "The Acting One," Acting Territorial Governor Thomas Francis Meagher led a colorful life until his death in 1867.

Diemen's Land (Tasmania). Four years later, he escaped to Brazil, made his way to New York City, gained U.S. citizenship, and fought for the Union during the Civil War. Appointed territorial secretary by President Andrew Johnson in 1865, within two years Meagher became acting governor. As historian Robert Athearn noted, "Governor Edgerton had been only too happy to hand this political menagerie over to any successor who might appear, and to get back to civilized parts as fast as available transportation would permit."[5]

On March 25, John Bozeman posted a letter to Meagher:

General: I take the responsibility of writing you a few lines for the benefit of the people of Montana. We have reliable reports here that we are in imminent danger of hostile Indians, and if there is not something done to protect this valley soon, there will be but few men and no families left in the Gallatin Valley. Men, women, and children are making preparations to leave at an early day. If you can make any arrangements to protect them, they will stay; if not the valley will doubtless be evacuated.[6]

Meagher responded by sending forty muskets and three thousand cartridges to the Gallatin Valley, making certain that newspapers mentioned his generosity; he also sent a bill to Washington, D.C., for the arms. Forming a local militia, the men built and fortified two little posts: one eight miles southeast of Bozeman which, in gratitude, they named Camp Elizabeth Meagher after the governor's wife; and another, Camp Ida Thoroughman, located four miles east of the present Livingston at the mouth of the Shields River as it flows into the Yellowstone.

Never one to overlook a situation he could exploit, Meagher made use of the single wire Western Union had strung from Salt Lake City to Virginia City and sent wire after wire to Secretary Stanton of the War Department warning of Montana's impending doom and imploring the military to rescue the settlers. The governor did not achieve the response he desired. Meagher's reputation for intemperate action and exaggeration had preceded him; he was generally regarded as a loudmouth and a rabble-rouser.

The governor wired President Grant: "The greatest alarm reasonably prevails. . . . Danger is immanent."[7] Back in the States, military men could discover no hard evidence that the Indians, those neighboring the Gallatin Valley or those further to the east, were planning hostilities.

Despite the hard work to equip Camp Meagher with guns and other military items, the little stockade could not have withstood serious attack. Bills for lumber, guns, ammunition, and any item remotely connected with community protection were forwarded for payment to the U.S. government. As Robert Athearn said, "It was a marvelous opportunity to raid the Treasury, and in a country where government funds were looked upon as fair game, the financial dredging proceeded with utmost avidity."[8]

When Montana Territory's demands for payment were totaled, the bill amounted to one million dollars. Seven years later, in 1874, the claims were settled for half that sum. Bozeman merchants who played this financial game included Nelson Story, Loren Tuller, Charles Rich, William Tracy, Lester S. Willson, W. J. Beall, P. W. McAdow, and Thomas Cover. Leander M. Black alone presented a claim for $100,000.

During the winter of 1866-1867, John Bozeman was a frequent visitor at the Thomas and Mary Cover cabin where the men discussed a number of business opportunities, which included the chartering of a ferry boat to cross the Yellowstone River near the present location of Big Timber. On April 1, 1867, the county commissioners granted them a charter for such a ferry, stipulating that it be completed by July 4.

Sometime that month, Cover convinced a reluctant Bozeman to accompany him on a trip east along the Bozeman Trail to Forts C. F. Smith, Phil Kearny, and Reno to secure government contracts for Gallatin Valley beef, wheat, and flour. One wonders why Cover chose to visit these military facilities at this time because the Bozeman Trail was essentially closed. Nelson Story had completed his

Early Bozeman businessman Thomas Cover was the last person to see John Bozeman alive.

cattle drive along the route the summer before; the last scheduled emigrant wagon train had come along the trail; and William J. Fetterman and seventy-four fellow army men had died in an Indian engagement just above Fort Phil Kearny, effectively scaring any extra-legal travelers from the closed route.

Bozeman did not want to go on the trip. He instructed Elmyra Frazier, with whom he was boarding at the time, that his gold watch should be sent to his mother if he did not survive the journey. Early on the morning of April 17, while Bozeman and Cover were saddling their horses in front of the City Hotel, George and Elmyra Frazier looked on. Elmyra handed the travelers lunches she had made for their first day on the trail. The noise of the horses and the bright sunlight wakened eleven-year-old Billy Frazier. Peeking from his bedroom window, Billy saw the two men mounted and ready to travel. He crept downstairs to watch, but his bare feet got cold so he hurried back upstairs to the window, where he saw his mother turn to his father and heard her say, "Isn't he a handsome man?" His father's reply was: "Yes, and take a good look at the son-of-a-bitch as this is the last you are going to see of him!"[9]

The first evening out, April 17, Cover and Bozeman stayed at a cow camp, part of Nelson Story's ranch on the Yellowstone, near the present site of Livingston. According to Bozeman's friend William McKinzie, a Blackfeet war party moved in at sundown, circled most of the ranch horses and drove them off. Three ranch hands went after the horse thieves and, after a brief skirmish, brought the animals back.

A nervous Bozeman bunked with McKinzie that night in "Brown's double cabin" and expressed his premonition that he would not return alive, an unusual attitude, McKinzie wrote later, since Bozeman "could never see danger."[10] McKinzie remembered that he laughed at Bozeman's fears, telling his friend that, more than anyone else, he would be the most secure in Indian country. "He offered me his horse, saddle and outfit if I would take his place. . . . I would have gone . . . but I had been out among the Crows for weeks without any change of clothing and was anxious to . . . get cleaned up a little."[11]

Early next morning, April 18, Bozeman and Cover started off toward the forts; the men were on horseback, leading an additional pack horse. On the

W. S. McKinzie

BOZEMAN.

John Bozeman's best friend and fellow Georgian William S. McKinzie became Gallatin County sheriff in 1878.
ETCHING FROM MICHAEL LEESON, *HISTORY OF MONTANA*, 1885.

way, they met Benjamin Bembrick, who had shot two deer. The hunter visited a bit with Bozeman, who had been a friend of his for some time, gave the travelers some venison, and left them to establish their noon camp on the Yellowstone near Mission Creek.[12] Well after midnight that night, Cover rushed back into the Story cow camp on foot, exhausted. Wounded in the shoulder, he reported to the cowhands that his traveling companion John Bozeman lay dead beside the Yellowstone River.

This is what happened, said Cover: as Bozeman was roasting the venison they had received from Bembrick, the men saw five Indians about two hundred and fifty yards away, leading a pony. Apparently, only one had a gun. As the five approached the campfire, a suspicious Cover told Bozeman he doubted any good intentions, suggesting, "We should open fire."[13] Cover held a Henry sixteen-shot rifle; Bozeman's Spencer lay on the ground beside the campfire. According to Cover, Bozeman said the Indians did not seem dangerous—they were not Sioux or Blackfeet. "Those are Crows, I know one of them."[14]

The five visitors shook hands with the affable Bozeman, then offered to shake with Cover, who rebuffed the gesture. The Indians, perhaps smelling the venison, asked for something to eat. Cover said that Bozeman began to fix them some food, but a few minutes later, Bozeman muttered to Cover and said, "I am fooled, they are Blackfeet. We may, however, get off without trouble." Cover reported he dropped his Henry gun near Bozeman, ran for their horses tethered nearby, and grabbed a pistol from his pack. At that point, the only Indian who was armed shot Bozeman in the right breast, then in the left breast, bringing Bozeman "to the ground, a dead man." The gunman then turned and shot at Cover.

Wounded in the left shoulder, Cover sprinted across open land to Bozeman, made sure that he was beyond help, and snatched up the Henry rifle. As he backed off, he aimed at the departing five Indians. The gun would not fire. He retreated fifty yards and aimed again. This time, the rifle worked. He killed one of the five, then ran for the safety of nearby willow brush and waited while the Indians moved out, carrying off their dead comrade and all the horses. They did not stop to scalp Bozeman, nor did they take his watch or the Spencer gun.

Early on the morning of April 19, Nelson Story's cattle foreman rode furiously into Bozeman to tell his boss of Bozeman's murder. Story immediately saddled up and hurried east to his Yellowstone property. Cover was still there and told the rancher he had covered Bozeman's body with a blanket, grabbed some venison, and struggled twenty-five miles upstream, fording both the Yellowstone and Shields Rivers. Story examined Cover's wound. It looked to him like a bullet had entered his shoulder from the front rather than the back, as Cover stated earlier to the cowhands. Unusual olive-green powder burns surrounded the entry, suggesting a discharge at close range.[15]

Story then sought out his veteran packer Spanish Joe at the bunkhouse. Had Joe heard the news? Yes, he had, when Cover arrived during the night. Story told Joe he was going to organize a burial party to travel to the death site, but he wanted Joe to leave the ranch immediately to examine the area before new tracks obliterated the old. Concerned not only about Cover's powder burns, Story wanted quick and accurate information as to the location and number of the Blackfeet and whether they meant to attack the ranch and make off with his cattle. Story said to Joe, "Don't talk with any member of the burial party. Return as soon as possible to the ranch." Joe had a quick breakfast, saddled up, and made for the Mission Creek camp.

When he returned, he told Story "no wild animals had disturbed the body during the night: he had particularly examined Bozeman's patent leather riding boots so that he could check which were his heel marks. He studied the campfire site. He could find no Indian tracks whatsoever. There was blood where Bozeman had apparently fallen, but he could find no blood signs from the Indian reportedly killed by Cover."[16] Joe then fanned south from the campfires to look for Indian or pony sign. Nothing. He climbed a nearby bluff to survey the scene. He followed the trail of the horses. He found Cover's boot impressions. He also determined that someone had lifted numerous stones from sod nearby and thrown them about, as if to force the horses down to the river. Joe rode out in the stream to a sandbar and whistled for them. "No answering neigh."[17]

For some reason, both Nelson Story and Spanish Joe kept silent about these discoveries. No coroner's jury formed to consider the murder, and no explanation was forthcoming about the fate of the horses. On April 22, Thomas Cover wrote a letter to Acting Governor Meagher, detailing the events leading to Bozeman's death, which was published in the *Montana Post* on May 4, 1867. Cover's memory did not seem to fit all the events.

McKinzie is said to have grumbled later that both Cover and Bozeman could have killed all five Indians, if such existed. Of Cover's wound, he said, "Whether he made it himself or not I do not know."[18] (McKinzie became Gallatin County Sheriff in 1878.)

Bishop Daniel S. Tuttle visited the Covers one year later and wrote to his wife of his impressions. Cover, the bishop said, suggested that John Bozeman had acted in a cowardly manner before his death; that the Indians were Crow, not Blackfeet; that they had three firearms, not one; and that they also shot arrows at Cover.[19]

To confuse the matter further, Crow interpreter George Reed Davis said years later in an 1896 memoir he saw five Blackfeet, or, as he characterized them, "Piegan renegades"—Mountain Chief, his three sons, and one other—enter Fort Laramie in May or June 1867 with a large Crow party and many horses. The Crow, Davis said, identified the five as the murderers of John Bozeman.[20]

The only part of the story that seems reliable is that John Bozeman was murdered along the Yellowstone at the age of thirty-two. None of the accounts of his death are fully persuasive. Was Bozeman truly fearful and despondent before this trip, or were these reports merely apocryphal upon hearing of an untimely death? Were the whispers true that Thomas Cover jealously thought John Bozeman's frequent visits to his cabin proved that the trailblazer was having an affair with his wife? Did Nelson Story really see powder burns around Cover's shoulder wound? Why didn't the Indians rush Cover when he had difficulty with his Henry rifle. Why did they leave a valuable gun and watch behind? Why did McKinzie say later that Bozeman took a shot in the stomach?

Did Spanish Joe truly find no Indian sign? What happened to the three horses? What were five Blackfeet, disreputable or not, doing with a party of Crow, their traditional enemies? And why, given the Blackfeet love affair with the horse, were these men on foot? Given Bozeman's earlier views on feeding Indians in the wilderness, why did he offer food to the five visitors?

Why did Nelson Story keep quiet about his version of these events until years later, when he told his son Thomas Byron of Spanish Joe's discoveries? And why did T. B. keep quiet about his father's suspicions of Tom Cover until the 1940s when he met with Jefferson Jones, the new publisher of the *Bozeman Daily Chronicle*? Did Billy Frazier have a clear memory of what he heard in front of the City Hotel that early morning of April 17?

Did someone pay, as has been suggested, to have John Bozeman killed? Or were there several men conspiring to murder the popular trailblazer? The death of John Bozeman will doubtless remain a mystery.

Because the road to Bozeman was nearly impassable that spring, John Bozeman lay in his Yellowstone grave for two years; at that point, his body was brought back to the town which bore his name and interred in the Story family plot at Sunset

Hills Cemetery. (Forty-four years later, William McKinzie would lie beside him under the marker, "Here lies two friends.")

Whatever did happen at the Yellowstone campfire on April 18, 1867, it set off a number of events: general panic in the territory ensued, caused in part by such newspaper headlines as appeared on May 2 in the *Helena Weekly Herald*:

Bozeman's murder announced in the Helena Weekly Herald, May 2, 1867.

Killing of Col. Bozeman and wounding of Thos. Cover by the Blackfeet Indians!

THE PANIC AMONG THE GALLATIN SETTLERS!

THEIR APPREHENSIONS OF A GENERAL ATTACK UPON THEIR HOMES.

Their Appeal to Governor Meagher and the People of the Territory!

Prompt and friendly response by the Governor, and Minute Men called for to meet the emergency!

THE PEOPLE OF MADISON COUNTY RALLYING!

300 Men from Edgerton, and 100 from Deer Lodge Wanted!

LET THESE COUNTIES DO THEIR WHOLE DUTY!

Thomas Meagher sent another telegram to the Secretary of War: " . . . Our Territory in serious danger from the Indians. Richest portion already invaded. Citizens murdered."[21]

The federal government finally succumbed to public pressure and ordered the military to establish a fort east of Bozeman to protect nearby residents from Indian attack and to lead forays into Indian country. Bozeman's businessmen, knowing that gold prospecting was no longer as profitable as it had been, were overjoyed with the chance to enrich themselves with government contracts for supplies. Moreover, the new resident soldiers would spend their wages in town.

The feared Indian War of 1867 did not materialize in the Gallatin Valley. Crow war parties did not rush through Bozeman Pass to attack the settlers en masse. Chief Red Cloud and the Sioux did not even come this way. Nonetheless, suspicion and hostility between whites and Indians raged. However he was murdered, John Bozeman's death was one of the events that led to a real battle nine years later at the Little Bighorn.

In spring 1869, Thomas Cover sold his interest in the flour mill to the McAdow brothers, moved to the land of orange trees in Riverside, California, and apparently enjoyed a life of considerable affluence. He, too, died under mysterious circumstances in 1884 while searching for the Peg Leg mine in the desert near Borrego Springs. Some

have alleged that the brothers of Boone Helm, a road agent that vigilante Thomas Cover helped to hang years before, tracked down the treasure seeker and killed him to avenge their dead brother. The bleached remains of Thomas Cover were later identified, the tale continues, because of a Masonic ring—supposedly Cover's—sparking in the desert sun, lying between skeletal fingers of his right hand.

A third curious death occurred in July 1867. Acting Governor Thomas Meagher arrived at Fort Benton on horseback to board the steamboat *G. A. Thompson*; he was going downstream to pick up ammunition for what has been called "Meagher's Indian War." He complained he did not feel well. A vigilante group had earlier expressed its anger with Meagher's pardon of disreputable brawler James Daniels, whom the governor thought innocent. Congeniality was not the mood as Meagher stepped upon the deck of the steamboat. After a few drinks, he was tucked into his berth by his friend and pilot Johnny Doran.

Meagher disappeared shortly thereafter. Did he fall overboard to drown by accident or was he pushed? For two months, a grieving Elizabeth Meagher patrolled the banks of the Missouri River, searching for the body of her husband. The deaths of John Bozeman, Thomas Cover, and Thomas Meagher have never been satisfactorily explained.

chapter

FOURTEEN

By the end of the summer of 1867, Gallatin Valley's frightened residents and enterprising merchants had gotten what they wanted: Brigadier General Alfred H. Terry, commander of Dakota Territory's army forces, had ordered Captain Robert S. Lamotte (LaMotte School was named for him) to establish a new military post three miles east of Bozeman. On August 27, Lamotte and 195 men of the Thirteenth U.S. Infantry set up tents and looked over the terrain for optimum building sites. They constructed a temporary stockade so that Bozeman residents felt they had a place to run to in case of Indian attack. George Flanders furnished logs from his new sawmill on nearby Bear Creek. The man in whose honor the new fort was named, Colonel Augustus Van Horne Ellis, never traveled west; he had died four summers before at the Battle of Gettysburg on July 2, 1863.

The presence of foot soldiers alone would not secure the area; four companies of the Second Regiment, U.S. Cavalry, would arrive at Fort Ellis in less than two years, the only mounted U.S. military force in Montana Territory at that time. In May 1869, Colonel A. G. Brackett (Brackett Creek in the Bridgers is named for him) started from Fort Sanders, Wyoming, with two hundred and fifty men and three or four hundred horses bound for Fort

Ellis. Companies F, G, H, and L traveled west by Union Pacific Railroad to the rail head at Carter in southwest Wyoming. There they started a long march to Idaho then north to Virginia City. As they passed near the gold fields on June 8, three of Brackett's men from Company G deserted, obviously more interested in mining than military service. (They were captured the following day.)

A young second lieutenant on Brackett's staff, Gustavus Cheyney Doane, would one day figure in a number of Fort Ellis adventures. His first wife Amelia accompanied him, the only woman on the trip. By the time the cavalry and Mrs. Doane settled in the fort, a number of buildings had been completed. Colonel Brackett described the construction:

> The fort is made of logs and surrounded with palisades with two block houses at diagonal corners. It is small, compactly built, and seems well adapted for frontier protection. The stockade was put up at the request of the citizens of the valley to serve as a place of refuge in case of an Indian invasion.[1]

Despite long, frigid winters, the extended periods of service, and the absence of notable Indian engagements, the officers of Fort Ellis lived in relative splendor for a military post. By the 1880s,

Fort Ellis officers lived in relatively substantial quarters. MARY LEE HUNTER DOANE PHOTO, C1894.

These frame barracks for the Fort Ellis enlisted men replaced earlier log quarters. MARY LEE HUNTER DOANE PHOTO, C1894.

Visitors watch soldiers on parade on Fort Ellis grounds. MARY LEE HUNTER DOANE PHOTO.

four hundred men lived in three log buildings, officers had quarters in seven spacious houses, and a two-story hospital held ten rooms. A substantial guardhouse and ordnance warehouse stood nearby, as well as a commissary and quartermaster's office. The soldiers built stables, granaries, a bakery, laundry, library, courthouse, sawmill, and workshops. They planted gardens, not totally reliant on farmers nearby. The stockade was torn down soon after the arrival of the cavalry.

Those in the Gallatin Valley who grew wheat, milled flour, bred horses, operated sawmills, and fattened cattle benefited by business with the new post. Pay day at Fort Ellis was a happy one for Bozeman businessmen. "The soldiers of the command at Fort Ellis were paid off yesterday. Results: the blue jackets are numerous on the street, and scattering greenbacks profusely."[2] Writer Eugene S. Topping summed it up succinctly: "From the moment this fort was definitely located, Bozeman's future was assured."[3]

Since no Indians appeared to fight the settlers, Fort Ellis soldiers worked at other tasks: they laid telegraph line, built roads, manned expeditionary forces, welcomed visitors to Yellowstone National

Park after it was established in 1872, and highlighted the Bozeman social scene at balls, parades, and sports events. Editor Maguire of the *Montana Pick and Plow* announced in his first issue that the Fort Ellis Amateurs were in rehearsal for their maiden theater production; dances and other social events were forthcoming. Mary Lee Hunter, soon to become the second Mrs. Doane, remembered that brisk dancing at the fort was a good remedy to keep down the mosquitoes.

One officer's lady described Fort Ellis life in *Harper's Weekly*: despite the rough log exteriors, the rooms inside were, to her surprise, "white coated and hard finished so that they glistened in the light and the floors were carpeted and rooms well furnished."[4] Immense chandeliers sparkled, bronze statuary glistened, and rare books and vases delighted. The orderlies wore white gloves. Fort Ellis officers led a different life from that of the Gallatin Valley farmer, rancher, and small businessman.

The officer's lady continued her account with the story of a smitten young lieutenant who attended an enlisted men's ball in order to dance with the pretty daughter of a Bozeman laundress. The next day, he came before the commandant who told the

Fort Ellis officers lounge on front porch of the commissary, c1870. From left to right: 1-Lieutenant Dugan; 2-Major Thompson; 3-Captain Wright; 4-Captain Gustave Doane; 5-Major Forsythe; 6-Dr. Baker; 7-Dr. Whiteford; 8-Captain Hamilton; 9-Major Eugene Baker; 10-Captain Ball; 11-Captain Tyler; 12-Lieutenant Jerome; 13-Lieutenant McClermond; 14-Lieutenant Schofield. WILLIAM HENRY JACKSON PHOTO.

hapless young lover that if he ever went to a soldier's ball again, he would be arrested and court-martialed.

A new sutler at the fort held a different view of Fort Ellis. Danish immigrant Peter Koch wrote his wife Laurie in November 1871, describing the post as "a miserable hellhole, where they have winter nine months in the year and cold weather the other three."[5] A few of the officers were not as bad as he had expected. The quartermaster, he wrote, "seems not to be infested by that intolerable stuck up pride, which so many of the officers of the regular army have, and which make them look down on all civilians (unless they have plenty of money) as inferior beings."[6]

A stronger military presence near Bozeman encouraged local business interests to expand their markets even further. Nelson Story bought 100,000 pounds of potatoes at one dollar per hundredweight and sold them to Fort C. F. Smith for ten dollars per hundredweight. Others profited as well. To their great joy, there was talk of a railroad coming this

way. Some of the Fort Ellis men stayed in the West after their service. James Forristell, for instance, opened a grocery on East Main Street.

By 1872, the little fort was already deteriorating. "The roofs leaked badly, and the dirt sifted down when the weather was dry."[7] Bear Creek lumberman George W. Flanders agreed to provide shingles and other materials for renovation. Flanders had come from Vermont six years before because of tuberculosis. He established his mill on Bear Creek near the mouth of Gallatin Canyon. It took almost a full year to get his shingle mill and parts from Erie, New York, transported first by rail to Omaha, then by steamboat to Fort Benton, then by freight wagons to Bozeman.

While waiting for his mill to arrive, Flanders befriended a Crow family living on Bear Creek; after hearing his cough, an old Crow woman prepared a number of herbal tonics for the patient which, although vile-tasting, may have cured his ailments. Flanders also went on an extensive camping trip with

Ike LeForge, husband of one of the Crow women and scout for Fort Ellis. As they moved through in the mountains along a trail that ran east to the Yellowstone River by way of Trail Creek, LeForge introduced to Flanders the pleasure of eating mountain sheep, a delicacy he enjoyed. Along the way, they met Indians from a number of tribes who preferred to travel along this route, thus avoiding Bozeman and the military men at Fort Ellis. Eventually, Flanders moved his shingle mill to Middle Creek, a better source of timber and water power.

* * *

On Christmas Day 1867, an intensely partisan election sealed the fate of struggling Gallatin City. The little Three Forks settlement had been the county seat since the time of Idaho Territory. Now, three communities, two real and one on paper, vied for county business. Charles P. Blakeley had long yearned to establish the county seat on his Middle Creek ranch; he called it Farmington. In fact, he had secured territorial designation for Farmington as the governmental seat one year before. Bozeman residents were outraged and actively promoted their town for the honor, knowing that more business would come their way.

Poor Gallatin City did not have a chance, though Bozeman politicians promised the declining settlement that, if another county were formed, they would support Gallatin City as its formal seat. Davis Willson reported the event to the *Montana Post*:

Christmas day was of all the most exciting Bozeman has seen. The polls were opened at precisely 8 o'clock, for the purpose of deciding where our county seat should be located. No election, I think, has ever occurred in Montana that elicited so much interest or called out so many voters. Teams were flying in every direction, bringing in the lukewarm, flags flaunted to the breeze from every quarter, whisky flowed like water and voters came in so rapidly that clerks could scarcely take their names. At one time, enthusiasm ran so high, that it was obliged to work itself off in a general street fight, when several knockdowns occurred, said to be very satisfactory to those most interested.[8]

BOZEMAN.

Charles P. Blakeley saw his dream of a county seat on his Farmington Ranch fade with the election of 1867.
ETCHING FROM MICHAEL LEESON, *HISTORY OF MONTANA*, 1885.

When it was over, Bozeman had received 475 votes, 200 more than Farmington. The winners pondered the delicious possibility of taking the territorial capital away from Virginia City, while Blakeley brooded over the loss of a county seat on his property. (The Territorial Legislature confirmed the election in 1869.)

* * *

A small group of territorial residents had long planned to explore the wonders of the Yellowstone area to determine if John Colter and Jim Bridger were correct in their reports of bubbling springs, giant geysers and waterfalls, and caldrons of steaming mud. In the early summer of 1869, a group of citizens planned in earnest such an expedition. Some pulled out, however, when they learned that a military escort from Fort Ellis would not be possible "owing to some changes made in the disposition of troops stationed in the Territory."[9] Others "began to discover that pressing business engagements would prevent their going."[10]

Three stockmen—David E. Folsom, Charles W. Cook, and Folsom's ranch hand William Peterson—decided to chance the journey alone. They started on horseback from Diamond City, fifty miles east of Helena, on September 6, 1869 with two pack horses, traveling south to Gallatin City, then to Hamilton (Manhattan) and across the Gallatin Valley. They climbed to the pass at Trail Creek, then descended to follow the Yellowstone River upstream.

Since they were in no hurry, they took their time, stopping to visit with a band of Sheepeater Indians as best they could, since neither knew the

The Lower Falls of the Yellowstone, which Folsom and Cook attempted to measure with a ball of twine.

Etching from *Livingston Enterprise*, Souvenir Edition, c1900.

other's language. They climbed high enough to see in the distance to the east the Bighorn and Wind River Ranges. They studied hot sulphur springs along the way, christening one group "The Chemical Works." They were mystified to hear dull underground explosions and watched with awe geysers spewing out perfect arcs of water.

They spent a day studying the two great falls in a grand canyon of the Yellowstone River. How far did the water drop? they wondered. Cook lay prone at the top of the Upper Falls, slowing playing out a ball of twine to Peterson, stationed at the bottom. They calculated the drop of the falls at one hundred and fifteen feet, fairly close to the present measurement of one hundred and nine feet. They moved to the Lower Falls, dropped the twine again, but swirling mist made it impossible to measure.

The ranchers spent a few days at Yellowstone Lake watching "crystal waves dancing and sparkling in the sunlight as if laughing with joy for their wild freedom . . . we felt glad to have looked upon it before its primeval solitude should be broken by the crowds of pleasure seekers which at no distant day will throng its shores."[11] Although the concept of a national park was unheard of at this point, these men discussed the need for the reservation of this land in some sort of public trust, as had Acting Governor Meagher as early as 1865. All knew that feverish businessmen would want to capitalize on the wonders of the Yellowstone.

On September 29, the three explorers started for home down the Madison Valley, well pleased with their adventure. When they returned on October 11, they learned with surprise that friends and relations were contemplating the formation of a search party to rescue them.

Like earlier Yellowstone visitors John Colter, Father DeSmet, Warren Ferris, Joe Meek, and Jim Bridger, the three men were reluctant to tell others what they had seen, not wanting to be branded as liars. When the word got out, they were branded anyway, at least by some. When an account of their journey was submitted to the *New York Times* and either *Scribner's Monthly* or *Harper's*, all publications rejected the manuscript because "they had a reputation that they could not risk with such unreliable material."[12] Chicago's *Western Monthly*

When the earliest explorers of the Yellowstone area predicted a wave of visitors soon, did they imagine
this steamboat that later appeared on Yellowstone Lake?

Magazine did not have such scruples and published the account in July 1871.

David Folsom did talk about what they had seen with Territorial Surveyor-General Henry D. Washburn, who did not discount their observations and was keenly interested in forming a future exploration party. He may have talked to Charles Cook as well, who wintered in the Gallatin Valley following the expedition.

* * *

Perhaps a military escort did not accompany the Folsom group because of preparations being made at Fort Ellis for quite a different kind of expedition. That fall, near Helena, popular rancher Malcolm Clarke was murdered and his son wounded, evidently by a band of Blackfeet as revenge for deaths of their own people. General Phil Sheridan ordered Major Eugene M. Baker to retaliate. "If you have to fight the Indians, hit them hard," Sheridan wired.

The major formed a mounted patrol of four Fort Ellis cavalry, picked up two infantry groups at Fort Shaw on the Sun River, and started north in subzero weather to the Marias River area to find the guilty band. Evidently, Major Baker drank a great deal during the march. Before dawn on a frigid January 23, 1870, his men found what they thought was the renegade camp. But scout Joseph Kipp recognized the lodges as those of Chief Heavy Runner, a band under the protection of the United States. When Kipp ran to Baker with this news, the major waved him away, telling him to keep quiet or be shot.

At first light, a drunken Baker ordered his troops to surround the village and to fire blindly into the inhabited area. Baker sounded the charge to move closer to the lodges where the soldiers fired, again blindly, into the entrances. When it was over, Baker and his men had murdered thirty-three Blackfeet men, ninety women, and fifty children. They had knocked down the lodges, some with frightened people still within, piled bodies on top, and set them afire. Also burned were Blackfeet food supplies set aside for the winter. They took more than one hundred and forty women and children as prisoners, intending to march them back to Fort Ellis. When Baker learned that some of the hostages might be ill with smallpox, he turned his prisoners loose with little food or shelter.

Everyone later learned what the major knew—that he had attacked the wrong band of Blackfeet. Word reached the East of what was now called the Baker Massacre; many found the behavior of the Fort Ellis men reprehensible and uncivilized. During the investigation which followed, however, Baker's superiors supported him; neither he nor his men received a court-martial. Lieutenant Doane was one of the party and later boasted he had taken part in "the greatest slaughter of Indians ever made by U.S. troops."[13] Montana merchants tended to support Major Baker's actions because they could see it as means to a possible end to Indian interference with their new markets.

* * *

Bozeman received one of its distinctive icons the next season, in 1870, almost by chance. A group of disillusioned Wyoming gold prospectors, having wandered about the Bighorn River and the Yellowstone Valley looking for color, disbanded their expedition in Bozeman, leaving behind a little 4.62 single-bore cannon in the care of miller Perry McAdow. It was christened almost immediately the Big Horn Gun.

Gunsmith Walter Cooper lovingly refurbished the small cannon, alleged to have been used on the Chihuahua and Santa Fe Trails and by General Zachary Taylor in the Mexican War of 1848.[14] Although the piece had no military markings, it may have been used by the Confederate army, one of many cannons manufactured in Europe in the 1770s, possibly in Sweden. The Big Horn Gun would travel again and again before reaching its present home in Bozeman's Pioneer Museum.

A grim end to the gold-seeking party was the suicide of expedition member Henry T. P. Comstock, sometimes known as "Old Pancake," who had earlier muscled in on some silver mines in Virginia City, Nevada, on a rich lode which came

to bear his name. He had spent what little money he received from the sale of the Comstock Lode and, after the ill-fated gold prospecting expedition in Wyoming, lived for a short time in a crude shack on East Main Street in Bozeman. He had no money; his meanness of spirit attracted few friends. He shot himself on September 27 and is buried in Bozeman's Sunset Hills Cemetery.

* * *

In 1870, another curious group of men wanted to see firsthand what Folsom, Cook, and Peterson had observed in the Upper Yellowstone country. Henry Washburn, United States surveyor-general, headed the expedition. Many members were between jobs. Nathaniel P. Langford had just been fired as territorial collector of Internal Revenue and had lost his bid for the territorial governorship. President Andrew Johnson had appointed him, but a fractious U.S. Congress said no. Former federal assessor Truman C. Everts and his assistant Walter Trumbull were also available, both having been ousted from their posts by President Grant's new administration. Everts was the oldest member of the expedition at fifty-six. Jacob W. Smith, former employee of the Montana Hide and Fur Company, said he could come. Attorney Cornelius Hedges wanted to be an expedition member, although he was frail and just starting his Helena law practice. Helena banker and civil engineer Samuel T. Hauser was interested in the trip. Benjamin F. Stickney left his Helena stationery store. Walter C. Gillette, freighter of mining supplies, told the surveyor-general he was ready to march.

Washburn assembled the expedition in Helena, issued each of the nine men a horse, a needle-gun, two revolvers, a hunting knife, and ammunition. Twelve pack horses carried bacon, dried fruit, and flour. Packers Charley Reynolds, Elwyn Bean, and cooks Nute and Johnny completed the party. They started off on August 17, 1870, heading for Gallatin City.

On the evening of August 19, they ate a late but elegant supper of chicken and trout with blanc-mange for dessert at Campbell's Hotel in Gallatin City. Some of the younger men called upon the few young ladies in the settlement. The next day, they crossed the valley to Bozeman. Nathaniel Langford described the valley:

> [It is] dotted with numerous ranches . . . large fields of wheat, oats, potatoes . . . droves of cattle . . . feeding upon the bunch grass which carpeted the valleys and foot-hills. Even the mountains, so wild, solemn, and unsocial a few years ago, seemed to be domesticated as they reared their familiar summits in long and continuous succession along the bordering uplands.[15]

Bozeman's merchants joyously welcomed this expedition, realizing the possibilities for future expansion of their markets. The party stopped for another elegant cold supper as guests of businessman Charles Rich. Melinda Rich presided at table, after which the party moved to the parlor where Emma Willson entertained them with songs as she played the piano. The men repaired to Guy House afterward to drink champagne with Major Eugene Baker and their military escort Lieutenant Doane. They were entertained with the singing of Samuel Lewis, who was accompanied by banjo and guitar.

Bozeman, Langford wrote, was "a picturesque village of seven hundred inhabitants . . . one of the most important prospective business locations in Montana . . . near the mouth of one of the few mountain passes of the Territory deemed practicable for railroad improvement." The residents, he reported, "are patiently awaiting the time when the cars of the 'Northern Pacific' shall descend into their streets."[16] Perhaps Langford exaggerated the population of the settlement, but his views were music to Bozeman merchants' ears.

All gathered at Fort Ellis on August 22 to pick up their military escort—Lieutenant Doane, one sergeant, four privates, and a dog named Booby. This nineteen-member expedition would be the high point of Doane's army career, although he held high hopes for even greater military stardom. The party followed the Folsom-Cook route to Yellowstone Lake, wandering through heavily forested areas. Expedition member Jacob Smith seemed to relish irritating Langford by sleeping on guard duty and shirking camp chores whenever he could; Langford testily noted his bad behavior in his later articles. Although he was not a good gambler, Smith loved to start games of twenty-one but ended broke, yet affable.

Lieutenant Gustave C. Doane, stationed at Fort Ellis, was head of the military escort for the Washburn-Doane expedition to the Yellowstone area in 1870.

As they journeyed up the Yellowstone River, Truman Everts had recovered from his gorging on berries picked on the way to Bottler's Ranch. Lieutenant Doane, however, had not been well since he left Fort Ellis. He was in constant pain from a felon, a deeply inflamed thumb. He tried to release the infection by poking at it with a dull pocket-knife, to no avail; each day it worsened. At night he paced back and forth near the sleeping men, his thumb wrapped in a wet bandage to ease what he called the "infernal agonies" of the infection.[17]

On September 4, Langford volunteered to become acting surgeon and sharpened his penknife. Doane stretched out upon an empty ammunition case, Cornelius Hedges and packer Elwyn Bean held him down, and, without any anesthesia for the pain, Langford sliced open the lieutenant's thumb to its base, the infected matter spewing out on all medical assistants. Doane gave out a violent shriek, then

Guarding the camp and watching for Indians. ETCHING FROM *SCRIBNER'S MONTHLY*, MAY 1871.

How Jake Smith guarded the camp. ETCHING FROM *SCRIBNER'S MONTHLY*, JUNE 1871.

These illustrations accompanied Nathaniel P. Langford's articles about the 1870 expedition to Yellowstone.

relaxed with "That was elegant."[18] After sleeping a day and a half, Doane felt fit to travel. He never again had full use of his right hand, however.

The dog Booby also had his troubles. Sore paws made it impossible for him to keep up with the men until someone fashioned four little leather moccasins. Booby recovered and later led some of the men back to camp when they lost their way.

Somehow, Truman Everts managed to get himself seriously lost. On the afternoon of

September 9, he became separated from the others, but found a stray pack horse and felt he was close to camp. After building a comforting fire, Everts spent a fairly restful night, not yet concerned for his safety. In the morning, however, the found horse bolted, carrying off Everts' gun, blankets, and matches. All he had was a small penknife and opera glass.

Everts walked one way, then another, but his nearsighted eyes could not follow the landmarks accurately. By the 11th, the expedition had started

The Rescue. ETCHING FROM TRUMAN C. EVERTS, "THIRTY-SEVEN DAYS OF PERIL," *SCRIBNER'S MONTHLY*, NOVEMBER 1871.

a systematic search for him, with no success. Along the way, they fired guns and built large fires to alert the lost man. Evidently, the searchers came close to Everts time and time again.

Despairing of ever being found, Everts ate thistle roots and starting warming fires with the lens of his opera glass. On at least one occasion, exhausted and cold, he lay down near boiling springs to get warm, getting too close and scalding his thigh. A hallucinatory figure, he said later, gave him comfort and advice on staying alive.

It would be thirty-seven days before he was found by trackers George A. Pritchett and Jack Baronett. The two men responded to the offer of a six-hundred-dollar reward and, following the trail of the expedition, found Everts within a few days. Baronett could scarcely believe that Everts was a human being. The man weighed fifty pounds, he had no shoes, his feet were frostbitten to the bone, his thigh was scalded from geyser burn, his blackened hands were claws, and his clothing was in shreds. For some days, he was delusional and unable to describe his experience alone in the wilderness. Baronett gently nursed the near-skeleton with weak tea and dosed him with warm bear oil to soothe his stomach damaged from thistle roots.

Brought back to Bozeman by spring wagon on October 26, Everts convalesced until November 4;

when his weight reached eighty pounds, he was able to return to Helena. Despite their care with Everts, Pritchett and Baronett never collected the six-hundred-dollar reward. Everts' colleagues became vague about the money; the again-healthy adventurer seemed ungrateful to the men who saved his life. (Everts remarried at sixty-five, fathered a child at seventy-five, and died peacefully at eighty-five.)

David Folsom had already planted the seed for the notion of a reserved area to guard the Yellowstone wonders. Members of the Washburn-Doane group discussed the idea further around a campfire and vowed to do something about safeguarding the lands about them—the waterfalls, geysers, and smoking mud-pots—perhaps in the way the U.S. Congress had protected the Yosemite landmarks in California, giving that state the right to form a park. They discussed whether the Upper Yellowstone should be added to Montana Territory. They knew they had to act quickly; too many promoters eyed the Yellowstone area as a potential for business ventures. Langford himself was in the temporary employ of J. W. Cooke, promoter of the Northern Pacific Railroad. Gold seekers were anxious to go prospecting. Others thought of hotels.

Accounts of Everts's adventures and his subsequent rescue served to romanticize the park idea. Langford planned a series of eastern appearances sponsored by J. W. Cooke to lecture on the beauties of the land he had just seen, but he gave only one speech. He turned to writing and completed a series of articles called "The Wonders of the Yellowstone" for *Scribner's Monthly*, the magazine that had turned down a similar article one year before for containing unreliable information. The growing number of those visiting the Upper Yellowstone talked of possible reservation of the area, but no one had yet used the words "national park," at least not in print. In less than two years, however, the U.S. Congress would do so.

Two recent arrivals to Bozeman decided in 1870 that they would chance a trip to the Upper Yellowstone alone. Since it was late in the season, house painter Henry Bird Calfee and bootmaker Macon Josey planned to start off the following spring. It took them ten days to get to Yankee Jim's cabin on the Yellowstone River because of the deep snow. They proceeded from there, stopping to look over Mammoth Hot Springs and going on to climb Mount Washburn with great difficulty; "being nearly snow blind we were in no mood to go into ecstasy over it."[19] They came down the mountain to camp for a time near the canyon falls then moved on to Yellowstone Lake.

Disaster struck at the Firehole River, when the men saw a deer trapped in a geyser cauldron. Feeling responsible for the animal's plight since it was running in fright from them, the men attempted to pull the deer from the boiling mess. The soft ground gave way and Macon Josey fell through the unstable crust. Calfee pulled him to safety but Josey was badly burned from the waist down.

Calfee dragged the scalded man to camp; he was horrified when he removed Josey's pants and socks to find "the flesh rolled off with them."[20] He poured flour on the burned man's wounds and built a travois to carry his friend out of the wilderness to medical aid. Before leaving the area, Calfee returned to Old Faithful, where he had "delivered our washing the morning before starting out. I found them all nicely washed . . . white as the driven snow."[21] Their woolen garments, however, were several sizes smaller.

Despite Josey's condition, the two explorers enjoyed watching geysers and boiling springs along the way back home. They suffered through swarms of flies and mosquitoes, avoided an angry female grizzly with two cubs, encountered a landslide and a flood, and saw settlements ahead that turned out to be mirages. Their final ordeal was a near-confrontation with a gang of bandits, intent upon robbing them. When they arrived in Bozeman, Sheriff John Guy listened to their story and went after the robbers, killing three and bringing back two for trial, together with a quantity of stolen goods.

Ferdinand V. Hayden, the young geologist on the Raynolds Expedition ten years before, attended Nathaniel Langford's sole lecture on Yellowstone back in the States. He had served as a Union physician during the Civil War; now at forty, he had gained considerable prominence as director of the Geological Survey of the Territories. Congress voted a forty thousand-dollar appropriation for Hayden to explore "the sources of the Missouri and

Yellowstone Rivers," which included a raise in his federal salary to an outrageous four thousand dollars per year.[22] Hayden planned two expeditions, one for the summer of 1871 and another for 1872.

Although the expedition money would not be available until July 1871, Hayden established an early camp in Utah, donned his beat-up but distinctive traveling frock-coat, and assembled men and supplies for the first of two ambitious trips to the . Yellowstone area. By the time he had traveled north and crossed the Gallatin Valley to Fort Ellis, he had with him thirty-four expedition members, as well as eighteen packers, cooks, guides, and military escorts. Along on a separate expedition were officers from the U.S. Army Corps of Engineers.

From Fort Ellis, Hayden led the party down Trail Creek to the Yellowstone River and Bottler's Ranch. They rested at Mammoth Hot Springs then continued on to the mouth of the Lamar River. To document what they might see along the way,

Hayden had hired talented twenty-seven-year-old photographer William Henry Jackson and landscape artist Thomas Moran. By the time the expedition had traveled over the Washburn Range to the falls of the Yellowstone, the artists had been busy with camera and sketchbook. Moran despaired of painting with accuracy the falls, but completed a watercolor that served as the basis for his later oil painting. The work of both men would subsequently serve to convince a reluctant U.S. Congress and lukewarm general public that a national park must be set aside with some haste.

The party stopped for a few days at Yellowstone Lake; while there they built a small boat, christened it the *Anna*, and ventured out on the water to take soundings. By the time Hayden and his men had returned to Bottler's Ranch and Fort Ellis, their baggage was filled with field notes, photographs, and sketches.

Back in Washington, Hayden distributed folios

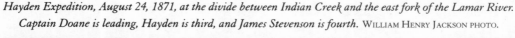

Hayden Expedition, August 24, 1871, at the divide between Indian Creek and the east fork of the Lamar River.
Captain Doane is leading, Hayden is third, and James Stevenson is fourth. WILLIAM HENRY JACKSON PHOTO.

of Jackson's outstanding photographs as well as copies of Langford's *Scribner's* articles in the halls of the U.S. Congress. As a matter of self interest, the Bozeman business community did its part to promote the notion of a national park. The usually slow-moving Congress sped up to vote favorably on the idea and, on March 1, 1872, Yellowstone National Park became a reality.

Hayden's second summer trek into the park was equally ambitious. He was to be joined by friends William and Mary Blackmore, a wealthy British couple with many social and financial ties to the West. But Mary Blackmore became ill in Bozeman and died of peritonitis on July 18. Her grieving husband bought five acres of land east of downtown and donated them to the city as a cemetery, now called Sunset Hills. Mount Blackmore, south of the cemetery land, is named in her honor.

* * *

Reports of these early expeditions inspired a number of high-ranking army officers to promote hunting forays to the West among wealthy sportsmen; some reasoned that the more animals hunted down and killed, particularly buffalo, the faster it would lead to the extermination of Plains Indians groups dependent upon bison herds for their livelihood.[23]

Such wealthy travelers as the Earl of Dunraven visited the area in 1874 for quiet reflection and a spot of hunting. Dunraven needed respite from his troubles in Estes Park, Colorado. Residents there objected to his ambitious plans to develop Estes Park into a recreation playground for the rich; in fact, "Mountain Jim" Nugent, friend of noted British traveler Isabella Bird, had been murdered because he opposed development. Local gossips whispered that the earl was involved.

Dunraven's party included his friend and personal physician George Henry Kingsley, his Scottish servant Campbell, his black valet Maxwell, and guide "Texas Jack" Omohondro. They traveled by train to Corinne, Utah, then by stage to investigate the fleshpots of Virginia City and across the Gallatin Valley on their way to Fort Ellis. A luncheon on the Gallatin River consisted of "fresh-broiled trout and some farinaceous food, taken in a concentrated and liquid form out of the black bottle," followed by a luxurious nap. This is the good life, wrote the earl: "You are not trespassing and nobody can warn you off. There is plenty of fish in the river, some whiskey left in the bottle, lots of bread in the

Up the Yellowstone Valley and into the mountains.
ETCHING FROM *LIVINGSTON ENTERPRISE,* SOUVENIR EDITION, C.1900.

buggy; and you run no risk of being disturbed, for there is not another human being within miles."[24] After this idyll, the party moved east to dine lavishly in the "clean, all-alive and wide-awake town of Bozeman."[25] When Dunraven reached Fort Ellis, he was well received by General Sweitzer, who showed him about the fort, which consisted of:

> a large square, two sides of which are occupied by the soldiers' quarters, while the remaining side is devoted to the officers' houses. All along the inside of the square runs a wooden sidewalk, beside which a few unhappy trees are striving to grow; and the interior space, the centre of which is adorned with a tall flagstaff, is gravelled, forming a commodious parade-ground; while the angles are flanked and protected by quaint old-fashioned-looking block houses, octagonal in shape, loop-holed and begirt with a broad balcony, upon which sentries pace everlastingly up and down.[26]

After watching a Crow ceremonial dance and visiting Bottler's Ranch, the earl moved into the park itself. He delighted in all that he saw. He described the thermal areas as:

> honeycombed and pitted with springs, ponds and mud-pots, furrowed with boiling streams, gashed with fissures, and gaping with chasms from which issue hollow rumblings . . . The crust feels as if it might break through at any moment and drop you into fire and flames beneath, and the animals tread gingerly upon it . . . .

This etching of a geyser fits with Dunraven's lavish descriptions of the area.
ETCHING FROM *LIVINGSTON ENTERPRISE*, SOUVENIR EDITION, C.1900.

Photographs of Yellowstone waterfalls, geysers, and tinted springs such as this 1897 stereograph of paint pots were distributed throughout the United States and many other countries by railroads, hotels, and merchants anxious for tourist dollars.

The air is full of subdued, strange noises; distant grumblings as of dissatisfied ghosts, faint shreiks [sic], satirical groans, and subterranean laughter; as if the imprisoned devils, though exceedingly uncomfortable, were not beyond being amused at seeing a fresh victim approach.[27]

Promoter N. P. Langford, now known as "National Park" Langford, was named park superintendent in May 1872 after Truman Everts turned down the appointment. For good reason.

Congress did not appropriate any money for salaries or maintenance. At first, Langford felt honored, but later became frustrated that he could not give the park any protection. Thereafter, he seldom visited the area. For years, certain criminal hunters slaughtered great numbers of elk, bear, moose, and other animals in the park, knowing they would not be apprehended. Other private interests slipped into the unattended area to prospect for gold. It was not a good beginning for the country's first national park. ▨

chapter

FIFTEEN

By the mid-1870s, Bozeman was on its way to becoming a progressive community, despite residents' complaints that Main Street was unbearably dusty in the summer, muddy in the winter, and always smelled of pig. One could cross the street by guesswork on wooden walkways or mere planks, seldom seen under the mud. After a heavy rain, four-horse teams were required to pull a coach or wagon through the puddles and gumbo. Some wag could be counted upon on these occasions to post a sign stating, "No fishing allowed." Women sewed a black dust ruffle to the hems of their long dresses, which trailed in the mud and could be taken off now and then for cleaning.

Since each merchant built his own wooden sidewalk, the heights of the walkways were not standard; hence, pedestrians bobbed up and down as they traveled down Main Street. Small boys, and some adults, fished for coins or a lost gold watch dropped through the slats of the sidewalks. Again, women's voluminous skirts were a hindrance, the hems ripping on loose nails along the way. Crude wooden bridges crossed Sourdough Creek (called Bozeman Creek where it ran through town) and another small stream to the west, now underground. Loaded sixteen-mule trains crowded the thoroughfare, on their way to Helena or Corinne, Utah. In order to reach Helena in one day, freighters

packed their goods and left a dark Main Street at 3 A.M.

Stage coaches bucketed into town "with four horses on the lope . . . the stage driver cracking his whip . . . with great style."[1] A ticket to Central Park cost two dollars; the trip to Three Forks cost four dollars; a ticket to Helena and back cost twenty; one way to Miles City was an exorbitant forty-two dollars.

With the establishment of William Tracy's brickworks just outside of town, followed by that of Carey and Lewis a few years later, business blocks made of brick began to replace a number of frame stores, giving an air of permanence to the town. Construction was made difficult on the swampy ground due to a high water table. The Metropolitan Hotel (later called the Grand LaClede) was one of the first brick buildings on Main Street. In 1872, gunsmith Walter Cooper astounded all with his elegant brick building at 118 East Main Street, south side. Each of the eleven doors of the Cooper Block was outlined with a gigantic Romanesque bay. Nearby, Spieth and Krug added a brick brewery to the east of their frame saloon in the 200 block of East Main, south side.

Architect Byron Vreeland designed and completed by July 11, 1880 a substantial brick county courthouse on West Main, at a cost of $24,750; also

Etching of Bozeman that appeared in the Pacific Rural Press, *San Francisco, March 16, 1872.*

Brick became the building material of choice once Carey & Lewis fired up its kiln, as did several new brickyards.
ETCHING FROM MICHAEL LEESON, *HISTORY OF MONTANA*, 1885.

123

BOZEMAN.

Walter Cooper's business interests were centered both in the Gallatin Canyon and town. ETCHING FROM MICHAEL LEESON, *HISTORY OF MONTANA,* 1885.

built to the east of the courthouse was a small and separate clerk and recorder building. Two years later, Vreeland completed another brick building for Smith's Palace Saloon.

As yet, no trees of any size grew in town. Cottonwoods and other saplings would soon be planted. Householders fenced their lots to keep wandering cattle and sheep from trampling their gardens. Family milk cows were tethered in backyards. On the front door of many homes hung a small decorative basket to hold calling cards from those stating their intention to pay a formal social visit. New Year's Day was particularly busy, with families calling on one another, the children fresh from a rare bath, women in their best dark wool, a few of the men in silk hats and dusters. Food and refreshments lined every table; by the end of the day, everyone was pleasantly stuffed. Fred F. Willson remembers that the custom "made for good feeling among citizens, and neighbors and friends, it preserved contacts."[2]

Everyday tables could offer cuts of either buffalo, antelope, bighorn sheep, moose, venison, bear, or wild fowl—a heavy meal, its gamey flavor cut by hanging or freezing the meat. Isabelle Randall wrote from the Three Forks area during one late July: "We have about twenty acres of peas to feed the pigs in winter but at present we are the pigs. We also live on fish, eggs and milk; meat won't keep a day in this weather; besides it is too hot to eat meat."[3] For special occasions—a wedding, a housewarming, a midnight supper at a ball—oysters highlighted the meal, at $1.35 per can.

Vegetables came from the garden and included peas, beans, cucumbers, potatoes, rutabagas, turnips, and cabbages, which were often "put down" in kegs for winter sauerkraut. Fruits were harder to come by and might be dried peaches or apples. Isabelle Randall remembers a sheepherder complaining about both the food and the weather: "Confounded country where it snows every month and dried apples are a luxury."[4] A can of peaches from the East might cost $1.25.

Sugar had to be shipped in and could be very expensive. Coffee beans came whole and green and required roasting. Eggs were often expensive in town, according to Bertha Clow's notes: "One dozen will get three pounds of coffee or four pounds of sugar. One egg will buy a glass of lager; six will get a square meal at Dutch John's; Brother Iliff will marry a nice couple for two dozen and the *Avant Courier* for one year can be had for five dozen eggs."[5] Yeast could be made from flours newly milled in the valley or from potatoes or hops. Some tried a yeast starter from corn meal.

Thirsty traveler A. K. McClure asked for a drink of water on his way through Bozeman to Helena in August 1867 and was told: "Water is all very well in its place—very good for baptizing babies where they have such things, and excellent for sluicing; but it don't do for a steady beverage up here where the air is so thin." After his wine, McClure wryly reported that "I could not deny the theory that sparkling wine refreshes the horses when imbibed by the driver or the rider."[6]

In winter, children brought their sleds and toboggans to career down Peet's Hill, below the cemetery, and Church Avenue. They skated on the pond next to the McAdow flour mill from

This 1872 view shows Walter Cooper Armory, front left, and his just-completed Cooper Block, near right, on the south side of Bozeman's Main Street.

November through March, unless a chinook wind melted the ice and snowbanks as if by magic. An indoor roller skating rink opened on West Main Street, which later became the first building to house the small classes of a fledgling college. Sleighs not only provided entertainment but often transported children to school and delivered milk and the mail. Both adults and children wore red woolen underwear through the winter, complaining of the itchy garments but unwilling to face cold weather without them.

In summer, young men on horseback raced one another down Main Street, although it was against the law. Youngsters learned to swim in a fifteen-foot-square wooden pool at Jerry Mathews's Hot Springs (now Bozeman Hot Springs) west of town. Fourth of July celebrations were splendid affairs. Catching a greased pig became an important athletic event. So, too, was another contest involving a greased pole where the victorious scrambler plucked

a five-dollar bill from the top. Bozeman's Silver Cornet Band, under the direction of A. P. Charpie, played throughout the day, their busiest holiday, although they came out to perform on any civic occasion.

Whether or not Bozeman saw the first bicycle in Montana, Davis Willson claimed that honor for the town in one of his dispatches to the *Montana Post*. Shelby Dogget constructed the first velocipede, but it did not work properly and he had to make adjustments:

Your correspondent can testify as to its locomotive powers by having mounted and tried the same, but owing to his inexperience or the bucking qualities of the creature, he was only enabled to perform certain rotary motions . . . by successive sommersaults and headlong plunges, much to the amusement of the small boys and apparent satisfaction of the older ones.[7]

The Gallatin County Court House, finished in 1880, once had a separate Clerk and Recorder building at the right rear, which was torn down to enlarge the main building.

126

When bicycles became a more tame form of entertainment, citizens formed wheel clubs for country outings and even long trips to such towns as Helena.

On Sundays, Bozeman's Chinese laborers would observe the day of rest by taking a walk from their small quarters in the alleys located between East Main and Mendenhall streets, bounded by Rouse and Bozeman. The men walked in single file, their hair plaited in a single braid, loose pants and tops flowing, each with a black umbrella to protect him from the hot summer sun. Seldom did these temporary residents cut their hair or adopt western clothing.

Few women were included in the 1,949 Chinese residents of Montana Territory in the 1870s, a figure representing ten percent of the total population. In Bozeman, four Chinese-born residents were here in 1870; the figure climbed to 27 in 1880, sixty-two in 1910, and dropped to 3 in 1930. A few young Asian women became prostitutes, a dangerous occupation often resulting in their deaths. Those Asian immigrants who did come as a families worked in laundries, small stores, or as servants to an emerging Bozeman gentry.

Such Chinese restaurants as the International

The substantial Bozeman Avant Courier *building, completed in 1881, was located on the northeast corner of Main Street and Tracy Avenue.*

Main Street Bozeman in the early 1880s: the Tivoli saloon at 17 East Main and Achilles Lamme's three business blocks.

Cafe at 135 East Main—Chin-Au-Ban, proprietor—were very popular with those who could afford to eat out. Many of the Chinese bathed each day and changed to clean clothes, a custom foreign to most western men of the time. Such tidiness meant little to the editor of the *Avant Courier*, who observed through cultural blinders that the "celestials," as he called them, were "worthless pagans . . . a detriment to any country outside the Mongolian empire," a view widely held then in the West.[8] The Territorial Legislature passed a law that Chinese-owned laundries would be assessed fifteen dollars per quarter in an obvious attempt to reserve such services for white women (a traditional way for widows to support their families).

Near Chinatown, a red-light district flourished for some sixty years, secure in the prevailing tolerant attitude that such establishments were a necessity. The six brothels paid a monthly fine to the magistrate's office. Madams such as Louise Courselle, who moved in from Helena in 1874, amassed sizable fortunes by investing in local real estate. Roberta Warren (known back home as Kitty Warn) and Lizzie Woods (known to her family as Frances Jackson) maintained "houses" north of East Main Street. Roberta Warren ran her "soiled doves" from a Mendenhall Street house featuring seven rooms, each with a stove, mirror, and brass bed. Lizzie Woods also operated on Mendenhall Street and was so successful that she added a branch eighteen-room boardinghouse in Livingston to her operation. Not many prostitutes lived to prosperous old age. Roberta Warren accidentally set herself on fire and died a painful death; a number of Bozeman women overdosed with morphine; and others were murdered by disgruntled customers.

In addition to Colonel Chesnut's popular saloon, drinkers could visit the Tivoli at 17 East Main where, after a dance, young men could take a glass of beer with a cheese sandwich—"the height of debauchery"—at tables covered with red-and-white checkered cloths.[9] Those with the money gambled at Matthias "Cy" Mount's Saloon, where gaming tables were inlaid with intricate wooden designs. On the balcony, a ladies' orchestra played; the musicians dressed in white mutton-sleeved gowns with pink and blue sashes. The diminutive Mounts himself dressed the part of a flamboyant saloonkeeper,

wearing high-heeled cowboy boots, checkered or plaid trousers, calfskin vests, long flowing ties, and a diamond stickpin, topping his costume with a large sombrero. For the more refined customer desiring a quiet evening of cards, cultured James W. Ponsford and T. B. Sackett operated a dignified saloon called Sackett's Harbor.

Affluent gentlemen were shaved by Samuel Lewis or one of two other Bozeman barbers at least twice a week, often Wednesdays and Saturdays, their jowls stubbled with short whiskers between visits. The barber shop was a men's haven where no respectable woman would think to enter. Each customer had his own shaving mug and brush, elegantly lettered in gold.

Fred Willson remembers his first experience with local theater; although he squirmed on the uncomfortable backless wooden benches in a little frame building just west of Spieth and Krug, he thrilled to an emotional rendition of *Uncle Tom's Cabin*.[10]

Members of the Young Men's Library Association started a reading room in 1872 above the Roecher and Alward Drug Store, hoping to attract visits from Bozeman's young ladies, who were now more carefully chaperoned than in earlier years. The books moved from office to office and ended up in Mayor Bogert's office when the association dissolved. In 1885, the Young Men's Christian Association (YMCA) met to form another private library committee. A room was rented in the Monroe Building located on the corner of Main Street at Tracy, which members of the Women's Christian Temperance Union (WCTU) decorated.

Bozeman women used the library during the afternoon; men patronized the room in the evenings. The collection of seventy books and a few periodicals became tattered with use; with the lack of funds, the library movement virtually came to a halt in 1888. The following year, a Bozeman Free Library was proposed and the remaining books moved to city offices. In 1890, Mayor W. M. Alward appointed a library board and the aldermen voted a one-half-mill tax for its support. With funds to buy books, the collection grew to 7,155 in 1903. Bozeman was one of the many towns across the nation to receive a $15,000 Andrew Carnegie grant in 1902, which included architectural plans for a Greek classic-style library on North Bozeman, completed in 1904.

A second Masonic organization formed in 1872, the fraternal organization's members long considered to be the power brokers in town; this time, lodge membership was open only to those whose sympathies had been with the Union during the Civil War. Down through the years, Lodge No. 16 has remained separate from the earlier Lodge No. 6, whose membership included those with Confederate sympathies. Other fraternal organizations sprouted—Odd Fellows, Eagles, Elks, Lions, Moose, and their auxiliaries for women.

Although the town of Bozeman was formally platted in 1870 and received corporate status from the legislature in 1874, the establishment of a city government in addition to county officers seemed unnecessary at the time. Other institutions were more important. The three lawyers in Bozeman formed a bar association in 1872. A physician in Helena saw no reason for more doctors in the territory and advised a young Yale medical graduate not to come to Montana, saying "Men are seldom sick and never die . . . the Vigilance Committee had to hang a man to start a cemetery."[11] Farmers in the valley went to Grange meetings in 1873, the first chapter to be established in the territory. Members of the Gallatin County Teachers Association started meeting in 1874. Families who had settled prior to 1868 joined the Pioneer Society in 1872.

On November 11, 1871, merchant Lester Willson and editor Joseph Wright sent greetings to Territorial Governor Benjamin Potts from Bozeman to Helena by the new telegraph. The men at Fort Ellis used the Bozeman service until the federal government strung wire with a direct line to Helena. Five years before, in 1866, wire had been strung from Salt Lake City to Virginia City; one year later, Helena was connected to the telegraph line, which became a valuable method of communication to the south and to the east, when the line worked. Joseph R. Farley started carrying the mail to Virginia City and back during the winter of 1869-1870. As yet, there was no electricity in town, nor telephones; no fire department had been organized.

In September 1877, a forest fire broke out up Middle Creek; one Bozeman paper reported philosophically, "We are now enveloped in a cloud of smoke, which is a rather agreeable diversion from the drifts of dust."[12]

By the end of the 1870s, Bozeman could offer accommodations at two hotels and two boardinghouses. Ten general stores offered a variety of goods, but specialty businesses had also opened— a milliner, a tailor, two boot shops, two watchmakers, and a jeweler. There were three blacksmith and wagon shops, a harness maker, two liveries, three carpenters, and a gunsmith. There was a brickyard, two tin shops, a sash factory, and a paint shop. There was a printing firm, a photographer, a bakery, a U.S. Land Office, and a faltering bank. Two doctors tended the sick; several dentists advertised painless surgery. In addition to the several saloons, two billiards parlors provided entertainment, and two restaurants catered to the carriage trade.

Children no longer attended classes in the back rooms of general stores or in private homes. By the mid-1870s, they had even outgrown the little frame building built in 1869 at Olive Street and Tracy Avenue. William Beall used his architectural training to design a two-story, four-room, brick schoolhouse with Colonel Chesnut supervising the construction.

The fifteen-thousand-dollar building, located in the 300 block of West Babcock Street, was finished just after Christmas 1877 and was almost immediately christened West Side School. The structure featured a square cupola, elaborate gabled finials, and carved wooden cornices. A heavy bell, originally freighted in to grace one of businessmen Story and Lamme's prospective steamboats on the Yellowstone—an abortive business venture—called pupils to class. Evidently, Beall's and Chesnut's construction skills did not mesh, for the school was declared unsafe almost from the beginning; the walls had to be reinforced with heavy iron rods. Officials no longer allowed dancing in the building. It would be another fourteen years, however, before a new West Side School would replace the old one.

By the fall of 1878, the school population had risen to one hundred and thirty, with principal W. W. Wylie and three teachers supervising their studies. A. D. Maynard taught some of the advanced forms at eighty dollars per month. Misses A. A. Sweet and H. M. Evans received seventy dollars per month. Horace Annis, the janitor, earned twenty dollars. Wylie himself was paid one hundred and

The first West Side School, a brick structure finished in 1877, was almost immediately declared unsafe.

fifty dollars each month.

Classes were finally graded; now pupils of similar age and skill studied together. Each week, those pupils whose work earned a "91" or higher were listed in the newspaper—these included a good number of Aldersons, Lammes, and Fraziers. Families loaned books for some of the classes; otherwise pupils had as supplementary readers such titles as *Dogs and Cats, Neighbors in Feathers and Furs, Neighbors in Wings and Fins,* and *Neighbors in Claws and Hoofs.* In 1879, school closed for several weeks because a number of children had come down with scarlet fever. An average school term lasted six months.

One wonders what happened in 1880 when the new school board felt compelled to pass a resolution on October 8 that stated:

that in future the reading of the Bible, or selections therefrom, or delivery or reading of prayers and singing or reading religious hymns and psalms shall be abolished in the public school of this District for the reasons that such exercises are out

of place in the public schools, of no benefit from the nature of the thing and offensive to many in the community having direct interest in the school.[13]

The poorly built West Side School also accommodated twenty-five students pursuing a high school curriculum; dropouts were common but, in 1883, two were finally graduated. A few private schools still offered education to those families who could afford the fees.

Both factions of the Methodist Church attracted congregations in Bozeman and in the valley. (The denomination split nationwide in the 1840s over the issue of slavery but reunited in 1939.) In addition to the two Methodist churches, other religious societies organized during the 1870s, using the little original Methodist building for their services until their own quarters could be finished.

The Presbyterian Church, organized in 1872, was one of seven societies of that faith established in the valley during a sixteen-day period by Sheldon Jackson. The first Bozeman church, on the southeast

The First Presbyterian Church was dedicated on October 24, 1880; parishioners collected five thousand dollars to build the structure, which has been replaced since that time.

corner of Willson and Babcock, was finished in 1879 at a cost of $5,000; a finer building replaced it in 1908.

The Episcopalians were growing in number by the mid-1870s. The Baptists organized in 1883 and worshipped in their new church two years later. In 1887, the Grand Avenue Christian Church formed, as did the Holy Rosary Catholic Church, although priests had been conducting Mass in private homes for a number of years. With the organization of church groups in the area, Bozeman was on its way to achieving a more stable society, different from Melinda Rich's description of the town's violent nights a few years before. ▦

chapter

SIXTEEN

During the summer and fall of 1873, Bozeman merchants retreated to the "Board Room" of Colonel Chesnut's saloon to discuss the gloomy financial news in the States and how it would affect old and new markets in the West. The long-awaited Northern Pacific Railroad had stopped laying rails at Bismarck, Dakota Territory, due to lack of capital. Jay Cooke and Company, Nathaniel Langford's old employer and financial arm of the railroad, closed its doors, contributing to the Panic of 1873.

Local businessmen took stock. True, Bozeman still supplied agricultural produce and supplies to the mining camps west of the county, but the market had declined since the boom days of the mid-1860s. Some of the gold settlements had become ghost towns, romantic but unprofitable. The market for fur pelts, dominated by gunsmith Walter Cooper, remained healthy, bringing in sixty thousand dollars per year. Fort Ellis was a stable source for commerce. The new national park looked to be a future moneymaker.

Recently established Indian reservations promised a lucrative source of revenue. Leander M. Black had become special agent for the Crow Indian Reservation in 1869, calling his new headquarters Fort Parker, located on the south side of the Yellowstone River a few miles from Mission Creek. One year later, Fellows D. Pease became Crow agent; C. W. Hoffman secured contracts from Washington,

D.C., for reservation housing. Nelson Story started freighting beef, pork, and flour to the new Crow reservation. Lester Willson, Charles Rich, and new partner J. V. "Vesuvius" Bogert also filled their wagons with goods, the Crow in mind. At one point, Washington considered moving the Crow Nation agency to a location farther from Bozeman, a possibility that gave local merchants a number of sleepless nights.

Reverend Alderson was on the Milk River in 1874, acting as agent for the Assiniboine and the Hunkpapa and Yankton Sioux. He was extremely pleased with his decision to establish a day school at Wolf Point. An unexpected financial boon for local merchants occurred in October 1871 when Chief Looking Glass and more than two hundred Nez Perce visited Bozeman, to the dismay of some residents. Happily for the shopkeepers, the chief bought considerable amounts of flour, sugar, coffee, guns, bullets, and powder.

But Bozeman as a commercial center was remote from most markets. Businessmen Leander Black, George W. Fox, C. J. Lyster, and John P. Bruce established the First National Bank of Bozeman in August 1872. Its prospects were not rosy; the new bank would close its doors after six years. Bozeman merchants looked to the east along the Yellowstone River for new financial life—if the Northern Pacific could not come to them, they would go to the railroad. But the Sioux and Cheyenne Indians were in the way; something would have to be done about them.

During the summer of 1873, a quickly formed Yellowstone Transportation Company planned to seek a route for a wagon road to connect with boats on the Yellowstone River at the mouth of the Tongue River to carry goods to Bismarck and beyond. The company did not get off the ground, but the notion continued to be discussed in Chesnut's saloon. By January 1874, a new Yellowstone Wagon Road Expedition, organized for the same purpose, had enough capital, supplies, and personnel to plan a departure date.

Professor J. L. Vernon, the Bozeman teacher who had earlier absconded with the school library fund, was back in town, this time as a gold prospecting promoter. Apparently, the book money was forgotten when he told local residents that he had found gold in paying quantities in the Wolf Mountains near the headwaters of Rosebud Creek, a tributary of the Yellowstone. As writer E. S. Topping says, "He was a smooth talker and convinced many of the truth of his story and quite a large number agreed to go with him to the Rosebud in the spring."[1] The stated goals of the expedition were to scout a wagon road and to look for gold; the other goal was less publicized: to clear out the Sioux

Some members of the Executive Committee of the Yellowstone Wagon Road and Prospecting Company, 1874.
TOP, LEFT TO RIGHT: *Unidentified man, Samuel W. Langhorne.* BOTTOM, LEFT TO RIGHT: *Walter Cooper,*
Nelson Story, Horatio Nelson Maguire.

and the Cheyenne or to provoke the Indians to such hostile acts that the U.S. military would be forced to come in to finish the job.

The executive committee of the Yellowstone Wagon Road Expedition was made, for the most part, of family men, still young but not rash enough to chase into Indian country themselves looking for the Sioux. They looked for others to do their work. J. P. Bruce was president of the committee; J. V. Bogert was treasurer and secretary; the rest were

familiar names: Horatio N. Maguire, W. L. Perkins, Walter Cooper, T. C. Burns, C. L. Clark, Nelson Story, Lester Willson, Charles Rich, D. H. Carpenter, Samuel W. Langhorne, S. B. Bowen. They sensed that the appeal of Vernon's "El Dorado" out yonder would attract the kind of men they were looking for and appended their names to the expedition.

Those who were recruited for the expedition were, for the most part, men skilled with firearms,

Advertisement, Bozeman
Avant Courier,
January 23, 1874.

YELLOWSTONE
WAGON ROAD
AND PROSPECTING EXPEDITION.

A large Expedition will leave

BOZEMAN, MONTANA,

On or about February 10th,

to locate a Free Wagon Road to Tongue River, and generally survey and prospect the country between Bozeman and that point. It will go well outfitted. Good men are invited to join it, and contributions of supplies are solicited. Men should come provided with transportation, arms, ammunition and supplies for a term of six months. Cattle, horse and mule teams will accompany it, and saddle outfits will be admitted.

Rich mineral deposits are believed to exist in the region referred to, and the best men of the Gallatin Valley are interested in, and have contributed $5,000 toward, the movement, which is endorsed by Messrs. Gemmell and Sharp, of Madison county, who have decided to move with this Expedition, which will be provided with 25,000 rounds of extra ammunition and three pieces of artillery.

All who intended joining the late Vernon Expedition are invited to join the Wagon Road and Prospecting expedition with their outfits. All that would have resulted from that movement will be obtained under this, and attention is hereby called to the reports published in the Bozeman and Virginia City papers of this week.

All who wish to join the Wagon Road and Prospecting Expedition are requested to correspond with the secretary IMMEDIATELY. Letters should state the amount of outfit the writer can supply, and the date he can report at Bozeman. As the Expedition will start by February 10th at latest, it is necessary that the suggested correspondence be attended to without delay. Those intending to contribute toward it must advise the Secretary fully immediately. Contributions should be sent to the Bozeman Depot without delay, and at the latest by February 1st, and all men and material MUST report at Bozeman before February 10th.

As this enterprise will do much to develop the various resources of the lower country, induce immigration and encourage railroad and steamboat approaches, the interest of every citizen will be consulted by assisting by men and material.

Executive Committee.

J. P. BRUCE,	N. STORY,	W. L. PERKINS,
L. L. WILLSON,	H. N. MAGUIRE,	CHARLES RICH,
J. V. BOGERT,	D. H. CARPENTER,	W. COOPER,
T. C. BURNS,	C. L. CLARK,	S. B. BOWEN,
	S. W. LANGHORNE.	

J. V. BOGERT, TREASURER AND SECRETARY.

BOZEMAN, MONTANA, January 2, 1874.

experienced in fighting Indians, or "turbulent and independent spirits" otherwise at liberty.[2] These young tough fellows could make the trip while members of the executive committee stayed home. Miners left their disappointing diggings and poured into town. The group received full backing from Bozeman merchants, who licked their financial chops at the possibility of gaining new markets at Forts Reno, Phil Kearny, and C. F. Smith. Farmers brought in enough produce and other foods to feed the expedition for four months. Carpenters came along to build a new "city" on the Yellowstone route near the Tongue River. Legally or illegally, Territorial Governor Benjamin Potts ordered an incredible amount of ammunition to be freighted to Bozeman for the venture. Down Main Street came "pack trains, mule teams, ox teams and miners with their picks, shovels and grub on the backs of restless steeds."[3]

The officers at Fort Ellis gave only lukewarm unofficial support. Because the United States had treaties with the Sioux and the Cheyenne guaranteeing them the lands along the Yellowstone, the military could not legally give aid. When word of the expedition reached Washington, the military wired Fort Ellis to stop the group; by then, it was too late. They were deep into Indian country.

On February 10, 1874, the Yellowstone Wagon Road and Prospecting Expedition, led by Texan Benjamin Franklin Grounds, left Bozeman to travel sixteen miles east to Ed Quinn's ranch near the Yellowstone River. Grounds had fought in the Rogue River wars and was highly respected by the men. By the time he gave the order to move out from Quinn's two days later, the party included 147 men, 22 wagons, 200 horses, mules, and oxen, Governor Potts' ammunition, a brass twelve-pound mountain howitzer from Fort Ellis, and the venerable Big Horn Gun.

Expedition member William D. Cameron, who was put in charge of the little cannon, looked around for a container that could be used to project shrapnel, as he had little proper ammunition. He found what he wanted on the shelves of General Willson's store—tinned oysters. The can was almost the right size to fit the cannon's bore. Willson magnanimously donated several cases of oysters for the project. After Cameron and his men feasted on the shellfish, a rare treat, they filled the cans with nails and other bits of metal, topped with small bags of gunpowder. When the party had a chance to fire the oyster cans in the field, expedition member Jack Bean remembers the sound they made: "Where is yee . . . where is yee!"[4]

Townspeople knew that all this activity for the scouting of a trade route to Bismarck would require engaging the Sioux and Cheyenne. Bragged the *Avant Courier*, "The men of that expedition are a host within themselves and hostile Indians had better keep out of their road."[5] When Editor Wright learned that some in Washington, D.C., disapproved of the expedition and its real intent, he mildly editorialized, "It is possible the boys may precipitate difficulties and possibly stir up a fight with the Indians."[6] So be it.

Grounds led his men along the north side of the Yellowstone River, past the mouth of the Bighorn, crossing the river near the present town of Forsyth, turning south to cross the river, heading for Rosebud Creek. Where was J. L. Vernon? The former schoolteacher had gone ahead with a small party, telling all he would meet them along the trail. He surfaced briefly near the expedition's camp near Porcupine Creek to pick up rations from the more than ample commissary; a few days later, near Skull Creek, he disappeared again, this time with companion James "Rocky" Rockfellow and two of Nelson Story's horses. The two rode furiously toward Fort Benton as if they feared that angry gold prospectors might be on their trail; there they stole a small skiff and started down the Missouri in some haste. Their journey was interrupted when Vernon quarreled with Rockfellow and badly cut him with a knife. The professor disappeared again, this time for good.

As the expedition leisurely moved toward the Rosebud, a newspaper reporter for the *Avant Courier* learned and got word back to Bozeman that a good number of Sioux had left the Red Cloud Agency. The paper told its readers this event gave "the boys renewed courage as it relieves us of the responsibility of causing an Indian war."[7]

For three months, members of the expedition fought the Sioux where they found them—small skirmishes and a few good-sized engagements. The men laid out pemmican and open cans of peaches laced with strychnine as they left some campsites, hoping that a hungry Indian would find and eat the deadly meals. They found Indian caches of food, which they also dosed with strychnine. At one battle site, they decorated a Sioux body with dynamite sticks, certain that warriors would arrive to carry away their dead. During a heavy engagement on April 12, Helena man Zachariah Yates died from Sioux gunfire, the only expedition member to fall on the trail. The fighters killed Indian horses and took Indian scalps until rainy weather and fatigue encouraged them to think of the comforts of Bozeman. Leader Frank Grounds began to feel that he was being unfairly used by the merchants back in Bozeman. When the returning party passed through Crow country, those Indian leaders expressed great joy at whatever casualties their Sioux enemies had suffered and received a gift of eight scalps from the expedition men.

On May 11, the Yellowstone Wagon Road and Prospecting Expedition crossed back over the pass to Bozeman; "no road was constructed, no gold was found, the head of navigation was not located, and no city was laid out."[8] The group brought back ten scalps and several pairs of severed ears. They may have killed from sixty to one hundred Sioux and Cheyenne. The *Avant Courier* boasted, "give us a few more men as we have and we will clean out the whole Sioux nation."[9]

During the summer of 1875, another expedition to the Yellowstone formed, a smaller group with fewer provisions; when they got to the mouth of the Bighorn River, they built a blockhouse, calling it Fort Pease. The men again took the Big Horn Gun with them; when they placed it on a flatboat, the little cannon sank near the fort. It took several days to recover the gun, which was then placed in the fort's stockade, an establishment soon abandoned, along with the cannon. Indians burned the facility, including the gun's wooden carriage. Four years later, Walter Cooper, on his way back from selling furs in Saint Louis, stopped at Fort Pease to search for the cannon. He found it rusting in a weed patch with nineteen rawhide straps attached, as if someone—a group of Indians, perhaps—had attempted to drag it away. Cooper brought it back to Bozeman and started to work on the cannon again.[10]

Some Gallatin Valley businessmen cut enough corners in their dealings with Indian reservations and other federal agencies that their activities were judged amoral, if not illegal, even by the loosest ethical standards. "There is no more malodorous chapter in the history of the frontier than that of the dealings involving supplies for Indian Agencies," says Mark Brown in his *Plainsmen of the Yellowstone*.[11]

The Yellowstone Wagon Expedition route.

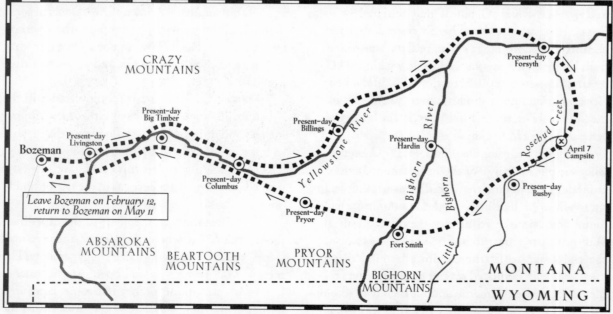

One such transaction involved Nelson Story, Leander Black, agent Dexter E. Clapp, and inspector Ed Ball, a captain attached to the Second Cavalry at Fort Ellis. Once business partners, Story and Black despised one another with a passion. Inspector Ball stated in writing that, when he opened Story's barrels of "mess pork," he found heads, tails, and trimmings along with the meat. Furthermore, some barrels were whiskey-barrel size, not regulation pork barrels; filled whiskey barrels weighed 231 pounds, compared to filled pork barrels, which weighed 450 pounds. Ball said later that Nelson Story offered him one thousand dollars to pass favorably on the lightweight barrels. Story's flour supplies were double-sacked; after Ball stamped his approval on the first sack, that was removed to present a new sack for the inspector to approve.

Merchant Story, of course, was not the only businessman allegedly guilty of such practices. Other complaints against Story and fellow ranchers included the running of cattle and horses in front of the inspector a second or third time to increase the count. Captain Ball, it was alleged, got his inspection post through the good offices of Leander Black. Both men supposedly asked Agent Clapp to falsify records. The *Bozeman Times* printed these allegations with an almost malicious pleasure.

After a Virginia City grand jury investigated the matter, neither Story nor Leander Black was indicted; Agent Clapp was transferred elsewhere. The presiding judge "rebuked" the grand jury "and insinuated that they had not done their duty."[12] Later, Nelson Story issued his own statement alleging that he offered no bribes, that Inspector Ball was a drunkard, and the judge's own behavior during the grand jury deliberations would not bear close scrutiny. Given the philosophy of the times, that it was not improper to swindle either the federal government or the Indians, it is perhaps not surprising that none of the principals got in trouble. Billy Frazier, who worked for Story at that time, said later, "Oh yes, he was dishonest with them all right, but so would any of the rest of us ... who had the chance he did. We all thought that any smart man would steal from the Indians in those days. We all helped him in any way that we could."[13]

During the 1860s, a number of enterprising men tried shipping goods to markets down the Yellowstone River on mackinaws, stout fifty-foot-long boats made of rough timbers. The military grouped along the river during the early 1870s, making a new potential source of business; however, fewer merchants tried shipping goods by mackinaw, fearing destruction of their products by increasingly angry Sioux and Cheyenne along the way. In May 1876, Colonel Chesnut decided to chance the route to sell to General Gibbon's troops. He and a crew of four loaded a boat near the present site of Livingston with vegetables, butter, eggs, tobacco, and a keg of beer for the officers. The mackinaw moved downstream without misadventure. The colonel's luxury items found a ready market with the men. The beer "put the voices of our singers once more in splendid tune. The time passed jollily, Colonel Chestnut [sic] was voted the best fellow going, and the occasion will long be remembered as one of the greenest of the green spots in the campaign."[14] A few others tried the Yellowstone run with less success. Upon their arrival with the goods, the troops enthusiastically called them

Leander M. Black. ETCHING FROM MICHAEL LEESON, *HISTORY OF MONTANA*, 1885.

L. M. Black

BOZEMAN.

137

"commodore"; after the men learned of the inflated charges, they called them old pirates.[15]

On June 28, 1876, former wolfer H. M. "Muggins" Taylor, scout for General John Gibbon, urged his horse west toward Fort Ellis and the telegraph with hastily penciled news of what had happened three days before on the Little Bighorn. On the way, Muggins, chased by an armed group of angry Sioux, was forced to flee toward the Yellowstone River. When he reached the water, to his great relief, he saw the *Far West* steamboat chugging upstream; he plunged into the river and reached the boat, safe from his pursuers. Later, the *Far West* would load fifty-two men wounded in the recent battle and make for Fort Lincoln near Bismarck, Dakota Territory, a seven-hundred-mile trip.

On July 1, Muggins Taylor again tried a western route to deliver messages from his officers in the field. When he reached the Stillwater River, near present-day Columbus, he found correspondent W. H. Norton, who listened to his news and wrote dispatches for both the *Helena Herald* and the *Bozeman Times*, sending Muggins on his dangerous way. Norton's partner Horace Countryman came with Muggins to carry the news to Helena.

When they arrived safely at Fort Ellis in the late afternoon of July 3, Taylor carried his messages to Captain D. W. Benham; for some reason, the account was sent by mail rather than by wire. The horsemen continued on into town and met with E. S. Wilkinson, editor of the *Bozeman Times*, who took Norton's material and published a single-sheet "special edition" that evening, detailing the deaths of Lieutenant Colonel George Armstrong Custer and five companies of the Seventh U.S. Cavalry. The grisly news was printed again in the regular July 6 edition.[16] Countryman reached Helena on July 4 with Norton's story and a copy of the *Times* extra; the *Herald* printed the story of defeat that evening.

Just before midnight, July 5, the *Far West* reached Fort Lincoln on the Missouri after a wild fifty-four-hour run downstream. The *Bismarck Tribune* published a detailed story the following day. Because of continued telegraph foul-ups, the news did not reach the States until July 7.

Custer's Battle and Death.

[TIMES EXTRA.]

Bozeman, Montana, July 3.1, 1876, 7 p. m.

Mr. Taylor, bearer of dispatches from the Little Horn to Fort Ellis, arrived this evening and reports the following:

The battle was fought on the 25th. Thirty or forty miles below the Little Horn. Custer attacked the Indian village of from 2,500 to 4,000 warriors, on one side, and Col. Reno was to attack it on the other. Three companies were placed on a hill as a reserve. General Custer and 15 officers, and every man belonging to the five companies were killed. Reno retreated under the protection of the reserve.

The whole number killed was 315.

General Gibbon joined Reno. The Indians left. The battle ground looked like a slaughter-pen, as it really was, being in a narrow ravine. The dead were very much mutilated. The situation now looks serious.

Gen. Terry arrived at Gibbon's camp on a steamboat and crossed the command over; and accompanied it to join Custer, who knew it was coming before the fight occurred.

Lieut. Crittenden, son of Gen. Crittenden, was among the killed.

The Bozeman Times, *July 6, 1876.*

James Shedd heard the news relatively early from stage drivers as they rode in from the east to cross one of his numerous toll bridges. Many in the Gallatin Valley did not hear the news until Independence Day. At a Bear Creek picnic, as the men turned the spits holding roasting elk, and the women arranged tables laden with vegetable dishes, pies, and cakes, they were interrupted by horseman Ike LeForge bearing the news he had learned at Fort Ellis of the Sioux victory over Custer forces. For many months after, an already fearful populace panicked with stories of growing numbers of Indian campfires nearby and visions of Sioux warriors streaming into the valley, riding toward their farms and settlements. Neither the campfires nor the warriors materialized.

chapter

SEVENTEEN

During the late afternoon of March 14, 1883, Nelson Story and other local merchants climbed into the tower of the courthouse, on the lookout toward the east. "There she comes!" someone yelled. A lone Northern Pacific locomotive chugged over the pass and down into town. One week later, on the afternoon of March 21, Bozeman made ready an official welcome to a full Northern Pacific train. Families from throughout the valley came in for the festivities. Flags and bunting decorated Main Street buildings; boughs of evergreen circled each gaslight. The Knights of Pythias solemnly marched down the street, accompanied by Company D from Fort Ellis. The Bozeman Cornet Band played stirring martial tunes with alternate selections by Smith's Band.

The crowds quieted to hear Walter Cooper, president of the new Board of Trade formed on March 8, as he introduced former *Montana Pick and Plow* editor Horatio N. Maguire, who discussed at considerable length the community's changes as it moved from camp to town; Bozeman was no longer remote, he stated, and would reap great financial benefit by trade with the East. He gave a pretty little history of the Big Horn Gun, which then roared an official welcome to the Iron Horse. After almost twenty years of waiting, Bozeman residents cheered as an engine pulling several cars steamed into town.

For a time, it looked as if the railroad men would choose a more northerly route recommended by the Isaac Stevens survey of 1853. With the activity at the gold camps in southwestern Montana Territory, however, Northern Pacific officials leaned toward a more southerly line and resumed laying rail from Bismarck, North Dakota, in 1879, the point where they had stopped five years earlier. When they learned about Colonel Chesnut's "black diamonds" in Gallatin and Park Counties, they became certain that the railroad should follow the Yellowstone River and through the pass near the coal fields that some residents once thought worthless.

The first depot, a simple wood-frame building on Ida Avenue (now Front Street) near Wallace, was described as "squat, squalid and stuffy."[1] No one wanted to brave the mud to the depot unless necessary, and eventually a wooden sidewalk was installed. A brick building replaced the first depot in 1891, its roof sharply sloping to the eaves and a projecting side wing.

Men were hard at work tunneling under Bozeman Pass in order that the grade into town would be more level. As it was, the grade was dangerous, as army wife Frances Roe reported in her memoirs:

The cars . . . still run over the mountain upon a

The first depot in Bozeman, a modest frame structure, was replaced in 1891 with a brick building.

The western approach to the first Bozeman tunnel during its 1882 construction. Pumping station is above. At this point, the tracks were 5,562 feet above sea level, the highest point on the Northern Pacific railroad from Lake Superior to Puget Sound. F. JAY HAYNES PHOTO, AUGUST 1882.

track that was laid only for temporary use. It requires two engines to pull even the passenger trains up, and when the divide is reached the "pilot" is uncoupled and run down ahead, sometimes at terrific speed. One day . . . the engineer lost control, and the big black thing seemed almost to drop down the grade, and the shrieking of the continuous whistle was awful to listen to . . . The thing came on and went screaming through the post and on through Bozeman, and how much farther we do not know. Some of the enlisted men got a glimpse of the engineer as he passed and say his face was like chalk.[2]

The tunnel laborers, mainly Chinese workers imported by the railroad, were plagued with mudslides within the bores, which made for construction difficulties. By building a three-mile ditch to siphon off the excess water and gumbo, the tunnel work proceeded.

When the tunnel opened, it was the highest point—at 5,562 feet—on the Northern Pacific run from Lake Superior to Puget Sound. A pumping station built at the top of the hill remained in place for some years. On January 22, 1884, the first train came through the John Muir Tunnel, so named for

the man who handled the contract (not the noted naturalist).

Bozeman had not supported a bank for five years; now that the railroad finally had arrived, a chain reaction of confidence in other good things to come stimulated business. The doors of two banks opened. The first of these was the Bozeman National Bank, capitalized in 1882, with Emory Cobb as president and a board that included C. H. Cobb, D. F. Sherman, Thomas Lewis, William H. Tracy, F. M. Esler, C. W. Hoffman, G. W. Wakefield, and Walter Cooper; Peter Koch was cashier. The bank prospered for eleven years until 1893 when it closed for four months, due to panic conditions back East. It returned to financial health however, and, in 1907, merged with the Commercial National Bank.

Also established in 1882, the Gallatin Valley National Bank was capitalized by Nelson Story, J. E. Martin, Lester S. Willson, E. Broox Martin, and Edwin B. Lamme, all familiar names in Bozeman's new booming economy. This bank also closed during the Panic of 1893 but, unlike the Bozeman National Bank, did not reopen.

In 1888, local businessmen supported the establishment of the Pioneer Savings and Loan Company. Carlisle S. Kenyon was secretary for this

The Bozeman roundhouse in the 1880s. The facility burned down in the late 1940s.

firm, which screened credit applications to buy or build homes in the area. Not only did this organization act as Bozeman's first watchdog "planning board," but it tended to insure "that Bozeman attracted only a certain type of population."[3] The town should remain what it already was, its founders thought, stable and staid; disruptions by the wrong sort should not be tolerated. It was said to be a good thing that "There are few millionaires in Gallatin County, and fewer paupers, and that disorderly element that is so conspicuous a feature of some Western communities is lacking here."[4]

One wealthy Bozeman resident took note that rich men in Helena were building grand and ostentatious mansions. Bozeman's Nelson Story followed suit and hired Saint Paul architect Cass Gilbert to design a large home appropriate to his family's social standing. When Gilbert specified that the building should be faced with limestone, Story became suspicious. Was Gilbert tied in with a limestone company? Story fired him, threw away the plans, and hired local architect Byron Vreeland

to design a massive, somewhat Gothic Second Empire building, which soon dominated the south side of the 300 block of West Main Street.

The mansion's foundation was torn out three times before Story finally approved it. When it was finished in 1888, the $125,000 structure supported stone arches decorating the windows and doors on three floors, a porte cochere, a Mansard roof, sixteen-foot ceilings, and "a kitchen big enough for a hotel."[5] It had a summer kitchen as well. The rooms featured red satin furniture, statues from the Continent, hand-painted walls, deep wool carpets, damask draperies, and many fireplaces. Coming home from a trip to Helena with his son Thomas Byron, Story surveyed his new home, saying, "By God, I like mine best."[6] After the Storys moved in, Nelson would become enraged, according to Fred Willson, when newcomers would come to his front door thinking they were entering the courthouse.

A new paper started weekly publication on January 27, 1883—the *Bozeman Chronicle*. Samuel L. Langhorne, one of the movers and shakers behind the Expedition of 1874, became its first editor and

The mansion that was Nelson Story's pride, finished in 1887. Cows grazed in back. Note early trolley.

Sweet Pea Carnival, c1907. The Ladies Imperial Band at left; at right the Women's Relief Corps perform "The Living Flag." Behind stands the former West Side High School, renamed Irving School.

publisher, with A. K. Yerkes as business manager. Langhorne, a transplanted Californian, also found time to run a drugstore, serve as probate judge and clerk and recorder, and become a legislator and speaker of the house. The following year, Langhorne turned over management of the newspaper to Yerkes. The Democratic *Chronicle* had strong competition from the Republican *Avant Courier*, which had gobbled up not only the *Montana Pick and Plow*, but also the *Bozeman Times*.

When the Rocky Mountain Telephone Company opened its offices in town in February 1884, twenty-four subscribers ordered telephones, but most of the users were in business; private residents showed little interest in the contraption. Five years later, the telephone company closed down, saying that the low demand for telephones—twenty-six businesses and eight residences—did not bode well for future prospects. The phone company changed its corporate mind in 1896 when forty-seven subscribers sought service. Four years later, 101 telephones were ringing in town. In 1908, a new facility was completed in the first block of North Tracy, west side, with room for a supervisor and five operators before a switchboard.

BOZEMAN.

Samuel W. Langhorne, first publisher of the Bozeman Chronicle. ETCHING FROM MICHAEL LEESON, *HISTORY OF MONTANA, 1885.*

143

Telephone operators. LEFT TO RIGHT: *Laura Haskins, Elma Bressler, Alma Moore, Ethel Yadow, Audrey Bragg, and Christine Waymes.*

An 1880s or 1890s view of downtown Bozeman taken from the roof of West Side School. The intersection at bottom left is Main Street and Grand Avenue. Bottom right is Benepe's hardware store. The building at center right is the William H. Tracy mansion, torn down in May 1971 to make way for a parking lot. The Story Hills appear beyond the town, shadowed by the Bridger Range.

Bozeman's school district flourished and grew. In order to catch the overflow of students spilling out of the once-handsome West Side School, a $11,900 brick-and-stone East Side School opened in 1883 on North Rouse Avenue and Mendenhall Street. In 1892, a elegant sixteen-room West Side School replaced the crumbling brick building on West Babcock at a cost of $37,800. The Story and Lamme bell was moved into the new tower, sometimes called City High School.

The course of study for the two Bozeman schools seemed straightforward: In the first two grades, Reading, Spelling, Writing, Numbers, and Language occupied the pupils. By third grade Physiology and Geography were added; by fourth, Arithmetic was studied. Grammar was part of the program in seventh grade; in eighth grade, students were introduced to U.S. History.

Offered at the high school level were Arithmetic, U.S. History, Bookkeeping, Geography, Rhetoric, Spelling, and Writing. In the second year, Algebra, English Literature, Latin, Physics and Geology occupied the pupils' time. In their senior year, aspiring graduates learned Geometry, General History, and more Latin and Rhetoric.

In the spring, the board of education forcefully resolved "that the Superintendent be instructed to notify pupils whose clothing were [sic] offensive from barns to change their clothing or sever connection with the school."[7] By 1898, part of the high school, now called the Gallatin County Free High School, was moved to the old academy building, where seventeen students received their diplomas. In 1902, a ten-room Gallatin County High School was completed near West Side; three years later, Longfellow School on South Tracy Avenue was built at a cost of $21,000, the most up-to-date building housing eight classrooms. To reflect the nation's respect for literary figures, East Side became Hawthorne School and West Side was renamed Irving School.

Bozeman had been incorporated on March 26, 1883, and was feeling quite sophisticated. On April 19 of that same year, John V. Bogert, the town's first mayor, watched the swearing in of eight aldermen with familiar last names from four wards: William B. McAdow, Will F. Davis, William H. Tracy, Walter Cooper, Nelson Story, William W. Alderson, Daniel Elliott Rouse, and Peter Koch. The new

John V. "Vesuvius" Bogert, first mayor of Bozeman, 1883.

mayor's first speech dazzled his audience; he called for a fire department, crosswalks and the grading of Main Street, an end to building wooden structures, a sidewalk to the railroad depot, a new cemetery, and community standards for public health.

On May 1, the aldermen passed their first ordinance, listing those activities contrary to public morals and decency: citizens could not cry "Fire!", swear, or use vulgar or indecent language within city limits. Disturbing the peace could result in a one-hundred-dollar fine. No dog or cock fights, since those too carried a fine: twenty-five dollars. It was now against the law to frighten people, to be drunk, or to pass out in public places. The smoking of opium or a visit to an opium den became illegal. No disruption of church services was allowed. Nudity in town was not allowed, either, and neither was dressing in clothes not appropriate to one's sex.

The ordinance disallowed possession of "lude" books or pictures; indecent plays would be shut down. Citizens might be arrested for abusing an animal or indecently exhibiting horses or bulls. Young men might be arrested for racing their horses

BOZEMAN FIRE DEPARTMENT.

The Bozeman Fire Department poses in front of its quarters in the Opera House.

through town—if they could be caught. No trapdoors could remain open unattended, no trade goods could block sidewalks, no horse teams could block any intersection. And finally, a precursor to Bozeman's modern sign ordinances: no commercial sign could project out at a right angle from any downtown building.

By February 22, 1884, twenty-four young men, the cream of Bozeman society, had volunteered as firefighters. They formed the Bozeman Hook and Ladder No. 1 with A. P. Clark as their chief; fireman Harry Healy once described this group as the "stag social center" of Bozeman.[8] To look the part, they ordered red shirts with black trim, special shields, belts, and caps. A crude homemade wagon was equipped with a few ladders and one hundred leather buckets. By June 10, a new fire wagon was in place and used until the 1900s.

In order to raise money for these enterprises and to purchase a fire bell, the men organized a

fireman's ball to take place on Thanksgiving 1884, which became the traditional method of fundraising, at a dollar or two per ticket. The following year, Alpha Hose Company organized, as did the Rescue Engine Company, raising the number of volunteer firefighters to seventy-five. A hand engine and hose carriage arrived by train that October. "Great was the rejoicing of this man killer," wrote D. E. Moser, fire department historian.[9] One thousand feet of Eureka four-ply hose arrived, at a cost of one dollar per foot.

When William G. "Billy" Alexander began his thirty-six-year stint as fire chief in 1889, he worked to modernize the department within certain budget constraints. In January, a steam engine arrived to replace the buckets and homemade trucks. Yet another company, the Omega, formed that year. In 1891, five hundred firemen from around the state held their meetings in Bozeman. Local hosemen, fiercely competitive with one another, vied with

Perhaps this is what caused a Northern Pacific investor to cry: "My God, this is Belgrade!"
Belgrade's Northern Pacific Avenue, 1893.

Northern Pacific Avenue, Belgrade, between Broadway and Weaver, c1892. Note Story elevator at right.

other hose teams but lost the championship; Chief Alexander, however, won the chief's contest. By 1897, the red-and-black uniforms were no longer considered classy and the firemen dressed in a more traditional blue. The men also raised funds that year for a hose drying tower.

Billy Alexander asked Bozeman's aldermen for a team and steam wagon in November 1901; for some reason city officials ignored his request. Feeling rebuffed for the first time, the fire department went on strike. They got their wagon one year later.

When fire broke out in Logan on February 19, 1903, the Bozeman firefighters loaded their steamer and equipment on a railroad flatcar and sped out to help control the flames. The hose companies dropped their separate identities two years later, combining into a single volunteer force. The Alexander men continued to compete whenever the state group met in Bozeman and staged competitions during Sweet Pea and other events.

* * *

At about the same time that the aldermen were passing new ordinances, a Bozeman realtor was looking over a natural gravel bed ten miles west of town. The bed ran from the East Gallatin River to the West Gallatin River and was six miles wide, making a far better building site than swampy Bozeman. Thomas Buchanan Quaw could see that construction of a new community at the center of the valley would not only provide a closer outlet for agricultural products in a growing farm economy but also serve as a better place to socialize when families from the various corners of the valley came to town to shop.

Quaw decided to name the still desolate spot along the new railroad "Belgrade" after Serbian investors who, he claimed, held an interest in the Northern Pacific. He wrote later that when a train of railroad dignitaries stopped at Belgrade, "one old fat fellow . . . looked around and saw nothing as far as the eye could reach but waving bunch grass and he said, 'My God, and this is Belgrade!' "[10] Whatever the origin of the name, he christened one of his sons Thomas Belgrade Quaw.

On New Year's Eve, 1886, Quaw hosted a winter ball which attracted two hundred couples to his new townsite. They divided into fifteen separate groups, each dancing to a different musical offering until 8 A.M. Midnight supper tables had to be reset six times. Most dancing and visiting of this kind took place during the winter months after harvest and before spring planting.

Quaw closed his Bozeman real estate office that same year to become general manager of the Belgrade Grain and Produce Company, capitalized by William H. Tracy and Frank Benepe of Bozeman. In three years, he would buy out Benepe's interests; it was an easy transaction because Nelson Story had convinced Benepe that Belgrade wouldn't amount to much. Quaw responded to such criticism by saying, "Belgrade in five years will outvote Bozeman" and "Belgrade will become the Hub of the Valley."[11] After Quaw bought out Tracy's interests in the grain

business, U.S. Senator T. C. Power took a keen interest in Belgrade and invested there.

By 1887 Belgrade had fourteen phone subscribers, a telegraph office, and a post office; town founder Quaw became postmaster. Six years later, the post office burned down; another was built. Seven years after that, the post office burned down again, and was again rebuilt.

Circuit preachers came to serve the community until local churches could be established. The Methodist Episcopal Church South was the first to organize. Belgrade's WCTU tried to close down the several saloons in town with no success. Perhaps the temperance group had something to do with the temporary closing of a fairly new kite-shaped horse racing track in 1892 because of "fighting and drinking."[12]

A more acceptable form of entertainment was the Belgrade Lyceum which, on Saturday evenings, offered readings, musical selections, debating, and dramatic presentations. In addition to the ninety people who lived in town, farm families came in on the weekends to attend the Lyceum. Sporting events also entertained. In July 1892, Belgrade watched the town's first baseball team play and win against the Flathead nine. Like others from elsewhere in the valley, Belgrade people enjoyed hiking in the mountains, planting trees on Arbor Day, and watching boxing matches. By 1900, a variety of fraternal orders had formed in the town, for both men and women.

A highlight of early Belgrade history was the arrival of Andrew Jackson Corbett, the Belgrade Bull, named for James J. Corbett, then heavyweight champion of the world. Raised by rancher Annie Miller, Corbett was the offspring of an ordinary milk cow. However, "as a calf, Corbett showed his championship possibilities. None of the boys was able to ride him as a calf and he had a terrible disposition."[13] Miller sold the Holstein to brothers Alva and Preston Johnston in 1892. It was not long before the Johnstons realized that they had a different kind of gold mine on their hands.

Within a few seconds, Corbett dumped every cowboy who tried to ride him: ". . . he went into the air head first, leveled off and then came down head first. . . . When bucking he always was ringing his tail."[14] Bets were placed and money changed hands,

Early Belgrade School, 1890s.

mainly to those of the Johnston brothers. Every Sunday, more and more spectators collected to watch Corbett throw cowboys. The fifty-dollar purse rose to one thousand dollars. Men came from one hundred miles to try their luck. No go. Corbett visited Anaconda, Butte, and Helena, but no one stayed the course.

Montana newspapermen had a field day with Corbett and his admirers. A Bozeman sorehead editor suggested that "Belgrade" change its name to "Bullgrade." Now and again, someone would claim to have stayed on Corbett. Some of these occasions occurred at midnight, however, with no witnesses. The Johnstons eventually sold the bull to a wild west show for three hundred dollars, but new stories about Corbett and his skill continued to be published locally well into the 1940s.

Among the many businesses booming in Belgrade during the 1890s was (surprise) a grain

Corbett, the Belgrade Bull. ILLUSTRATION BY G. M. WHITE

149

Morning in Belgrade, where farmers are waiting to unload their wagons.
CHARLES KINSEY PHOTO, 1909.

Teacher Oliver Crawford poses with his charges at the Baker Creek School near Manhattan.

warehouse owned by Nelson Story. Evidently Story changed his mind about Belgrade and sent his brother Elias to manage the new firm. The Story family's wood-frame flour mill in Bozeman had flourished there, but Nelson Story was always on the alert for potential competition. He decided to move his mill business closer to the valley's grain farmers.

* * *

During the 1880s, a group of young Britishers, many of them second- and third-born sons of noble families, streamed out of England for adventure in faraway places. Some went to Africa or India seeking the riches that could not be theirs at home because of an older brother's right to the family fortune. Others were summarily ordered by their parents to leave home and not return to England until they had mended their frivolous and dissolute ways. Whether of serious or wild disposition, most brought with them the almost inbred condescension toward outsiders that has characterized English relations for many generations.

Word had spread throughout Great Britain by

way of travel books and the press of the fine opportunities in the American West for cattle raising and horse breeding. Do not be fooled by the short brown grass covering western high prairies, the publications forewarned prospective livestock men. It is more nutritious than our green acres at home. Besides, they wrote, the air is pure and champagne dry—even the occasional rains do not thoroughly dampen—and most suitable for healthy herds as well as healthy men. What a chance for the good life and for easy income! Montana Territory is the place; the railroad has just arrived there. Do not delay.

By 1885, the land surrounding "Old Town" near the Three Forks of the Missouri became an English colony almost overnight. The year before, four Englishmen—John A. Chater, Everhard Hennager, Lord Duncan T. Hunter, and Major Andrew Cracraft Amcott—spent ten thousand dollars for the Paul and Hanley hotel site in Old Town and registered their business as John A. Chater and Company. Lord Hunter became its manager, incorporated the area, and called it Three Forks. With a practiced eye to assessing good rangeland for horses and cattle, the men bought seven hundred additional nearby acres from James Smart for a dazzling eighteen thousand dollars. By the time they finished negotiations with the Northern Pacific Railroad, they owned seven thousand acres of the land surrounding Old Town. They had spent about fifty thousand, an amount that did not go unnoticed by American settlers. More land near Clarkston was also purchased by the would-be British horse breeders.

John Chater's brother Henry established what historical writer Lyle Williams calls the area's first dude ranch. Henry C. Chater negotiated with a number of English families who wanted to get rid of a wayward son or two; he would house them, he offered, teach them about the breeding of horses, and possibly reform them for a fee of about $250 per year. A good number of these fun-loving, devil-may-care, irresponsible playboys found life in the Gallatin Valley to their liking; they came ostensibly to raise thoroughbred horses or oversee cattle ranches. They filled westbound baggage cars with numerous trunks and, likewise, loaded stock cars with high-quality jumpers and fine cattle as if they meant to stay. However, they weren't settlers in any

traditional sense, but lived in the area just long enough to irritate their hard-working American neighbors with their superior manner.

No doubt, "the natives," as the British called the Americans, may have been a bit jealous of the newcomers' wealth and leisure. (Moreover, settlers from the States felt they could call Indian tribal members "the natives" with impunity but they didn't like being called "the natives" themselves.) One young English gentleman, at a loss when he discovered he was expected to dine with ranch hands, was overheard to state that he did not care to eat with "cow servants."[15] This compliment spread from ranch to ranch, and western cowboys experienced much merriment with each retelling.

The newcomers bought more land at the Hamilton stage stop, southeast of today's Manhattan, and renamed it "Moreland" after an English settler. Britishers James Lowndes and Frank Randall incorporated the Moreland Ranch Stock Company on March 20, 1884. Frank Randall had settled in the area in 1880 and was waiting for his brother James to come from England. By the time his brother and new wife Isabelle arrived with their servants in the fall of 1885, the area was more English than American.

Lady Randall was both excited and apprehensive about her new life in the wild West when her husband Lord James Randall—she called him "Jem"—proposed that they raise horses in Montana. Frank had bought the Culver place for them, which had housed the select Gallatin Valley Female Seminary ten years before. All was in readiness—the house, the company, and the horses.

Despite her description of the Gallatin Valley as "a barbarous region,"[16] Isabelle loved ranch life, the hearty Montana weather, long rides down the valley on her beloved thoroughbred racehorse Daisy, and visits from fellow Englishmen. But, like many of her class, Isabelle Randall did not know how to treat anyone who was not in it. She received her first American lady caller in the kitchen and did not invite her to sit in the parlor. After all, the American was delivering butter at the back door. But apparently, she noted in letters back home, "they are all ladies here."[17]

The next female visitors merely left their cards; Lady Randall escaped upstairs just in time to avoid

Known for years as the Culver Place, this once-elegant building, built around 1872 two miles northeast of Manhattan, housed the Crittendens' Female Seminary in 1874; ten years later, Britishers Jem and Isabelle Randall would own the property.

MERRILL G. BURLINGAME PHOTO, 1933.

their social call. However, she did spy on them from a bedroom window as they left and observed their heavily rouged faces covered with pearly powder, a practice, she erroneously supposed, learned "from the Indians."[18] Ah, for more Englishwomen in the neighborhood, Isabelle wrote home, or at least ladies of a better class from the States.

Shortly after Christmas, the Randalls were invited to a bachelors' ball in Bozeman; Lady Randall noted, however, that most of those listed on the ball committee were tradesmen, so, of course, the Randalls could not attend. Needless to say, news of the British settlers' attitude toward Americans, male and female, spread throughout the area and fewer invitations from Gallatin Valley residents arrived at the ranch.

The Morrises, the English servants whom the Randalls had brought with them from abroad, did not share their employers' social class or views. They were invited here for tea and there for supper at American tables; these outings intensified Lady Randall's outrage and sense of propriety. "How can anyone keep servants in their place," she wrote home,

"when the people, whom we associate with, invite them to their houses as equals?"[19] It was not long before the Morrises left the Randalls for more agreeable employment opportunities.

At that point, Lady Randall took over all household chores, stating that she enjoyed the robust work. She did much of the outside ranch work as well because Jem was gone for days at a time, sometimes moving horses into the Horseshoe Hills, sometimes taking others to market.

When Isabelle Randall did return home to England for a time, she edited her letters and sent them along to W. H. Allen and Company; *A Lady's Ranche Life in Montana* was published in 1887. The book did not receive rave reviews in the *Avant Courier*:

The ladies of Gallatin Valley have a right to feel indignant, as the writer's ridicule and unwarranted statements had no foundation in fact and were intended to cast slurs on the integrity and virtue of a class of ladies far superior in intellect, culture and refinement to her English "ladyship."[20]

Other *Courier* comments featured Isabelle's need to henpeck her husband, her alleged inattention in church, and a lack of attention to her grooming, i.e., grease spots on her suits, rips at the seams—vicious revenge for her earlier snubs.

Although they had little to do with their American neighbors, the Englishmen had a lot of fun among themselves. They "rode to hounds" seated on their curious little English pancake saddles, dressed in the traditional hunting crimson; instead of the bushy-tailed fox, they chased jackrabbits and coyotes across the plains. From time to time, some of the gay blades raced through Moreland or Three Forks on horseback at midnight, shouting, "Let's wake up the blooming duffers of Americans!"[21] Residents of that time remember the day a number of young nobles flew through town shooting at a fat pig which, by the time the fun was over, dropped with fatigue but, miraculously, was not bloodied with bullet holes. Those Americans who had fled to their root cellars at the first sound of gunfire were not amused.

Gallatin Valley residents did have an opportunity to witness an event at which the Britishers came out the losers. It was a typically American bunco: one afternoon, after a British romp along the valley terrain, a number of horsemen spied a whiskery old man seated in a dilapidated pine board wagon, dressed in clothes, according to writer Edward B. Reynolds, "which hung on him 'by the Grace of God' and the lack of a high wind."[22] His disheveled sorrel could barely stand and looked as if it was more than ready for the glue factory. Ah, what sport, cried the Britishers. Let's have a race between the crowbait and one of ours! The old man was heard to mutter that he would take on all comers; the American observers settled down to enjoy themselves.

The Britishers laid out a four-mile course and started to place their bets with the old man, who miraculously brought from his tattered pockets several $20 gold pieces. Just before the race, another man showed up, announcing to all that he would place his gold certificates on the sway-backed sorrel. Furious betting and side-betting ensued. The Americans did not bring out their purses, however.

The race lasted twelve minutes. Somehow the sorrel straightened up, jumped the gun, and proceeded to neatly cross four five-foot fences, an irrigation ditch, a gate, and two hurdles. The British horse never had a chance.

The nobles were totally confounded, but paid up with good humor and repaired to a nearby saloon for refreshment. A bit later, the Americans watched the old gentleman and the man with the gold certificates carefully lead the sorrel into a waiting boxcar bound for Chicago.

* * *

During the fall of 1886, local residents noticed that geese were flying out of the valley several weeks too early. Many saw Arctic owls in the valley, a sure sign, they felt, of unusual weather to come. Some pondered the reason for the beavers gathering and storing more than the usual number of twigs for winter suppers; muskrats had heavier-than-normal fur.

It had been an unusually dry hot summer resulting in poor grass for cattle and horses. Creeks and lakes dried up. The stock imported from Texas and the Midwest did not thrive. Furthermore, the price of beef was dropping in eastern markets. The *Rocky Mountain Husbandman* commented, "Beef is very, very low, and prices are tending downward, while the market continues to grow weaker every day. . . . But for all that, it would be better to sell at a low figure than to endanger the whole herd by having the range overstocked."[23] A few ranchers warned that too many cattle on the range would require hay for winter feeding; few heeded the prediction.

It seemed a normal cold Montana winter—a few wicked storms and a few mild days—until the middle of January 1887. Chinook winds then raged across the plains, followed by a seemingly endless series of bitter frigid storms. Sunny days melted the top of the building snowbanks, causing freezing crusts at night; cattle and horses sank through the drifts, cutting their legs to bloody shreds. Snow buried downed telegraph lines; mail delivery was discontinued.

Most ranchers could not get to their herds to assess the damage until late spring. What they found were "Dead animals . . . piled in coulees, along streams and against fences."[24] The Anceneys found 76 of their 2,400 cattle alive on the Meadow Brook

153

Ranch. Pilgrim cattle imported from milder climates were virtually wiped out. Many expressed outrage at those who had left animals without winter fodder to violent killer storms. When it was all over, the *Cheyenne Daily Sun* expressed the view: "A man who turns out a lot of cattle on a barren plain without making provision for feeding them will not only suffer a financial loss but also the loss of the respect of the community in which he lives."[25]

In the Gallatin Valley, those Britishers who came for a lark as well as to make money left the area as quickly as they had come. What remained of their once beautiful thoroughbreds and sleek cattle, now emaciated and feeble, was shipped to Canada by rail. Lord Duncan Hunter seems to be one of the few who made money on his ventures; he sold his ranchland to Marcus Daly of the Anaconda Copper Company for a reported ninety-five thousand dollars. Daly had in mind building a smelter in the Three Forks area; he changed his mind, however, and constructed the plant at Anaconda, thus sparing the Gallatin Valley from pollution, at least for a time.

Since Lord Hunter owned the bridges acquired with the Paul and Hanley purchase just a few years before, he tried to interest Gallatin County in purchasing them. Since the county was not buying, and no other businessmen stepped forward, Hunter finally donated them to the county in order to avoid taxes. The Randalls gave up their venture, too. Lady Isabelle came back briefly in 1889 to sell the Culver ranch; she was on her way to New Zealand.

Most of the Britishers went back home, reformed or not; some went on to one of the African colonies or to life of the Raj in India. Little remains in the valley, either in buildings or in institutions, to memorialize this short period of British residence. Will o' the wisp, they came and went, leaving behind a vision of young men and women, riding on little flat saddles, dressed in jackets of hunting crimson, dashing about the Gallatin Valley, shouting and laughing, looking for jackrabbits. ▨

chapter

E I G H T E E N

The financial boom of the 1880s renewed territorial residents' interest in statehood, for which they had yearned since the 1860s. A change from territory to state would bring better representation in Washington, fewer outsiders appointed to important posts, and greater taxing authority. With the railroad had come a healthier economy; the territorial treasury even had a surplus of $130,000. More people were moving in.

A convention was called in November 1883 to write a state constitution, which was widely approved the following year. Politics back in the District of Columbia delayed the statehood process, however. Before they would grant statehood, the Republicans were waiting for a clear majority in Congress and for evidence that more Republicans than Democrats were moving into Montana Territory. National Democrats opposed any moves toward giving statehood to western territories that would bring more Republican senators to Washington. After another territorial constitutional convention in 1889 and significant Republican success at the national polls, Congress at last granted statehood to the "northern tier" states—North Dakota, South Dakota, Washington, and Montana—on November 8, 1889, despite Montana's heavy Democratic registration.

The forty-first and "Treasure" state did not grant women the vote at that time for fear that Congress would find woman suffrage enough of a frightening issue to deny statehood. The failure to guarantee women the right to vote did not sit well with a large group of Bozeman women. By May 1884, their newly formed local branch of the Women's Christian Temperance Union (WCTU) had met several times. Not only did they band together to protest the use of alcohol; they also saw an opportunity to gain political power through woman suffrage, a movement that had spread throughout the nation. "We believe in one standard of morals for men and women, in equal rights, in a living wage, in an eight hour day, and equal pay for equal work."[1]

Strong stuff for 1884, even though neighboring Wyoming Territory had granted women the right to vote fifteen years before. Within one year, the local WCTU membership had increased to eighty-four women whose last names suggested social prominence—Rich, Beall, Willson, Spain, Edsall, Wylie, Koch, Street, Tracy. The group met every other Thursday afternoon at the Presbyterian Church.

The temperance group established a coffee house where residents could take a break with a drink different from that served in the flourishing twenty-one saloons around town. The women also established and maintained a curious cast-iron multilevel drinking fountain at Main and Black. The bowls measured five to six feet in diameter, and were about one foot deep. The lowest level accommodated dogs and other small animals; horses drank from the middle trough; the upper level, complete with fountain, provided a resting place for human passersby, who could dip a cup into the flowing water, winter and summer.

Within a few years, the number of saloons had decreased from twenty-one to sixteen but the WCTU was not content; its members wanted to tax the remaining "water holes" out of existence or close them outright.

* * *

In Bozeman, plans were completed in 1887 for an elegant two-story brick-and-stone building to be built on the southwest corner of Main Street and Rouse Avenue. It was to house the fire department, the police department and municipal jail, the city library, offices for officials, and an opera house—all

under one roof. It took three years of confusion over construction bids, additional bond issues, and fights between the mayor and the aldermen, to complete the building. John "Vesuvius" Bogert was again elected mayor in 1887, along with successful passage of a first ten thousand-dollar bond issue for constructing the "City Hall." Architect Byron Vreeland supervised construction for a three-hundred-dollar fee.

The *Bozeman Chronicle* predicted the building would be in the "French Renaissance style of architecture with a handsome bell tower and bristling spires, entablatures, Gothic windows, triglyphs, spandrels, façades, friezes and cornices, handsomely combined."[2] Architect Vreeland explained that, although the structure would look like a three-story building from the outside, the inside height of the second floor would accommodate the opera house auditorium and balcony. A handsome metal mansard roof would finish the structure.

Despite continuing troubles with bids and

Finished in 1890, the Opera House also housed the fire and police departments, a jail, and a library.

more bond issues, the cornerstone was dedicated on July 4, 1888. A new architect, W. H. Babcock, took over construction supervision due to the death of Byron Vreeland. Arguments centered around the design of the opera house stage—should it tilt toward the audience or should it be level?—and the folly of housing so many municipal departments together. The *Avant Courier* called the effort a "Comedy of Errors," a mild criticism considering the arguments between the mayor and the aldermen.[3] But Bozeman residents wanted their opera house completed and no longer fretted about the building costs, which had risen to a whopping $45,000.

By September 1890, the fire department had moved in, placing a fire bell in the tower. Behind the fire rooms, a windowless, no-frills jail stood ready for occupancy. City officials furnished their rooms and rented out others; the library had temporary quarters upstairs. Singer Emma Willson tried out the acoustics of the auditorium and pronounced them perfect. On September 19, members of the Queen City Band, many of whom had played with the earlier Bozeman Cornet Band, entertained at a benefit concert to raise money for a stage curtain and scenery backdrops. The official dedication had to be delayed because of "the uncertainty of the electric lights. Water was low in the creek which supplied the generator."[4]

The first performance by a company that came from out of town, on October 13, featured the Mendelssohn Quintette Club of Boston. The *Avant Courier* looked over the new building that evening and reported to its readers: "It is without a doubt as handsome as any in the state. The curtain is a beautiful piece of art, representing a Venetian scene,

Bozeman's firefighters in dress uniforms, bedecked with flowers and ribbons.

157

and the scenery and stage furniture are very handsome."[5] The auditorium, with its serpentine balcony, could seat 675 patrons. Subsequent events included plays, operas, benefits, graduation ceremonies, and political rallies.

The following March, 1891, the elegant Bozeman Hotel across the street had its grand opening. Designed by architect George Hancock, it cost $105,000 to construct and could accommodate 136 guests. Each room had an electric light, call bell, steam heat, and fire escape. Built for the opening was a temporary footbridge from the second floor of the hotel to the second floor of the opera house, in order that dancers could stroll back and forth without destroying their finery in the famous Main Street mud. Attempts to solve the mud problem resulted in the laying of brick crosswalks at intersections, but mud collected there as well.

Across the street, on the northeast corner of Rouse and Main, stood another elegant brick building, built by John W. Tilton for offices in 1889. The three buildings constituted the center of activities on Main Street for a number of years.

Offerings at the opera house for the next few seasons varied from classy to downright trashy. The *Avant Courier* complained that some productions "traveled on the strength of pink tights and foul words."[6] Within eight years, the Bozeman Opera House no longer enjoyed its reputation for elegance only. The metal roof produced unsettling noises whenever it stormed and, moreover, it leaked. Performers complained they bumped their heads on the low ceilings of the dressing rooms, and the loft over the stage was not high enough for the most

Across Main Street from the Opera House bordering Rouse Avenue is the new Bozeman Hotel on the left (1890). On the right is the Tilton Building, completing the most urban corner in town. Chief Alexander leads the procession of firefighters in a touring wagon.

splendid sets; there was no place to store scenery. The building would have to be remodeled.

Helena architect C. S. Haire felt he could solve many of the problems by raising the outside brick walls by fifteen feet; the sloping metal roof could be covered by another flat roof; he was awarded a $5,633 contract to do the work, a makeshift solution at best.

* * *

During the fall of 1890, Henry Altenbrand with several other New York businessmen looked over the Gallatin Valley as a prime spot to grow malting barley. They found conditions just right for a superior crop of their product, used in the brewing of beer. Moreland became the center of their operations; they changed its name to Manhattan in 1891.

The resulting Manhattan Malting Company bought thirteen thousand acres of benchland for barley production, then capitalized the West Gallatin Irrigation Company which, in turn, bought another twenty-eight thousand acres of grant lands from the Northern Pacific. Some of the New York officials constructed summer homes in the area, to which they could come to rest from the cares of urban life in the East, the first of such migrations to the valley which would continue into the 1980s and 1990s.

Manhattan was platted with spacious streets and areas with the malting industry in mind. By 1893, a malting house and adjoining grain elevators were ready for business. Some of the malt was brewed in Montana, to be sure, but much of the product went by rail to the East, another exploitation of Montana raw materials by outside interests. Barley straw was not wasted but provided another industry in the valley, feeding the Gallatin Valley Pulp and Paper Mill. The straw contained too much silicon, however; the resulting paper was of an inferior grade and could not compete in the national market.

Employees of the Manhattan Malting Company pose for a winter portrait, sometime before 1915.

A prosperous malting operation in Manhattan.

Manhattan businessmen also acted as volunteer firefighters, running to fires with two hose wagons, 1906.
They were unable to save their own building, in background, in 1918, when it burned to the ground.

No minors allowed in this Manhattan tavern.

Amsterdam, 1915, with John Verwolf residence in foreground.

The Dutch Reformed Church commands the hill at Churchill, March 17, 1911.

Since the malters needed agricultural workers to operate the irrigation canals and grow the barley, they looked to the Netherlands for a labor supply. By May 1893, they had encouraged enough Hollanders to settle in the valley to work the prospering fields. At first, the Presbyterian Church helped to bring Dutch farmers to the area; soon, however, the immigrants encouraged the Presbyterians to quit their ministry, since they wanted to worship in a church similar to those they had left behind. The resulting Dutch Reformed Church was formed from families with names still familiar in the Gallatin Valley—Kimm, Kamp, Broekema, Alberda, Braaksma, Weidenaar, and Van Dyken. By 1903, the new church had organized with nineteen families and five bachelors.

Within a few years, a larger church opened its doors to forty Hollander families in a growing community called Church Hill (later spelled Churchill). Because of the building of a railroad spur nearby in 1911, another town called Amsterdam developed to accommodate more Dutch families.

Together, the two communities form what is still called the Holland Settlement, a closely knit, conservative, religious society whose children have attended private schools since 1911. Amsterdam was never incorporated and had no post office, nor did Churchill (previously called Godfrey, then Rotterdam); both still receive their mail addressed to Manhattan.

* * *

The Anceneys decided to try it again. Still smarting from the loss of Meadow Brook, they considered leaving the valley for opportunities elsewhere. But a Bozeman bank changed all that; it granted them a loan of $38,000 to start over. With the funds, the elder Anceney went to Saint Paul to buy Gallatin Canyon land from the Northern Pacific. His son traveled to Oregon and Nevada to buy cattle, which he trailed back to Montana, crossing desert land as he came. They established what they called the "Home Ranch" in Madison County on eleven thousand acres. By 1894, they had

The Red Stone house on the Flying D Ranch, 1908. LEFT TO RIGHT: *Frank Eckley, Anna Vogel Fechter, John Fechter, David Vogel, and Anna Eckley. In front are Louise and Fred Eckley.*

163

accumulated sixteen thousand acres. They incorporated their land as the Charles L. Anceney Land and Livestock Company.

The elder Anceney died the following year from injuries when a saddle horse fell on top of him. His son, left alone to carry on, went into partnership with Helena banker Harry W. Child. Child was to raise the money for their ventures; Anceney was to manage the livestock. In 1908, Child won the concession to winter nine hundred Yellowstone National Park horses on their ranch. In 1913, the men started an ambitious program to buy another eighty thousand acres, naming their venture "The Flying D Ranges," an area covering ten townships, six in Madison County and four in Gallatin County. Ultimately, the Flying D stretched from the Gallatin River on the east, across the Madison Range (twenty-four miles), to the Madison River on the west. From north to south, the ranch measured twenty-six miles, from the Camp Creek road on the north to the Spanish Peaks on the south.

The owners inherited five school districts, several mines and mill sites, an indeterminate number of whiskey stills, and a Methodist Church, complete with stained glass windows. As Charles

Anceney III says, "it was a cattleman's heaven," with as high as 14,000 animals on the land, the largest stock operation in Montana.[7] Much of the area is still called Cowboys Heaven today.

When Yellowstone National Park became motorized in 1917, the men continued to raise horses, but the concentration was on improving strains of cattle. By 1920, the Flying D covered 100,000 acres with leases on 400,000 more. The ranch owned part of little Salesville nearby; Charles Anceney II sat as president of the Salesville State Bank. The Northern Pacific Railroad built a branch railroad from Manhattan to the northern border of the Flying D, naming the last stop "Anceney." Cattle could also be driven to the eastern border of the ranch at Salesville, renamed "Gallatin Gateway" in 1927. With such optimum shipment possibilities, Flying D cattle could be in the Chicago yards in as little time as sixty-one hours. In a glowing, often inaccurate article in *Forbes Magazine* in 1923, B. C. Forbes described Anceney as "Boss of Half-a-Million Acres . . . one of the 'Men Who Are Making the West.'"[8]

In 1931, Harry Child died; five years later, Charles Anceney died, too, in an auto accident.

Alta Young and Lou Davis look over a barn on the Flying D, c1912.

The interior of Wilson Creek School near Salesville, April 17, 1914.

Carriages line up before the Canyon Hotel, August 1913. The drivers wear dusters. F. JAY HAYNES PHOTO.

Ranch accountant Frank Stone took over as manager until 1944, when California investor James Irvine bought the Flying D for a reported $1.5 million. Irvine leased the property to George Sinton, then to Bill Foxley of Omaha, Nebraska. Other locals leased parts of the extensive holdings from time to time, groups that included former Senator Zales Ecton, Sr., and the CA Ranch. In 1971, Robert Shelton of Kerrville, Texas, bought the Spanish Creek Ranch; seven years later, he reunited it with the rest of the Flying D by purchasing all the former Anceney range. E. Bert "Bud" Griffith managed both operations under a new name, Shelton

Ranches, Inc., although most valley residents continued to call it the Flying D.

* * *

Not everyone flourished during the boom years of the 1880s and 1890s in the Gallatin Valley. Some souls, less enterprising than Bozeman's first merchants, came to improve their lot in the new state, but failed to achieve the good life. When Charles D. Loughrey came to Montana Territory in 1882, his dream was to become a professional photographer; most of the time, however, he worked as a field hand for others. He spent his early years

Charles D. Loughrey dreamed of becoming a professional photographer.

on his family's Compton, California, vegetable farm. He helped to clear the land, plant and irrigate it; he freighted water, repaired fences, saw to the farm animals, and performed other chores necessary to keep the truck farm going.

Loughrey apparently found farm life lacking in excitement. Early in 1882, he took the train from Los Angeles east to Arizona, then traveled by stage to Tombstone to look for work in the mines. There he found too many men for too few jobs. To get back to his family in California, Loughrey hired out as a water freighter and played his guitar to entertain drinkers in Tombstone saloons. Back in California, he still dreamed of opportunity elsewhere. He turned his attention to Montana. His laconic diary entry for May 8, 1882, read: "I pack my trunk again, take a bath, and start for Montana."[9]

He took the train north to San Francisco, then went on to Salt Lake City by stage. He arrived in

Dillon on May 20 and immediately looked for work. He chopped wood and did other odd jobs until August, when he told his diary that his new life in Montana was virtually the same as his old life in California.

After that, Loughrey drifted about for a while and wandered into Bozeman on New Year's Eve, 1882. He performed what he regarded as more tiresome odd jobs on the Erskine farm in the Gallatin Valley, same old routine. But the Erskines did have a shy teenage daughter named Ida he may have noticed. By September 1883, Loughrey had earned enough extra money—eight dollars—to buy a small cabin from John B. Koch. Later, he lived on an old farmstead at the mouth of Bridger Canyon, at the present site of the fish hatchery.

Loughrey got to know Jack Bean and heard enough of the guide's former exploits, real and fictional, to become his solid admirer. Jack had been

Ad in the Avant Courier, *May 26, 1887.*

with Hayden in Yellowstone in 1872; he had been one of the tough young men hired to kill Sioux on the Expedition of 1874. In 1876, he was part of a grisly detail to clean up after the Battle of the Little Bighorn. With such experiences, he could not fail to attract the attention of British hunting parties who came to kill game in the wild West.

Bean had married Dora, one of the Erskine girls, in 1881; when Loughrey started courting her sister Ida, he invited the Beans and Ida to toboggan near his Bridger Canyon farmstead, a perfect way to spend a moonlit winter evening. When Loughrey married Ida on February 27, 1887, Jack Bean was his witness. His diary entry for the romantic day, "Ida and I were married at half past three by Mr. Stevenson."[10]

Most of Loughrey's diary entries were just as spare. He recorded the weather each day, listed the grubby jobs he did for Jack Bean and others, mentioned family social events, and described the photographs he took. He loved ice cream and cake

and took note whenever it was served. He hated the east winds. "Cuss that wind. Rats! Rats! Rats!" He cut hair for both family and friends. He didn't like to go to dances but submitted to a few to please Ida. She and her sister went to all the balls, with or without their husbands.

Loughrey was quiet but stubborn. When cars of the Northern Pacific killed his calf, and, later, a cow, he spent months trying to get a settlement from the company. He possessed a sense of humor: "March 8, 1889: I am going to take a bath tonight if Providence will permit." On the subject of fishing from Shedd's Bridge, he wrote, "March 8, 1889: John [Jack Bean] caught twelve, Amos caught six and I accidentally caught one." He also recorded sad notes: "Thursday, March 24: Went with John to Fort Ellis to get remains of his infants from the cemetery. Brought them down and dug grave on a little point and Henry and I interred them there."

In April 1887, Charles Loughrey decided to open the Sunbeam Photograph Gallery on

167

The Loughrey, Erskine, and Bean families enjoy a Fourth of July picnic, 1893. CHARLES D. LOUGHREY PHOTO.

Bozeman's Main Street; his partner was J. B. Proctor. They found a space to rent, cleaned it out, did some painting, papered the walls, laid carpet, and put in a stove. They moved their photographic gear in. One of their first customers was General Willson. In July, the Sunbeam Gallery closed; Loughrey's partner left town. For whatever reasons, the photo studio was not a success.

Most of the time Loughrey and Bean farmed an inhospitable acreage just below the Story Hills, land that wanted to be left alone in gorse and weeds. Bean had a full 160-acre homestead; in 1889, Loughrey bought an adjoining 5 1/2 acres for $130.25 that had taken him two years to save. The men dug a ditch to use water from Rocky Creek and grubbed out tree roots up to the grassy slopes of the Story Hills. They cut hay and hauled it to town for sale. They planted potatoes, melons, tomatoes, corn, and set out fruit trees. They built

chicken houses and fences to contain their few horses and cattle.

Loughrey also worked hard to improve a house for Ida. He added another room, rebuilt and papered the walls, and finished cabinets. When it was ready to be seen, the Loughreys invited their friends to a dance in the small cabin on May 19, 1889, which featured an oyster supper at midnight; they continued dancing until well after three in the morning.

Despite the hard farm work (which again reminded Loughrey of earlier days in California), the families had time for fun. The Loughreys would visit the Beans and stay overnight. One diary entry: "The girls make molasses candy and the baby cries."[11] Or they would visit Erskine relatives in the valley, or stroll over to Fort Ellis to watch a parade. They followed the railroad tracks into town to visit a circus and marvel at a balloon ascension. They

Guide Jack Bean and one of the Englishmen pose over a downed elk in front of fire-blackened trees. CHARLES D. LOUGHREY PHOTO.

watched a dog show and listened to the "medicine men." They circled the curious Bozeman "light plant."

In August 1889, Jack Bean got a job guiding two Englishmen on a hunting trip through Yellowstone Park. Evidently, Bean's reputation had spread, for he had guided a number of Britishers in previous years. This time Loughrey went along as camp cook and photographer. He bought a new camera for $30.55 and additional equipment for $22.05. He made a five-dollar down payment on a new lens and built a wooden case to carry his materials on the trail. Bean hired Nelson Catlin and Edmonds as assistant guides.

It was easy to spot the Englishmen Beach and Lennard when they arrived on the train to Gardiner. Their tweed suits were neatly pressed, their caps almost new, and Mr. Lennard sported a monocle over his right eye. The Montanans wore tattered jeans and shirts; their boots were well worn.

The party wasted no time and took off for Tower Falls, their first camp. No sign of elk or any

game. The air was heavy with smoke from nearby forest fires. Loughrey tells his diary: "So smoky the sun refused to shine!"[12] He complained that his eyes stung and his throat was raw. The party moved on to Yellowstone Lake. With each camp, Loughrey unpacked the gear, built a mess table, rolled out bread to rise, and started a pot of beans. Sometimes, as Loughrey looked up from his daily chores, a band of Indians silently passed him, filtered by dim sunlight through the trees.

By the middle of September, the Englishmen had bagged their elk and antelope. Bean had killed a fox and Mr. Beach brought in six sage hens and a mess of trout, a change of menu for the supper pot. The mornings were crisp and cool now, sometimes frosty. Loughrey surprised the men at breakfast one morning with his loaded camera. Lennard made sure his monocle was in place and stared sternly in the direction of the photographer, but the others did not look up, intent upon their breakfast. The hunters traveled through the park, south through the Tetons, and over to Rexburg, Idaho, where they took the

This formal portrait, taken in Rexburg, Idaho, was later burnished by Loughrey and sent off to England. The Englishmen, Lennard and Beech, are top row, middle and right. Note Mr. Beech's monocle. Jack Bean in tattered jeans, lower right. CHARLES D. LOUGHREY PHOTO.

train to the East and home.

Back in camp, the remaining four packed up their gear "with the wind howling and all hands cursing."[13] By the end of September, the men had passed the Upper Madison and made for home and their wives.

Where were their wives? Ida and Dora were not at the homestead dutifully waiting for their husbands. They had taken the buggy and gone into town. Loughrey looked over the garden, checked the potatoes, and waited for Ida to come home. On October 2, Loughrey was back at work cleaning out the chicken coop and digging the potatoes for market.

The hunting trip with Jack Bean may have been Loughrey's high point during his twelve-year stay in Montana. He left his five-and-a-half acres to return to California to work the Compton farm. Ida worked out in the fields beside her husband; it seemed they worked even harder than they had in Montana. In his later diaries, Loughrey never again mentioned the art of taking photographs. Many of his photographs returned to Montana in the 1970s, however, when Jack Bean's grandson donated more than one hundred Montana and Yellowstone National Park scenes to the Gallatin County Historical Society. ▣

chapter

NINETEEN

The establishment of a college in the Gallatin Valley was clouded by dogfights in the State Legislature over which political party would choose Montana's senators and where the state capital would be located. Although the Morrill Act funding for land grant institutions passed years before in 1862, it seemed that Montana communities did not sense that a university—even a so-called cow college—would bring money into local coffers. The most hard-won fight at the time brought a penitentiary to Deer Lodge, considered a true moneymaker. Miles City got the reform school, Boulder got the school for the deaf and dumb, Twin Bridges built the state orphanage, Columbia Falls added the soldiers' home, Butte saw a new school of mines, Dillon got a normal school, and Missoula was settled with the state university.

On February 16, 1893, Governor John E. Richards signed a bill providing for a land grant college to be established somewhere in the Gallatin Valley area with the proviso that the site be picked in ninety days. Washington, Bozeman learned, would not expend any money to buy land. Under the terms of the second Morrill Act of 1890, the federal government would send some eighteen thousand dollars if college instruction would begin on or before July 1, 1893. Under the terms of the Hatch Act, another fifteen thousand in funds could

be had for an extension service. Further state restrictions precluded any money for college buildings or for instruction. Thomas H. McKee, one of the first students to enroll in the Agricultural College of the State of Montana, remembers that the notion of a college came in the spring of 1893 with neither "'purse nor script nor shoes.' It was only an idea, a disembodied one, with no house to dwell in, without teacher or student, and, worst of all, without a dollar. . . . It needed money to get started and couldn't get money until it did start."[1]

The governor appointed five local men to serve as an executive board of education to find its way through this educational maze—Peter Koch, Lester Willson, Walter Cooper, George Kinkel, Jr., of Manhattan, and E. L. Talcott of Livingston. They considered three sites. The military reservation of 640 acres at Fort Ellis, which had been abandoned five years earlier, looked promising; perhaps the buildings could be renovated for classroom use. Would Washington give the land for an agricultural college? Probably not. They considered a tract near Belgrade, but it seemed far from the center of things.

Bozeman itself had been planning to beat both Helena and Anaconda in the contest for state capital and had built a parkway along Eighth Avenue leading to forty acres, where, they hoped, a moneymaking Capitol and state complex would

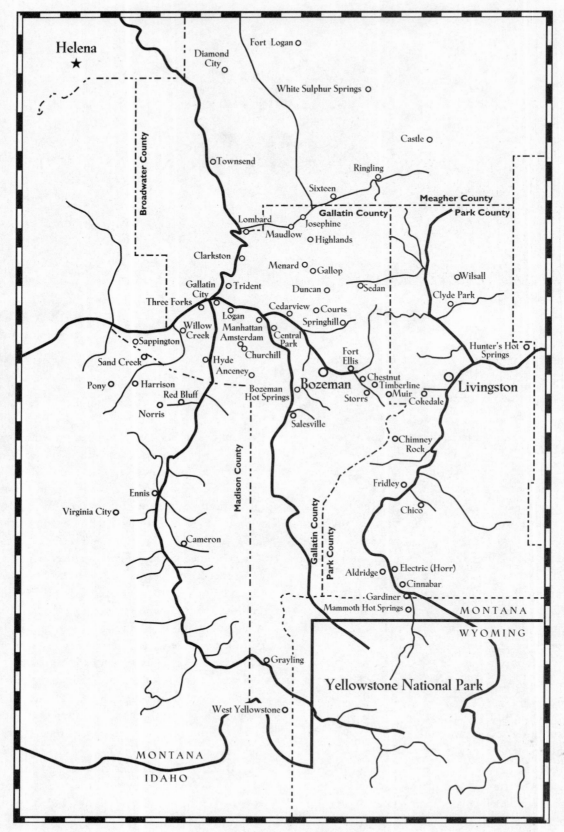

Helena
★

Fort Logan ○

Diamond
City ○

White Sulphur Springs ○

Castle ○

Townsend ○

Ringling ○

Broadwater County

Sixteen

Meagher County

Lombard ○

Josephine ○

Gallatin County

Park County

Maudlow ○
Highlands ○

Clarkston ○

Menard ○
Gallop ○

Wilsall ○

Gallatin
City ○
Trident ○
Three Forks ○

Duncan ○

Sedan ○

Clyde Park ○

Cedarview ○
Courts ○
Springhill ○

Willow
Creek ○

Logan ○
Manhattan ○
Amsterdam ○

Central
Park ○

Sappington ○

Churchill ○

Fort
Ellis ○

Hunter's Hot
Springs ○

Sand Creek ○

Hyde ○
Anceney ○

Bozeman ○

Chestnut ○
Timberline ○
Muir ○
Cokedale ○

Livingston ○

Pony ○
Harrison ○
Red Bluff ○

Bozeman
Hot Springs ○

Storrs ○

Norris ○

Salesville ○

Chimney
Rock ○

Madison County

Gallatin County

Fridley ○

Ennis ○

Park County

Chico ○

Virginia City ○

Cameron ○

Aldridge ○
Electric (Horr) ○

Cinnabar ○

Gardiner ○

MONTANA

Mammoth Hot Springs ○

WYOMING

Grayling ○

Yellowstone National Park

West Yellowstone ○

MONTANA

IDAHO

Gallatin County, 1910.

First built as a roller skating rink, this Main Street building housed the Bozeman Academy, then served as the first classroom for the new college in 1893. Holy Rosary Church now occupies the site.

bring new business to the area. Alas, Helena won that long-fought battle the following year in 1894.

Adjoining the Eighth Avenue land was 160 acres owned by the county, on which the County Poor Farm was situated. Perhaps this was the right location for an agricultural experiment station adjoining the proposed college. The five board members, aided by local merchants, cajoled the county to donate its property for the experiment station and local citizens to contribute money to buy the forty acres. Nelson Story crowned the effort with a generous fifteen-hundred-dollar donation.

Now for the summer deadline for the start of instruction. Board members needed a temporary classroom. The Bozeman Academy, a private high school of sorts located in a former roller skating rink on West Main, seemed a good choice. Nelson Story owned the roller rink building and Peter Koch and Lester Willson served on the academy board. In March, 1893, well before the July deadline, the board announced that a ten-week college course would commence on April 17. Five young men and three young women, all Academy students, "suddenly found themselves attending college instead of prep school."[2] They were not happy with this change in their curriculum and they regarded the "upstart college as 'an annex to a barber college.'"[3] So began the Agricultural College of the State of Montana.

The executive board laid down rules for admission: students must be at least fourteen years of age; no one would be denied entrance because of race or gender; an entrance fee was ten dollars. Luther Foster came from South Dakota to be acting president for the summer; S. M. Emery directed the new experiment station for a yearly salary of twenty-five hundred dollars; Homer G. Phelps was hired to teach business; Benjamin F. Maiden of the Bozeman Academy became one of the first faculty members.

Because of financial hard times, the bank where Peter Koch worked as cashier was forced to close for four months; therefore, he had the time and energy to watch over the fledgling college. He was formidable. When mining engineer Augustus M. Ryon became president in the fall of 1893 at a yearly salary of three thousand dollars, a healthy one for that time, he and Koch clashed with one another almost immediately. The men had totally different views of the direction the college should take and both "had the flexibility of a hungry badger."[4]

Ryon envisioned the college as a center to train engineers in the sciences and business skills. He saw the need of a preparatory department, given the sparse numbers of students registered in the state's twelve high schools. The new president told his first students he would treat them as adults and, if they failed, it was their fault, not his. His aloof manner enraged Koch, who thought Ryon's narrow vision

173

*Peter Koch determined the early course
of the college at Bozeman.*

*Augustus M. Ryon, first president of the
new agricultural college.*

not in keeping with the kind of college he and the executive board wanted.

Having studied at the University of Copenhagen, Koch wanted a broader curriculum to include agricultural subjects and a variety of trades. He begrudgingly accepted the notion of a preparatory school but hoped to close it down at the earliest opportunity. And then there was the "ladies' course." Sometimes called domestic science, or home science, the field of study would finally have meat on its academic bones in the 1930s when it became "home economics."

Both Ryon and Koch felt they were right, but the banker won the contest of wills. Ryon resigned at the end of the first year, although he stayed on to teach for a short time. James R. Reid became the college's next president and stayed for ten years, giving a sense of stability to the institution. He got

along well with local business leaders, insisting that the development of high morals went along with intellectual training. By the end of his first year in office in 1896, the Agricultural Experiment Station (now called Taylor Hall), was completed at a cost of four thousand dollars. One hundred and thirty-nine students had started their education at the Montana State College of Agriculture and Mechanic Arts.

But Peter Koch was not finished with Professor Ryon. Because of continued friction among the small faculty, he prevailed on the State Board of Education in February 1896 to call for the resignations of every member of the teaching staff; the following month, the state officers accepted three resignations and rehired the rest. Augustus Ryon was out; so was preparatory teacher Benjamin Maiden and experiment station chief Luther Foster. Despite the infighting, the cornerstone for Montana Hall had

Montana Hall is finished. Members of the Epworth League move toward the new building, c1899.

Montana Agricultural College's first football team, 1897. TOP, LEFT TO RIGHT: *Jim Arnold, Scott Millis, Ralph Boyles, Reno H. Sales, Herman Waters, Ellie Moore, Irvin Cockrill, Will Brandenburg.* MIDDLE ROW: *Harry Patterson, Will Flaherty, John Seyler, Tom O. Caldwell.* BOTTOM ROW: *C. D. Flaherty, John Peat.*

The Bobcat "Boosterines" in their finery, c1909.

The college women's champion basketball team of 1903.

Mrs. Eliza Owen's cooking class, c1896.

been laid, although it would be a year or two before the students, who were meeting their classes at various downtown locations, moved to the campus. Four students were graduated at the end of the 1895 term with a Bachelor of Science degree, two women in the "ladies' course" and two men in applied science. By 1904, forty-four men and women had been graduated.

* * *

An electric plant of sorts opened in February 1886, powered by water from the old McAdow mill north of Main Street on Bozeman Creek. The Bozeman Electric Company charged $2.50 per month for five light sockets and fifty cents each for extra outlets. The lights came on around dusk and went off at midnight. Within a few years, the facility moved one mile south of Main Street, still on the creek, and eventually was established on the East Gallatin in 1891.

With an increase of additional power and an arc lighting machine, three street lights replaced the gas lamps on Main Street at Tracy, Bozeman, and

Rouse Avenues. Michael Langohr, Sr., remembered that "people came from miles around to see these wonderful lights which were quite a curiosity at that time."[5] Local power continued to be used until 1906 when the Madison River Power Company completed its dam and power plant at the head of Bear Trap Canyon on the Madison River.

On a summer Thursday afternoon, July 27, 1892, three sparkling new electric trolley cars rumbled down Main Street, covered with bunting, American flags, and political ads, accompanied by men on horseback, families in buggies, and excited small boys running alongside. Those privileged to make the first run—ministers, merchants, newspapermen—waved to the downtown crowds. The previous April 5, Minneapolis financial interests had bought the Gallatin Light, Power and Railway Company, which incorporated under a fifty-year franchise with the immediate goal of putting three forty-horsepower trolleys on the streets of Bozeman; the dream was to build eventually an interurban line to serve the Gallatin Valley, the only train of its kind in Montana.

177

This photograph may have been taken on the first day of operation of Bozeman's three trolleys, July 27, 1892 at Rouse Avenue and Main Street.

The Bozeman trolley leaves the depot.

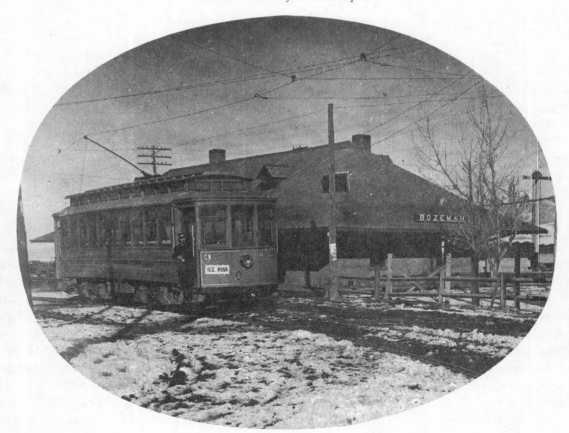

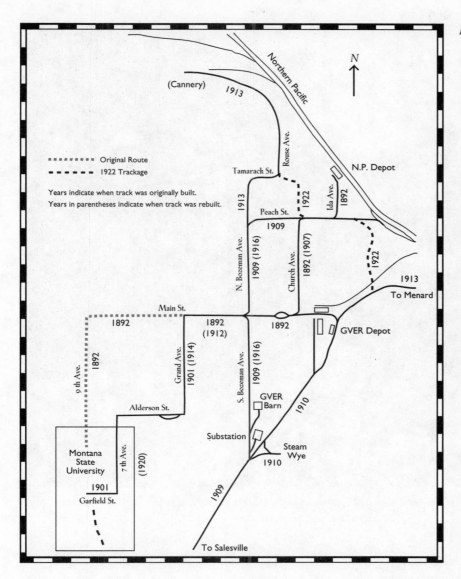

Bozeman's trolley routes.

During the month of June, one hundred workers laid rail on North Ida Avenue near the Northern Pacific depot and on into town to accommodate a method of transportation that some feel even today should never have been abandoned.

From Ida Avenue, the line moved west on Peach Street, then south on Church Avenue, turning west on Main Street, a distance of 1.3 miles; another 1.2 miles of track ran up Capitol Hill by way of Ninth Avenue. The *Avant Courier* described the view from the top of the hill, seventy five feet above Main Street, saying, "If all the citizens of Montana could be congregated at once on this charming elevation, especially at this season of the year, there would be no further contest about the future location of the capital."[6]

The line was moved from Ninth to Grand Avenue in 1901, and Michael Langohr remembered "what fun we used to have helping the car make the grade up Grand Avenue during the winter months."[7] Motorman Larry O'Brien took a personal interest in his customers; on the run out, he would stop the trolley, walk to various residences to wake up those he knew had to make a connection to the train. As O'Brien returned on his run, sleepy but grateful travelers lugged their suitcases to the trolley stop. The streetcar line cost $50,000 to build; it would be another $150,000, a return to local ownership, and seventeen years before the interurban line would begin its service outside the town in the valley.

* * *

In May 1893, curious sleigh riders down Bridger Canyon stopped at the canyon mouth to

The homestead in Bridger Canyon where Charles Loughrey stayed as a bachelor was leveled for hatchery buildings.
CHARLES D. LOUGHREY PHOTO.

see what the men from Washington, D.C., were doing. For some years, the federal government had supported the establishment of four fish hatcheries to stock rivers, streams, and lakes. They needed a fifth site in the western states that was free from pollution and near railroad transportation. The first prospectors looked over Warm Springs Creek, Silver Bow Creek, and Deer Lodge Creek and dismissed all as severely polluted from the mining industry. Davies Springs on Bridger Creek seemed ideal; one spring flowed with a cold water temperature, the other with a warmer temperature; the stream was ten feet wide, ten inches deep, with a flow of two cubic feet per second. For $3,500, the government bought seventy-seven acres from the W. J. Davies family, the spot where Charles Loughrey had lived before he married Ida, and where, with Jack and Dora Bean, they had sped down the canyon by sleigh on moonlit evenings.

Soon the crumbling homestead shacks were torn down, and a residence for the superintendent was built, along with an ice house, pond system, hatchery, and outbuildings. Winter mud and slush hampered construction; many of the workers found that traveling about on horseback was an easier method of transportation than mucking about by foot.

At first, steelhead eggs, wrapped in ice and moss, were shipped from San Francisco; from the East came brook trout eggs to start the hatchery population. Just as it had been with pilgrim cattle, sheep, and horses in the Gallatin Valley, fish eggs from another part of the country did not fare as well as the later deliveries of native cutthroat trout from Henry's Lake. Valley residents on a Sunday tour up canyon added a visit to the new federal fish hatchery to their outings.

* * *

The class of 1903, Gallatin County High School.

Few of the earliest doctors practicing in the Gallatin Valley held professional credentials. Perhaps they had read a book on the subject, perhaps not. Those who held degrees from a medical school or certification of any sort seldom ventured west to practice medicine. A few came, as others did, to see the sights, to mine for gold, or to try a different line of work. Achilles Lamme, who had received a medical degree from Rush Medical College in Chicago, preferred not to practice medicine but engaged in the mercantile business instead, first in Gallatin City and then in Bozeman. Others came to open drugstores or to start livestock operations in the valley.

Dr. Andrew Jackson Hunter came to Bozeman with his family in August 1864, but left almost immediately to look for gold in Alder Gulch. Next, he tried Confederate Gulch at Diamond City, a congenial place in which to express his Southern views, but not an easy spot to make money in the mines. He returned to the practice of medicine, first in Canyon Ferry and then in Bozeman. His real interest, however, was the development of the hot springs in the upper Yellowstone Valley. He dreamed of a medical facility at that spot similar to those he had seen in Arkansas. In 1870, Hunter moved his family to a spot twenty miles east of present-day Livingston, built a home and a number of bath houses. He homesteaded the land in 1878, after a survey was official; his rights to the land and the springs were still shaky, since the Northern Pacific Railroad disputed his claim, but he won his case in 1882. Three years later he sold Hunter's Hot Springs and returned to practice medicine in Bozeman.

The establishment of Fort Ellis brought an unusual number of well-educated medical personnel—doctors, dentists, midwives—some of whom stayed in the community after their military contracts expired. A makeshift first hospital at the fort could accommodate seven patients, surprisingly

Dr. Andrew Jackson Hunter realized his dream of a hot springs spa on the Yellowstone, but sold it in 1885.
ETCHING FROM MICHAEL LEESON, *HISTORY OF MONTANA*, 1885.

few beds for a military post that often housed four hundred and fifty men—a population sometimes larger than nearby Bozeman. The men were generally healthy, however, save for those who consistently drank too much—both officer and enlisted man—and those who contracted tuberculosis or pneumonia. Arthritic complaints were common during periods of sub-zero weather. Both post and town doctors conferred when scarlet fever or diphtheria threatened to become epidemic. Eventually, Fort Ellis supported a larger hospital but with few amenities. Dr. Robert M. Whitefoot supervised most of the medical activities at the post and eventually settled in Bozeman.

Dr. George Washington Monroe came to practice medicine in Bozeman in 1872, but also found time to become county superintendent of schools, mayor, and registrar for the U.S. Land Office. Dr. J. M. Waters set up medical offices in town but was also interested in establishing a Sweet Pea Carnival, building a Presbyterian Church, and starting a pea canning factory. By 1880, six doctors attended the Bozeman sick.

Dr. Henry Wright Foster called his first small and cramped medical facility the Bozeman Sanitarium for Women, but it soon shortened to the Bozeman Sanitarium in order to encourage male patients as well. The twenty-four-year-old Foster had come to Bozeman in 1882 from his native Minnesota, and despite his tender years, was a credentialed surgeon, educated at the Detroit Medical College.

In 1893, Dr. Foster astounded the local medical world by performing a successful Cesarean section, the first operation of its kind in Montana. Three years later, he completed a second successful Cesarean at the Sanitarium; eastern medical journals published accounts of these medical procedures performed in "the wilderness." As word spread of the doctor's impressive record, patients came in from many parts of the Northwest to consult with Dr. Foster. The influx of those needing hospitalization forced the doctor to think of new quarters. Money was tight, however, owing to bank failures in the East; the Panic of 1893 was spreading west.

Dr. Foster had his account with the Gallatin

Dr. Henry Foster's second sanitarium opened in 1896.

Four nurses proudly wear their new hats from a Salt Lake City hospital. FRONT ROW: *Two sisters from the Gallatin Valley, Wilda Smith Niven and Anna Smith Heiskell.* BACK ROW: *unknown.*

Valley National Bank, which closed that summer, greatly upsetting the young physician. Upon meeting banker Nelson Story on Main Street one day, the two exchanged harsh words; the doctor suggested that the banker should be hanged; the encounter escalated when Story cane-whipped the doctor in public view. In order to avoid a court appearance and suit, the banker settled privately with the doctor. It must have been a generous settlement because Dr. Foster immediately made plans to build a handsome, $20,000, three-story brick facility on the northwest corner of Lamme Street and Tracy Avenue.

Opening in 1896, the twenty-bed hospital was an elegant refuge for the ill; since Dr. Foster would not allow carpeting or wallpaper in the rooms for sanitary reasons, the floors and trim were hardwood and the walls and ceilings featured frescoes with restful colorful scenes. Hot water heated the building, the cleanest method, and electric lights lit up each room—"an ideal place to get well," pronounced the *Avant Courier*.[8] Five years later, the Bozeman Sanitarium increased its size with an additional wing at either side of the building.

* * *

The trip from Switzerland to the Gallatin Valley almost ended in disaster for the family of Mary Flora Kopp and her husband Josef Hagen. They and their children, ranging in age from nine years to nine months, boarded the French ship *Paris* in 1882. In the middle of the Atlantic Ocean, the ship's boiler broke down, forcing the vessel to travel at half-speed. When the passengers ran out of drinking water, many became ill, including the Hagen's baby Mary.

The Hagen family and employees of the Bozeman Steam Laundry.

After twenty-two days, the exhausted immigrants arrived in New York City, took the train to Salt Lake City, then to Dillon, and on to Virginia City by stage. Mary Flora's brother, Joseph Kopp, Jr., brought them in to Bozeman by wagon. Their father had established the Kopp Brothers Meat Market in town. Mary's husband Josef found work as a laborer during the construction of Hawthorne School in 1883. The family was forced to move from their first home near the McAdow mill when the new railroad preempted the land.

Eventually, the Hagens bought four acres near Sourdough Creek and moved into a little house on Church Avenue. Soon cattle roamed their small farm; flocks of chickens and a large garden supported the growing family of eight small Hagens. Josef Hagen yearned to move farther west, however, and took his family to Astoria, Oregon. He died there in 1888, leaving Mary Flora with eight children to support.

The widow returned to her family in Bozeman, where she operated a dressmaking shop with her daughter Lena. Mary Flora's next business venture was to cook for a large number of bachelor coal miners in Chestnut. In 1900, Mary Flora, with tailor Henry Topel as partner, opened the Bozeman Steam Laundry, the first of its kind in Montana. When the laundry machines arrived from the East, the two men charged with installing the equipment decided to run the widow out and take over the business themselves. Mary Flora figured out their intentions and fired them; before they left, however, the men sabotaged some of the parts. With help from her family, she got the machines running smoothly and developed a thriving business that still operates today as the Gallatin Laundry.

In 1897, Bozeman bought the town's existing waterworks from private hands for $104,000. Officials looked over some of the wooden pipes laid as early as 1883 and found them to be in surprisingly good condition. The following year, the spring waters of Lyman Creek were collected in a reservoir

Bozeman Steam Laundry's new machines, which Mary Flora Hagen had to repair after the deliverymen sabotaged them.

Mystic Lake reservoir and tower housing pump, built by Elias Hardin Williams.

and piped into town to provide drinking water for the residents. As the town grew, Bozeman officials would secure rights to Sourdough Creek and its Mystic Lake headwaters, and additional supplies from Middle Creek (later called Hyalite).

* * *

By the 1880s, Bozeman no longer laughed at Colonel Chesnut when he predicted a prosperous coal industry east of town. Since that time, twenty years before, when he and two blacksmiths developed the first mines, coal as a moneymaker was taken seriously.

As wood grew scarce and costly, householders began to burn coal in their stoves. The railroad men needed fuel and found that the bituminous character of the Bozeman-Livingston coal field was of sufficient quality to use in their engines. It wasn't inferior brown lignite after all, as earlier supposed. Those who dug the Muir railroad tunnel needed coal to power their machines. The emerging copper industry in Butte and Anaconda also needed coal in the form of coke to smelt its ores.

As new mines opened and the older sites expanded, districts formed: Chestnut, Cokedale, Meadow Creek, Timberline, Bridger Creek. Most of the shafts were inclined, sloping down to an average of three hundred feet. Timberline mine No. 3 was unusual in that the incline dropped to a depth of nine hundred feet. Below ground, rooms with supporting pillars were carved out, strengthened by timbering; the logs were freighted in from nearby sawmills. Miners undercut each coal vein by chopping a kerf below it; knocking out chunks above made the use of dynamite less necessary, a dangerous practice in shafts containing pockets of poisonous gas. At first, horses and mules pulled little cars filled with coal chunks to the tipple above ground. Later, steam-powered winches lifted the cars to the surface.

Unfortunately, most of the veins were thin or fractured from numerous faults; the resulting coal contained a great amount of ash which meant that the chunks had to be washed before they were ready for market or for coking. Wood-timbered coal washers—some of them cost $100,000 to build— soon towered above the growing little company

Surface buildings at a mine in the Meadow Creek-Trail Creek area, 1900-1915. REX R. LABERTEW PHOTO.

Coke ovens and mine buildings at Storrs, c1903. GEORGE CAROLUS PHOTO.

towns at Chestnut, Timberline, Mountainside, Cokedale, and Storrs.

In 1882, William Henry Williams built the area's first coke oven near Cokedale, a crude beehive-shaped burner made of limestone slabs and lined with fire brick imported from the East. (The ruins can be seen today.) By the 1890s, Cokedale had one hundred and thirty ovens; Storrs had more than one hundred, some of which were never fired up.

Coal operators built tramways and spur lines to the mines in order to get the ore to market more efficiently. By 1882, Timberline had a spur rail to its mines, its small Baldwin locomotive called "Heppie" replacing freighting by mules. From 1899 to 1919, a ten-mile track, dubbed the Turkey Trail by locals, ran through Chestnut, Mountainside, south to Storrs, Maxey, and along Trail Creek to Chimney Rock. Now that it was easier to transport coal to the main line, the price to homeowners came down, making it a more attractive fuel. At Cokedale, a

diminutive Baldwin locomotive named "Ella" replaced the mules to carry coal on a narrow gauge track to the coke ovens. Below Ella ran the Coal Spur Line, built in 1887 to connect to the main Northern Pacific road, where cars were loaded with washed coal for home use or coke bound for Anaconda and Butte.

As the mines became more productive, the Northern Pacific bought many of the sites for its own consumption. The railroad owned all of the coal interests at Timberline, with Robert McKee as its superintendent. Colonel Chesnut sold his one-third interest for a tidy $15,000 in 1883; Daniel Maxey sold his developed mine that same year to the Northern Pacific Railroad for $22,000.

Some of the camps in the Livingston-Bozeman Coal Field became miniature company towns, resembling the larger constructions in Utah, Colorado, and the East. Small, identical wooden homes sprouted like the neat little rows of a vegetable

This small Baldwin locomotive "Heppie" freighted coal and supplies along the ten-mile Turkey Trail,
from Timberline to Chestnut.

garden, each with running water and electric power. Storrs, named for railroad geologist Lucius S. Storrs, was a company town built by the Anaconda Copper Mining Company. At Timberline, Robert McKee built twenty-five four-room houses and a store; although his basic salary was modest, the rents and the company store profits added to his bank account. Those workers who saved enough money to homestead on ranches nearby tended to stay in the area when the industry closed. A few miners made their homes in the area's caves. Hotels and boardinghouses opened at Chestnut, Cokedale, Chimney Rock, Storrs, and Maxey.

The company towns owned general stores where groceries and other goods could be bought with scrip, paper vouchers issued by the company. But there were independent butchers and farmers selling produce as well. Former Fort Ellis man Julius Beltezer peddled eggs and butter from his place near Storrs. Frank Buttrey established a grocery near Trail Creek, the first store in the modern Buttrey Stores chain.

Most settlements had at least one saloon; one of four Chestnut watering holes sported a sign reading "All Nations Welcome but Carry Nation." Sylvester Gasaway opened a handsomely decorated Chimney Rock Saloon and Hotel on Trail Creek. No saloon was built at Timberline, at least for a time; Robert McKee was a strong Presbyterian and did not consider a saloon an asset.

Almost all the coal communities supported schools for beginning students. At Timberline, a two-room school housed a number of boisterous miners' children for more than twenty years. One teacher remembers them "as wild as Indians and as lousy as sheep."[9] Those lucky enough to continue their education came into Livingston or Bozeman for further training. In 1903, 132 students attended school at Chestnut. All the camps had post offices for a short period of time. And almost all had a baseball team.

Cokedale and Timberline were proud of their silver cornet bands. Despite the modest incomes of the miners at Timberline, they raised money for

Company houses at Storrs.

Members of the Cokedale Silver Cornet Band pose in dress uniforms.

handsome white uniforms with gold braid for their twenty-one member band, which traveled all over the state to perform at fairs and parades. Some say that the bands were a medical necessity because the miners needed to blow the coal dust from their lungs.

Circuit preachers occasionally visited the little towns. Cokedale at its height numbered five hundred; eight hundred people lived at Storrs in its heyday. Timberline once supported a population of three hundred families.

Miners came from England, Wales, Ireland, Scotland, Germany, Italy, Sweden, and Denmark. A few Chinese immigrants cooked at the boardinghouses. Miners from Montenegro achieved local notoriety for their famous pork and beer parties.

In 1884, the Knights of Labor, precursor to the United Mine Workers of America, organized at Timberline, which was at its height of production. Within two years, the labor group could not help but become a powerful force because of changes in company policy. Robert McKee had been removed from management and replaced by Logan M. Bullitt as company man. Almost immediately, Bullitt reduced wages and raised prices at the company store. He encouraged five saloons to open their

doors, which quickly led to violent shootouts and other criminal acts. Observers noted, "It is becoming painfully apparent that worse conditions of morals exist in Timberline than was ever known in Montana."[10]

As was usual at that time, the railroad did not recognize any labor organization; instead, it brought in Pinkerton Detective Agency men to work as miners and spy on the men. On July 6, 1886, the Knights of Labor declared a strike; it lasted until May 23, 1887, not as long as some coal strikes in the West but long enough to cause hardship to mining families. Bullitt tried to hire scabs from other mines and from workers in Bozeman, but, since most were sympathetic with the miners, he was unsuccessful. Along the tracks leading to the mines, dummy figures with nooses swung in the breeze to warn prospective scabs with signs reading "This is what we do to blacklegs."[11] In the 1890s, and again in 1910, more labor problems affected some of the coal communities, but they did not have the disastrous effect that they did in larger coal fields.

Sometimes the aging Martha Jane Canary, occasionally known as Martha Burke or Martha Dorsett but always known as "Calamity Jane," lived

*Sylvester "Ves" Gasaway's Chimney Rock Hotel and Saloon, once elegant, served as storage shed in 1919
for hay to feed the sheep milling about. Both the hotel and saloon later burned down.*

at Horr, a coal camp later called Electric at the southeastern edge of the field. Seldom sober, Calamity reeled from camp to camp, selling her memoirs printed in a little pink pamphlet entitled "Life and Adventures of Calamity Jane by Herself." In 1901, she fell ill in Bozeman; apparently considered indigent, the famous western woman was sent to the County Poor Farm, an insult she did not suffer long. She escaped to continue her alcoholic travels until her death in 1903.

From 1890 to 1910, the Bozeman-Livingston Coal Field was a lively place, supporting a total population of one thousand to fifteen hundred. However, by the latter date, some mines had closed, a sign of things to come. Soon, the copper industry developed a smelting method that required less coke. Orders decreased and many of the ovens lay idle. Some of the coal measures played out; only the fractured veins remained, requiring a difficult and expensive method of extraction. Strip mining of coal, elsewhere in the region, was less costly and more attractive to the businessman. The railroad turned to diesel to power its engines. Natural gas became

the home heating fuel of choice. One by one, the mines shut down. Wooden washers and tipples burned down, some under suspicious circumstances; a few were rebuilt, only to burn again. Deserted buildings were taken away to serve other purposes. Ted Swainson carted off one tipple to a West Boulder farm for a lambing shed. The little company houses at Storrs were auctioned off.

From time to time, local newspapers predicted a resurgence of the coal industry in Gallatin and Park Counties. New companies formed here and there to develop what they hoped would become profitable ventures. During the hard times of the 1930s, coal was again extracted for a short time. Many of the mining families moved away; the few who stayed bear names associated with the days when coal trains bustled and coke ovens smoked—Williams, Maxey, Brooks, Hoffman. Today, crumbling coke ovens at Cokedale and Storrs give evidence to earlier more prosperous days when Colonel Chesnut finally convinced the doubters that he had indeed found "black diamonds." ▣

191

chapter

TWENTY

In the 1870s and 1880s, immigrants from Germany settled in significant numbers in Bozeman. The Spieths and the Lehrkinds established breweries. Rudolf Vogel managed the Tivoli Saloon; August Richter repaired shoes and boots. The Papkes farmed in Bridger Canyon and the Kiefers entered the meat business. John Stuve started a cigar factory. Whenever this congenial group got together, they drank beer, sang, danced, played a variety of instruments, and picnicked in the mountains.

Because of their love of music, these new residents helped to found a number of musical organizations, including the choral group Sangerfest, the Bozeman Silver Cornet Band (1880s; Frank Benepe, director), the Queen City Band, the Bozeman Brass Band (1893), and the Bozeman Men's Band. When John Fechter settled in Bozeman as the new manager of the Tivoli, he had just completed a tour as an oboe player with John Phillip Sousa's Band. He directed the German Band which played at community picnics; in later years, he would become the first conductor of the Bozeman Symphony.

German names—Schlechten, Spieth, Hoffman—dominated the membership of the Ladies Imperial Band, organized August 28, 1906 by Jesse Thompson. His wife Carrie played French horn. They wore costumes designed to complement

their performances; sometimes they appeared in tuxedos, sometimes in soft corduroy suits. An underage Fred Willson remembers peering in the doors of a saloon to glimpse the women attired in elegant flowing white dresses and picture hats, playing on the mezzanine. No one seemed to object to the women performing in a saloon, since either their father or uncle owned it. The Ladies Imperial Band made its debut in the second Sweet Pea Carnival in 1907, marching proudly down an unpaved Main Street, part of a twenty-four-block parade.

The Sweet Pea Carnival had been organized the year before in 1906 by merchants eager to publicize Bozeman and the Gallatin Valley. They chose the sweet pea flower as a symbol because of its beauty, fragrance, and ready availability. During the first celebration, the fraternal Woodmen of the World gathered from throughout the state to attend their yearly convention and participate in the festivities. Pink, white, and green bunting lined Main Street; pennants fluttered from upstairs windows; shops featured elegant displays of their wares, enhanced with bouquets of sweet peas. August 11, 1906, dawned warm and bright, a perfect day to welcome visitors and their pocketbooks.

It took some time to organize the first parade of two hundred sweet pea-covered floats, waiting to come down Main Street. There were flower-

Employees hoist a mug at the Julius Lehrkind Lager Beer Brewery.

German sons and daughters enjoy a picnic. William C. Glawe photo.

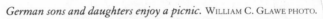

German Band plays at Dutch Picnic, Vogel's Grove, August 16, 1908. August Richter (accordion), director John Fechter (fourth from left), David Vogel (right of drum), and Rudolph Vogel, Jr. (trombone), among others.

The parading Bozeman Men's Band in white uniforms.

Kathryn Hanley is crowned first queen of Sweet Pea, August 1906.

A Sweet Pea parade gets organized.

One of the first floats moves through giant arches built for the carnival.

Dressed in demure, white, layered dresses, the Ladies Imperial Band marches down Main Street.

One Sweet Pea entry poses in front of the county courthouse.

bedecked pony carts, bicycles, carriages, and wagons drawn by goats, sheep, and dogs, patiently suffering with headdresses of flower garlands. The Bozeman Fire Department stood in parade dress beside its float entry, waiting for the signal to march. The parade was delayed for one hour, however, because the Butte Special train carrying visitors and the drill team was late.

Finally, trumpets heralded the start of the parade, led by queen Kathryn Hanley's carriage, drawn by six showy white horses. The queen's court followed, then came town dignitaries in medieval costume and boys on horseback waving floral arches. Mrs. Charles A. Backes floated by in her rig decorated with 30,000 fragrant sweet pea blossoms, "tastefully banked into the colors of the carnival."[1] Blacksmith Adolph Huber demonstrated the art of shoeing a horse on his float. The Fair Store display was in the shape of a flower-bedecked butterfly.

The only incident marring the event involved a persistent young man's attempt to get his rig into the parade at Main Street and Rouse Avenue. He backed into a carriage driven by Agnes Mitchell, whose horse bolted and threw Miss Mitchell from her seat. During the melee, Marie Corwin and eight-year-old Lee Wood were knocked to the ground by the runaway rig; the young son of William Beattie fell beneath the carriage wheels. Mrs. Kate Cowan was also thrown from her rig as it finally blocked and stopped Miss Mitchell's carriage. Miraculously, no bones were broken. An anticlimax to these unscheduled events was a twenty-dollar first prize awarded the butterfly float.

That afternoon, Bozeman and Livingston baseball teams faced each other; the Bozeman nine

won and received a one-hundred-dollar prize. Members of the fire department's hose team showed their expertise by running down a four-block stretch to lay down three hundred feet of hose in one minute and fifty-seven seconds. Concluding festivities in the evening featured a band concert in Bogert's Grove, a confetti fight among Bozeman's young people, and a series of splendid balls around town.

The following year, the Montana Elks Grand Lodge met in convention during the Sweet Pea Carnival; sweet peas for the event were purple and white, the Elks' traditional colors. Queen Myrtle Foster and her court led the parade, followed by the Elks carrying bright purple umbrellas shading spotless white suits. A group of Blackfeet joined the parade in full ceremonial regalia. Merchants happily welcomed an estimated ten thousand visitors that summer. In 1908, the outstanding attraction was the "living flag," a group of 175 school girls called the Women's Relief Corps, who swayed in unison to show off the colors of the American flag. In 1909, the parade included Nelson Story, Jr.'s new automobile, appropriately smothered with blossoms.

To advertise each summer's Sweet Pea Carnival, boxes of the fragrant flowers were transported to nearby communities. In town, handsomely dressed young women handed bouquets to female passengers coming through on the trains, a tradition that lasted long after the carnival. Some civic groups spent many long winter hours making artificial flowers to be ready for the next summer's gala. Grocers saved brightly colored tissue from their fruit stands for use as next year's paper flowers. Bands from throughout the state arrived each summer to play at Sweet Pea to compete for honors with

A field of sweet peas beside the original Nash Ranch.

Bozeman's musical groups.

In 1912, the Montana Saengerbund, a group of German singers throughout the state, held their convention during Bozeman's Sweet Pea Carnival. Evening festivities included their two-hundred-voice choir serenading Queen Rausie Roecher and her court. Gene Quaw, son of the man who founded Belgrade, wrote two operettas for the occasion. That summer, he offered "The Sweet Pea Girl," followed by "Sweet Pea Land" in 1913.

By 1914, the yearly event had lost its luster: a blight caused failure of the sweet pea crop; the approaching world war lessened the town's enthusiasm for the summer celebration. In 1916, Bozeman merchants sponsored a modified Sweet Pea celebration; that summer, Lela Maxwell reigned as the last queen for some time. (The Sweet Pea Festival re-emerged in 1977 and has continued as a tribute to the arts of the area.)

For some years, it became abundantly clear that an unpaved dusty Main Street and Sweet Pea activities did not mix. Residents complained that a dirty thoroughfare did not impress visitors; besides, they were tired of it, particularly women with long skirts. Bozeman had wooden sidewalks, even a few cement walkways, installed by 1904. On July 4, 1907, a resolution was put to the aldermen for the paving of Main Street, from Church to Grand avenues. Some proposed blocks of creosoted wood would do the job at $3.85 per square.[2]

For more than a year, arguments raged at city hall as to the proper material to use on Main Street. Opposition to creosote blocks surfaced at the August 8, 1907 meeting, with Alderman E. Broox Martin crying in exasperation ". . . for God's sake pave the street with something."[3] In January 1908, the papers printed a long scholarly article on various street paving materials. Finally, on July 8, 1908, the aldermen settled on cement for Main Street and macadam for Wallace Avenue and let a contract.[4]

Cover of Sweet Pea song by Louis Howard and T. Byron Story.

Within a few weeks, a headline read, "Main Street Paving in Full Swing."[5] By November, before winter set in, the job was completed. The curious drinking fountain that had been installed by the WCTU ladies had to be removed.

* * *

Since the installation of the trolleys in town, Gallatin Valley residents had talked about the possibility of an electric railway into the valley that would serve several interests. Agricultural produce and stock could more easily get to market with a connection in Bozeman to the Northern Pacific or at Three Forks to the proposed extension of the Milwaukee Road. Students could commute daily to classes at Montana College of Agriculture and Mechanic Arts. Valley ranchers certainly looked forward to such a prospect. Farmers and ranchers

had raised $50,000 by October 1907; now it was Bozeman's turn to come up with $100,000. Meanwhile, railroad men outside the valley watched developments with a great deal of pleasure and very little expenditure of capital, waiting for their chance to move in. As had happened before in Montana, "local residents built the line and outside interests realized the benefits."[6]

In March 1908, the Gallatin Valley Electric Railway Company was capitalized and "was ready to make the dirt fly."[7] The line would run west from Bozeman, then south to Salesville, a distance of seventeen miles. Railroad stops along the way included the Patterson Ranch, Ferris Hot Springs (formerly Jerry Matthews's Hot Springs), Balmont, Chapman, Potter, Blackwood, Gilroy, and Atkins. When ground was broken for the line on April 21, 1909, Vera Anderson smashed a bottle of champagne

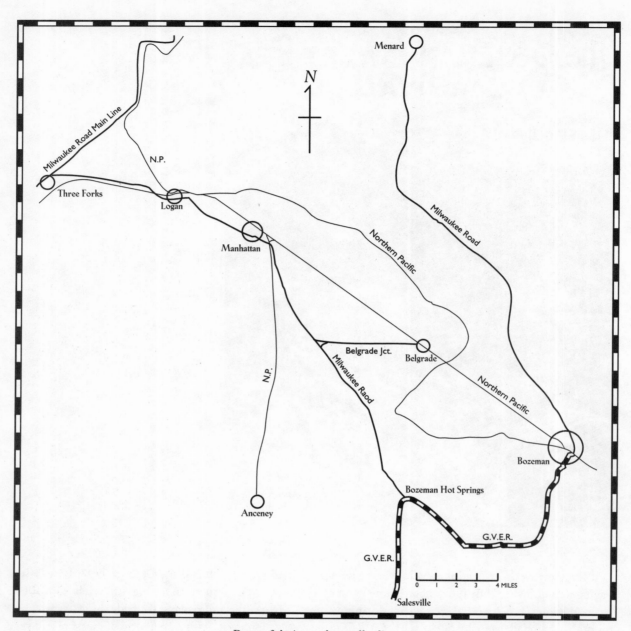

Route of the interurban trolley line.

over a plow pulled by four coal-black draft horses. To celebrate, trolleys in town carried passengers all day without charge.

By this time, the Madison River Power Company had completed enough generator stations to supply electricity to the entire valley, including Bozeman. Plant No. 1 was called the "Nunn" plant, after L. L. Nunn, president of the Telluride Power Company in Colorado, who provided the expertise for construction. Even though the line had not been completed to Salesville, car No. 10 was carrying passengers on tracks just installed to the Hot Springs

and back five times each day for fifty cents per round trip. It was worth the price just to look at the car No. 10's golden oak interior with rattan seats. Overhead, bronze baggage racks gleamed. Made by the American Car Company of Saint Louis, No. 10 could accommodate forty-two passengers, including twelve in the smoker. Its companion box motor No. 11 had already brought its first tonnage of barley into town to the Bozeman Brewing Company.

One year later, without much fanfare, the Chicago, Milwaukee & St. Paul Railroad moved in to buy the entire stock of the little interurban and

Young and old pose with the new Car No. 10 at the Salesville depot.

Wicker seats and brass trim were part of the interior of Car No. 10.
FROM IRA SWETT, "MONTANA TROLLEYS," *INTERURBAN MAGAZINE*, 1920.

The Montana Railroad.

Bozeman's streetcar lines; at the same time, they announced plans to extend the rails from Ferris Hot Springs to Three Forks, where its main line stood ready to receive goods from the Gallatin Valley. Thus, the interurban became a branch line, renamed the Gallatin Valley Railroad, with general offices far away in Chicago and Seattle.

Despite the sale to outside interests, car No. 10 continued to carry passengers from Bozeman to

Salesville and back until 1930. The Milwaukee Road's steam trains carried passengers and freight from Bozeman to the Hot Springs, then on to West Gallatin, Holland, with a short branch line to Belgrade, on to stops at Camp Creek, Manhattan, Logan, and Carpenter, terminating at Three Forks. With auto ownership on the increase, the interurban to Salesville (called Gallatin Gateway since 1928) had been operating in the red. Instead of sidelining car No. 10 to wait for a happy home in a local museum, the Milwaukee Road ordered it scrapped.

At the northern end of the county, another railroad stirred up an otherwise quiet, even desolate, landscape. Virginian Richard Austin Harlow came west to Helena for his health; he recovered from his illness, only to be bitten by the railroad-building bug. Realizing that money could be made transporting silver ore from Castle, a then bustling mining camp near the present White Sulphur Springs, to the smelters at East Helena and Butte, and after a number of false starts, Harlow capitalized the Montana Railroad Company in 1895, with a promising $3.5 million in shares. The line would start north of the three forks of the Missouri at Lombard (named for chief engineer A. G. Lombard), travel northeast to Maudlow (named for Harlow and his wife Maud), thence to Josephine (named for a Harlow relative) and Sixteenmile Creek (so named because the mouth of the creek is sixteen miles from the three forks), on to Leader (later renamed Ringling to honor the famous circus family who wintered there), continuing northeast to terminate at Lewistown.

Seldom was this railroad called by its proper name; folks called it the Jawbone Railroad because Harlow, encountering construction problems, bad weather, angry ranchers, and dwindling finances, talked himself out of bankruptcy numerous times; the name "Jawbone" stuck.

Before the railroad, the area near Lombard, at the mouth of Sixteenmile Creek, was called "Painted Rock." At its height, Lombard bustled with switching yards and repair barns, although no road connected the community with its neighbors—just the train. For a number of years, Chinese immigrant Billie Kee presided over the Lombard Hotel, post office, and general store there, which catered to railroad workers and the exhausted passengers who had traveled the Jawbone.

In 1908, after a few years of negotiation, Harlow sold the 157-mile Jawbone line to the Chicago, Milwaukee, & St. Paul Railroad, who moved the rails higher to the top of Sixteenmile Canyon. At the close of World War I, the fortunes of the little railroad plummeted. The 1918 influenza epidemic struck particularly hard in the region. A June 27, 1925 earthquake, with its epicenter just

The town of Lombard was the western terminus for the Jawbone Railroad.

Men pose before Lombard's post office and Tulloch's general store; in background is the Lombard Hotel.

Lombard hotelkeeper Billy Kee and his family pose in their Sunday best. Formerly a court reporter in Helena, Kee made enough money to leave the area a rich man.

Maudlow scene, June 1925.

north of town, leveled many of the buildings in Lombard. As railroad historian Don Baker concludes, "The economy of this section of Montana wasn't only depressed, it was demolished."[8]

Maudlow looked like what it was—a small railroad town in the middle of Sixteenmile Canyon. Western writer Ivan Doig describes the land around Maudlow: "Here around the corner from the Bridger Mountains, the country went wild in a hurry."[9] A settler named Brammer and a man named Dave Bagby homesteaded in the area many years before Harlow thought about a railroad through Sixteenmile Canyon.

A two-story section house was almost as tall as the grain elevator. The town supported two saloons, two general stores, a hotel, blacksmith, lumberyard, livery, post office, barber shop, pool hall, and dance hall. When Maudlow School was built in 1909, it held forty-nine pupils, most of them with the last names of Brainard, Scheytt, Callantine, Badgett, Doig, Durham, and Morgan. A teacher taught elementary students on the first floor; the first two years of high school were offered on the second floor.

The road from Maudlow to Belgrade had an unhappy reputation because of its seasonal ruts and gumbo. It usually took ten hours for team and wagon to make it from the town to Belgrade. In Ivan Doig's autobiographical *Heart Earth*, he recounts a day in the 1940s when the old family Ford got stuck in the mire. The Doigs pulled some boards from a dilapidated cabin nearby and shoved them beneath the wheels of the auto. The mud still held the car. Hours later, relative Bob Campbell rode by, attached a rope from the Ford to his saddle horse, and pulled it out.

From Maudlow to Ringling, enough ranchers settled in this lonely region to support a number of schools: Lincoln School at Sixteen, Pass Creek School, Morgan School, which was moved to Pass Creek when the school there burned down, Josephine School, with students numbering from two to an all-time high of ten, and a school in a basin with the unusual name of Belly Ache. Since no roads were built to connect the small settlements until 1948, children rode horses to school.

The stepchild community of Sedan, located east of Flathead Pass, has threatened to secede from Gallatin County from time to time; its fortunes seem more closely linked with Livingston and Park County; even its creek waters drain east into the Shields River. John Maddox and his family, formerly of Sedan, Kansas, settled the area in 1884 as did James and son Joshua Woosley in 1885. Three years

Ralph Tycer drives six-horse-hitch near Pass Creek.

later, sixteen students attended a log cabin school at Sedan; almost fifty came to class in 1895. More schools opened in the lonely area—East Flathead School in 1911 and Sunnyside School (sometimes called Sagebrush) in 1921.

Perhaps this feeling of being cut off from the world encouraged some twenty-five residents to order magneto telephone service in 1905, stringing the wire themselves. A log cabin served as Sedan's Methodist Church where a circuit minister sometimes came to preach. Lumber for most of the area's buildings came from Joshua Woosley's sawmill.

In 1914, the Shields Valley Cheese Company opened in the Sedan area; Leo and Al Meyer served their customers until 1936. On the second floor, away from the cheese making, the Yeoman's Lodge and Social Center met; there neighbors played cards, danced, watched plays, and listened to the yodels of Swiss cheese-maker Walter Boegli. Dairy farmers brought fresh milk to the factory, emptying their cans and filling them with whey to take home to their pigs.

On the site of Sedan's first log school, Wes and

Myda Inabnit built a general store in the 1930s. On the outside wall, an unusual exhibit featured an assortment of rabbit ears, strung artistically along wires, collected during periods of heavy jackrabbit habitation when competitions were held. Shooters divided into two groups; hunters who dispatched the most rabbits enjoyed a whiskey party provided by the losing team. In the early 1920s, residents flocked to the Sedan Rodeo, held in three acres of corrals. "It was not until 1949 that electricity came up the valley to Sedan, and then not everybody took it. One old timer lived without it until 1975, and he was 88 years old. No phone either."[10]

Before the 1870s, Bridger Canyon lay undisturbed, except for the occasional Indian party using the area as an escape route after a successful horse-stealing raid. A few prospectors wandered the area, on the lookout for color. The Jim Bridger wagon train was the first of a number that rattled down the roadless canyon, on its way to Virginia City. Soon after Fort Ellis was established, twenty soldiers were sent up the canyon sixteen miles to build a sawmill, freighting down logs to the post for

A view of Sedan, c1926. At left is the schoolhouse; at middle is the cheese factory; at right is Woosley Ranch building.

Sedan hunters display their winning collection of rabbit ears.

Bridger Canyon Road, rough and uneven, c1890. CHARLES LOUGHREY PHOTO.

various construction projects. They also built a crude wagon road from the canyon to Fort Shaw on the Sun River, twenty-four miles west of Great Falls. Officer's wife Frances Roe remembered a difficult trip up the snow-packed canyon to the sawmill. She was discouraged to go—women were not hardy enough—and enjoyed herself thoroughly. Gunsmith Walter Cooper maintained a twenty-four-foot powder house nearby, a safer place to store gunpowder than in town.

In 1875, James Proffitt brought his wife and three sons from Johnson County, Missouri, to settle in the Bridger Canyon area. Proffitt was a Josephite, a sect split from the Mormon church; he wanted to settle away from a strict Mormon community, just as Melvin Ross had done in the Springhill area. Soon Proffitt was selling hay in town and to Fort Ellis; with his proceeds, he stocked his homestead with Merino sheep.

When David Bertie Christie left Minnesota in 1883 to come west for his asthma, he was so ill he had to be carried off the train at Miles City. After a three-hundred-mile wagon trip to Bozeman, he was walking and feeling much better. He worked as a ranch hand in the valley. His wife Emma Mary's nephew Myron Stratton had already established a homestead in Bridger Canyon and convinced David Christie that the area was a good place to settle. Two years later, Emma and their five sons and baby daughter came to Bozeman by train and were obliged to stay overnight at a Main Street hotel, Saint Paul House, before the canyon trek. David had written her, "They dont keep much of a Hotell, but then they are good folks."[11] Reflecting later on the spare conditions up Spring Creek at Stratton's cabin, Emma was grateful for the respite.

It was not long, however, before the Christies moved into their own cabin, built another home for the senior Christies who came out from Minnesota, planted a successful garden, and brought stock from town—chickens, sheep, and dairy cows. David Christie's son Will brought in more dairy cows; his

A man stands on his head atop Maiden Rock at the mouth of Bridger Canyon. The landmark was later blasted away by road crews.
CHARLES LOUGHREY PHOTO.

business prospered and formed part of the founding base for the modern Darigold firm.

In the 1890s, W. J. Davies, the man who wrote about John Bozeman, and his son Dewey built and operated a lime kiln in the canyon, which produced construction products until 1907, when the growing operation across the valley at Trident made the Davies operation no longer profitable. Charles Papke went into the quarry business, providing stone work for Gallatin County High School and the new Catholic Church on Main Street. Coal businessman John Maxey brought his mules over from Trail Creek to haul coal from his newly opened mine a mile above the lime kiln. He abandoned this effort when he discovered that the coal held too much sulphur

to be marketable. In 1905, Belgrade founder Thomas B. Quaw built an elegant summer home on stilts near the mouth of the canyon, naming it the Three Bears, after his daughters. Later, his son, songsmith Eugene Quaw, converted the house into an inn. Eventually, boisterous parties there gave the hostelry a bad reputation; the Three Bears burned in 1932.

With the modest influx of settlers to the canyon region, two schools opened; in 1886, a log cabin housed the Upper Bridger School, which was replaced by a frame building in 1900. The Lower Bridger School opened on the Murray property in 1896 with Kate Ferris as teacher. Weather limited the school curriculum, because classes could meet for only four months each year.

209

Looking up at The Needle,
Bridger Canyon.
CHARLES LOUGHREY PHOTO.

A small, white, frame church opened its doors in 1906; services were held each Sunday afternoon. Because of the difficulty in getting to town for at least part of the year, residents in Bridger Canyon formed a close-knit social circle. The women met regularly to visit at the Happy Day Club. Church picnics and school programs were well attended. The young people married into other pioneer families in the Canyon; the descendants of Christie, Stratton, Oma, Sparr, Murray, and Stone were intertwined.

Another village in the western part of the north country started its modest life as a stage stop. Dry Creek once had a store, post office, gas station, and school. The Baptist Church at Dry Creek got there by unusual means. The 1889 structure was built at the nearby hamlet of East Gallatin; by 1904, however, most of the Baptists had moved around Dry Creek. A year later, it was decided to move the church to the people. On a mild January day, Henry Cramer and Bill Brownell shored up the wooden building with two giant bobsleds and hitched six teams of horses to pull the church eight miles. The Dry Creek Bible Church holds services to this day.

A staunch supporter of the Dry Creek Church traveled thirteen times from Gentry County, Missouri, to Virginia City before she settled in the valley. Mary L. Wells Yates, later called "Granny," originally hailed from Virginia but left in 1834 at seventeen to marry Solomon George Yates, a Missouri landowner who had been widowed after

the death of Mary's sister Rachel. Although it was not uncommon for men to marry a sister after one had died, the Virginia family searched the Bible for guidance before they would agree that it was ethical for Mary to wed George. The growing Yates family moved from county to county in Missouri until just before the Civil War when George died. Mary was left to care for Rachel's three children plus ten of her own. With each trip back to Missouri, Mary gathered up more of her children and encouraged others to come to Montana.

On the first trip to Virginia City, the forty-eight-year-old widow sold the six cows she had trailed from Missouri and the butter that had churned in wooden crocks tied to the wagon during the bumpy ride west. On one occasion, she brought three barrels of apples from Missouri and sold them for one dollar each to the miners, hungry for a sweet. On another trek, she met a man along the trail from Salt Lake City who seemed to be in a hurry and did not stop to visit, let alone tip his hat. Shortly thereafter, a number of Vigilantes dashed by, tracking a man who, Granny found out later, was wanted for murder in Alder Gulch.

Since there was no Baptist Church in Virginia City—only a Methodist building filled with Republicans, according to Granny—she moved to the East Gallatin in 1875 on land eight miles north

of Belgrade in order to worship in the Dry Creek Bible Church. Granny Yates could neither read nor write, but challenged anyone who dared to correct her when she quoted from the Bible. When asked why she did not remarry, she said she would consider it if a Southern general would come to court her.

North of Dry Creek stood the little village of Menard, named for settler Teleford Menard. Once a railroad stop for the Milwaukee branch line from Bozeman, affectionately called the Turkey Red Special, named after the type of wheat grown nearby, Menard had its short heyday from 1913 to 1915, supporting a store, post office, blacksmith, grain elevator, dance hall, depot, and baggage building.

Nestled in a small valley fourteen miles north of Logan was the settlement of Magpie, home to cattle and horse breeders, sheep herders, and a few railroad men. The hardy pioneers who settled this arid land with little winter snow bragged of their large mosquitoes, gophers, rattlesnakes, and mountain rats. In 1866, James H. Gallop trailed forty-five head of cattle from Oregon to the Magpie area; his homestead included a post office which Gallop operated in the front room of his residence until 1908. Ed Sawyer also brought in stock, establishing the River Side Ranch Company; his brand Circle S decorated the little general store he opened at Magpie. George Geddes brought his

Moving the church from East Gallatin to Dry Creek, a distance of eight miles.

Mary Wells, known as "Granny Yates," and four generations of her family.

horses north from Willow Creek to feed on the short bunch grass in the valley, the same grass that British horse breeders learned was very nutritious despite its appearance.

W. Guy Clark came with the railroad in 1910, filled with plans for business expansion in the little three-mile-wide valley. He found the town name of Magpie odious, so he changed it to Clarkston, after himself. He took over the post office and Sawyer's Circle S Store, supervising construction of stockyards and an elevator. Enough settlers eventually homesteaded the area to support four schools: Pole Gulch (sometimes called Evergreen), Garden Gulch (or New Garden Gulch), Prather (or Harbison), and Clarkston. Except for Clarkston School, none of the schools had more than ten pupils at any one time; sometimes one child had the class to himself.

Although riding horseback was one way in and out of the Clarkston Valley, the easier method was to flag down the stub, a small train which included a passenger car, baggage car, and diner. At some point, residents discussed constructing a ferry across the Missouri, but nothing came of it. South of Clarkston, a few houses clustered around a flag stop called Rekap. Together, the Clarkston and Rekap families formed a community. They rode horses, took sleigh rides, celebrated holidays with elaborate feasts, and, on occasion, danced until daybreak, their small children muffled under coats at the edge of the dance hall. Sadly, as was true in other settlements in this area, influenza took an unusually high toll in 1918, followed by the violent earthquake of 1925.

To the south, Trident started as a collection of tents. In 1907, Dan Morrison surveyed the limestone deposits that Sacagawea talked about to Lewis and Clark one hundred years before. Morrison started to build a cement plant in 1908 which he called the Three Forks Portland Cement Company; by 1910, he was producing respectable quantities of "Red Devil Cement." Soon, company houses sprouted on the low benches in neat rows; American workers moved in. Austrian and Italian employees were not welcome there and were forced to live apart in what

The Martin Brothers threshing crew takes a break at Gallop. LOWRY PHOTO.

was called derisively "Woptown."

Despite social division, Trident supported a pool hall, bowling alley, ice house, grocery, depot, band, and baseball team. Residents could hike into Three Forks to see silent films at the Ruby Theater. Evidently, the settlement once attracted a preacher who felt that the families there could benefit from his religious instruction. Offered a bed for the night, he discovered it was home for many lice; he departed the following day. During its short history, Trident has often been flooded in the spring when the Missouri River fills with ice jams. In 1917, the Ideal Cement Company bought the industry; their first year of business was marred by the explosion of 1,025 pounds of black powder, which killed nine workers.

The population of little Three Forks swelled from time to time, depending upon the fortunes of a mining settlement across the border in Broadwater County. As early as 1863, newly elected county commissioner Al Nichols had found promising copper specimens in his wanderings through the area. The following year, fellow commissioner Dr. D. H. Ketchum, ferry-builder James Gallagher, and others consolidated their finds, calling it the Green Eagle. But successful copper mining required expensive stamp mills; placer sluicing was the only method available at that time.

Twenty years later, James Aplin, the man who hauled the anvil used at the fur trading post in 1810 at the Three Forks, Frank Akin, John Emmerson, and Samuel Seaman discovered a boulder of copper quartz six feet high and twenty feet around. Samples of this boulder assayed well and they sank a shaft twenty feet down, but found no veins of copper or gold. Good news or bad, the rush was on, resulting in a camp called Copper City.

Newspapers predicted that some lucky miner would make it rich; what was needed was adequate capital for exploration. Lyle K. Williams describes Copper City as "a perennial plant with its summers and then the winters when it lies dormant until a springtime of new investors starts it budding."[12]

Italian and Austrian workers at Trident were not allowed to live in these tidy company houses
but forced to make do with shacks beyond the railroad tracks, center left.

Locating a find near Copper City seemed to be a weekend avocation for farmers, ranchers, hotelkeepers, and judges. When they did find the type of quartz that held either copper, gold, or silver, they tried to interest those outside the valley with money to invest. Deals were struck; deals faded. During the hard times of the 1930s, more prospectors appeared in the area, looking for the big strike. Alas, Copper City became a ghost settlement almost before it was established. Only the excavation scars remain.

With railroad lines constructed by 1908, Three Forks became Old Three Forks because it was not close enough to the tracks; residents began to move their homes and businesses one mile up river to form a new Three Forks. Within a year, eight hundred citizens called the new town home; merchants operated from tents before their buildings could be completed. All this construction attracted a business which depended upon a supply of bachelor workers, so a few "girls" sold their services from tents until

they moved to a wooden residence called Green House, where they stayed until forced out in 1917.

It was not long before five streetlights lit up downtown. A small library operated from an abandoned boxcar. A man with a famous name, John Quincy Adams, agent for the Milwaukee Road, built a hotel in 1910, which he named the Sacajawea Inn. Parts of the old Madison House were moved to the inn site by rollers and teams of horses to form wings at either end of the structure. Four years later, a memorial to Sacagawea herself was dedicated across the street from the hotel.

Residents in the Three Forks area have never felt a strong bond with a county government located miles to the east in Bozeman. Perhaps they still smarted from the loss of the county seat at Gallatin City in 1867. In 1913, citizens tried to form a new "Wilson County" with no success. Again, in 1918, another attempt to establish a "Pershing County" failed. The grumbling has continued down through the years.

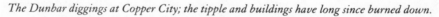

The Dunbar diggings at Copper City; the tipple and buildings have long since burned down.

215

Because the Northern Pacific branched at Logan with lines to Butte and to Helena, busy engines chugged back and forth from the roundhouse to switching lines. Population boomed in 1907 to three hundred. More businesses opened to accommodate the needs of the railroad workers; additional teachers were hired to instruct their children. In 1917, a disastrous fire broke out in downtown Logan, destroying eight businesses. The once-elegant Beanery was torn down in the 1970s.

Sappington, a settlement at the westernmost point on the county line, located near Sand Creek, once experienced busy times. First a stage station; it became a train stop named for rancher Henry Hiter Sappington, a settler from Sappington, Missouri. Cattle went to market from this spur. Nearby, a lime quarry operated in 1902 for a short time across the border at Sand Creek, a hamlet of 125 workers. During the 1930s, gypsum was mined at Sappington; now a talc plant operates there.

Willow Creek also experienced a temporary boom when the Milwaukee Road completed its lines there in 1908 (the Northern Pacific Railroad had come to Willow Creek in 1887). Throughout the state, a new wave of homesteaders called honyockers by some—not a compliment—filed on land parcels along the railroads. Willow Creek real estate men also sold lots to the newcomers, hoping they wouldn't realize, at least not right away, that Montana's periodic drought could devastate crops on marginal lands not served by irrigation ditches.

For a time, the town flourished with more saloons, general stores and blacksmiths, a millinery, five barbers, a dance hall, and one doctor. In 1914, partners Eugene Thorndike and Fred Nelson opened the Willow Creek State Bank. Electric power, sometimes erratic, came to Willow Creek in 1918. When it worked, the lights went on at 4 P.M.; by 10 P.M., the town was dark again. At the time of the sinking of the *Lusitania* in 1915, members of the local Spiritualist Church joined in a grand seance in an attempt to contact those who had drowned. A more cheerful activity engaged the four hundred Willow Creek residents in the 1920s when they gathered to root for their baseball team. During periods of drought, which seemed to be increasing, fires were put out by two men who ran with a hose cart; this fire wagon was used until well into the 1950s.

The new farmers, unable to sustain crops on marginal lands, moved on as they did throughout the state. Some of the businesses lost their clientele and closed; teachers had fewer students to instruct. The Thorndike and Nelson Bank failed in 1923. The hard times of the Great Depression came early to Willow Creek. ▦

Sacajawea Inn, Three Forks, with memorial to the Shoshone woman in front.

chapter

TWENTY-
ONE

By 1900, big business had come to Belgrade. So much so that some Gallatin Valley farmers grumbled about their treatment by banking, grain, and farm-machinery interests. Forty farmers met in 1904 to discuss their grievances against those businessmen they claimed were not giving farmers a fair shake in the profits. Perhaps they should cooperatively buy seed and other materials they need in order to skip the middleman.

The resulting Gallatin County Farmers' Alliance had a rough start but, within a few years had grown to ninety members. Z. S. Morgan became president; A. L. Corbly was named vice president; long time residents John Verwolf and Henry Monforton sat on its board. When the Belgrade Company, Ltd. asked to join the Alliance, the board turned them down, deciding that no businessmen would be considered for membership.

Farmer dissatisfaction was growing throughout the country and expressed itself in such organizations as the American Society of Equity and the Non-partisan League. By 1908, the Alliance operated two grain elevators, one in Bozeman and one at the western edge of Belgrade. On the other side of town loomed the Story elevator, also known as "Big Red" because of its exterior paint job; Nelson Story was one of the grain merchants the farmers regarded as the enemy.

The Alliance began to market its own crops and cooperatively buy more and more equipment, and started an insurance company especially designed for farmers. This effort did not last too many years, however; the group suffered from poor management and spread itself over too many activities. As one man put it: "A few farmers have been loyal to the Alliance while the majority have done nothing to support it."[1] By 1910, the Alliance elevators were up for sale.

When Glen D. Powers started Belgrade's first newspaper, *The Gallatin Farmer and Stockman* on September 20, 1902, he told his new readers that no politics would be discussed in the weekly, just news relating to farmers. Price: five cents.

Editor Powers assessed the development of Belgrade in glowing terms:

> Belgrade is once again the scene of a hustling grain business. The streets are daily crowded with loaded wagons of the various cereals which are lined up along the side tracks awaiting their turn to unload, from early morning until late in the afternoon. Last year Belgrade made a wonderful record in grain shipment, but this year bids fair to greatly surpass all preceding records.[2]

That year, the town welcomed Dr. J. H. Featherston and A. J. Palmer's construction of the

Belgrade was bustling in the 1880s, although its streets were yet unpaved.

The Belgrade State Bank commanded the street.

Jim Isbell waits for customers in the New Belgrade Store.

Gallatin Valley Milling Company's new elevator and flouring mill, the biggest plant in the area. Soon, the business was operating both day and night. The Benepe-Owenhouse company also built an elevator in Belgrade, hoping to compete with Nelson Story's "Big Red." In 1903, almost by chance, Featherston and Palmer sold their new elevator and flouring mill to the wealthy Fisher family.

Oliver W. and Oliver D. Fisher, father and son, crossed the Gallatin Valley after a spot of fishing. Son O. D. told his father there was a mill for sale nearby. "I'd like to see the valley but I don't want to go to Belgrade. . . . If I step into the mill, I'll probably buy it—and I don't want to own a flour mill."[3] Grumbling, O. W. did visit the mill; one and one-half hours later, he bought it for $35,000. At first O. D. supervised the Belgrade operation but, within a few months, brother Dan became the local manager. In May 1904, he bought the first auto seen in Belgrade, cruising around town in his bright red Rambler. The elder Fisher built a mansion for his family in Bozeman on South Willson and lived there until 1914.

In 1908, with power supplied by the Madison River Power Company, the Fisher operation, as well

as others, was able to increase both production and profits. Although the processing of cereals became the chief industry in Belgrade, business boomed in other areas. Three tons of turkeys were shipped to market in 1903. Carloads of sheep left Belgrade for eastern sale. This business activity spurred the development of Belgrade in other ways. The Belgrade State Bank opened its doors in 1902, followed by the Farmer's Bank of Belgrade in 1916. Wooden sidewalks lined the streets by 1904.

The town's incorporation in 1906 highlighted the need for good water and sewer pipes as well as electricity. Fire in a town with five grain elevators and wooden buildings was a frightening and real possibility to residents who remembered that, in 1900, much of downtown Belgrade was consumed by fire with no source of water to put it out. Six years later, Ben Hager of Livingston designed a water system for Belgrade, which included an underground wooden pipe, ten inches in diameter, running from the south branch of Ross Creek eight miles into town. Now the town had drinking water; housewives skimmed out the foreign matter collected in the buckets, including a number of small fish.

219

The Milwaukee Depot, Belgrade.

Neighbors study a train wreck near Belgrade, November 4, 1909. CHARLES KINSEY PHOTO.

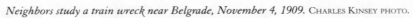

Two years later, the water system froze. The editor of the *Belgrade Journal*, successor to the *Gallatin Farmer-Stockman*, was sharply critical of Ben Hager, insisting that he should have buried the water pipe six feet deep, instead of five. Harsh words were exchanged and Hager stopped his subscription to the *Journal*. This waterworks was used for twenty years; after that, farmers continued to plow up sections of the old pipe when they prepared their fields in the spring.

Hager was also responsible for the construction of power poles to bring electricity to Belgrade from the Madison River plant. In February 1911, forty streetlights illuminated the Belgrade night, causing great excitement and celebration.

In 1910, Frank Johnstone and his wife announced their intention to build a two-story hospital which would include private rooms for ten patients, a ward, an operating room, and offices for two doctors, an unusual institution for a town the size of Belgrade. The following year, the Johnstone Hospital opened its doors and was busy for a time; however, it eventually failed and the building was made into apartments.

There had been a grade school in Belgrade since 1885, operated by the Southern Methodist Church. In 1892, a grand two-room structure opened, housing more than fifty-five pupils. In 1908, a brick structure was completed to augment the crowded frame school nearby. Each year, another grade was added until 1914, when all twelve grades were taught.

Membership in fraternal organizations attracted residents in the Belgrade area: the Masons, Woodmen of the World, American Yeomen, Independent Order of Odd Fellows, Organization of the Royal Highlanders, and the Knights Templars. Belgrade churches included the Southern Methodist, Presbyterian, Christian, Episcopalian, and Baptist.

Belgrade was proud of its musical tradition, exemplified in the Belgrade Band, a succession of all-male groups starting in 1900 and lasting until World War I. Residents gladly donated money for elaborate uniforms for the musicians, who appeared to parade at all local functions, for Sweet Pea events in Bozeman, and other gatherings in the valley. By 1914, the Belgrade Commercial Club had collected

George Williams delivers rural mail to one hundred and thirty families on Route No. 1. CHARLES KINSEY PHOTO.

The Belgrade Band, 1901. VAN VOAST PHOTO.

Cephus Inabnit stands before the Treasure State Land Company and the Manhattan Post Office. He is admiring a 1913 Model T Ford.

enough money to build a little bandstand for summer performances.[4]

* * *

Manhattan was also maturing as a major Gallatin Valley community. By December 1906, the town had its own newspaper, the *Manhattan Record*, under the editorship of F. D. Geiger. Two banks served the area: the Manhattan State Bank was capitalized in 1905 and Walter White's Home State Bank opened in 1913. The area got telephone service in 1909 and electricity in 1910; two years later, concrete sidewalks replaced wooden ones. Malter Henry Altebrand contributed land for a municipal park in 1915. The Manhattan water supply seemed secure; it flowed through wooden pipes from springs located south of town on Meadow Brook Ranch. In the fall of 1910, the Manhattan Bachelors Club gave the first of many picnics; the menu included roast duck, baked clams, and fried fish.

Henry William Becker delivered the mail to rural areas in a Model T Ford; no longer did he make the route by horse and buggy. During periods of bitter cold, residents would heat bags of salt or bricks to keep Becker's feet from freezing as he made his rounds. They did the same for Jake Krol, who carried mail to the Holland Settlement.

In 1914, Manhattan children attended classes in an urban $32,000 brick building, replacing a small wooden school built in 1890 and a two-story school, built in 1896. In 1916, high school youngsters moved to their own handsome brick building; that year three Manhattan girls were graduated. Both schools were severely damaged in a 1925 earthquake.

Three years later, Manhattan suffered major flooding in March 1928 from spring runoff. Amsterdam and Maudlow had badly flooded the year before.

Henry Altenbrand, manager of the malting plant which provided most of the jobs in the area, was initially opposed to incorporation for the town—he thought it premature—but he changed his mind and voted for it in 1911. Three years later, in August 1914, Altebrand was forced to close the plant for a season because of labor troubles with the malters' union based in Butte. He opened again but would close again later upon passage of the Volstead Act, federal prohibition against the manufacture of alcoholic beverages. Although Manhattan had been regarded as a company town, a growing business diversity kept its economy going. The farmers surrounding Manhattan did not suffer as they thought they would and easily found other markets for their grains. At least one illegal entrepreneur was exposed in 1934 when a still exploded at the west end of town.

Trident was not the only town to install an electric theater. Manhattan's Electra attracted moviegoers as did as the Kid Theater, a 1915 building constructed by Dave "Kid" Johnston, ex-prizefighter and animal trainer. One of his more notable feats was to train a mountain lion to pull a small cart. The Kid Theatre featured boxing matches, wrestling, Saturday night dances, and basketball games as well as movies. The Vogue, another theater, opened in the late 1930s.

In 1908, one of Manhattan's unusual characters died. Sammy Williams had hopped off a freight train in the 1890s, looking for work as a cook. The Heeb family hired Williams and, except for an occasional drinking binge, the cook became famous for his light breads and cakes. When Williams succumbed to a heart attack, however, the undertaker made a startling discovery—Sammy was a woman. Manhattan soon learned that Sammy was, indeed, Ingeborg Wekan, an immigrant from Norway, who had been known earlier in Wisconsin as "Billy." Evidently, Ingeborg had suffered an unhappy love affair and decided that life would be easier wearing men's clothing, a not uncommon occurrence in the West.

* * *

Before any settlement of the Gallatin Valley, Indian hunters from the valley ventured into the Gallatin Canyon during the summer months, but they did not establish permanent camps there. From the south, Sheepeaters slipped in quietly from time to time, but when cold weather threatened, they returned to the Yellowstone Park area. Later, fur trappers visited the canyon, but they took their pelts and knowledge of the terrain with them.

Walter W. DeLacy and other prospectors traveled through the canyon in the 1860s, on the watch for color in the streams plunging into the West Gallatin, but they did not find gold in paying

Kid Johnston shows off his trained mountain lion.

Two 1910 Model Glides parked in front of Danley and Nason Machine Shop, Manhattan.

Early blacksmith shop, Manhattan, August 1, 1882. LEFT TO RIGHT: *Jesse Nelson, Ed Connell, Hamp Hecox, unidentified boy.*

quantities. Geologist Ferdinand V. Hayden brought his 1872 survey party through the canyon after his second trip to the Yellowstone area, seeing little sign of human residence there. A small number of stockmen ran cattle as far south as Taylor Fork. None of these operations compared with the Anceney cattle enterprise at the mouth of the canyon.

Because of its rugged nature, the upper Gallatin and its narrow canyon lay undisturbed as other areas of southwest Montana were settled and exploited. The wider Yellowstone Valley to the east and the Madison Valley to the west lent themselves to easier economic exploitation. Not that there weren't businessmen on hand who dreamed of riches to be gained by one scheme or another in the canyon. Some wanted to dredge the river for gold; others wanted to dam it. Prospectors were convinced that great caches of gold, silver, and copper lay hidden in the farthest reaches above. Why not run a railroad through the canyon to carry the tourist trade to the park?

Bozeman residents Walter Cooper, Peter Koch, and George Wakefield tried to interest the Northern Pacific Railroad in 1881 in a railroad through the canyon to carry tourists to the new park—a potential bonanza. On August 19, the three businessmen trekked through the canyon to study its geology, to survey a rail route, and to hunt. By the time they reached the park, four days later, they had shot at four lynxes with no success and saw no other game. On August 25, the party started back through the canyon; Cooper kept a journal of the next few days.

August 26—Smoky and hazy ahead . . . must be approaching forest fire, probably not in our path. Might be cut off if we go back.

August 27: Smoke awful. Horses nervous. Birds with seared wings flying past us. . . . See red glow ahead and very nervous. . . . Taking turns now sleeping. . . . Afraid to travel before daylight for fear we might get off our course and get lost in the increasing smoke.

225

Early homestead, Gallatin Canyon. CHARLES D. LOUGHREY PHOTO.

August 28—Fire creeping toward us from every direction; all around us. . . . Travel through hot ashes. Steer horses down creek bed whenever possible.

August 29—Flames jump canyon from one side to the other. Spectacular sight but an inferno. See small game with seared fur and bewildered elk and deer race by. We hardly halt for food. Cannot now travel any part of way in stream. Hot ashes falling everywhere. Noise of fire deafening. No feed left in upper or lower part of Gallatin basins. Timber practically burned out . . . one mountain completely bare of timber. We are naming it baldy. Fire out here. Some smouldering patches still and hot ashes everywhere. Some places the largest trees still standing. One wonders how they escaped.[5]

Heavy, acrid smoke poured into the Gallatin Valley, leaving no doubt of what was happening in

the canyon. Later, the three men were disappointed to learn that, for whatever reason, the Northern Pacific chose not to lay track through the canyon but was looking at the wider Yellowstone Valley to carry tourists to the park boundary.

Desolate places often attract those who prefer the lonely life to that of ordered society. "Buckskin Charley" Marble hunted and guided in the canyon; he and his wife Lizzie lived year-round in a cabin up Taylor Fork. In 1886, he met young Theodore Roosevelt in Bozeman and offered to guide the sportsman for forty days up the canyon to hunt mountain sheep, elk, and black bear. Roosevelt was most impressed that Marble could imitate the bugle of an elk. In 1892, Marble and his partner Dick Rock, sometimes known as "Rocky Mountain Dick," described themselves in Bozeman ads as "Mountaineers, Guides, and Collectors of Wild Animals." Marble left the canyon in the early 1900s to open a taxidermy shop on Bozeman's Main

A buggy on the road into Gallatin Canyon.

Street. And Rock, after years of supplying elk, buffalo, geese, swans, mountain goats, and deer to zoos throughout the country, suffered a violent death in 1902 when he was gored by one of his "tame" buffalo.

Lewis Cass "Big Lew" Bartholomew, a shell-shocked victim of the Spanish-American War, may have earned his reputation for eccentricity by his fondness for fried gophers. He was also famous for his one-course diets; sometimes he ate only cucumbers; at other times, he limited himself to apples or peanuts. He didn't like clocks and told time by his sundial. Although he lived in different parts of the canyon, he spent a number of years operating a sawmill located near the mouth of Greek Creek, which he had bought from Albert Greek.

Polish immigrant Andrew Levinski—his name was pronounced "Leven Sky"—a canyon loner who appeared not to like people, regularly scared them away from his meager gold diggings during his residence of thirty-five years. Sometimes he lived near his claims located two miles south of Porcupine Creek, but he had built lean-tos and dilapidated shacks throughout the canyon area.

227

Dick Rock might have trained these bison before he was gored to death by one.

Helen and Grace Trent with Andrew Jackson "Jack" Smith at his cabin one mile north of the West Fork in the Gallatin. A Confederate soldier, Smith came to Montana from Missouri in 1872. He ran cattle in the canyon and later served as a deputy game warden there.

Sometime in January 1917, Levenski killed two young men, Gladstone Stevens and Strauss Miller, who, the old man said, were attempting to jump some of his claims. He turned himself into the sheriff, was tried for murder, and acquitted. Claim jumping was not popular anywhere in the West. One year after the trial, he disappeared under mysterious circumstances. He may have died in the canyon or he may have left the area.

Hunter and trapper Albert Wagner, referred to by some as the "Duke of Hellroaring," was alleged to be an Austrian count and his wife a Russian duchess. At least, she wore embroidered "Russian" clothing and smoked foreign cigarettes; the couple may have survived by the sale of Mrs. Wagner's jewels. In the 1890s, they lived in a commodious cabin built by the duke near Hellroaring Creek. The "duchess" augmented their meager finances by serving meals to those few visitors who ventured up the difficult trail. After years of privation, they left, selling their property to George Dier, proprietor of the Bozeman Hotel in town, who wanted a summer canyon retreat. The duchess may have returned to Russia; the Duke of Hellroaring surfaced again as a guide in the park.

In March 1897, Central Park businessmen Vardiman Cockrell made a successful two-hundred-dollar bid to the county to build two bridges in the canyon, one over the West Fork, the other on the Gallatin River, one mile downstream from the mouth of the West Fork. In addition, the county commissioners saw the logic of building a road to the proposed bridges and again awarded a contract to Cockrell for eight thousand dollars to construct a road from the mouth of Squaw Creek upstream to the park boundary, a distance of thirty-two miles. Cockrell was to complete the work by July 1898. By August, the contractor had built the road to Taylor Fork, just four miles short of his goal.

Four years later, Bozeman businessman Walter Cooper, a man whose variety of financial interests earned him the title of capitalist, with the backing from Helena investors, bought Taylor Fork land from the Northern Pacific Railroad to log there and provide ties for the railroad. Cooper established three tie-cutting camps on the Taylor Fork, subcontracted for other camps on nearby drainages, and provided bunkhouses, cookhouses, and commissaries for the

Railroad ties pile up at Walter Cooper's Taylor Fork lumber camp.

It looks easy at the moment. Sending lumber downstream to Central Park.

The job is almost done.

loggers. At the main camp, Cooper established the Eldredge Post Office, which remained open during the years of the logging operation.

During the winter months, Cooper's men piled up timber they had logged from Taylor Fork land and other tributaries nearby behind retaining dams just off the main Gallatin, waiting for the spring runoff. For several years, during high water, experienced lumberjacks imported from Oregon and Canada floated downstream with the logs, jumping to break up the timber jams as they came downstream and across the valley to Central Park to Cooper's sawmill. As historian Michael Malone says, "It was a colorful, boisterous operation, but it didn't last long."[6] By 1907, Cooper had withdrawn from the lumber business in the canyon and concentrated on Bear Canyon as a logging source.

At the mouth of Gallatin Canyon, little Salesville, which had benefited by the logging activities upstream, suffered financially when lumber interests decided to move elsewhere. The Salesville State Bank, capitalized in 1911 by three Bozeman businessmen, was controlled by 1917 by cattleman Charles Anceney, who became its president. In later years, ranch manager Frank Stone served as bank president. Anceney also bought real estate in town, including the hotel, where visitors to the Flying D Ranch could stay. He had an interest in the general store and in the old Tomlinson lumber mill.

When the Gallatin Valley Electric Railway Company extended its interurban line to Salesville in 1909, residents boarded the train to shop and visit friends in Bozeman; youngsters could extend their education by attending college in the big town. When the Milwaukee Railway took over the interurban one year later, the company extended its lines north to Three Forks, connecting the village to transcontinental railroad traffic.

Not everyone who chose to live in the remote canyon was unsociable or eccentric. Pete Karst came from Wisconsin in 1898 and settled on a homestead ranch in the Lower Basin which he received from

Visitors lounge in front of Karst's Cold Spring Resort.

Cabins circled the 320 Ranch quarters, 1940s. DOROTHY NILE PHOTO.

Packed mule train leads the way for a 320 Ranch outing in the mountains, 1940s. DOROTHY NILE PHOTO.

Walter Cooper in lieu of pay for his freighting activities. Karst delivered the mail and supplies on a rough wagon road which had been carved through the canyon that year to Taylor Fork; the road was another project of Walter Cooper and Peter Koch. Karst and fellow ranchers Tom Michener and Sam Wilson pondered the possibility of a new business in the canyon that would not depend upon outside capital for railroads, cattle raising, gold mining or dredging, river damming, or clear cutting. Why not entertain eastern dudes for a price?—say, twelve dollars per week for room and board and six additional dollars for a saddle horse.

In 1901, Karst was ready for the first dudes; he called his place Karst's Cold Spring Resort, the first dude ranch in Montana. Tom Michener's ranch became Michener's Camp, and Sam Wilson named his the Buffalo Horn Resort. In time, Pete Karst

shortened the name of his resort to Karst Kamp and built a swimming pool for his guests; during Prohibition he maintained a mountain still. Tom Michener left for New Mexico to prospect for oil and the Buffalo Horn Resort became the 320 Ranch; other havens for dudes included Elkhorn Ranch on Sage Creek, Nine Quarter Circle Ranch on Taylor Fork, Rainbow Ranch, and Buck's T-Four Ranch in the Lower Basin.

In 1910, James M. Moore and his nephew William blazed a trail from the Taylor Fork to the sleepy little village of Riverside, later to be renamed West Yellowstone, thus connecting the Gallatin Valley to the west entrance of Yellowstone National Park. The area came to life in 1908 when the Oregon Short Line Railroad chugged in from Monida and Henry's Lake, Idaho, following an earlier stage route; travelers could stop at Dwelle's Hotel or go

320 Ranch guests help with branding, 1940s. DOROTHY NILE PHOTO.

Bozeman architect Fred Willson designed Eagle's service station and cafe, West Yellowstone.

The Gallatin Gateway Inn was completed just in time for this photograph, 1927.

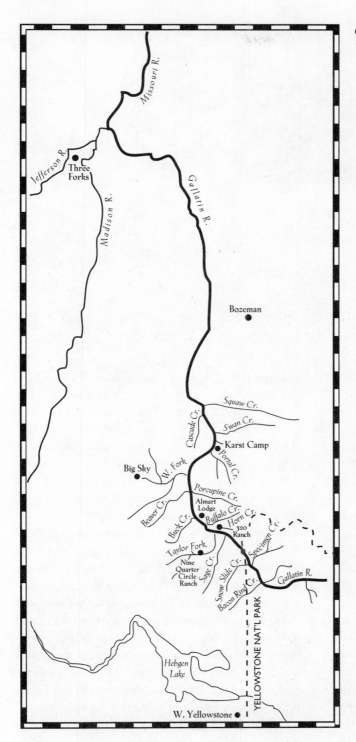

Gallatin Canyon.

on to Riverside to transfer to a stage coach for a trip through the park.

Fourteen miles northwest of Riverside, a post office was established at Grayling in the ranch house of Peter Kerzenmacher, serving the few homesteaders in the area. His wife Lulu Darling served as postmaster for forty-four years. Other Kerzenmachers continued as postmasters until 1951.

Work began to build a better road through Gallatin Canyon in 1919 and continued to be improved until the 1930s. In 1924, Karst opened his profitable bus line, which carried tourists from Salesville to West Yellowstone. In 1927, with tourists in mind, the Milwaukee Road built an elegant inn at Salesville, a stopping place for those on their way to the park. The grand opening attracted two thousand celebrants to a magnificent ball. Since the company called it the Gallatin Gateway Inn, nearby Salesville changed its name to Gallatin Gateway.

During the administration of President Theodore Roosevelt, the former canyon game hunter enraged many Gallatin Valley residents, as well as those living in the canyon, by directing the creation of Gallatin National Forest. They felt a loss of control over their lands and they saw the end to some of their financial schemes for the canyon, although many farmers liked the idea of having the source of their irrigation water protected. In the years to come, Gallatin Canyon would become the site of a number of business schemes which would change the character of the once-quiet region.[7]

chapter

TWENTY-TWO

The Bozeman Opera House would soon see hard times. After a spectacular 1905 season of fifty-five performances, highlighted by *Uncle Tom's Cabin*, *The Mikado*, *Bohemian Girl*, a John Phillip Sousa concert, and a dog and cat circus called *The Funny Folks*, road shows called less often at Bozeman. Vaudeville and minstrel productions still came west, but live "legitimate" theater bookings only lit up the auditorium two or three times each month.

And more: something called "the electric theater" had come to town. The Lyric Theatre opened at 25-27 East Main Street in June 1908, offering moving pictures for five and ten cents' admission; live entertainment could not compete with such low ticket prices. "Our Pictures Do Not Flicker" read the ads; manager Jacob Jagorda promised to change the offering at least three times each week. The Bozeman Orpheum movie and vaudeville house opened in December of that year, also featuring evening shows and matinees on Saturdays. More electric theaters, the Gem, 126-130 West Main, and the Globe, 230 West Main, began to compete for public entertainment. Each advertised that its seats were more comfortable, and that its movies were five-reel, not one. The theaters added complementary attractions to draw more customers: The Lyric opened a bowling alley in its basement; the Orpheum countered with a pool hall. An electric marquee flashed on and off at the Lyric.

In 1910, the Gem Theatre featured the first performance of the Bozeman Symphony. In 1919, the owners of the Gem decided to construct a more elegant building for live and movie performances. Nelson Story, Jr., T. B. Story, H. R. Greene, E. H. Kleinschmidt, and Otto Schmidt put up $150,000 for "one of the first and most complete show houses of the size in the Northwest," named to honor the Story brothers' mother, Ellen.[1] They hired Fred Willson to design the Main Street theater, which included a confectionery shop next to the entrance, a stage which could accommodate vaudeville as well as movie presentations, spacious dressing rooms, and balcony and loge seats, some of which were permanently reserved for members of the Story family. Upstairs, the hardwood floors for a private banquet hall and dance floor were underlined with felt to deaden any noise to theater patrons below.

The Ellen Theater opened on December 1, 1919, with George Loane Tucker's movie *The Miracle Man*, followed by a Pantages vaudeville show. Edgar Bergen and Charlie McCarthy came to the Ellen, as did the musical *Kismet*, during which live elephants paraded across the stage. Under faint lights and a blue spot, Sally Rand floated through her notorious fan dance. Overcome by his temporary

236

The popular Gem Theater.

power, spot operator Ed Pegram flooded the stage with "a bright white light" at the precise moment Miss Rand had little on but a few fans; the audience cheered but the dancer was not amused.

In 1925, the Ellen installed a $16,000 Wurlitzer organ which, on opening night, featured organist Adolph Evans, Jr., and the Bozeman Symphony playing Rossini's overture to *William Tell*. Evans also played the popular hit "Follow the Swallow" as the audience sang along, reading words flashed on the screen. The movie *Her Night of Romance*, starring Constance Talmadge, concluded the ceremonies. In 1929, the Ellen management installed a sound system and Bozeman audiences heard their first "talkie," featuring Fred Waring and his Pennsylvanians.

The Opera House also showed movies and had done so since 1897. A short kinetoscope of the Corbett-Fitzgibbons fight attracted an audience, as did news clips of the Spanish American War the following year. More renovation of the auditorium included a new proscenium arch and curtain and a cleaner property room, just in time for the January 1916 showing of *A Birth of a Nation*. Politicians still held rallies at the Opera House, high school graduates continued to walk across its stage, and Gene Quaw offered one play after another. Clarence Darrow shouted his opposition to Prohibition there on October 26, 1916; Al Jolson appeared in *Robinson Crusoe, Jr.* the following year. Boxers and wrestlers made occasional appearances at the Opera House, which, because of neglect, was showing its age. Colorful posters still lined the walls, dusty and curling, reminiscent of earlier good times. The cooing of pigeons replaced the sounds of band instruments tuning up.

The firefighters who shared the Opera House building with police and city government needed

The Ellen Theater was an elegant addition to Main Street.

John Fechter leads the Bozeman Symphony Orchestra at the glamorous Ellen.

Posters from the Opera House interior walls could not be saved.

more room; the fire chief ordered construction of dormitories for the men on one side of the theater's balcony. An additional courtroom filled the other side. Jail cells replaced old dressing rooms. In the late 1930s, architect Fred F. Willson prepared plans to renovate the stage area, but Bozeman, like the rest of the country, was tightening its financial belt, and a bond issue failed.

The severe 1959 earthquake at last weakened the structure. Six years later, the old Opera House, long a source of civic pride, was slowly dismantled: first, the top brick addition was removed, revealing the old mansard roof that had made so much noise during rainstorms. Second, the interior walls came down. Theater buffs tried to save the posters that lined these, but they were firmly glued to the brick interior and wouldn't come off whole. Finally, in the 1960s, the structure was razed by a demolition crew.[2]

* * *

When the United States entered the war in Europe in April 1917, teachers and faculty left their posts for war-related jobs. Students left school to work in the valley's fields, heavily planted in wheat and other grains to feed the troops abroad. Women throughout the valley formed Red Cross societies. The men who stayed behind drilled with military precision to be ready for enemy invasion. Rumors of trouble ahead spread in much the same way that stories of Indian menace traveled in the 1860s.

The Gallatin Valley did not escape the anti-German sentiment so prevalent throughout the nation and especially Montana during the days of World War I. By 1917, more Montana men, including those of German descent, volunteered or were drafted for military service than any other state of the Union relative to its population—40,000— or ten percent. Members of the local German community were subjected to the hysterical wrath of those who felt it was patriotic to revile their neighbors, even young children. Bozeman resident Helen E. Fechter, daughter of an American mother

Cyrus "Si" J. Gatton, football hero and all-around athlete at Montana Agricultural College in 1915, became a pilot during World War I. He was lost over France one week before the Armistice. Gatton Field at Montana State University is named in his honor.

and a German immigrant, remembers being taunted by "You're a little Hun," "Your father is a German."[3] German texts were weeded out of school and public libraries. Music teachers excised German tunes from class songbooks, leaving holes throughout the texts. On campus, the German Language Department closed. Sauerkraut was called "liberty cabbage" and hamburger became "liberty steak." All pacifists were suspect. Jeannette Rankin, Montana's Congresswoman and the first woman to sit in the U.S. House of Representatives, dismayed many of her fellow Montanans by voting against the declaration of war.

In July 1918, people in the Gallatin Valley began to hear that some American soldiers on their way home from Europe were getting sick—just a runny nose at first, followed by a high fever and chest congestion. In fact, this was no ordinary flu; victims turned very dark in the face just before they died. The disease seemed to strike those in their twenties, thirties, and forties, although other age groups were not immune. In September, a man from a threshing crew developed the symptoms and was brought into town; the Spanish influenza had spread to the valley.

The Opera House was kept dark, and theaters throughout the area closed to avoid spreading the germs. No public meetings of any kind were scheduled by order of the health department; the town's schools closed; Montana State College shut down. Ministers advised their parishoners to hold family services at home. Those who ventured out wore protective masks. The newspapers, either by innuendo or by outright statement, told readers that influenza was spreading through the valley carried by strangers who brought the germs here from the East.

Classrooms on the top floor of Gallatin County High School were cleared of desks in October and beds were moved in to house the sick. Wards opened at the college as well. Manhattan's school also became a hospital. Teachers and other Good Samaritans nursed the victims. One Belgrade ice cream shopkeeper stubbornly kept The Fountain open against all advice; he died from the disease. Kate Hanley, who had been Sweet Pea Carnival queen in 1906 and had become Mrs. Robert McComb, succumbed, as did her husband. The illness tended to run through families: L. E. Brown, his wife, and all five children died of the disease within days of one another.

On October 25, ninety-four people needed hospital care; two weeks later, that number rose to one hundred and fifty nine. Quite possibly, more got sick because of the temporary lifting of the curfew on November 11 to celebrate the Armistice. By the end of November, ninety-six new cases were reported. Although the newspapers reported the progress of the disease through the community, they tended to downgrade the seriousness of the epidemic, hoping to lessen anxiety. Taking advantage of the situation, makers of a new product placed ads in the local papers: "How to use Vick's Vaporub in Treating Spanish Influenza."[4] According to the Vick's people, "Those Who Don't Go to Bed Soon Enough, or Those Who Get Up Too Early" were likely to contract the illness.

As the holiday season approached, the traditional shopping period for many families, merchants began to pressure public health officials to lift curfews so that customers might spend money in their stores. But the doctors were not so moved. On November 28, county health chief Dr. Joseph A. Piedalue remained firm: the quarantine would remain in force for schools, churches, poolrooms, and other spots of public assembly, most particularly the electric theaters. Some days later, the doctors did relent somewhat on the reopening of downtown stores. Shops could serve those who dared to venture forth if merchants promised not to advertise bargains or special sales that would attract large numbers of shoppers.

New cases and subsequent deaths were still reported in December and into the new year; by late spring 1920, however, Spanish influenza was becoming an unpleasant memory. Life returned to normal for most; shoppers ventured forth; by March, the local children were back in school.

* * *

During the summer of 1919, construction began on what was to become a centerpiece of Gallatin Valley entertainment for twelve all-too-short years. Thomas Byron Story and his brother Nelson, Jr. got together with R. P. McClelland and Lester Work to build a stadium and grandstand on a four-block tract just south of the present county fairgrounds. The site cost three thousand dollars and the construction expenditure rose to twenty-eight thousand dollars. The grandstand would seat 2,800 people; the stadium would accommodate 15,000 to 20,000 customers. The builders had to act fast; the Elks would be in town for their yearly convention in mid-August—a good time to make money. On July 14, the Kenyon Noble lumber yard brought in the first load of wood for construction. The Story brothers hired returning veterans to do the work, but they were non-union and had to cross picket lines. Despite the labor troubles, the stadium and quarter-mile racetrack were finished twenty-eight days later, ready for the first Roundup celebration.

August 12 began with a morning parade down Main Street, featuring rodeo cowboys and cowgirls, Flathead Indians in full regalia, Roundup queen Peg McGovern, and other local and state dignitaries. After the parade, the crowds enjoyed a baseball game and an Elks carnival. The actual Roundup rodeo competition took place in the middle of the afternoon, with cowboys and cowgirls competing for purses of several hundred dollars each in bronc and bull riding, horse racing, trick riding, and bulldogging. In the evening, local residents and visiting Elks watched a minstrel show, the latest Gene Quaw musical revue called *Hello, Bill*, and danced in the middle of Main Street and Central Avenue (now Willson Avenue).

For the next six years, Bozeman had a good position on the rodeo circuit; cowboy stars regularly performed here as they did in Madison Square Garden in New York; Calgary, Alberta; Pendleton, Oregon; and as far south as Mexico. A small number of female performers charmed crowds along the way. Dressed in costumes of their own design, trimmed with bits of fur, sequins, and bright sashes, topped with giant brimmed hats, these women dared to compete in bronc riding, bull riding, and bulldogging, events not open to women today. Each afternoon, after the rodeo clowns, the crowds

241

A parade to kick off the Bozeman Roundup crosses South Willson Avenue at Main Street.

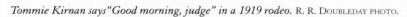
Tommie Kirnan says "Good morning, judge" in a 1919 rodeo. R. R. DOUBLEDAY PHOTO.

Alice Sisty laughs as she performs the Roman Jump over a 1935 Cord auto. Note the "suicide" door.

Cowgirls in elegant costumes pose for R. R. Doubleday.

Rose Henderson performs for rolling cameras with the Bridgers in the background. FOSTER PHOTO, MILES CITY.

Cowboy Byers spins the double loop, 1919. W. H. KITTS PHOTO.

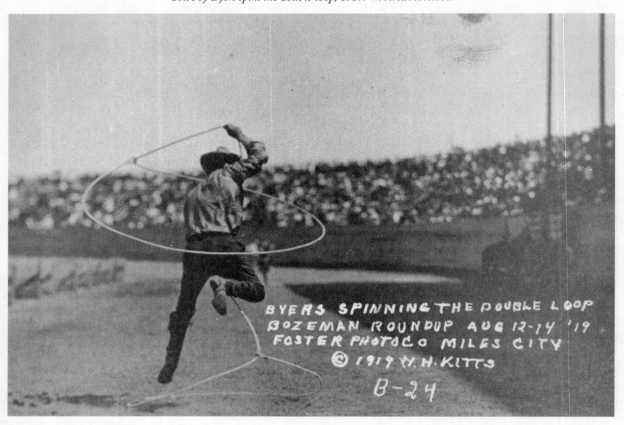

Having a good time at the Bozeman Roundup, 1919. W.H. KITTS PHOTO.

warmed up the festivities, shouting the slogan, "She's wild! she's wild! she's wild!"

The stadium was surrounded by decorated Indian tepees. Not too far away, crowds thronged around something called the "Slippery Gulch," a gambling operation which included two roulette wheels, a chuck-a-luck wheel, two faro tables, and one for blackjack. Threading through the people, rodeo officials, distinguished by their white silk shirts featuring brightly colored butterflies embroidered on the sleeves and a bucking bronco on the back, saw to it that their customers had a good time without breaking too many laws. Bogert's Grove, a park and auto camp south of East Main Street near Church Avenue, filled with tents.

The history of the Bozeman Roundup was exciting but short, ending in 1926. Had the building and grounds been kept up, Bozeman might have remained on the national rodeo circuit. In 1921, the stadium was sold to Richard T. Ringling, member of the circus family, who continued the yearly events until August 5 and 6, 1926. Shortly thereafter, lightning struck the grandstand, badly scarring the wooden structure. The building was condemned and

torn down for salvage lumber in 1932. As writer AnnaBelle Phillips concludes, "when they hauled away the last board, a little bit more of Bozeman's early, colorful past died."[5]

* * *

The automobile had come into its own, changing the face of the Gallatin Valley. Henry G. Merry, resident of the coal camp at Electric, astounded all, including the horses, when he drove his 1897 Winton car into Mammoth Hot Springs, the first motorized vehicle to enter Yellowstone National Park. Sam Mendenhall made local automotive history on May 12, 1905, when he drove his new car along rutted roads from Butte to Bozeman, a seven-hour trip of one hundred miles. That same year, Walter Story showed off his new Stanley Steamer, "the fastest thing on wheels"; its kerosene-powered lamps made night driving possible. Cars appeared on the main streets of Manhattan and Belgrade. Since early autos had no windscreen, passengers adopted protective hats and long coats, reminiscent of earlier cattle drives.

Not all were pleased with the prospect of autos

Church dignitaries face the camera in a Buick touring car in front of the Catholic Church at Logan, c1908.

The Bozeman Fire Department is motorized. The chief's car, a c1909 Model T customized Ford, is white with gold trim.

cruising down roads and highways, disturbing wagon and carriage traffic. One legislator tried to pass a law during the 1907 session of the Montana Legislature banning autos from the state's roadways. The bill failed. Two years later, a bill to license autos failed as well. In Manhattan, local authorities passed an ordinance in 1911 allowing motorists to cruise in town at ten miles per hour unless they encountered an animal; at that point they were required to come to a full stop. Finally, in 1913, the legislature passed the first state car regulations, which specified that drivers could travel thirty miles an hour on state roads and eight miles an hour within city limits. A license was required for each vehicle. At first, licenses were homemade; the state issued the auto owner a number, and he was responsible for affixing a placard on his vehicle. In time, the state issued metal plates. (In 1944, in order to save metal for the war effort, licenses were made of pressed soybean fiber, a tasty meal often enjoyed by wandering horses and cattle.)

By 1917, more than forty companies sold cars to more affluent Americans at an average cost of $605. Two years before, Yellowstone National Park converted to motorized White touring buses; gone were the elegant stagecoaches drawn by three and four teams of horses. Stage coach driver Berg Clark, who had piloted visitors to the park for years, retired from the job, saying, "All I know is horses. I don't know anything about cars."[6]

The Story family, long known for its ability to make money with new projects, joined the industry. In 1907, the Story Motor Supply was capitalized, selling cars, auto supplies, and "Powerized Hot Shot Gasoline and Veedol Motor Oil." The company branched out with service stations and motor supply houses both in Bozeman and the Gallatin Canyon. A number of liveries and blacksmiths closed their doors. Horseless school buses carried children to schools. Members of the Bozeman Fire Department raised enough money to buy Chief Alexander a 1914 elegant Model T Ford touring car, sparkling white

First site of the Story family service stations, northeast corner of Main Street and Grand Avenue.

with gold trim, which was modified for responding to fires. Tourist camps opened throughout the valley to accommodate vacationers visiting the area by auto. Bogert's Grove became a popular auto camp. In 1920, a state highway commission formed and kept the thirty-mile-per-hour speed on highways but raised in-town speed from eight to twelve miles per hour.

* * *

In 1911, the Jerome B. Rice Seed Company of Detroit sent William A. Davis to the Gallatin Valley to determine whether or not peas, a crop blighted by disease in the East, could be grown here profitably. Seed peas could be chancy to grow, affected by too much or too little water, easily damaged by hail. Farmers had tried raising sugar beets in the valley a few years before, but the area's short growing season and the heavy soil made them a difficult crop. Davis's pea experiments were so successful that, two years later, farmers harvested seventeen thousand acres of seed peas, spawning

such new industries as the Gallatin Valley Seed Company at 209 South Wallace, the Associated Seed Company at 407 North Broadway, and Brotherton & Kirk.

With the outbreak of war in Europe, businessmen T. B. Story, L. L. Brotherton, and Lester P. Work sensed the opportunity to bring new federal money into local coffers—long a method of financing used by merchants with profit since the 1870s. Why not can peas for the table? In 1917, they incorporated the Bozeman Canning Company and built a cannery on South Rouse the following year. As the first 16,334 cases of sweet peas rolled off the production line, the government bought most of the supply to feed the troops abroad. From July through September, the cannery hired some two hundred to two hundred and seventy-five men, who earned forty cents per hour operating heavy machinery in the cannery and in the field. Once harvest began, all hands had to work fast; the peas would turn sour if not canned quickly. After the peas

Smith's Department Store, 125 West Main, in the 1890s.

The Bungalow, 14 West Main, was always a popular spot.

*John Kapamas's Sugar Bowl, 42 East Main, looks more like a tavern than a candy and ice cream store.
Mabel Grass is serving, 1915.*

249

were extracted from the pods, the screenings went back to the farmers to feed their pigs and cattle.

The growing industry attracted a large number of local women who had seldom worked outside their homes before. They sorted peas at thirty cents per hour. Housewives enjoyed the sociability of working with others and also seemed pleased that they were contributing to family income. After harvest, the women moved to staff the seed companies, cleaning, sorting, and packaging seed peas. During the Depression, canning and seed pea management would ration hours from family to family in order to spread weekly paychecks around; this "kept a lot of people from going hungry in those days."[7]

Bozeman's pea industry had its ups and downs until its official demise in 1961. During the late 1930s, farmers soon learned the dangers of single crop production; blight destroyed some of the once-vigorous pea fields. The Gallatin Valley Seed Company absorbed the Brotherton-Kirk operation as well as the original Rice Seed Company, and the smaller firms went out of business. (L. L. Brotherton moved to Oregon where he founded PictSweet, Inc., a pioneer in the frozen vegetable field. The Bozeman cannery was a PictSweet company until it closed in 1958.)

Another industry dominated the local market for a longer period of time than did the pea business: flour. First crude grist mills operated in every part of the valley where water power was available—Salesville, Willow Creek, Gallatin City, Belgrade, Springhill. Nelson Story had acquired the McAdow flour mill in the 1860s; by 1872, he cut out some of the competition by acquiring the Tomlinson mill at Salesville and closing it down. His penchant for double-sacking to Indian and other federal customers notwithstanding, he aimed for a more

Nelson Story's flour mill employees pose with manager Elias Story, Jr. (with book), sometime before 1897. The family sent Elias for a much-needed rest in Hawaii. He died there from a ruptured appendix.

sophisticated operation at the mouth of Bridger Canyon in 1882, knowing that Northern Pacific engines would chug by within one year. He built a two-mile canal which conducted water from Rocky Creek, Bozeman Creek, and Bridger Creek to power his Valley Mills complex. The railroad, in turn, built a spur to Nelson Story and Company, the first of forty-one such industrial spurs in the valley. Story advertised that his was the largest elevator in Montana, producing one hundred bushel barrels of flour per day. The business came to a temporary halt on August 27, 1901, when a spark from a passing engine burned the mill down.

The family rebuilt the Story mill almost immediately, this time of brick and masonry. Son Thomas Byron Story took over the rechristened Bozeman Milling Company, adding to it a cereal mill on North Rouse. Production was up to six hundred and fifty bushel barrels per day. Now the Milwaukee Road also called at the mill complex. Within three years, production rose to one thousand bushel barrels per day.

The Story family sold its lucrative business to Montana Flour Mills in 1919. At the time, more than seventy-five men and women were assured of a job. In 1967, however, the eighty-three-year-old flour business was sold to ConAgra, which closed it down within thirty days in order to lessen competition.

* * *

The Story mill burns, August 1901.

The Montana Agricultural College, uncharitably characterized as a "barber college" in its infancy, had come a long way since 1893. It was beginning to look like a real campus. Small outbuildings surrounded its first structure, the Experiment Station. The cornerstone for Montana Hall was dedicated on October 21, 1896; the building was finished two years later. By 1906, the campus consisted of the Experiment Station, Montana Hall, a heating plant, an engineering laboratory, and a chemistry building (which burned in a spectacular fire on October 20, 1916).

The _College Exponent_ became a weekly student publication in 1912. Downtown classrooms were no longer needed, nor was the preparatory department, which closed in 1913. A growing faculty, some of whom were recruited from Harvard University, helped expand the curriculum. Young women debated suffrage and other subjects of the day at meetings of the Cliolian Society. Young men formed a social group called the Stags; the women responded with a club of their own—the Does. Although President Reid frowned upon dancing on campus, another men's group, Les Buffons, staged formal dancing parties downtown. There were literary societies, musical groups, a football team and a baseball nine, and a camera club.

Bozeman's streetcar and, later, the interurban line, played a major part in transporting students to the campus from all over the Gallatin Valley. Local conductor Larry O'Brien assumed a fatherly role in seeing that students arrived and departed the campus on time. At the end of social gatherings on campus, President Reid would announce, "Young people, Larry is waiting at the foot of the hill."[8]

When James McClellan Hamilton assumed the presidency in 1904, the college had begun to develop a broader curriculum. Although Hamilton's goals included introducing more technical subjects without sacrificing agricultural, engineering, and domestic science courses, he could also see that students needed to expand their knowledge of

The Montana Agricultural College campus, c1906. LEFT TO RIGHT: _the heating plant and engineering laboratory, Montana Hall, the three-story brick chemistry building (which burned in 1916), and a drill hall._

literature, history, the arts, mathematics, and physics—without stepping on the academic toes of the University of Montana at Missoula, that is. A course in forestry taught by George Patrick Ahern was in place, the first systematic treatment of the subject in the nation. Professor R. A. Cooley began his tick research in 1907, looking for a treatment for Rocky Mountain spotted fever.

The students, not unlike young people everywhere, had fun. On one occasion, they led a cow up the four flights of stairs in Montana Hall. On another, a group busily took apart, then re-assembled a Fort Ellis cannon in the middle of the library. The "M," one hundred feet tall and two hundred and forty feet wide, long a symbol of student pride, was first constructed on the face of the Bridgers in October 1915.

In 1930, Una B. Herrick, the college's first dean of women, did not expect trouble when she proposed that young ladies should be in their rooms at eleven

o'clock on weekend nights, rather than midnight. She misjudged the times. There followed an all-campus strike featuring rallies, picket lines, and class boycotts, all happening while President Atkinson was out of town. President Atkinson was still at the helm when another event challenged his somewhat limited sense of humor. The crowning glory of student whimsy led to the publication of the infamous yearbook of 1933. Editor Dave Rivenes met regularly that spring with Atkinson and an advisory committee to plan a yearbook. Unknown to the committee, however, Rivenes, local photographer Chris Schlechten, and a few others laid out an annual with quite a different format. In this version, no campus institution was sacred. As historian Merrill G. Burlingame recalls:

Through the entire book, a bearded shaggy creature in tattered clothes appeared. He was photographed in many situations, through

The college tennis team, 1905.

Mjork and sorority girl.

superimposition, he appeared sprawling on the laps of girls sitting in their sorority living room, peering over the shoulders of students and faculty in impossible situations, playing games with the best of teams, and, being in short, the hero of the school.[9]

When the yearbook went on sale, the campus was in an uproar. Editor Rivenes was placed on probation, his fraternity started proceedings to oust him, and Chris Schlechten was declared persona non grata. The National Association of College Annuals, however, declared the work the most original of 1933. Other awards followed. Today, those fortunate enough to own a copy know they possess an irreplaceable collectors' item.

What the yearbook staff thought of the basketball team of 1933.

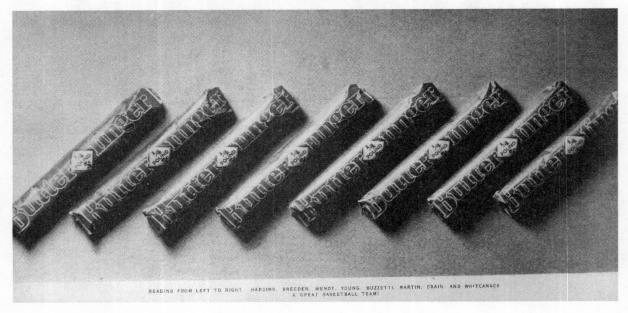

READING FROM LEFT TO RIGHT   HARDING. BREEDEN. WENDT. YOUNG. BUZZETTI. MARTIN. CRAIN AND WHITCANACK
A GREAT BASKETBALL TEAM!

TWENTY-THREE

Although Montana did not accord women the right to vote until 1914, a few Bozeman matrons had been voting along with the men since 1883. Women of property could vote in school elections throughout the valley, but were specifically denied the franchise during the tax assessment election in 1874. Somehow, that restriction was left out of the voting requirements for the incorporation election of March 1883. Word of this omission quietly circulated around town and, as the *Avant Courier* reported, "several prominent ladies of Bozeman, whose names appear on the assessment list, exercised the right of suffrage."[1] A few grumbling males called for annulment of the election or, at least, for the removal of the female votes. Since the final tally for incorporation numbered 123 to 18, the complainers realized that nothing would be accomplished by tracking down the few female voters.

Just as the Women's Christian Temperance Union members were interested in female suffrage in addition to closing down saloons and liquor stores, so did a new Bozeman women's group have a multiple purpose. Established in 1894 with the motto "Our Kingdom is Our Home," the Bozeman State Housekeeper's Society vowed to "encourage and stimulate interest in more scientific methods of housekeeping," as well as studying history, literature, and modern methods of child care. The group of local businessmen's wives—Mariam Skeels Cooper, Ellen Trent Story, Mary Long Alderson, and Nellie Koch—also discussed national women's issues, such as "rational dress" to allow females greater freedom of movement. After all, said Mary Alderson, quoting national feminist leader Celia B. Whitehead, "until woman is allowed to have ankles, there is no hope for her brains."[2]

Bozeman women began to study local and state government, concentrating on voting rights and a new municipal concept—community zoning. They discussed setting aside land for public parks, improving local schools, and encouraging public health. In 1920, another women's group was established. The Women's Club of Bozeman would in a short time become a powerful force in municipal policy.

* * *

In 1865, the shape of Gallatin County was that of a large square block covering most of south-central Montana, one of the largest county units in the nation at that time. Its jurisdiction has been whittled down since then, to its present measures of one hundred and sixteen miles long and from twelve to forty-nine miles wide. The northern part of the county was sliced off to form Meagher County in 1867. To the east, the 1872 legislature carved out Park County; that same year, the U.S. Congress preempted lands to the south and the southeast when it created Yellowstone National Park. Big Horn County had its own government by 1877. Yellowstone County was established in 1883. By 1924, Gallatin County had shrunk and moved west to its present "key" shape, essentially unchanged since 1924.

* * *

Although early Montana did not generally favor jail construction—banishment or instant hanging seemed better alternatives—Gallatin

Lu Sing, sentenced to hang for the murder of Tom Sing in 1906. Evidently, the rope was not adjusted properly; it took fifteen minutes for Lu Sing to expire.

County's first criminals were housed in a drafty log cabin just off Mendenhall and Rouse. A city jail on East Main held municipal offenders, located at the back of the Opera House's lower floor near the janitor's quarters. Two narrow rooms, each with bricked-over windows and a single light bulb hanging from the ceiling, accommodated male prisoners, whose only ventilation was a peephole in the heavy metal doors. Women under arrest were held upstairs.[3]

With the completion of the brick county courthouse in 1881, prisoners occupied a basement cell block next to the sheriff's office. Eventually, a small exercise yard was built at the back northwest corner of the courthouse, surrounded by a brick wall. The *Avant Courier* described it: "A fence around the jail yard is complete. It is of brick, twelve feet high and two feet thick. On the top it is rendered somewhat disastrous for prisoners to scale by having a row of broken glass imbedded in mortar."[4] Both the city and the county jails were crowded and dirty, inadequate to meet even the most basic needs of the prisoners.

The privacy of the accused was casually treated, at least by the *Avant Courier*. When news was sparse, the paper listed guests of the jail, or, during the tenure of Sheriff Charles P. Blakeley, "Brother Blakeley's Boarders." Those awaiting trial were listed according to crime, without the word "alleged"; their home states were also mentioned.[5]

The first legal county hanging occurred in the prisoners' exercise yard behind the courthouse on December 27, 1883. John A. Clark had been arrested and convicted for the robbery and subsequent murder of a prospector at a camp near Trail Creek. Just before the noose was placed around his neck, Clark stated to the sheriff, three guards, and a Presbyterian minister, "I suppose you all know what I am here for . . . I am an innocent man . . . Goodbye to my dear mother in her sunny home."[6] The *Avant Courier* did not spare the reader; each grisly detail of the hanging was chronicled, including the later digging up of Clark's grave, which, the *Courier* supposed, was for the money local physicians would pay to secure a corpse for study purposes.

Twenty-three years would pass before another hanging—that, in 1906, of resident Lu Sing, who was convicted of the murder of laundryman Tom Sing (no relation) with a hatchet. Reported motives for the crime varied: some alleged it was over a woman, either Tom's wife or another; others suggested it was a Tong killing to punish Tom, who had recently cut off his long braid, a first step toward Americanization. Observers noted that Lu Sing appeared to be mentally deranged. Whatever the cause of the murder, the *Avant Courier* celebrated the event with a photograph of Lu Sing, with rather racist commentary describing the killer as "a fat ugly looking specimen of the Celestial kingdom."[7]

The trial was held on November 10, 1905; by the end of the day, the jury pronounced him guilty. Lu Sing was sentenced to hang the following April 7, 1906. Again the prisoners' exercise yard was used.

This time, one hundred and fifty persons, many of whom had received a black-edged invitation to the hanging, witnessed the event, including two waitresses from the Chinese restaurant who, the *Courier* piously stated, "should not have been there."[8] The hanging was more of a strangulation; it took fifteen minutes for Lu Sing to die.

In 1911, Gallatin County officials commissioned young architect Fred Willson to design and supervise construction of a brick jail to be built just west of the courthouse. Willson's plans for a Bastille-like structure took shape in the spring and construction started almost immediately. Just before Christmas of that year, the building was completed; the prisoners moved in, and Willson presented his bill to the commissioners for $33,932.49. The jail was touted as one of the best in the West. Ten days later, however, six prisoners escaped their cells in the early morning hours, ran through an underground tunnel connecting the jail and the courthouse, broke out of the boiler room,

Four high school students take in the sun. The jail is at their left, and the old courthouse is in the background, c1922.
The young man at the right is Frank Cooper, later known to Hollywood as Gary.

and, presumably, left town on one of the trains passing through at dawn. Four of the escapees were eventually apprehended and returned to jail.

The third and last legal hanging in Gallatin County took place on July 18, 1924, inside Fred Willson's Bastille. Auto mechanic and habitual petty criminal Seth Orrin Danner was arrested in June 1923 for the murders of John and Florence Sprouse. Although the crime had been committed three years before, Danner's wife Iva did not immediately come forward. When she did, Mrs. Danner led the sheriff and his men to the Sprouse grave, in which was also buried their little dog. Danner's trial for the murder of Mrs. Sprouse ended with conviction the following October 1923. A prosecution team which included State Attorney Wellington D. Rankin sought conviction for the murder of Mrs. Sprouse only. With Iva Danner as chief witness, Danner was convicted and sentenced to hang. After exhausting a number of appeals to higher courts, he was hanged the following summer, a day

Jack Allen, who died from a criminal's bullet.

Confiscated stills displayed in front of the county jail.

Pomeroy Vreeland had plans for an architectural career before he died trying to subdue a criminal.

after he had converted to the Catholic faith. This time, twenty-two people watched the proceedings, but the hanging itself was shielded by a black curtain.

As elsewhere, law enforcement was not without its casualties. Special Deputy John A. Allen, "Jack" to his friends, had turned thirty-seven when he went to work for newly elected Sheriff William J. Fransham in January 1897. Allen had been the constable at the Marysville gold camp near Helena. For a number of months, two young toughs had terrorized the Belgrade and Manhattan areas with vicious beatings, saloon robberies, and roadside holdups. Sheriff Fransham learned that the two men might be hiding at Carpenter's Ranch, twenty-five miles west of Bozeman in the Cherry Creek basin. Off he went with Jack Allen, confident he could take the two into custody.

When they arrived at the horse ranch, gunfire ensued; Deputy Allen's gun misfired and, unprotected, he was shot in the head. After further exchanges of gunfire with the sheriff, the gunmen rode off. While Fransham came back to Salesville

to organize a larger posse, Dr. Chambliss rode out from Bozeman to attend Allen, bringing him back to Bozeman by horse-drawn ambulance. After many days of agonizing pain and convulsions, Jack Allen died on February 2, 1897. The gunmen were never apprehended.

In 1919, Pomeroy Vreeland was on his way to becoming an architect, as was his father Byron before him; he trained in Fred Willson's office. In October, he signed on as a special deputy sheriff. So had Frank Curtice, a career lawman. Some time later, ranch hand Buford Webb shot his employer Harvey Plumlee after an argument over fifteen dollars in wages. When Vreeland and Curtice went to the ranch to arrest the disgruntled employee, who was hiding in one of the ranch outbuildings, Webb shot and killed them both. One hundred and fifty farmers advanced upon Webb's hiding place and dynamited the structure; he ran outside and was killed from multiple gunshot wounds.

* * *

In 1920, Bozeman and the Gallatin Valley seemed a stable, thriving community. The war was over, the influenza epidemic had abated, population growth was slow but orderly, and abundant crops of potatoes, wheat, and peas promised good times ahead. Nothing appeared to mar the idyllic picture until the 6,183 citizens of the valley's leading community learned that their city government was one-half million dollars in debt.

Bozeman officials had issued numbered warrants that could not be cashed until sufficient municipal funds became available; some of these warrants were five years old. When bond issues to retire the debt failed to attract local banks, council members realized that something drastic would have to be done to pull Bozeman out of bankruptcy. Bozeman had eight council members—two from each of four wards—with a mayor elected at large. Evidently, the members had practiced municipal "pork barrel" politics—"you vote for improvements in my ward and I'll do the same for you"—without considering the overall picture of municipal finance.

In January 1921, Bozeman's new Rotary Club learned about the benefits of the city manager form of government, a relatively new innovation in municipal governance promoted nationwide by the National Short Ballot Organization. Although the city manager form of government was regarded in some circles as radical and untried, Rotary Club members spoke before a number of civic groups to promote it. Council members and Mayor Chester W. Sweet became convinced of its promise. Members of the Chamber of Commerce came to the same conclusion. Opposition to a change in government was quiet but strong, centering in neighborhoods in the north part of the community. Most of the council members lived in homes on Bozeman's south side. Neither the *Daily Chronicle* nor the *Courier* took a stand on the issue. The election was held on June 28, 1921. Out of 3,500 registered voters, only 913 cast ballots. With a plurality of just 35 votes, Bozeman voters chose a commissioner-city manager government, the only one in Montana at that time.

The transition seemed easy at first. Three former council members were elected to the three-person city commission. The highest vote went to

Sam Mendenhall was Bozeman's first city manager.

banker Amos Hall, who became mayor. The next highest vote went to high school principal E. J. Parkin, who garnered a large block of female voters. The third place was won by architect Fred Willson. On January 26, 1922, the three men hired engineer Samuel A. Mendenhall as the first city manager, but evidently the local papers didn't consider it a newsworthy item at the time. Mendenhall kept the former city engineer, fire chief, and health officer in place, but he replaced the police chief and city attorney with—of all things—Democrats. The editor of the *Courier* objected to the new appointments, writing that, surely, there were qualified Republicans available to do the job. Thereupon, a taxpayers' committee appeared before the March 9 commissioners' meeting to object to the city manager's appointments. These skirmishes died down, however, when residents learned that Mendenhall and his appointees had "kept an eye on the cash drawer," that outstanding city warrants had been retired, that operating costs were healthy, and that the police chief had returned to his earlier job as an officer.[9]

When Mendenhall resigned at the end of 1923, the city's debt of $474,002.92 had decreased, although it was not until 1938 that the red ink had moved down to $19,295.90, notwithstanding hard times during the depression. Looking back on this period, the statewide fiscal watchdog magazine *Montana Taxpayer* concluded in 1948 that Bozeman's change to city manager government was praiseworthy:

Having operated through a depression as well as the inflated war and post war years, the city of Bozeman has paid off the entire debt, gained an AA-1 credit rating as a municipality, has built up its services to a place where it ranks with any city of its size in this country, and has accumulated surplus funds for postwar developments.[10]

Despite the growing fiscal health in Bozeman's city government, residents in the Gallatin Valley faced the hard times of the Great Depression long before Wall Street foundered in 1929. Until 1917, "nature was kind" to those growing wheat, with luxuriant rains in May and June, bringing in "the best wheat in the nation." During the month of June 1919, however, a mere .09 inches of rain fell and "the green little town of Bozeman was parched."[11] With the dry summer came hot damaging winds and fires. When precipitation did fall, it was in the form of hail, death to wheat fields and seed peas. For several years, the lack of rain brought farm foreclosures.

During the mid-1920s, the rains returned but, beginning in 1929, drought and the hot winds again prevailed for the next ten years, with the summer of 1936 the hottest on record. Farmers and ranchers also endured periodic scourges of army worms, cutworms, and grasshoppers. Moreover, the blight to seed peas had spread to the Gallatin Valley. By 1935, one-fourth of all Montanans were on relief.

In the early evening of June 27, 1925, a major earthquake, measuring 6.75 on the Richter scale, hit the valley, its epicenter at the northwest corner of the county, severely damaging school and church buildings in Three Forks and Manhattan. Brick chimneys twisted and fell; church bells swung to and fro, ringing wildly. Telephone lines went down.

Those who were on the streets said later that the roads moved in waves like water. The Milwaukee Road tunnel just east of Lombard collapsed. Residents as far away as Butte felt the aftershocks. Some frightened families slept outside in tents for a time. In Bozeman, officials took down the heavy bell from Irving School, fearing another temblor would tumble the tower on students or passersby. Downtown businessmen removed turrets and other ornate motifs decorating their store buildings, leaving them "mute and chastened."[12] The number of damaged commercial buildings, schools, churches, and railroad facilities took a heavy economic toll in the Gallatin Valley.

In addition to earthquakes and grasshopper plagues, a series of floods ravaged the Gallatin Valley. First hit were Maudlow and Amsterdam, heavily flooded in the spring of 1927. The following year, Manhattan streets became waterways during the March thaw.

To make matters even worse, bank failures were

A young farm girl feeds the chickens.

What the earthquake of 1925 did to the high school in Manhattan. F. B. LINFIELD PHOTO.

Three Forks residents take a good look at the nearly demolished Methodist Church.

rampant. Historian Merrill G. Burlingame concluded, "During the war boom state banks had multiplied like rabbits; in the early twenties they collapsed like flies."[13] Manhattan's Home State Bank closed in 1924. Willow Creek's bank had closed the year before. The bank in Belgrade closed in 1932, not to reopen for three years. The Martin and Hall Bank in Bozeman came close to collapse in 1926; it avoided default when other bankers quietly took charge of its assets and liabilities to head off a local banking crisis. James E. Martin told everyone he had decided to get out of the banking business and tend to his sheep herd.

Registration at the college remained relatively healthy, however, throughout the depression. Young people who could not find jobs got an education instead. Upon graduation, their prospects were still slim. Said President Atkinson in 1931, "To be perfectly frank, the outlook for a lot of them is a bit dismal."[14] Of the ninety who earned teaching degrees, not more than thirty got posts. Hardly any of the sixty-five graduating engineers readily found employment. Women with Home Science degrees found jobs in their field scarce.

On the morning of Friday, July 22, 1932, just before ten, two men decided to solve their financial hard times by unusual means. They entered Bozeman's First Security Bank and Trust Company with guns drawn and left four thousand dollars richer, after having forced several bank officers into the vault. The alarm sounded when the bandits sped away in a sporty green Model A roadster with red wire wheels, the top down; within fifteen minutes, every law enforcement agency within two hundred miles knew of the robbery.

It was not long before Pete Karst of the Karst Kamp in Gallatin Canyon phoned Sheriff O. L. DeVore to report that two suspicious men had just bought eight gallons of gas; one had a gun in his lap. Paul Bohart, working as a road patrolman for the Forest Service, hopped on his motorcycle and chased the roadster, dodging bullets as he careened down the highway.

The robbers left their auto, hiked into forest land, ending at the Bud Henke summer cabin near Cinnamon Creek at ten o'clock that evening. They interrupted a congenial card game, demanded that Mrs. Henke prepare food for them, and gave Mr. Henke ten dollars, ordering that he go down to the main road in the morning, buy supplies, and leave

Manhattan streets filled with water during spring flooding, 1928.

them at a specified spot in the woods. This Henke did; on the way down the trail, he met the sheriff's posse. He pleaded with the searchers, "Don't go to the cabin; they will kill my wife and our four guests."

When one of the robbers appeared near the cache of food the next afternoon, he was killed by Seth Bohart, Paul's brother. As the sheriff and his party continued to hike toward the ridge above, the second criminal came out from behind the sagebrush and shot and wounded DeVore in the neck and thigh. Two of the sheriff's deputies then killed the fugitive with rifle blasts. News of the two deaths was not well received by all residents, who felt the bank robbers could have been apprehended without killing them. Even so, the unidentified bodies were laid out at the Dokken funeral home, where crowds passed by to view their remains. A service was held

to note their passing; the room was filled with summer bouquets, most with no cards attached.

* * *

On September 5, 1934, some one hundred and fifty young men marched north from West Yellowstone through Gallatin Canyon to Squaw Creek. With military precision, they quickly built a spike camp of tents and settled in. This was Camp F-57, Company 1963, Missoula District, of the Civilian Conservation Corps (CCC), established by President Franklin Roosevelt and Congress the year before to provide job training for young men whose prospects would otherwise have been slim. The recruits received thirty dollars per month in pay, twenty-five of which was sent home to their families. For some, it was the first time in their young lives

*Seth Bohart poses with the family motorcycle that his brother Paul probably
used to chase the bank robbers up Gallatin Canyon.*

they had eaten properly; they grew taller and gained weight. The men had varying levels of literacy and mechanical skills. It was not long before the camp was called the "University of Squaw Creek," because everyone seemed to be studying: some were learning to read and write; some hoped to pass a sixth-grade proficiency test; others crammed to earn a high school diploma; still others studied university-level courses.

The CCC men first built a two-mile road from their camp to the Squaw Creek Ranger Station—a ten-day effort. Next they replaced their tents with sturdy cabins. They built beds, tables, and chairs to furnish their quarters. By November 1, with snow swirling about them, all had moved in, including three lieutenants, a camp surgeon, and a district ranger. They improved the water supply, constructed

a creosote plant to treat telephone poles, established a sixty-five-mile long copper telephone line, built hiking trails, and developed plans for a new ranger station and a bridge across the Gallatin River. By the end of November, small crews were in the field studying the winter habits of elk and other wildlife or analyzing the fish population.

Within two years, everyone at the Squaw Creek camp could read and write; eighty-eight men had completed their elementary school education; thirty were working toward a high school diploma. Members of the camp orchestra rehearsed regularly, as did glee clubs and dramatic groups. Some of the men met with counselors to put right formerly chaotic lives. In general, the morale was high at Squaw Creek; the men's pride in their work was self-evident. Those who were violently opposed to the

Young Montana men pose in front of spike tents, one of the first constructions by the Civilian Conservation Corps at Squaw Creek.

The Civilian Conservation Corps begins work on a bridge across the Gallatin River, c1935.

Mabel Cruickshank, the first woman to represent Gallatin County in the Montana Legislature.

creation of the Civilian Conservation Corps ended praising the effort. In the 1990s, these veterans of a depression training camp met regularly to renew friendships and reminisce about the days when they were involved in a successful government program.[15]

* * *

In 1936, a small, plumpish, quiet woman decided to run for the Montana Legislature, the first woman in the Gallatin Valley to do so. Mabel Van Meter Cruickshank ran a no-nonsense campaign; she raised no campaign funds and printed no handbills—such things were a foolish expenditure of money, in her opinion. She dressed in shapeless dark blue with modest lace collars that did not call attention to herself. Instead, she went after the votes. Democratic Party officials did place a slate ad in the _Bozeman Daily Chronicle_ during the campaign, in which they assured voters that candidate Cruickshank had not forsaken her homemaking role, "a task she has never stinted."[16]

Females in state office were unusual, but not rare in Montana. Jeannette Rankin had already served her first term as congresswoman representing Montana in Washington, D.C., in 1916. Mrs.

Cruickshank and her carpenter husband Pete settled in Bozeman in 1899. Born in Hudson, Wisconsin, probably in 1872—later on, she shaved three years off her age and said she was born in 1875—she moved to Lisbon, North Dakota, where she met and married Pete. In Bozeman, she reared sons James and John and found time to go back to school at Montana State College, taking courses in music education. She augmented the family income by taking beginning piano students; however, her heart was not in the musical training of Bozeman youngsters. She began to look over other opportunities in the community. Quiet husband Pete Cruickshank was content to stay at home. In fact, he seldom drove the large family car, but sat in the back seat as Mabel chauffeured him about town. She usually drove in the middle of the road at a high rate of speed.

It was not surprising that Mabel Cruickshank easily secured the votes to go to Helena. Working hard in local Democratic politics, she became state committeewoman for Gallatin County. She was active in the Presbyterian Church, in Eastern Star, and in Women of the Shrine. During World War I, she supervised the making of surgical dressings for the Red Cross. She joined the Business and Professional Women's group and served on its state legislative committees.

In 1928, Mrs. Cruickshank became president of the Women's Club of Bozeman, now at the height of its power. One of her concerns was the lack of any zoning commission in Bozeman; construction, she felt, was helter-skelter; there was no protection for existing land use. Just before Christmas 1929, Mrs. Cruickshank and other club members notified the city commission that they expected an immediate draft to establish a zoning commission. Recognizing the prestige of the Women's Club, the

Arnold Swanson and his assistants wait for customers at his service station at East Main and Church Avenue.
Note the Bozeman Hotel and Tilton Building in the background. Also note that gasoline is 24 cents per gallon.

Bozeman continues its musical tradition. Emerson School symphony, 1930s.

commissioners moved on March 7, 1930, perhaps not as quickly as the women required, to establish a zoning ordinance; the resulting commission and a board of adjustment were in place by 1935.

In Helena, Mrs. Cruickshank sponsored Bill 233 to establish adult education schools or classes through the state. It passed, but her Bill 232 to establish nursery schools and kindergartens in Montana did not. Her political career ended when husband Pete suffered a heart attack in July 1938 and she returned from Helena to care for him.

In 1989, a group of Gallatin Valley women, many of whom had succeeded the quiet legislator in office, dedicated a shelter in Kirk Park in her name and planted a tree to memorialize the first woman to win election to represent Gallatin County in the Montana Legislature. ▨

chapter

TWENTY-FOUR

In the late 1930s, Pete Karst helped launch the region's skiing industry from his Cold Spring dude ranch in Gallatin Canyon, now called Karst Kamp. Downhill skiing would spread from Karst's to Bear Canyon east of Bozeman, to the Story Hills, and to Bridger Canyon. Skiing became a mania for many men and women in the Gallatin Valley, as it had in other mountain communities across the nation. Karst pulled out a 2,500-foot-long cable from his idle asbestos mine nearby and threaded it through a pulley attached to a Nash auto engine and up to a bull wheel anchored to a large pine tree at the top of Karst Hill. This became Montana's first tow for downhill skiing.

Local skiers wanted a jump as well. "We built the first jump and we didn't know how the hell to do it," remembered Charles Anceney.[1] In order to figure out how best to improve the construction of the ninety-foot jump, a few of the braver skiers dared to try it. After lying dazed at the bottom of the hill for a time, they pulled themselves up and made suggestions for changes. Lou Bartholomew, the Gallatin Canyon resident who had earlier enjoyed cucumber diets, tried out his seven-foot-long homemade skis on the jump without great success. For the next two years, spectators from around the Gallatin Valley gathered at Karst Hill on the weekends to watch the ski jump exhibitions, despite

temperatures well below zero.

During that time, the Bozeman Ski Club formed and sponsored championship jumps at Karst Hill. Most competitors were novice skiers and made up for lack of experience with theatrical flair, sailing down through the air in loose floppy clothing, waving their arms, as Anceney said, "like you were swimming through the air, clawing at it to show you weren't afraid, you were a Viking."[2] Occasionally, an experienced Norwegian skier would compete at Karst and jump with practiced skill smoothly and simply, without the theatrics. Local skiers learned from watching the veterans.

Kay Widmer remembered the first Sunday afternoon she and husband Gib parked on the road below Pine Hill in the Story Hills to watch "tiny dark figures against the snow. Some were walking up a slope . . . some were gliding down with gentle turns, some were falling."[3] The first downhill skiers used wooden skis that were easily damaged by the many rocks on the trail. Kay and Gib Widmer bought their first pine skis from Montgomery Ward; his cost $7.50, hers cost $5; bamboo poles were $2.50 per pair. It was a herringbone climb to the top of Pine Hill until Adolph Peterson built a short tow up one of the gentler slopes.

Bozeman Fire Department Chief Bill Pentilla skijumped at Karst's, but also helped to develop a

Spectators watch action at the big jump at Karst Hill.

downhill run in Bear Canyon just before the start of World War II. Using another old car motor donated by Adolph Peterson, the Bear Canyon skiers built a rope tow. Each trip up the tow cost twenty-five cents, which some residents thought was a bit high. Realizing that someone should be on hand to help when the novices got in trouble, Pentilla established the Bear Canyon Ski Patrol. In addition to teaching members the usual first aid practices, he also demonstrated how to form a splint for a broken leg with ski poles.

Despite construction of a warming log cabin and other amenities partially funded by the Works Progress Administration in 1938, facilities at these early ski areas were spartan, appealing to the hardy and athletic. Saturday nights found tired skiers around the fireplace, eating chicken and dumplings.

In November 1941, Kay Widmer started to write what would become a regular skiing column

for twelve years in the *Bozeman Daily Chronicle* entitled "Dope on the Slope." Nighttime skiing became popular at Bear Canyon when a number of skiers set out railroad flares to light up at least part of the run. Widmer wrote, "We could see well enough as we were approaching the flares, but the instant we skied past them—complete blackness. Jimmy Livers and Sandy McCracken collided on the dark side of a flare and knocked each other out. They lay unconscious in the snow for some time before someone else skied into them."[4]

It was only a matter of time before a natural snow-filled bowl was discovered by skiers from the air. Barney Rankin and Gib Widmer flew over the Bridger Mountains in May 1948. Above timberline, they saw "a long slope with steep bowls on either side of it."[5] They realized that snows in Bridger Canyon were deeper and more reliable than elsewhere and that it was a natural place for a ski area.

Linda Kundert tries the Bridger ski tow, c1956.

Such a venture seemed out of reach for Bozeman's ski community, but they applied to the state and received six hundred dollars for road construction. By 1954, Bridger Bowl had its own board of directors who, after a number of land transactions and with $6,500 in donations, built a first 2,600-foot-long rope tow which climbed 800 feet up a hill; a tow ticket cost $2 a day for adults and fifty cents for children. Skiers could climb the slopes in 1957 by another rope tow, 1,500 feet long, rising 900 feet. The first chair lift was in operation by 1964. Although state and national competitions met at Bridger Bowl during this period, local residents called the growing development the skiing world's best-kept secret and hoped it would stay that way.

Many of the plans for developing ski slopes in the mountains surrounding the Gallatin Valley were on hold during World War II. Skiers went off to war. Karst Hill fell into disuse during and after the war. The men who served as wranglers and guides at the dude ranches left for military service as well.

Because of the rationing of gas, many of those who operated service stations closed them as they left town to fight in either the European or Pacific theaters. People traded rationing coupons for sugar and shoes.

As elsewhere in the nation, Gallatin Valley residents drew together to support the war effort. Householders saved scrap metal. Children made balls of tinfoil to send to armament factories. As farmers left for boot camps, women took their places in the fields, knowing of the national need for agricultural products. Some left for "Rosie the Riveter" jobs in Seattle factories.

Campus enrollment dropped at Montana State College, despite military cadet and nursing programs. Fraternities closed. Town women rolled bandages for the American Red Cross. Blackout instructions were read with care. Rural electrification programs continued during the war; some areas of Gallatin County received electric power for the first time.

* * *

271

A group of Gallatin County inductees pose in front of the courthouse, May 13, 1942.

Growing urbanization in Bozeman required the services of city planner S. R. DeBoer of Denver in the late 1950s. By 1940, 21.8 miles of Bozeman streets had been paved; in ten years that mileage would climb to 31.1 miles, a 43 percent rise. New sewers increased by 12.3 miles leading to the first sewage treatment plant, built in 1948 for $300,000. In 1957, more reservoirs were completed to serve growing miles of water mains to new residences. The fight over the fluoridation of Bozeman's drinking water ended in 1953 when a ballot, mailed with residents' water bills, was returned with a favorable vote. From 1940 to 1950, the population of Bozeman rose seven percent, from 8,665 to 11,325. In 1960, the number of residents rose again to 13,400, a jump of 2,000, or 15 percent.

With the rise of population, the city budget grew dramatically; from 1950 to 1957, yearly funds totaling $850,000 were allocated. The 1958 budget mushroomed to $2.7 million. Planner DeBoer stated that, given the beauty of the Gallatin Valley, population was certain to boom even higher;

planning for growth would be a wise investment. A zoning ordinance had been in place since 1935 and a planning board selected in 1957, but DeBoer must have gone back to Denver frustrated. Although the signs of future acceleration of growth were evident, few expressed their concern.

Seven police officers protected Bozeman residents in 1940; they had one cruiser, but it did not have a radio. If an emergency occurred after 10 P.M. and before 8 A.M., someone called the telephone operator to detail the nature of the problem; after hearing what was wrong, the operator would throw a switch controlling three colored light bulbs located on Main Street—one in front of the Opera House, another near the phone company on North Tracy, and the third in front of the Baxter Hotel—in hopes that the lone officer on night duty would pass by the glowing lights and call his dispatch. Twenty years later, the force had grown to thirteen men and three radio-equipped cruisers. The department now owned cameras and fingerprint equipment.

By 1940, Bozeman no longer relied on a volunteer fire department; its chief and six firefighters were paid, but twenty-four volunteers helped with larger fires. Their equipment consisted of one hose truck and a chemical wagon, which answered some one hundred fire calls each year. Twenty years later, thirteen professional firefighters were on duty, but the volunteer group, which had fought fires since the 1880s and was a dominant part of Bozeman's social fabric, was forced to disband when Bozeman became a first-class city. By state law, only professional firemen could be employed. Three additional mobile units had been added, each with a pumper; one truck carried a seventy-five-foot aluminum ladder. The chief drove a station wagon which was also equipped to fight fires.

In 1953, city residents were shocked to learn that municipal cashier Donald L. Henry had embezzled $82,052.91. After his arrest, most of the misappropriated funds were replaced either by him or by bonding companies.

After years of knowing that the decaying Opera House could not continue to house all municipal facilities, Bozeman commissioners presented a $986,001 bond issue to voters in 1961, which called for the construction of new city offices, separate police and fire stations, a city shop, and a parks and cemetery building. The measure failed. The commissioners tried again at another election held later that year. This time the bond issue was reduced to $753,646, most of which was earmarked for a municipal building. Again, the measure failed. Three

The old in contrast to the new. The foundation is in place for the new Art Deco Willson School, 1937.
Soon to be torn down is Nelson Story's mansion.

273

years later, a third bond issue for $475,000 to build a city hall passed by only 779 votes. With land on the northeast corner of Main Street and Rouse Avenue acquired through a trade, the commissioners built a no-nonsense square building and dedicated it on June 29, 1966. That same year, the Opera House came down and a park was established in its place.

As in other parts of the country, Art Deco and Art Moderne became the preferred architectural styles in Bozeman. Fred Willson designed a county courthouse to replace the old brick building; built with some funding from the Works Progress Administration, the Art Deco structure was dedicated in 1936. Willson also designed four schools, partially funded by the WPA, despite some local reluctance to accept federal money. Willson School was completed in 1937; the building was located just yards from Nelson Story's ornate mansion, which was razed the following year to provide a playground for the school. Irving School was finished in 1939; Hawthorne and Longfellow Schools, formerly of brick, also were rebuilt as flat-roofed Art Moderne structures.

The Baxter Hotel, another Fred Willson design, was already a landmark. Dedicated in 1929, the elegant building cost $300,000 to construct. Its distinctive electric roof sign, thirty-two feet high and forty-two feet wide, costing $3,600, was to serve as a beacon for travelers throughout the countryside. (Today, winter visitors may wonder about a flashing blue light located just below the giant sign. It is turned on when snow has fallen in Bridger Bowl within the last twenty-four hours.)

* * *

Since World War I, Gallatin Valley fairgoers had watched with awe and some fear as stunt pilots performed high above them. Air hero Charles A. Lindbergh visited Butte and Helena in 1927, and the accompanying enthusiasm for air travel spread to Bozeman and the Gallatin Valley. A modest airfield to serve the region, however, seemed out of reach. Local businessmen and military groups talked to city and county commissioners about developing an airport. The U.S. Department of Commerce sent a representative to Bozeman in July 1928, as it was doing throughout the nation, to talk to local officials about the establishment of a local airfield. It seemed

poor timing, considering the financial hard times for many residents who worried about enough food and clothing for their families.

In the fall of 1927, E. A. Stiefel and E. R. Kahla decided that a parcel of land one-half mile north of Belgrade seemed ideal for a regional airport. It was flat with a gravel base and few springs to muddy landing strips; moreover, less snow fell there, making its removal less of a problem. The site was reasonably close to Bozeman.

While Stiefel and Kahla were completing their plans, Wayne Siefert graded a modest airstrip southwest of Belgrade. He and other local men removed rocks from the new air strip and loaded them into wheelbarrows to prepare for the dedication of Siefert Airport on April 21, 1928. Three thousand people came to watch the ceremonies, which included 675 five-minute rides in one of four airplanes. Siefert took in $2,500 that day. But when federal officials visited the little airfield to determine whether it was suitable for mail delivery, they noted high-tension lines nearby and decided it was too dangerous for regular mail flights.

Meanwhile, Stiefel and Kahla had rented the site north of Belgrade from the state for seventy-five dollars per year. More loading of rocks into wheelbarrows was necessary to grade six runways, each one hundred feet wide and about a thousand yards long. On April 20, 1929, another dedication took place with eight thousand people on hand to marvel at the new airport's rotating beacon, the only one operating in Montana's thirteen airports at that time. For two days, enough autos collected around the airport to produce Gallatin Valley's first traffic jam. Visitors cheered marching bands, parade floats, and stunt aviators. Despite a more advantageous position, Stiefel and Kahla could not persuade federal officials to designate their airfield suitable for airmail delivery, either.

On the afternoon of January 10, 1938, a Northwest Airlines transport plane, on its way west from Billings to Spokane, crashed and burned in Bridger Canyon's rugged terrain, one-half mile west of the Flaming Arrow Ranch. This was the first air crash in Montana history; all ten people aboard died, and the mail pouches were charred. The bodies and debris had to be carried out by sled.

That same year brought renewed federal

All that's left of the Northwest Orient Airlines plane that crashed in the Bridgers in 1938.

Lynch Flying Service trained air cadets from Montana State College.

An early hangar at Gallatin Field.

interest in developing a regional airport in the Gallatin Valley. The pending world war required the training of pilots throughout the country. With the cooperation of Montana State College, an air cadet program was launched in 1940, with John Lynch of Lynch Flying Service as chief trainer. By October 1940, a city-county airport board was in place; its first members included Dean Chaffin, E. R. Anderson, Gardner Waite, Eric Therkelson, and Bozeman mayor Frank Hoey. Bozeman's city commissioners bought 354 acres from the Ponderosa Pine Company near Belgrade for $15,000, the first expenditure for the future Gallatin Field. By 1941, the site had grown to 1,200 acres. The federal government provided $397,851 to build the air field.

Even though the new airport administrators operated from a Quonset hut, another dedication occurred on October 11, 1942, which included a wagon train parade and chuckwagon breakfast. A half-mill levy assessed in May 1942 would bring in $7,087 each year to maintain the airport—$1,500 from Bozeman, $87.50 from Belgrade, and $5,500 from the county. A successful bond issue in November 1944—it carried two-to-one—allowed the Airport Board to build an administration building for $104,044, which was completed in June 1951 and dedicated with an elegant dinner at the

Gallatin Gateway Inn, costing each diner $2.50.

On June 22, 1947, Northwest Airlines inaugurated its first regular passenger flight to Gallatin Field. On board was copilot C. R. Kahla, whose father had dreamed of air service to the Gallatin Valley twenty-four years before. (Freight had been handled by Gallatin Field for some years. A runway could handle the landing of the first jet in 1967.)

As was true in other parts of the country, the fortunes of airlines grew and railroad passenger traffic declined. In 1974, a two-mill levy was proposed and the resulting $4 million bond issue passed, providing funds for a terminal, new roads, taxiways, and aprons. In 1978, the present air terminal was completed. Stone for the facade of the new building was quarried in the Portal Creek area of Gallatin Canyon. When artist Jim Dolan submitted his sculptures of ten geese in flight to the Airport Board, the Gardner Waite family provided the money to buy the distinctive art. In 1982, the terminal received an award of excellence from the Montana branch of the American Institute of Architects. The Federal Aviation Administration also gave an award for the design of the terminal. In the 1990s, Gallatin Field expanded its facilities to accommodate the growing tourist trade.

The Airport Board acted as a separate body to

On hand to welcome the first commercial flight into Gallatin Field, June 22, 1947 are members of the Airport Board, the Bozeman Chamber of Commerce, and Northwest Airlines personnel.

oversee the airports at Three Forks and West Yellowstone. Three Forks' first airport was located southwest of Old Town, operating at that location during the 1920s and 1930s. By the late 1940s, a new Three Forks airfield developed called Pogreba Field, named to honor airman Dean Pogreba, who flew during World War II, the Korean conflict, and the Vietnam war, where he was declared missing in action. The airport at West Yellowstone is open only in the summer.

* * *

A number of Bozeman businesses have kept their doors open down through the years, which has contributed to financial stability in the area. Perhaps the oldest business house still in operation is Waite and Company, an insurance and real estate firm. Founded in 1880 by E. M. Gardner, who adopted a covered wagon and team as his trademark, the company received its customers at 5 East Main Street. P. C. Waite joined the firm in 1908, followed by E. J. Parkin in 1920. Gardner C. Waite began his

career in the insurance company in 1931.

In 1866, Willson and Rich sold general supplies to its local customers, extending its business to other towns and mining camps with a string of loaded mule trains. Eventually, the firm became The Willson Company, dealing in dry goods, located at 105 East Main Street, northeast corner. At first, the Willson Company employed only men; slowly it added women to its sales force. By 1915, the company had from twenty-four to thirty employees, who served customers from 8 A.M. to 6 P.M., except on Saturday, its busiest day, when the store remained open until 9 P.M. to accommodate farmers and ranchers, some of whom came to town by train. Willson's became McDonald's department store in 1955, which in turn closed its doors in the late 1970s.

Benepe and Davidson opened for business in 1879, featuring a wide array of general merchandise; that same year, Frank L. Benepe, Sr., bought out Davidson, and began to specialize in hardware. E. J. Owenhouse, who had been repairing saddles

277

for the Fort Ellis men in the 1880s, joined Benepe in the hardware business in 1890. Benepe Owenhouse Company also stocked farm machinery by 1892. Business arrangements were more casual in the 1890s. For example, in July 1891, Owenhouse received a letter from William Ennis, resident of the Madison County town which bore his name: "Please send me two pair of fly nets. Cotton. Large size. Send in morning if possible by coach. Please send bill of all I owe and I will send you a check.... I wish you would tell Phillip Dodson to send me a case of good lemons. And I'm obliged. It is awful hot here."[6]

When Swiss brewer Julius Lehrkind came to Bozeman in 1892, he bought the Bozeman Brewing Company from Spieth and Krug, moving the business from East Main Street to North Wallace Avenue and Plum in order to be closer to the railroad. He built a handsome brick building to house the brewery and other financial interests; for a time, it was the largest building in Bozeman. Next to the brewery, Lehrkind built the family residence, a Queen Anne brick structure with bays, turrets, colored and leaded glass, and multiple rooflines. The onset of Prohibition forced the Lehrkind family to invest in other businesses such as the Lehrkind Coal and Pure Ice Company. After repeal, the Lehrkinds resumed producing Old Faithful Beer and lagers, eventually turning to the soft drinks industry, which is the firm's main source of revenue today.

Bozeman grocer Michael Langohr started growing lettuce and other vegetables as a hobby next to the family home at 315 South Tracy in 1881. Even though he served as a ranger with the Forest Service, Langohr had time to expand his South Tracy operation. He and his son Don built additional greenhouses to grow more vegetables and flowers for the retail trade. Don Langohr, Jr., continued to expand the nursery until he sold it outside the family in 1979. The business still exists under the name of Langohr's Flowerland.

Phillips Book and Office Supply Store started business in 1892 under the name of Gallatin Book and Stationery Company. In 1897, Sherman G. Phillips and Augustus G. Ryon, former president of the new college, became partners in the venture. One of their specialties was the sale of a typewriter with an unlikely name—the Blickensderfer.

That same year, in 1892, Squire C. Kenyon bought the Pray Lumber Company from George Flanders, the man who had supplied Fort Ellis with wood in the 1880s from his sawmill on Middle Creek. In 1906, the firm became Kenyon-Noble. When the company bought a truck in 1918, it offered free wood and coal delivery to its customers.

Jeweler Henry A. Pease started his firm in 1864 in Virginia City, selling watches and bits of finery to the miners, until he relocated in Bozeman in 1882 and took in partner Claude P. Steffens. In 1945, the business was acquired by Miller's Jewelry, which still operates at 2 East Main Street.

Long a Main Street institution, the Bungalow opened in 1912 at 14 West Main Street as a confectionery and drugstore. It quickly became a gathering place for generations of young people, who dawdled over root beer floats, Green Rivers, and banana splits. The Bungalow was redecorated in the 1940s in the popular Art Deco style. A series of large black-and-white photographs of regional scenes—some were ten feet long—covered the walls. (Some of these photographs are now on display at the Pioneer Museum on West Main Street.) The Bungalow continued to serve confections from its old fashioned soda fountain until it closed in 1994.

In the early 1930s, discouraged by financial hard times, twenty-one local dairy farmers and others formed the Gallatin Cooperative Creamery, hoping to benefit by pulling together to market their products. After looking over several locations for the creamery, they contacted the Milwaukee Railroad to rent its empty passenger depot to house dairy equipment for the yearly rent of three hundred twenty five dollars. Almost immediately, the dairy men were successful. They sold milk to Wilcoxson's in Livingston, which made ice cream; they sold dairy products to Yellowstone National Park and to the CCC. Butter, at thirty-five cents per pound, went to Seattle. By 1941, 239 dairymen were members of the cooperative. Six years later, the cooperative bought the Jersey Dairy and marketed its products under the label "Gallatin Gold" and, later, "Darigold." Today, the cooperative is the largest milk producer in Montana.

On the last day of January 1945, a group of livestock men met at the Baxter Hotel to discuss how they might bring together agricultural interests

278

Art Deco comes to the Bungalow. Many of the photographs that hung at this popular fountain are now displayed at the Pioneer Museum.

once each year and focus on businesses that contributed to the farming and ranching economy throughout the state. The resulting Bozeman Livestock Show Association set up a tent to house their festivities that year, which nearly collapsed in a heavy spring snowstorm. By 1947, the event had a new name—the Montana Winter Fair. Each year, in either January or February, events were scheduled to take advantage of a warm spell during the middle of winter. Sometimes it worked. With 1.5 percent set aside from each year's receipts, a building fund accrued so that a number of exhibition halls were constructed on the Gallatin County Fairgrounds to house needlework exhibits, artwork, wood carving, photograph contests, bake-offs, and booths where business houses displayed the latest in equipment.

People from all over the state participated in hoedowns, cabarets, stage shows, fiddle competitions, and turkey shoots. Farmers competed for champion ribbons for the best in dairy cows,

swine, sheep, horses, rabbits, and beef animals. One woman from each county displayed her skills in sewing, cooking, and flower arrangement to vie for the title of Mrs. Montana. The Montana Winter Fair of the 1990s still offers prizes for the best cake, candy, jams and jellies. New breeds of domesticated animals appear in the show barns each year, most recently, llamas.

* * *

The Big Horn Gun, resting in front of the county courthouse, made its presence known again during the early morning hours of March 20, 1957. Unknown persons loaded a tin can with explosive powder and a slow burning foot-long fuse, shoved it into the cannon, lit the fuse, then melted into the darkness at 12:38 A.M. The resulting blast tumbled Sheriff Don Skerritt and his deputy out of bed at the jail next to the courthouse and wakened many residents in the area. Was it a defective boiler, or

279

Snow can't stop the Montana Winter Fair, 1952. Bob Overstreet (at left), Judge Wilbur Spring, Jr. (at right).

Handler Gib Rehm displays two champion steers, 1953. CHRIS SCHLECHTEN PHOTO.

4-H groups from around the state compete at Farm Bureau Hoedown at Romney Gym, 1953.
CHRIS SCHLECHTEN PHOTO.

Al Malmborg wins the 1954 contest for Old Time Fiddlers. Jack Lutes is on guitar.

Bozeman candidates for Mrs. Montana smile for the camera, 1956. 7-unidentified; 8-Ethel Hamilton; 9-Helen Buckmaster (Joe); 10-Marie Ridder; 11-Marie Buckley (Art); 12-Jeri LaPalme (Jules). 6-The winner, Ann McCormick Ayers (Dan); 5-Doris Seibel Brew; 4-Barbara Burnett; 3-unidentified; 2-Aileen Burke Crouse, (Lester); 1-Elizabeth Spring Lemon. BURGESS PHOTO.

Visiting is an important part of the Winter Fair. Left to right: Tom Lehman, Bob Metcalf, and Bud Burkhart.

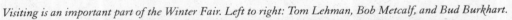

had a safe been cracked open?

After hours of exploration, police officers discovered broken windows at the courthouse and nine shattered panes across the street at the old Gallatin County High School. The burned fuse was found lying on the school lawn. To prevent another midnight blast, the sheriff's men filled the bore of the Big Horn Gun with cement. Years later, any number of men smiled at the memory of the midnight blast, but no one has come forward to admit to the deed. In 1994, the Big Horn Gun found a new home at the Pioneer Museum; rancher Don Weibert supervised the rebuilding of a carriage for the old cannon and the cement was drilled from its bore.

* * *

Monday, August 17, 1959, had been a busy day for dude ranches in the Gallatin and Madison Canyons. Guests relaxed after a day of hiking, fishing, or seeing the sights on horseback. Eighteen thousand visitors to Yellowstone Park had picked up their nighttime reservations; fishermen dotted the Madison and Gallatin Rivers until dark, when they climbed the banks to return to their cabins; campers filled three Forest Service sites in the Hebgen Lake area, peacefully sitting around their campfires, enjoying an unusually bright moonlit night. Shortly before midnight, at 11:37 P.M., an earthquake hit the area, rattling southwest Montana, central Idaho, and northwest Wyoming, the third most severe temblor experienced in the United States to date, measuring 7.8 on the Richter scale.

At Hebgen Lake in the narrow Madison Valley, the force of faults moving during the quake rocked and tilted the lakebed eighteen feet to the northeast, forming a series of seiches, which have been described as water violently sloshing in a jiggling saucer. This agitated water roared down the seven-mile stretch of Hebgen Lake and, on at least four occasions, leaped to a height of thirty feet over the earth-filled Hebgen Dam. The dam itself dropped more than nine feet. At about the same time, one half of a 7,600-foot mountain located six miles below

The Big Horn Gun after its third known renovation. On exhibit at the Pioneer Museum, Bozeman.

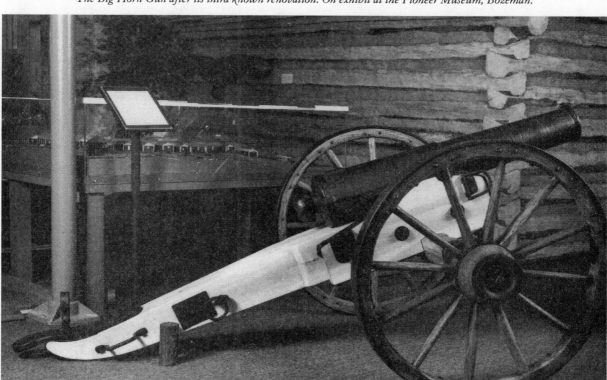

the dam crashed down upon the canyon to dam the Madison River, and "cascaded, like water, up the opposite canyon wall, hurtling house-size quartzite and dolomite boulders onto the lower portion of Rock Creek Campground."[7]

Thirty-eight to fifty million cubic yards of rock piled up in the canyon in less than a minute, covering a mile of both river and highway from one hundred to three hundred feet deep. The roar of the earthquake could be heard throughout the Gallatin Valley. Aftershocks continued every five minutes throughout the night. Roads leading to West Yellowstone broke apart; boulders moaned, then crashed down to cover roadways in the park.

Seventy-year-old Grace Miller, a widow who ran the Hilgard Fishing Lodge on the north shore of Hebgen Lake, woke with the first shock, wrapped herself in a blanket, kicked open her jammed front door, and jumped over a widening five-foot crevice just as her house slid into the lake. Grover C. Maults, seventy-one, and his wife Lillian, sixty-eight, were asleep in their trailer at the Rock Creek Campground when they awoke with the first jolt. It's bears, they thought; no, it's an earthquake. The trailer catapulted into the rising creek and the couple climbed to its roof as they began to float downstream. Grover Maults grabbed at a tree limb and hoisted Lillian to the branch just as the trailer swept away. There they spent the night, nearly covered with cold water, surrounded by the roar of avalanches, violent winds, and a thunderstorm. The bright moonlight was darkened by dust and flying debris. At eight o'clock the next morning, the frightened and exhausted couple was picked up by

Where the mountain fell, August 17, 1959. The rubble below is a graveyard for those who perished. Quake Lake is beginning to form, slowly drowning trees. On a hillside are the remains of a campsite left in a hurry. DOROTHY NILE PHOTO.

boat; they were hardly able to move their arms and legs, which had been numbed from clinging to the tree.

At West Yellowstone, many residents were thrown from their beds; those out strolling at that late hour found it difficult to walk on the rolling roadways. Guests at the Baxter Hotel in Bozeman nervously collected in the lobby after the first tremor. At the north edge of the park at Mammoth, Superintendent Lemuel A. Garrison was reading in bed. As brick chimneys and rock tumbled about, he put his uniform coat over his pajamas and got his wife and daughter out of the house. They could hear coyotes howl with each aftershock. Park employees were staging a beauty contest that night; Miss Old Faithful had just been crowned when the quake hit. Seven hundred and fifty guests at Old Faithful Inn spent the rest of the night huddled in

their cars or in the park buses.

Telephone service and electricity were out, but ham radio operators almost immediately gave the news to the outside world. A few rescuers started toward what was left of Rock Creek Campground on horseback. Just before dawn, Bozeman radio executive William Merrick, Sheriff Don Skerritt, and flying service owner Al Newby took off from Gallatin Field in a single-engine Cessna 172 four-seater to assess the damage and take pictures. When they flew over Hebgen Dam, they could see it was still intact; in fact, survivors had printed with stones on the top of the dam, "OK SOS." But the road entry at Duck Creek leading to West Yellowstone was now a giant rift. As they passed over what was left of Rock Creek campground, a small forlorn group waved at them. Merrick remembers seeing a few campers searching the rocks for either survivors

The remains of Grace Miller's house. GENE BROOKS PHOTO.

285

or their belongings. Since there was no way to get to these people by road, Merrick suggested that the Forest Service be contacted to order smokejumpers to the area.

Soon, eight smokejumpers equipped with first-aid supplies parachuted into the canyon to locate the injured and survey the damage. Back in Bozeman, Merrick prepared a story for radio station KBMN, which was broadcast to one hundred and sixty stations across the country. Photographs of the event were sent to *Life* magazine, which published the earthquake story on August 31, 1959.[8]

All during the day of August 18, sheriffs, rangers, construction men, firemen, military men, nurses, doctors, and Red Cross workers appeared at West Yellowstone and at Bozeman to help the wounded and calm frightened children. All in all, some three hundred people came out from the Madison Canyon; those requiring emergency care were airlifted by helicopter to the West Yellowstone Airport and then to Bozeman Deaconess Hospital, or hospitals in Butte, Anaconda, Livingston, and Idaho. An accurate number of fatalities has never been determined, but it is generally agreed that twenty-eight or twenty-nine visitors known to be camping in the area have never been accounted for. Others may have perished as well. When it was over and the aftershocks had subsided, all were relieved to learn that a damaged Hebgen Dam continued to hold. Below the dam a new body of water formed, later aptly named Quake Lake. Crews began clearing rocks, trees, and debris from roads inside and outside the park. Naturalists came to study the changes in both new and old thermal features. Since the earthquake of 1925 centered north of the Gallatin Valley and the earthquake of 1959 centered to the south, scientists regard the region as prone to major temblors. ▦

chapter

TWENTY-
FIVE

During the 1960s and 1970s, Bozeman City Commission meetings grew longer and longer. The review of subdivision after subdivision, which they approved with little opposition, occupied the commission's time. In 1975, city planner Paul Bolton told a small audience that, in other parts of Montana, communities had begun to fight subdivisions built on agricultural lands. He added, somewhat disparagingly, "But in Bozeman, I have never seen a subdivision request denied. I guess what it takes to stop leapfrog development is gutsy people."[1]

By 1970, the city limits had expanded with the annexation of 1,390 acres, as well as some additional 300 acres acquired by the college. Bozeman had almost doubled its area since 1960, from 2,640 acres to more than 5,000. Five hundred and sixty city acres had been carved into 840 lots. In addition, just outside the city boundaries, 180 acres were divided into 360 lots. Commissioners wrestled with the paving of new streets and sidewalks to these subdivisions, as well as extension of streetlights and other services. To handle the heavier workload, membership on the commission increased from three to five in 1970, and the first city-county planner was hired.

No longer did West Main Street end in open country at Ninth Avenue. On North Seventh Avenue, two rows of young ash trees, planted to beautify a major entrance to the city, were removed when the street required widening. Farther out in the valley, more and more farmland turned into subdivisions. From 1971 to 1975, population growth within Bozeman rose four to five percent; in the "planning area," however, that land lying within a four-and-a-half mile radius from the city limits, population rose eighteen percent, with four thousand acres of farmland turned into housing tracts.

* * *

Problems with the right to divert water in the Gallatin Valley continued to plague water court judges, the Montana Supreme Court, and the users who came before them. Since settlement, water law had muddled along, generally favoring the Doctrine of Prior Appropriation, "first in time, first in right," until 1921, when Helena resident Anna Mettler sued the Ames Realty Company, claiming her right to divert water because it flowed by her property. When the Montana Supreme Court heard the case, it decided against Mrs. Mettler, stating, "Our conclusion is that the common law doctrine of riparian rights has never prevailed in Montana since the enactment of the Bannack Statutes in 1865, and that it is unsuited to the conditions here. . . ."[2]

Many local ranchers and farmers and their

287

descendants had been diverting water to their lands from the Madison, Gallatin, or East Gallatin Rivers, Middle Creek, or their tributaries since the beginning of settlement by way of ditches they had dug themselves. They reckoned their right to divert water by the Doctrine of Prior Appropriation according to the seniority of their claims. Ditch companies figured their right from the time the canal was first dug, not when it was completed. Some of these families holding senior rights did not register their claims, however, assuming that everyone in the valley knew whose right came first.

As the region filled with more and more would-be irrigators, the Montana Legislature, feeling that "the Territory is now getting too old and too thickly settled for such important matters to be left to the memory of the settlers,"[3] passed a bill in 1883 to require registration of prior rights, but Governor John S. Crosby vetoed it, stating the law could lead to water exploitation. John M. Robinson, an irrigator on Middle Creek, was outraged enough with the governor's veto to seek and win election to the legislature in 1885, where he offered a similar bill which passed, but this time without a veto.

With provision for a state engineer or a water court to determine what irrigator could have how much water during each growing season, however, the farmer still relied on county registration or a casual posted notice of his early right to divert water. When a neighbor also claimed the same water, a not-uncommon situation during years of drought, all interested parties would go to court, present their claims, and a judge would adjudicate rights to divert water based on the seniority of claim. Many local ranchers thought adjudication a costly and unnecessary expense. John Robinson and his Middle Creek neighbors probably spent thirteen thousand dollars to prove up their rights. Lawyers charged what ranchers thought were exorbitant fees to adjudicate water rights.

Many fights over water rights in the Gallatin Valley ended in violence or court action or both. But altercations between Joseph M. Lindley and Nelson Story, as historian Merrill G. Burlingame concluded, had their "comic opera episodes."[4] Both men were real estate developers, in addition to other and varied pursuits. Lindley owned acres southeast

of Lindley Place, called the Ice Pond area, just south and west of Church Avenue, including major rights to Bozeman Creek water.

Nelson Story wanted to divert water from Bozeman Creek to Mill Creek to power his flour mill north of Main Street. He ordered some of his men to cut down large cottonwood trees lining Bozeman Creek to effectively dam it. Not only did the cottonwoods dam the creek, but the resulting jam forced water to flood East Main Street and much of Joseph Lindley's land.

An angry Lindley hired blacksmith James Pratt to make a bomb which he hoped would blast out the cottonwood dam. When the bomb did not explode, Lindley ordered some of his employees to chop out the offending trees. An irate Story arrived at the site and proceeded to club some of the woodchoppers with his dragoon Colt 44 revolver. Shortly thereafter, he was forced to pay the men for damages in order to avoid suits, a not unusual occurrence for Nelson Story, whose short temper often landed him in court.

Lindley further enraged Story by posting notes on downtown telephone poles which described banker Story's less attractive attributes in violent language. Story returned the compliment by adding his own profane evaluations of Lindley's character. On one occasion, while Lindley was nailing his most recent missive to a pole in front of the bank, Story dumped a pailful of water on him from the second floor. On another occasion, after a violent shouting match, Story chased Lindley down Main Street with the intention of cane-whipping him, as he had assaulted Dr. Foster a few years before. But the fleet-footed Lindley evaded him by running in the front door of the Phillips store and out the back. The two developers continued to fight over water rights, in court and out.

Until well into the 1970s, Gallatin Valley ranchers and farmers with early water rights fought any legislative attempt to centralize statewide regulations on water diversion, fearing that their senior right advantage might be lost. With passage of the Water Use Act of 1973, and its amendments passed in 1979, Montana finally achieved a central role in water use. Water users throughout the state were obliged to re-register their claims to divert water. Gallatin County District Court Judge W. W.

Lessley became the first chief Montana Water Court judge and spent the rest of his life attempting to address the complex issues regarding seniority. When Judge Lessley died in 1990 at the age of eighty-two, Bruce Loble took his place as Chief Water Judge to continue the task of unraveling the tangled threads of water rights.

About ten percent of Bozeman water users still depend on surface diversion of Lyman Creek, the first water supply acquired by the City of Bozeman one century ago. It is conveyed to a reservoir by means of an eighteen-inch cast-iron intake pipe, where it is treated with chlorine and fluoride. As Bozeman grew, the city acquired rights to divert water from Bozeman Creek in 1917. By 1922, shares of reservoir water from Mystic Lake increased water supplies, which flowed down Bozeman (Sourdough) Creek to Sourdough Reservoir at the mouth of Bozeman Creek Canyon. In 1976, however, a sinkhole developed on the face of Mystic Dam's right abutment, and the city was forced to partially breach the dam at that site six years later. The City of

President Roland R. Renne guided the fortunes of Montana State College from the post-war years to 1964.

Bozeman also stores water in the Middle Creek (Hyalite) Reservoir, which is used mainly during summer months. Water from these sources is treated with chlorine and fluoride at a newly expanded water treatment facility, one-half mile south of Nash Road.

* * *

When Montana State College became Montana State University in July 1965 (the last land grant institution in the nation to become a university), the action was not merely a change of name. Twenty years of expanding the campus and broadening the curricula had preceded the move, an "extraordinary transformation," concluded the three authors of the university's most recent history.[5]

This effort was largely the work of Roland R. Renne, who served as college president from 1943 to 1964. Just after World War II, enrolled students numbered a modest 1,155. Twenty years later, 5,250 students took classes at a university whose faculty had grown from 132 to 389 and whose campus acreage had doubled. Although Renne's accomplishments were many, he attracted substantial controversy, partly because of his strong leadership, partly because he was "politically contentious," and partly because of his willingness to undertake projects offensive to some of Gallatin Valley's conservative community.[6]

In the years shortly before his presidency, a number of county residents drew together to form a group opposed to the use of federal money for any local project, university or otherwise, a far cry from those early Bozeman merchants who welcomed funds from the federal treasury. When the Chamber of Commerce and the *Bozeman Daily Chronicle* recommended in 1936 that the county courthouse be replaced with the present Art Deco structure, partially using federal money, Bozeman was flooded with flamboyantly written handbills distributed by the Committee for Opposition of Courthouse Bonds: "Has the *Bozeman Daily Chronicle* become so arrogant and selfish, that it sees nothing and hears nothing but the ring of the cash register. Has it become a self-styled political organ and recognizes no master but the Bozeman Chamber of Commerce, and a willing tool to place greater tax burdens on the faithful patrons of the soil."[7] Doubtless, these same citizens were dismayed in 1940 when Renne, as president of the local school board, successfully obtained federal funds to help build new Hawthorne, Irving, and Longfellow Schools.

At war's end, Renne anticipated higher enrollments, as veterans returned for further schooling. Montana State College needed more classrooms, more places for single and married students to live, and a broadening and strengthening of its courses. President Renne reviewed the curricula with a critical eye. They were too narrow, he said, "turning out agricultural students who slaughter the English language, home economists who can't spell, and engineers who have had so little biology that they do not know . . . how or why they are born."[8] With federal money, the new thirty-eight-year-old president assembled makeshift classrooms as well as trailers, barracks, and Quonsets for student housing. He began to interview for additional faculty; applicants knew ahead of time, however, that salaries were low and teaching schedules heavy.

With state surplus funds, a new $400,000 library was built in 1948. That same year, a Montana State Legislature-recommended mill levy raise and a $5 million bond issue to build permanent additional university classrooms was approved by the voters; construction finally began in 1952 on the first permanent classrooms to be built since 1927. With another successful bond issue, passed in 1954, residence halls were built, as well as additions to the student union building—a bowling alley, a small theater, a health unit, and a larger bookstore. The bond issue was repaid from revenues collected from these new enterprises. During the late 1950s and early 1960s, more buildings sprouted on the expanding campus, including Reid Hall, a dairy center, a medical-science research building, more residence halls, a library addition, and a fieldhouse.

Although President Renne ran the campus as what has been characterized as a "one-man show," he was reluctant to expand overnight liberal arts programs from service-centered to full status because of the expected wrath from the University of Montana at Missoula, which objected to a name change for the "cow college." Instead, he concentrated on a Department of Education for teacher training, a reconstituted School of Business, and a doctoral program in chemistry and chemical engineering. He instituted classes in geography,

geology, agricultural engineering, industrial arts, architecture, and military science. When Roland Renne left the college for an unsuccessful run for the U.S. Senate, a new more conservative president, Leon H. Johnson, expanded upon Renne's legacy.

When the college became Montana State University in 1965, President Johnson told the faculty, "I got you the name and you're going to live up to it."[9] Johnson provided the structure for change by instituting four-year degrees in English and history, followed by a Bachelor of Arts degree in music, government, philosophy, foreign languages, and a Bachelor of Science degree in economics, psychology, and sociology. Doctoral programs expanded and research grants reached the $2 million mark. In the 1990s, Montana State University is home to a greatly expanded Museum of the Rockies—it too started in a Quonset hut—and has greatly expanded not only its foreign student program but also its ties with educational institutions abroad.

* * *

Just as the establishment of Yellowstone National Park and the introduction of railroads changed the character of the Gallatin Valley, another development would substantially affect both urban and rural life. In late 1969, rumors spread throughout the valley of the possible construction of a resort complex in the Gallatin Canyon at the foot of Lone Mountain. After Christmas, rumors gave way to a solid story. The *Gallatin County Tribune* and *Belgrade Journal* put out a special red-letter edition on January 17, 1970, with the headline "Lone Mountain Looms Over Site of Proposed Big Sky Complex." Retiring national newscaster Chet Huntley said "Good night, David" for the last time the following July and assumed the title of Chairman of the Board of Big Sky Corporation, a $20 million recreational development to be built on the West Fork of the Gallatin River. Detroit's Chrysler Realty Corporation, Meridian Investment and Trust of Georgia, Burlington Northern, Northwest Orient Airlines, Continental Oil Company, Montana Power Company, the General Electric Pension Fund, and other industrial giants would fund construction of Meadow Village and Mountain Village, a golf course, an air strip, a skeet shooting range, indoor swimming pools, tennis courts, Sam Smedling's Lone Mountain Dude Ranch, ski runs, condominiums, and private residences.

Recreational resorts such as that proposed at Big Sky had become potential lucrative business ventures throughout the West. Almost immediately, public meetings were scheduled in the Gallatin area, many of which Chet Huntley attended. Letters to the editors multiplied, detailing views for and against the project. The Bozeman Chamber of Commerce expressed its full support. Some were thrilled with the possibility of new jobs in the building and service industries. Local merchants assessed prospects of an increase in their businesses, although some feared that the money to be made would leave Montana as had happened in the past. Within a short time, land prices near the proposed development shot up.

Other residents had many questions about Big Sky. Should such a resort be located within and near national forest boundaries, and the Spanish Peaks Primitive Area? What would happen to the elk range? Was this to be a playground for the rich? Was it true that "Some people who bought bargain land built bargain structures?"[10] What about the capacity of Gallatin Field? Where will the garbage go? Would life in the Gallatin Valley be forever changed? "Leave us alone!" Louise Keightley wrote to Huntley in a letter to the *Bozeman Daily Chronicle*:

> . . . taxpayers resent having to donate over $800,000 to help build the road through your rich man's resort . . . and they dislike having to pay and pay thereafter to enlarge the local airport to accommodate Big Sky super jets, to widen and straighten Highway 191 to Big Sky, to furnish extra police protection, to enlarge local schools, to maintain and snow-plow the road through your subdivision, to furnish litter disposal along the canyon.[11]

Chet Huntley was astonished at the variety and tone of criticisms expressed against Big Sky development. He became upset over what he called "ninety-day-wonder ecologists and smart-alec editors."[12] On one occasion, he complained to a reporter, "the ringleader of the opposition claims I'm going to bring in marijuana and heroin and naked

The Crail Ranch before construction of the resort at Big Sky.

women." To the contrary, he said Big Sky would strengthen Montana's depressed economy. "Dammit, we can't build a fence around Montana."[13]

Nevertheless, a group of conservationists gathered signatures on petitions. Editorials for and against such a resort tended to polarize opinion. "Montana is for sale in the classified sections of national magazines," said the *Great Falls Tribune*.[14] Lawsuits abounded. A Bozeman-based National Forest Preservation Group filed a number of complaints in federal district court.

Early construction problems multiplied. The Arnold Palmer-designed golf course, remembers David Penwell, chief legal counsel for Big Sky, was another comedy of errors. "The first time the course was seeded, a rainstorm washed it out. The next year there was a drought. The following season, the seed was mixed with too much fertilizer and failed to grow."[15] The first condominiums didn't sell as quickly as had been predicted. The early ski runs did not attract many practiced skiers, who looked for more

advanced slopes. And "Big Sky was considered troublesome because of all the publicity."[16]

By the mid-1970s, many of Big Sky's problems had been resolved. The land swaps between Burlington Northern and the Forest Service had been completed. For a time, President Richard Nixon had delayed the land exchange, reportedly because he was vexed that Huntley would not support him in the next election. After years of strong citizen protest, the road between the two resort villages was resurfaced at Big Sky (rather than taxpayer) expense; later, the road was paved with state money. Chairlifts to the first ski runs were operating. But construction of many of the facilities was delayed because of a variety of lawsuits. Big Sky was in a $4.58 million capital deficit and was losing money each year. But the area was still growing; the student population at little Ophir School jumped from nine to fifty-four.

Due to economic problems, the first Big Sky investors, Chrysler and others, couldn't wait it out

Lone Mountain looms over first buildings at Big Sky. RICHARD HARRISON PHOTO.

for first financial returns. Chet Huntley died of cancer in 1974. Two years later, Everett Kircher of Boyne USA, a Michigan-based firm, bought Big Sky for a reported $7.4 million. Big Sky continued to experience intermittent problems in the 1980s and 1990s. In 1995, continuing problems with the area's sewage system resulted in a building moratorium while a new environmental impact statement attempted to sort out solutions to upgrade the plant and correct the leaking of half-treated sewage.

Despite Big Sky's legal and effluent problems, the massive resort continues to attract recreation-minded tourists for both winter and summer activities. In 1995, construction of a $2 million tram which snakes 1,450 feet up to the barren summit of Lone Mountain at 11,166 feet was completed. Skiers who desire advanced challenges can now be whisked up the mountain in six minutes' time—fifteen each trip—to explore 1,200 acres of new terrain on the south side of the peak. On a clear day, those hardy souls who have no problem with vertigo can ascend to the peak in a purple-and-black tram car to view the Grand Teton, about one hundred and thirty miles away—unless, of course, high winds or an electrical storm dictate prudence.

On unrelated matters, Big Sky made national headlines for a number of months in 1984, when Kari Swenson, a member of the U.S. Women's World Championship Biathlon team, disappeared on the afternoon of July 15, 1984, as she was running along a trail at nearby Ulery's Lake. The twenty-three-year-old Olympic athlete had worked as a waitress at Lone Mountain Ranch while she pursued pre-veterinarian studies at Montana State University and practiced her skills in biathlon, a sport that combined ski racing and target shooting. When she did not return for work that evening, Gallatin County Sheriff John Onstad and Madison County Sheriff John G. France mounted a massive search.

Reality was stranger than fiction: Kari had been kidnapped by two self-designated "mountain men," Dan and Don Nichols. The following day, as one of the searchers, thirty-six-year-old Alan Goldstein, approached the kidnap site, kidnapper Don Nichols shot and killed him. In the excitement, son Dan Nichols leveled his gun at Swenson, chained by the waist to a tree, and accidentally shot her through her lungs. "Oh, my God, I shot her," yelled the younger Nichols, the victim later reported. The two men shoved her into a sleeping bag and left her. A helicopter pilot spotted her from the air and rescued her shortly before noon.

Swenson began a long recuperation, greatly aided by her athletic condition, and law enforcement officials from both Gallatin and Madison County jurisdictions began the long hunt for fifty-three-year-old Don Nichols and nineteen-year-old son Dan, who had reputedly taken the biathlete so that she could be a wife for the younger man. Big Sky management advised their guests that fall to go on no hikes alone and take no lonely horse trails until the two were caught. The Nichols men, known for their ability to survive in rugged mountain terrain and armed with rifles, pistols, and knives, were finally apprehended on December 13, and were tried and convicted for kidnapping and murder the following May in Virginia City. Kari Swenson returned to her interrupted education and successfully completed a degree in veterinary medicine at Colorado State University.[17] The remote trail beside Ulery's Lake where Swenson was abducted is now filled with resort homes and condominiums.

* * *

Just a few decades earlier, in the late 1960s and early 1970s, a number of unsolved murders in the Gallatin Valley caused an uneasiness among residents. On March 19, 1967, thirteen-year-old Bernard Poelman and a friend were playing on the Nixon Bridge near Manhattan. Young Poelman fell into the water. At first, lawmen assumed the boy had accidentally drowned; but his friend reported that Bernard had been shot down from the bridge. After the youngster had been fished from the river, the coroner found a bullet lodged in the victim's heart. On the following May 6, 1968, twelve-year-old Michael Raney, camped with two hundred fellow Boy Scouts at Headwaters State Park, was found stabbed in his tent, the canvas ripped open where he slept. On June 25, 1973, seven-year-old Susan Marie Jaeger, camped with her Farmington, Michigan, family also at Headwaters State Park, disappeared from her tent, its canvas slashed. From time to time, a number of young women reported to law enforcement authorities that, as they drove home at night, someone would follow them closely, attempting to force them off the road. In Manhattan, nineteen-year-old Sandra Dykman Smallegan disappeared in February 1974.

A series of phone calls and an analysis of burned bone fragments found at the Lockhart Ranch in the Horseshoe Hills finally led to the arrest of David Gail Meirhofer, a twenty-five-year-old Manhattan resident, on September 27, 1974. The news spread through the valley, shocking all, at the same time relieving some that perhaps there could be an end to the apparent killing of youngsters. After a taped interview with County Attorney Thomas Olson, Special Agent Byron "Pete" H. Dunbar, Federal Bureau of Investigation, and Meirhofer's attorney, the suspect confessed that he had indeed shot Bernard Poelman, stabbed Michael Raney, kidnapped and strangled Susan Jaeger, and kidnapped and killed Sandra Smallegan. Yes, he had called the Denver Federal Bureau of Investigation office to demand a ransom for Susan Jaeger. Yes, he had called the Jaeger residence in Michigan and talked to Susan's mother, Marietta. No, he was not responsible for the disappearance of eight other youngsters in the southwest Montana area.

Investigators hoped to clarify details of the crimes and Meirhofer's motives at a subsequent interview. On Sunday morning, September 29, however, David Meirhofer was found dead in his cell, hanged with a towel that had been issued him. With no closure to these grisly events, some residents wondered what more could have been discovered had Meirhofer stood trial. Marietta Jaeger went on to write a book called *The Lost Child* and devoted herself to helping other parents who had suffered the death of a child.

* * *

A new railroad tunnel was built next to the old one east of Bozeman in 1944. Within twenty years, trains would concentrate on the freight business. Passenger travel throughout the Gallatin Valley dwindled, then died. The Milwaukee Road stopped booking reservations in 1963. The Northern Pacific dropped customer service in May 1971. The Turkey Red train to Menard stopped running altogether in April 1978. For a time, Amtrak picked up passengers in Bozeman; after October 1979, however, the government-run train service concentrated on its line stretching across northern Montana.

As in other parts of the country, tourists turned

A Northern Pacific train on its way to Belgrade, January 26, 1941.

Waiting for the first train to rumble through the new tunnel, 1944.

to their cars for travel and stopped for the night in tourist camps along the way, later replaced by little bedrooms with doors opening to parking lots, now called motels. Bozeman's two main hotels, the Bozeman and the Baxter, converted their rooms to office space and apartments. The town's smaller hotels closed as well.

At the end of the 1970s, Bozeman's downtown merchants nervously watched construction of a new shopping complex at the western edge of town. The Main Mall opened in 1980, followed by additional strip businesses stretching along West Main Street, North Seventh Avenue, and Huffine Lane. JC Penney's, long an anchor in downtown Bozeman, moved to the mall. Some storefronts remained empty for a time.

But the continuing rise in population in the Gallatin Valley provided new customers for at least some downtown business ventures. Several merchants rediscovered the brick that lay beneath more modern facades and renovated their buildings to recall the Main Street of the 1880s and 1890s. The face of the central district changed from year to year but continued its strong economic role in the valley. ▓

chapter

TWENTY-
SIX

"Some day the valley will be one big city," predicted rancher William Brainard in 1985.[1] In the 1990s, more and more lights glitter after dusk in the Gallatin Valley. They light up the face of the Bridgers to the border of Forest Service land and glow from subdivided tracts surrounding Bozeman, Belgrade, Manhattan, and on to the Madison River. Some call it progress; others call it light pollution and complain they can seldom look up on a November night to watch the Northern Lights move across the sky as they used to.

Once a rare traffic jam occurred when Gallatin Field was dedicated. Now cars daily clog Bozeman arterial and collector streets. Coping with commuter traffic from Bozeman to nearby towns and subdivisions is a serious daily chore, handled by some as if they were still grimly racing down an urban freeway. Pedestrians have developed a new agility, scampering across formerly quiet roads during the occasional lull between spates of traffic. Bozeman streets are no longer quiet when the students from Montana State University leave for home during the summer months. Now campers and cars with license plates from across the nation cruise the area. Freelance writer for the *New York Times* Dan O'Brian gave this advice to the incoming tourist:

Perhaps the best thing a tourist can do to insure a good time in Bozeman, Mont., is to stop at the airport on the way into town and rent a car with Montana license plates. . . . A pickup truck would be even better, especially if it has no lightning bolt decals and is carrying enough dust.[2]

Growth has mainly occurred in once-rural areas. From 1980 to 1990, Gallatin County's population rose to 50,463, a rise of 17.7 percent. During the next five years, the population rose again to 59,406 with an average annual rate of 3.4 percent, the highest urban increase in Montana. During the decade of the 1980s, Bozeman population grew to 22,660, up 4.7 percent. Since the 1990 census, an estimated 2,407 more people have moved to town. By the year 2000, perhaps 29,000 citizens will live in Bozeman and more than 60,000 people will call the Gallatin Valley home.

In 1950, 1,129 farms and ranches dotted the valley; in 1992, that number dropped to 798. Moreover, some of the land is worked by "hobby farmers," owners who work in town but tend small crops during their leisure hours. One serious rancher, Ray White, former county commissioner and descendant of one of the five Cornish brothers who settled in the valley in the 1860s, has told his children they may be the last generation of his family to ranch in the Gallatin Valley.[3] White foresees the day when residences replace much of the agricultural operations.

Harry Brainard, whose ancestors settled the Maudlow area in the 1880s, sold 26,000 acres of his land there in 1938.
He talks to one of his cats at his Dry Creek ranch near the Horseshoe Hills. DOUG LONEMAN PHOTO.

As the Blackfeet resented other hunters stalking game in one of their favorite areas, some people in the valley despair of the steady growth in population and what they perceive as unrelenting intrusion into their lives. Anti-newcomer attitudes are also voiced by recently arrived residents, themselves part of the problem. Settlers from California have received much of the brunt of criticism. Said local artist H. J. Schmidt in 1993, "You were in your place and it got ruined. Now you are coming to my place to ruin it."[4] Lest Schmidt be regarded as a grouch, he appears to have anticipated the rapid rise in crime, traffic-congested streets, and the crowding of area schools. Writer William Kittredge wrote, also in 1993, "We had our hundred years of solitude, and now the West is turning itself into a make-believe place where celebrities and tourists and retirees can roam and find homes. Beverly Hills in the highlands.... They want to buy into our functioning culture on the cheap."[5]

Some would-be Gallatin Valley residents, fleeing urban crime and, perhaps, problems of their own, leave almost as soon as they arrive. Housing is too costly for them; wages are too low. In 1993, Gallatin County was thirty-third of Montana's fifty-six counties in per-capita income—$17,032. The winter months, which sounded romantic at first, are indeed long and cold. Life here is not what they expected. They have not done their homework. Other newcomers, usually older and wealthier, have done theirs. Perhaps they have vacationed here for a number of years. They have sold their homes in other states at inflated prices and arrive with enough

Early morning on Bozeman's Main Street, framed by two former hotels: at left down the street is the Baxter; at right is the venerable Bozeman. RICHARD HARRISON PHOTO.

Afternoon traffic moves out of Bozeman. RICHARD HARRISON PHOTO.

POPULATION

Year	Gallatin County	Bozeman	Belgrade	Manhattan	Three Forks	West Yellowstone	Montana
1870	1,578	168					20,595
1880	*	894					39,159
1890	6,246	2,143					142,924
1900	9,553	3,419					243,329
1910	14,079	5,107	561		674		376,053
1920	15,864	6,183	499	591	1,071		548,889
1930	16,124	6,855	533	501	884		537,606
1940	18,269	8,665	618	646	876		559,456
1950	21,902	11,325	663	716	1,114		591,024
1960	26,045	13,361	1,057	889	1,161		674,767
1970	32,505	18,670	1,307	816	1,182	756	694,409
1980	42,865	21,645	2,336	988	1,247	735	786,690
1990	50,465	22,660	3,411	1,034	1,203	913	799,065

* Change in County Boundaries
From the Montana Census Department

Subdivisions surround Belgrade in the 1990s. RICHARD HARRISON PHOTO.

299

money to build an expensive home or renovate an older one. A few have second or third homes around the country and live in each one for a portion of the year.

With each investment in local real estate, the newcomers drive up property values and, therefore, property taxes for all. In 1987, residential taxes accounted for 39.7 percent of the county tax base. In 1994, that share rose to 54 percent.[6] For some, the newcomer is merely resented because he is rich or famous or, perhaps, fatuous. For others he is blamed for older residents' inability to keep up with the rising taxes on their homes or farms. A few arrive with enough money to start a business they hope will boom. Some of these would-be entrepreneurs, however, misread the economic climate and the taste of its customers and leave town, disappointed, with lighter wallets.

In 1977, the road through Bridger Canyon was widened; gone were the cattle guards and gates that characterized it as a rural lane. Part of Maiden Rock, a local landmark at the entrance to the canyon, was

blasted down because engineers feared it would fall down onto the road on its own one day. New canyon residents include those families who have retired, attracted by the beauty of the area. Other newcomers still work, managing their business interests by computer. More and more vacation homes sprout on the hillsides, some of which are visited but a few times each season.

Bridger Bowl, one of the few nonprofit ski areas in the United States, is no longer a recreational secret held by local skiers. Plans for expansion of the facility are strongly opposed by some and actively promoted by others, resulting in spirited meetings of the Bridger Canyon Property Owners Association, the Bridger Bowl board, and sessions with the Gallatin County Commissioners. Involved are questions of the number of overnight accommodations and individual homesites, additional land for parking and other amenities, new lifts, and water and sewer systems. Lawsuits highlight the controversy. Almost all agree that increased traffic has changed the character of the canyon and will continue to do so,

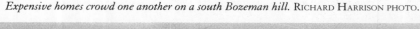

Expensive homes crowd one another on a south Bozeman hill. RICHARD HARRISON PHOTO.

whatever the nature of the development finally agreed to by all parties.

No longer do Sedan residents stage jackrabbit hunts and pin rabbit ears to the local store. The cheese factory, which opened and closed any number of times, stopped making cheese for good in 1938. Four Sedan-area elementary students finished their classes in 1967, after which they were bused to schools in Wilsall, Park County. In the 1990s, a developer bought land in the area and subdivided it, but the high price of the lots has discouraged most prospective buyers.

The Maudlow region, which writer Ivan Doig earlier described as around the corner from the Bridger Mountains, an area which "went wild in a hurry,"[7] is still populated by Brainards, Doigs, Callantines, and Morgans. Ranchers can no longer load their cattle on local railroad cars; the trains are gone. Maudlow School closed in 1975; what few students are there go to Manhattan for their education. The Dry Creek Road to Maudlow was rebuilt in the 1960s, which makes it a little easier to come to town during the muddy season. In 1968, telephone service was extended to the region.

The Climbing Arrow Ranch, the largest privately owned acreage in Gallatin County, still operates at three locations, spilling over into Madison, Meagher, and Broadwater Counties. By 1960, Buck Anderson had amassed 70,000 acres at Francis Ranch, his summer pasture land northeast of Maudlow. Anderson's Madison Ranch, on irrigated lands near Three Forks, provides some grain and hay for his stock. His Hudson Ranch, located on a wind-blown plateau overlooking the Madison River, mostly snow-free, is winter feeding grounds for some three thousand Hereford-Angus cattle.

Lonnie Ewin sorts calves for branding at the Climbing Arrow's Francis Ranch.
RICHARD HARRISON PHOTO.

The Springhill community, never incorporated, remains a cohesive society, many of whose residents bear the names of the earliest settlers. In 1989, in order to protect themselves from what they regarded as subdivision frenzy, landowners formed a Community Planning and Zoning District. Fifty-one percent of those eligible to vote agreed that no further subdivision may take place unless it meets the terms as set forth in the Gallatin County Comprehensive Plan, approved in 1991. The Springhill Church holds services each Sunday; the local school has remained open since its inception, serving from five to ten students each year. The Springhill Women's Club flourishes and publishes a newsletter, the *Springhill Community Coverall*, for its members. Each fall, the women put on a festival to raise money for the school, the church, the fire department, and the cemetery. The

venerable pavilion is available for wedding receptions and other local events.

Belgrade, still called founder Thomas Quaw's "Hub of the Valley," experienced phenomenal growth in the 1980s, from 2,336 residents to 3,411, an increase of forty-six percent. From 1990 to 1994, it led the valley with an additional twenty-one percent gain of new residents to 4,134. Town boosters do not like Belgrade to be called a bedroom community serving Bozeman, but the subdivision and construction activity there make it a fair characterization. Families with modest incomes can still find less expensive housing in Belgrade than in Bozeman, although it is becoming more difficult to do so. Schoolrooms are bursting past capacity. The town with the Serbian name continues to serve the agricultural community, although it aims to attract more jobs in light industry as well.

Bringing the cattle down to winter range. RICHARD HARRISON PHOTO.

Manhattan continues to be a stable community of 1,137 people, with a ten percent rise in population since the 1990 census. New homes, built by residents who work in Bozeman, circle the town. The Christian Reformed Church, established by those Holland families who came to grow barley for the Manhattan Malting Company in the 1890s, still dominates the religious community. In 1967, James Taylor bought twelve thousand acres west of town, some of which once belonged to the malting interests, stretching across Gallatin County and into Broadwater County. His crescent-shaped Wytana Ranch runs twelve hundred Hereford-Angus crossbred cows and even more yearlings.

In the 1970s, a developer bought ten thousand acres in the Clarkston area, subdivided them into ten-acre lots, called the enterprise Ponderosa Pines Ranch Subdivision Properties, and advertised "A Once in a Lifetime Opportunity" in newspapers based in Guam, Japan, and Hawaii. With five hundred dollars as down payment on a five-thousand-dollar investment, the buyer would make monthly payments of $57.43. "Are we selling some densely wooded jungle, or swamp useless land?" continued the advertisement. "No, indeed, this is prime land."[8] The ad for November 2, 1972, in the *Japan Times* started with "Escape! This is the year to get away to the wide open spaces of Montana, the Big Sky Country." Some Americans completing their military service overseas were encouraged to buy a lot by mail, sight unseen. A few did, hoping for inexpensive home sites. When they visited their new property, they discovered that land near the Horseshoe Hills had little irrigation prospects and few roads. The Clarkston subdivision has changed hands in recent years, from developer to developer. A few homes have been built in the area.

The settlement at Logan, never incorporated, has steadily declined since the railroad discontinued its operations there. Where once thirty trains filled the Logan yards within a twenty-four-hour period, the introduction of diesel engines in the 1940s made it no longer necessary to stop over in Logan. Waitresses known as the "Beanery Queens" gave up serving meals at the once-elegant depot cafe, which was torn down in the 1970s. The local school closed

Flying D men line up at the Home Ranch under a darkening sky. LEFT TO RIGHT: *Johnny Flowers, Larry McDonald, Bill Shunk, Roy Laird, Howard Lewis, Stanley Laird, Grady Woirhaye, Jim Pratt.*

its doors in 1988; students travel either to Three Forks or Manhattan for their education. Hikers still climb the nearby Buffalo Jump, perhaps imagining great numbers of bison falling to their death thousands of years ago.

Gone are most of the company houses at Trident. The plant is now owned by a Swiss firm and was the focus of a campaign in the 1990s to keep the company from receiving a permit to burn hazardous waste at the site. The company subsequently abandoned those plans.

By 1990, Three Forks had lost residents, down 3.5 percent, a total of 1,203, although its reputation for a population of voracious mosquitoes seemed intact. More storefronts with empty windows than was economically healthy lined its main street. Local resident and sometime mayor William Fairhurst said, "When I look at Main Street, I'd hate to think these are the good times.... It looks like the *Grapes of Wrath*."[9] Although Pogreba Air Field expanded to ten hangars, it had no freight service and served private planes only. The schools in Three Forks have maintained a steady enrollment of from two to three

hundred pupils, receiving students from surrounding dying neighboring school districts, including some in Broadwater County.

In 1994, however, the sleepy little town experienced a modest building boom with thirty to forty modular homes under construction, which attracted new residents, expanding its population to an estimated 1,357. Several of the old Main Street buildings are under renovation, including the old Ruby Theater. Noted fisherman Bud Lilly, a descendent of constant traveler Granny Yates, has converted his late mother Violet's railroad hotel into the Anglers Retreat, a cozy haven for fishing guests, featuring a century-old cathedral organ. A refurbished Sacajawea Inn attracts visitors looking for a quiet place to stay. After dinner, when weather permits, they can sit in one of the many rocking chairs on the Inn's long front porch. Or they can stroll down the quiet street to visit the Three Forks Museum.

Willow Creek families still send their children to local schools, although pressures to consolidate with Three Forks mount each year. One of the first settlements in the Gallatin Valley, Willow Creek seems to have limited opportunity for new growth. A new development in the quiet town is the establishment of a bird sanctuary, where injured birds receive medical attention or are free to breed without danger of new construction.

When cable television mogul Ted Turner bought the historic Flying D Ranch in 1989, he encountered a mixed reception from local residents, old and new. Some resented his replacing traditional Santa Gertrudis cattle herds with bison, but he countered with his view that bison were less destructive to the acreage. Others applauded his placing part of the Flying D Ranch in a conservation easement to insure that the once-flourishing Anceney Ranch would not be subdivided into housing tracts.

Other landowners have followed a similar path to protecting their land from development. In 1995, Marjorie and Ken Goering were one of three owners who granted an easement involving 416 acres of their Middle Cottonwood Canyon land west of the Bridgers to the Gallatin Valley Land Trust, an organization devoted to removing Gallatin Valley land from the threat of subdivision. Thus far, the Trust has acquired conservation easements on 1,570 acres, ranging from land near Trail Creek Road to the east, to Green Mountain in the Bridgers, and west to the Springhill area.

Gallatin Gateway, once the scene of Saturday night fights between cowboys and loggers, still experiences a rowdy night now and then at Stacey's Bar. Although a number of new subdivisions circle the community, those who live in the drab buildings of old town are fiercely loyal to "Gateway." Gallatin Gateway Inn, sold by the Milwaukee Road in the 1950s, renovated in the 1980s, is elegant again after a number of hard years. Valley residents gravitate toward the Inn for special occasions; visitors still stop on their way to Yellowstone National Park.

West Yellowstone grew 24.2 percent in the 1990 census to 913 year-round residents. In the 1990s, the population rose again to an estimated 999. A local-option resort tax of 3 percent has changed the appearance of "West," making possible paved streets, a new school, and other amenities. The community used to close down during the winter months, resting from its summer influx of tourists, but the rising

popularity of snowmobiling has made it a year-round tourist stop. Not all residents welcomed entrepreneur Lewis Robinson, who proposed a park for grizzly bears, located between the town limits and Yellowstone Park boundary. The Grizzly Discovery Center continues to expand and attracts its share of tourists.

On clear days, it is still possible to see the Bridgers or Spanish Peaks from downtown Bozeman. It is not uncommon now to see deer feeding on rose bushes and other greenery in Bozeman backyards, displaced from their former grazing areas by new high-country residences. In earlier days, sighting a mountain lion was considered a rarity; as deer move closer to town, so do their predators. Fifty years ago, town dwellers could glimpse the bright flash of bluebirds in their yards. They can still enjoy watching song birds, but more sparrows, pigeons, and starlings also live in the city.

Children still slide down Peet's Hill in the winter; however, the area has become overused and citizens are making plans to renovate it. An expanded Gallatin Field brings in more visitors, some with expensive fishing and hunting gear. On Main Street in Bozeman, dime stores and department stores have been replaced by art galleries and specialty boutiques. More and more young saplings line the street. The evergreens in front of the courthouse, planted there in 1928, tower above neighboring buildings.

In town, early morning coffee klatches abound, each with its particular political makeup. In addition to reviewing the national scene, members may blast "the Californios" and other incoming residents, or they may turn their attention to assessing the effects of whirling disease and how it might change fishing in the region's premium trout streams. They might also discuss the effects of the newly passed impact fees, designed to impose charges on those who would build more residences in the Gallatin Valley.

On Bozeman sidewalks, most people still look one another in the eye when they pass and say "Good morning." In the country, motorists salute one another with a brief hand lifted off the steering wheel. When the British horse breeders came to the Gallatin Valley in the 1880s, they reported back home that the air here was like dry champagne. It still is. ▣

ENDNOTES

Chapter One

[1] John Bozeman, "Letter from the Gallatin," *Montana Post*, February 3, 1866.

[2] Quoted by Walter Cooper, "Early History of the County," *Bozeman Daily Chronicle*, February 23, 1921. The same quotation also has been attributed to Theodore Roosevelt.

[3] Peter Watts, ed., *A Dictionary of the Old West* (New York: Knopf, 1977), p. 125; Winfred Blevins, *Dictionary of the American West* (New York: Facts on File, 1993), pp. 306-307.

Chapter Two

[1] Explorer and Catholic Father Jacques Marquette called the Missouri River the Pekihanoui in 1763. He called the Indians who lived near its mouth the Oumessourit, or those "living at the mouth of waters." From Hiram Martin Chittenden, *American Fur Trade of the Far West*, vol. 2 (Stanford: Academic Reprints, 1954), pp. 762-763n.

[2] Donald Jackson, *Among the Sleeping Giants* (Urbana: University of Illinois Press, 1987), pp. 103 and 109.

[3] Thomas R. Wessel, "Introduction," *Agricultural History* 51 (January 1977): 1.

[4] Chittenden, p. 745.

[5] For a spirited discussion of Powell and his views, see Joseph Kinsey Howard, *Montana: High, Wide and Handsome* (Reprint. Lincoln: University of Nebraska Press, 1983), pp. 31-37.

[6] Isabelle Randall, *A Lady's Ranche Life in Montana* (London: W. H. Allen & Co., 1887), pp. 75-76.

[7] Perhaps the Blackfeet were describing the thorny hawthorn, a rugged, spreading bush that grows in abundance on north valley hillsides.

Chapter Three

[1] H. M. Wormington, *Ancient Man in North America*. Popular Series No. 4, 4th ed. (Denver: Denver Museum of Natural History, 1957), p. 251.

[2] Carling Malouf, *Archaeology in Montana* 16 (January-April 1975): 27.

[3] Peter Koch, "Historical Sketch: Bozeman, Gallatin Valley and Bozeman Pass," *Contributions to the Montana Historical Society*, vol. 2 (Helena: State Publishing Company, 1896), p. 127.

[4] Wallace Stegner, *Wolf Willow* (Reprint. Lincoln: University of Nebraska Press, 1980), p. 73.

[5] Michael P. Malone, Richard B. Roeder, and William L. Lang. *Montana: A History of Two Centuries* (Rev. ed. Seattle: University of Washington Press, 1991), p. 17.

[6] Malone, Roeder, and Lang, p. 21.

[7] Walter Fleming, "We Knew You Were Coming: A Native Perspective of European Settlement in North America," speech given at annual conference of the Montana Historical Society, Helena, Montana, October 25, 1991.

Chapter Four

[1] Robert Athearn, *High Country Empire: The High Plains and Rockies* (Lincoln: University of Nebraska Press, 1960), p. 4.

[2] Athearn, pp. 13-14.

[3] Athearn, p. 3.

[4] Earlier discussions of Lewis's pet referred to the dog as "Scammon," or "Scannon," a mistake probably due to the difficulties of interpreting the penmanship in the journals.

[5] Letter from Meriwether Lewis to William Clark, June 19, 1803, as quoted in Donald Jackson, ed., *The Letters of the Lewis and Clark Expedition, with related documents, 1783-1854* (Urbana: University of Illinois Press, 1962), p. 58.

[6] Entry for May 14, 1804 in Gary Moulton, ed., *The Journals of the Lewis and Clark Expedition*, vol. 2 (Lincoln: University of Nebraska Press, 1986), p. 227. Readers may wish to consult other editions of the Lewis and Clark journals: Nicholas Biddle, ed., *The Journals of the Expedition under the Command of Capts. Lewis and Clark* (New York: Heritage Press, 1962); Reuben Gold Thwaites, ed., *Original Journals of the Lewis and Clark Expedition, 1804-1806* (New York: Dodd, Mead and Company, 1905); Bernard DeVoto, ed., *The Journals of Lewis and Clark*, available in several editions.

[7] Entry for Friday, July 12, 1805, in Moulton, vol. 4, p. 377.

[8] Entry for Monday, July 22, 1805, in Moulton, vol. 4, pp. 416-417.

[9] Entry for Tuesday, July 23, 1805, in Moulton, vol. 4, p. 420.

[10] Entry for Thursday, July 25, 1805, in Moulton, vol. 4, p. 428.

[11] *Ibid.*

[12] Entry for Saturday, July 27, 1805, in Moulton, vol. 4, p. 434.

[13] Entry for Sunday, July 28, 1805, in Moulton, vol. 5, pp. 7-8.

[14] Entry for Sunday, July 28, 1805, in Moulton, vol. 5, pp. 8-9.

[15] Nicholas Biddle, ed., *The Journals of the Expedition Under the Command of Capts. Lewis and Clark*, vol. 2 (New York: Heritage Press, 1962), p. 233.

[16] *Ibid.*

[17] Entry for Sunday, July 13, 1806, in Moulton, vol. 8, p. 180.

[18] Entry for Monday, July 14, 1806 in Moulton, vol. 8, p. 182.

Chapter Five

[1] Some sources say Courtin was an American.

[2] W. J. Ghent, "'Jeremy Pinch Again," *Oregon Historical Quarterly* 40 (December 1939): 308.

[3] Donald Jackson, ed., *Letters of the Lewis and Clark Expedition with Related Documents, 1783-1854* (Urbana: University of Illinois Press, 1962), pp. 433, 437n.

[4] Dale Lowell Morgan ed., *The West of William H. Ashley* (Denver: The Old West Publishing Co., 1964), pp. xxxi-xxxii, 227n; Dale Lowell Morgan, *Jedediah Smith and the Opening of the West* (Lincoln: University of Nebraska Press, 1953), pp. 122-123, 123n.

[5] Thomas James, *Three Years Among the Indians and Mexicans* (New York: L. P. Lippincott Co., 1962), p. 29.

[6] James, p. 26.

[7] John Bradbury, *Travels in the Interior of America* (Liverpool: Smith & Galway, 1817.), p. 19n.

[8] *Ibid.*

[9] James, pp. 34-35.

[10] Burton Harris, *John Colter: His Years in the Rocky Mountains* (Basin, Wyo.: Big Horn Books, 1977), p. 133.

[11] James, p. 25.

[12] Harris, p. 142.

[13] James, p. 34.

[14] Hiram Martin Chittenden, *History of the American Fur Trade of the Far West*, vol. 2 (Stanford: Academic Reprints, 1954), appendix, p. 963.

[15] James, p. 35.

[16] Chittenden, p. 898.

Chapter Six

[1] Hiram Martin Chittenden, *The American Fur Trade of the Far West*, vol. 2 (Stanford: Academic Reprints, 1954), pp. 744-745.

[2] Don Berry, *A Majority of Scoundrels* (New York: Harper & Bros., 1961), p. 87.

[3] Peter Koch, "Historical Sketch of Bozeman Gallatin Valley and Bozeman Pass," *Contributions to the Montana Historical Society*, vol. 2 (Helena: Montana Historical Society, 1896), p. 132.

[4] *Ibid.*

[5] Chittenden, vol. 1, p. 263.

[6] Letter of Joshua Pilcher to Major Benjamin O'Fallon, July 23, 1823, quoted in Chittenden, vol. 1, p. 154.

[7] Berry, p. 28.

[8] Chittenden, vol. 1, p. 252.

Chapter Seven

[1] Larry S. Thompson, *Montana's Explorers: The Pioneer Naturalists* (Helena: Montana Magazine, Inc., 1985), p. 29.

[2] L. C. Butscher, ed., "An Account of Adventures in the Great American Desert by His Royal Highness, Duke Paul Wilhelm von Wurttemberg," *New Mexico Historical Review* 17 (1942): 206, 217.

[3] Hiram Martin Chittenden and A. T. Richardson, eds., *The Life, Letters and Travels of Father Pierre-Jean DeSmet, S.J., 1801-1873* (New York: Francis P. Harper, 1905), p. 235.

[4] S. D. McKelvey, *Botanical Explorations of the Trans-Mississippi West, 1790-1850* (Jamaica Plain, Mass.: Arnold Arboretum of Harvard University, 1955), p. 803.

[5] McKelvey, p. 806.

[6] T. C. Tessendorf, "Red Death on the Missouri," *American West* 14 (January-February 1977): 52.

[7] *Ibid.*

Chapter Eight

[1] Robert Athearn, *High Country Empire* (New York: McGraw-Hill, 1960), p. 52.

[2] Charles J. Kappler, *Indian Affairs, Laws and Treaties*, vol. 2 (Washington, D.C.: Government Printing Office, 1904), p. 736.

[3] Mark H. Brown, *Plainsmen of the Yellowstone* (New York: G. P. Putnam's Sons, 1961), p. 113.

[4] Brown, p. 114.

[5] Report of First Lieutenant H. E. Maynadier, 10th Infantry, on route between the Yellowstone and the Platte Rivers, 1859, in "Report of Brevet Colonel W. F. Raynolds, U.S.A. Corps of Engineers, on the Exploration of the Yellowstone and Missouri Rivers in 1859-1860," 40th Cong., 1st sess., Ex. Doc. No. 77, pp. 140-141.

[6] John Lyle Campbell, *Idaho, Six Months in the New Diggings: The Emigrant's Guide Overland* (New York: J. L. Campbell, 1864), pp. 19-20.

[7] Cornelius Hedges, "Early Masonry in Montana," *Rocky Mountain Magazine* 1 (September 1900): 13.

[8] Campbell, p. 36.

[9] Campbell, p. 39.

[10] As quoted in Daniel N. Vichorek, *Montana's Homestead Era* (Helena: American Geographic Publishing Company, 1987), p. 8.

[11] Peter Koch, "Historical Sketch: Bozeman, Gallatin Valley and Bozeman Pass," *Contributions to the Montana Historical Society*, vol. 2 (Helena: State Publishing Company, 1896), p. 135.

[12] Emily R. Meredith letter in historical section, *Frontier and Midland*, 17 (summer 1937).

[13] Edward B. Neally, "A Year in Montana," *Atlantic Monthly* (August 1866).

[14] *Montana Post*, September 3, 1864.

Chapter Nine

[1] George W. Irwin, II, "Overland to Montana in 1863," *Butte Miner*, January 1, 1888.

[2] W. J. Davies, "John Bozeman: Peculiarities of His Character," in "Sketches of Early Days," *Bozeman Avant Courier*, January 21, 1893.

[3] William S. McKinzie, "John M. Bozeman," *Bozeman Avant Courier*, December 19, 1891.

[4] Irwin.

[5] Davies, *Bozeman Avant Courier*, December 19, 1891.

[6] *Ibid.*

[7] McKinzie.

[8] Davies, *Bozeman Avant Courier*, December 19, 1891.

[9] W. J. Davies, in *Bozeman Avant Courier*, March 8, 1891.

[10] Granville Stuart, "The Yellowstone Expedition of 1863," *Contributions to the Montana Historical Society*, vol. 1 (Helena: Rocky Mountain Publishing Co., 1876), pp. 187-188.

[11] James Kirkpatrick, "A Reminiscence of John Bozeman," *Frontier* 9 (May 1929): 356.

[12] Robin McNab, "Trailblazer Bozeman Bent the Rules," *Bozeman Daily Chronicle*, April 1, 1979.

[13] Kirkpatrick, p. 354.

[14] Knoch became a longtime Bozeman resident, gunsmith, and cabinet maker.

[15] Grace R. Hebard and E. A. Brininstool, *The Bozeman Trail*, vol. 1 (Cleveland: Arthur H. Clark, 1961,), p. 219.

[16] Grace Stone Coates, in *Bozeman Avant Courier*, June 5, 1931.

[17] William White Alderson, diary, titled "Across the Plains to Montana in 1864, to Gallatin Valley, Montana, 1864-1879" in the collections of the Gallatin County Historical Society, Bozeman, Montana, p. 2.

[18] William White Alderson, address at the laying of the cornerstone of the City Hall and Opera House, July 4, 1888, as quoted in Rosa Barker Beall, "Montana's Early History," *Contributions to the Montana Historical Society*, vol. 8 (Helena: State Publishing Co., 1917), p. 296.

[19] Alderson diary, p. 7.

[20] Esther C. Niebel, comp., *The First Methodist Church, Bozeman, Montana: A Century of Service* (Bozeman: First Methodist Church, 1966), p. 1.

[21] Frank Kirkaldie letter to Elizabeth Kirkaldie, as quoted in Dorothy E. Johnson, "The Patience of Frank Kirkaldie," *Montana, the Magazine of Western History* 21 (Winter 1971): 12-27.

[22] Johnson, p. 16.

[23] Minutes, East Gallatin Claim Association, August 9, 1864, in collections of the Gallatin County Historical Society, Bozeman, Montana.

[24] Minutes, East Gallatin Claim Association, September 14, 1864.

Chapter Ten

[1] Michael P. Malone, Richard B. Roeder, and William L. Lang, *Montana: A History of Two Centuries* (Rev. ed., Seattle: University of Washington Press, 1991), p. 79.

[2] Merrill G. Burlingame, introduction to Lew. L. Callaway, *Montana's Righteous Hangmen: The Vigilantes in Action* (Norman: University of Oklahoma Press, 1982), pp. xv-xvi.

[3] *Proceedings of the Grand Lodge, A.F. & A.M.* (Butte: Grand Lodge, A.F. & A.M., 1914), p. 164.

[4] Nathaniel P. Langford, letter to Colonel W. E. Brackett, April 8, 1896, in Merrill G. Burlingame Special Collections, Renne Library, Montana State University at Bozeman.

[5] Dorothy Johnson, introduction to rev. ed., Nathaniel P. Langford, *Vigilante Days and Ways* (Missoula: Montana State University Press, 1957), p. xxii.

[6] Wesley P. Emery, "The Execution of Bill Hunter," *Contributions to the Montana Historical Society*, vol. 7 (Helena: State Publishing Co., 1910, p. 171; also read Merrill G. Burlingame, "Montana's Righteous Hangmen: A Reconsideration," *Montana: The Magazine of Western History* 28 (autumn 1978): 36-49.

Chapter Eleven

[1] Edward L. Nowels in the *Bozeman Daily Chronicle*, August 10, 1954.

[2] *Montana Post*, January 13, 1865.

[3] Thomas Wessel, "Introduction," *Agricultural History* 51 (January 1977): 2.

[4] William White Alderson, diary, entitled "Across the Plains to Montana in 1864 and Settlement in the Gallatin Valley, Montana, 1864-1879," in the collections of the Gallatin County Historical Society, Bozeman, Montana, p. 19.

[5] James Kent, *Commentaries on American Law*, vol. 3. Ed. Charles M. Barnes (13th ed., Boston: Little, Brown & Co., 1884), p. 439.

[6] Robert G. Dunbar, "The Search For a Stable Water Right in Montana," *Agricultural History* 28 (October 1954): 139.

[7] Montana Territory Session Laws, 1869-1870, p. 57.

[8] Dunbar, p. 140.

[9] *Montana Post*, September 17, 1864.

[10] Merrill G. Burlingame, *Gallatin County's Heritage: A Report of Progress, 1805-1976* (Bozeman: Gallatin County Bicentennial Publications, 1976), p. 41.

[11] Bogert quoted in Burlingame, *Gallatin County's Heritage*, p. 95.

[12] *Bozeman Avant Courier*, July 2, 1876.

[13] Cecilia Carter, "Springhill: An Early Gallatin Valley Community," paper in the collections of the Gallatin County Historical Society, Bozeman, Montana.

[14] Dee Brown, *The Fetterman Massacre* (Lincoln: University of Nebraska Press, 1971), p. 134.

[15] Burlingame, *Gallatin County's Heritage*, p. 95.

[16] Joseph Kenney, letters to Susan Kenney, in the collections of the Gallatin County Historical Society, Bozeman, Montana, p. 3.

[17] Kenney letters, p. 68.

[18] Kenney letters, p. 8.

[19] Kenney letters, p. 63.

Chapter Twelve

[1] Rosa Barker Beall scrapbook, in Merrill G. Burlingame Special Collections, Renne Library, Montana State University at Bozeman, p. 112.

[2] Emma Hart in *Bozeman Avant Courier*, March 12, 1891.

[3] Sarah Jane Bessey Tracy, *Bozeman 1869: The Diary and Reminiscences of Mrs. William H. Tracy* (Bozeman: Gallatin County Historical Society, 1985), p. 20.

[4] Melinda M. Rich, speech given to the First Presbyterian Quarterly Centennial, 1872-1897, prepared by P. C. Waite and W. M. Cobleigh, p. 57.

[5] *Bozeman Avant Courier*, February 7, 1873.

[6] *Ibid.*

[7] *Montana Pick and Plow*, December 31, 1869.

[8] *Ibid.*

[9] *Ibid.*

[10] *Ibid.*

[11] *Bozeman Avant Courier*, September 13, 1871.

[12] *Ibid.*

[13] Edward Laird Mills, *Plains, Peaks, and Pioneers* (Portland, Ore.: Binfords & Mort, 1947.), p. 4.

[14] William White Alderson, diary, "Across the Plains to Montana in 1864, to Gallatin Valley, Montana, 1864-1879" in collections of the Gallatin County Historical Society, Bozeman, Montana.

[15] Lester Willson, letter to his mother, December 26, 1866, in Merrill G. Burlingame Special Collections, Renne Library, Montana State University at Bozeman.

[16] Merrill G. Burlingame, *Gallatin County's Heritage, 1805-1976* (Bozeman: Gallatin County Bicentennial Publication, 1976), p. 41.

Chapter Thirteen

[1] John Bozeman, letters to his mother, in the collections of the Gallatin County Historical Society, Bozeman, Montana.

[2] Merrill G. Burlingame, "John Bozeman's Son," research note dated December 18, 1973, regarding his conversation with James Hamilton, President of Montana State College, who reported an earlier conversation with Rosa Barker Van Vlierden Beall. In Merrill G. Burlingame Special Collections, Renne Library, Montana State University at Bozeman.

[3] *Montana Post*, February 9, 1864.

[4] William White Alderson, diary, "Across the Plains to Montana in 1864 to the Gallatin Valley, Montana, 1864-1879," entry for March 23, 1867, in the collections of the Gallatin County Historical Society, Bozeman, Montana.

[5] Robert G. Athearn, *Thomas Francis Meagher: An Irish Revolutionary in America* (Boulder: University of Colorado Press, 1949), p. 147.

[6] Michael A. Leeson, ed., *History of Montana, 1739-1885* (Chicago: Warner, Beers & Co., 1885), p. 119.

[7] James L. Thane, Jr., "Thomas Francis Meagher: The Acting One" (Master's thesis, University of Montana at Missoula, 1967), p. 69.

[8] Athearn, *Thomas Francis Meagher*, p. 162.

[9] Author's interview with Roy Walton, November 15, 1993. Mr. Walton stated that he had a conversation with Billy Frazier sometime around 1916. Frazier was in his sixties at the time and was a regular patron at the Tivoli bar, where he enjoyed an evening of poker. Sixteen-year-old Walton was the Tivoli bartender.

[10] William S. McKinzie, "John Bozeman," *Bozeman Avant Courier*, December 19, 1891.

[11] *Ibid.*

[12] Marshall Bennett, "Benjamin Bembrick's Knowledge of the Death of John Bozeman" in Merrill G. Burlingame Special Collections, Renne Library, Montana State University at Bozeman. Bennett is the great grandson of Bembrick.

[13] Thomas Cover, letter to Acting Territorial Governor Thomas Francis Meagher, April 22, 1867, printed in the *Montana Post*, May 4, 1867.

[14] *Ibid.*

[15] Jefferson Jones, "The Murder of John Bozeman," paper delivered to the Quest for Knowledge Club, Bozeman, Montana, December 13, 1955. In the collections of the Gallatin County Historical Society.

[16] *Ibid.*

[17] *Ibid.*

[18] Merrill G. Burlingame, *John Bozeman, Montana Trailmaker*, rev. ed. (Bozeman: Museum of the Rockies, 1983), p. 37.

[19] Daniel S. Tuttle, *Reminiscences of a Missionary Bishop* (New York: Thomas Whittaker, 1906), pp. 196-198.

[20] George Reed Davis, statement to Grace Hebard and E. A. Brininstool, April 1, 1896. In Grace Raymond Hebard Memorial Collection, American Heritage Center, University of Wyoming at Laramie.

[21] Thane, p. 70.

Chapter Fourteen

[1] Michael J. Koury, *Military Posts of Montana* (Bellevue, Nebr.: Old Army Press, 1970), p. 31.

[2] *Bozeman Avant Courier*, June 13, 1872.

[3] Eugene S. Topping, *Chronicles of the Yellowstone* (St. Paul: Pioneer Press Co., 1888), p. 68.

[4] Fran Denning, "Social Life at Fort Ellis," *Three Forks Herald*, June 5, 1991.

[5] Peter Koch, letter to Laurie Koch dated November 5, 1871, in the collections of the Gallatin County Historical Society, Bozeman, Montana.

[6] *Ibid.*

[7] George W. Flanders, Jr., manuscript, "A History of the Flanders Sawmill," in Merrill G. Burlingame Special Collections, Renne Library, Montana State University at Bozeman.

[8] Davis Willson to the *Montana Post*, December 27, 1867.

[9] David E. Folsom, "The Valley of the Upper Yellowstone," *Contributions to the Montana Historical Society*, vol. 5 (Helena: State Publishing Co., 1904), p. 357.

[10] *Ibid.*

[11] Folsom, p. 367.

[12] Aubrey L. Haines, *The Yellowstone Story*, vol. 1 (Boulder, Colo.: Colorado Associated University Press, 1977), p. 101.

[13] Anne Garner, *Who's Who in the Bozeman Cemetery: A Guide to Historic Gravesites* (Bozeman: The Bozarts Press, 1987), p. 13.

[14] Letter from Virginia Bunker Barnett, granddaughter of Walter Cooper, to Lou Ann Westlake, president of the Gallatin County Historical Society, March 1994. In collections of the Gallatin County Historical Society, Bozeman, Montana.

[15] Nathaniel P. Langford, "The Wonders of the Yellowstone," *Scribner's Monthly* 2 (May 1871): 2.

[16] Langford, p. 3.

[17] Haines, p. 115.

[18] Haines, p. 120.

[19] Henry Bird Calfee, clipping from the *Great Falls Tribune*, possibly 1890s, in the collections of the Gallatin County Historical Society, Bozeman, Montana.

[20] *Ibid.*

[21] *Ibid.*

[22] Haines, p. 141.

[23] See David D. Smits, "The Frontier Army and the Destruction of the Buffalo: 1865-1883," *Western Historical Quarterly* 25 (Autumn 1994): 313-338.

[24] Earl of Dunraven, *The Great Divide: Travels in the Upper Yellowstone in the Summer of 1874* (London: Chatto & Windus, 1876), p. 53.

[25] Dunraven, p. 55.

[26] Dunraven, pp. 55-56.

[27] Dunraven, p. 229.

Chapter Fifteen

[1] Fred Fielding Willson, paper presented to Quest for Knowledge Men's Club, October 15, 1940, in the collections of the Gallatin County Historical Society, Bozeman, Montana, p. 20.

[2] Fred Willson, p. 3.

[3] Isabelle Randall, *A Lady's Ranche Life in Montana* (London: W. H. Allen & Co., 1887), p. 96.

[4] Randall, p. 74.

[5] Bertha Clow, *Foods of the Montana Pioneers* (Bozeman: Gallatin County Historical Society, 1988), p. 6.

[6] A. K. McClure, *Three Thousand Miles Through the Rocky Mountains* (Philadelphia: J. B. Lippincott & Co., 1869), p. 277.

[7] Davis Willson, undated clipping from the *Montana Post*, in the Merrill G. Burlingame Special Collections, Renne Library, Montana State University at Bozeman.

[8] Quoted in Anne Garner, *Who's Who in the Bozeman Cemetery: A Guide to Historic Gravesites* (Bozeman: Bozarts Press, 1987), p. 16.

[9] Fred Willson, p. 24.

[10] Fred Willson, p. 25.

[11] *Helena Herald*, May 28, 1880.

[12] *Bozeman Avant Courier*, September 27, 1877.

[13] Verris A. Wessel, *A Brief History of Bozeman Schools* (Bozeman: Gallatin County Historical Society, 1963), p. 17.

Chapter Sixteen

[1] E. S. Topping, *Chronicles of the Yellowstone* (St. Paul: Pioneer Press Co., 1883), p. 104.

[2] Topping, p. 122.

[3] *Bozeman Avant Courier*, February 6, 1874.

[4] John Barker Bean, "Adventure in Early Montana: the Reminiscences of John 'Jack' Barker Bean," manuscript in the collections of the Gallatin County Historical Society, Bozeman, Montana, p. 5.

[5] Bean manuscript, February 27, 1874.

[6] Bean manuscript, March 27, 1874.

[7] Bean manuscript, February 27, 1874.

[8] Merrill G. Burlingame, *The Montana Frontier* (Bozeman: Big Sky Books, 1942), p. 209.

[9] *Bozeman Avant Courier*, May 1, 1874. For accounts of this expedition, see Eugene S. Topping's *Chronicles of the Yellowstone* (St. Paul: Pioneer Press Co., 1883) and Don Weibert, *The 1874 Invasion of Montana: A Prelude to the Custer Disaster* (N.p.: Don Weibert, 1993).

[10] Letter from Virginia Bunker Barnett, granddaughter of Walter Cooper, to Lou Ann Westlake, president of the Gallatin County Historical Society, March 1991. In collections of the Gallatin County Historical Society, Bozeman, Montana.

[11] Mark Brown, *Plainsmen of the Yellowstone* (New York: G. P. Putnam's Sons, 1961), p. 436.

[12] Brown, p. 438.

[13] Bessie Benham, "Interview with William 'Billy' Frazier," April 3 and 4, 1940. In collections of the Gallatin County Historical Society, Bozeman, Montana.

[14] Lieutenant James H. Bradley, in *Contributions to the Montana Historical Society*, vol. 2 (Helena: State Publishing Co., 1896), p. 203.

[15] *Ibid.*

[16] *Bozeman Times*, July 6, 1876.

Chapter Seventeen

[1] *Bozeman Avant Courier*, September 5, 1891.

[2] Frances Roe, *Letters from an Army Officer's Wife* (New York: D. Appleton & Co., 1909), p. 313.

[3] James R. McDonald, *Bozeman's Historical Resources* (Bozeman: County Planning Board, 1984), p. 61.

[4] "The Gallatin Valley, Montana," *The Coast* 15 (June 1908): 426.

[5] Fred Fielding Willson, paper presented to the Quest for Knowledge Men's Club, October 15, 1940, in the collections of the Gallatin County Historical Society, Bozeman, Montana, p. 28.

[6] Fred Willson paper.

[7] Verris A. Wessel, "A Brief History of Bozeman Schools," (Bozeman: Gallatin County Historical Society, 1963), p. 26.

[8] Harry Healy quoted in the *Bozeman Daily Chronicle*, September 23, 1951.

[9] Moser, D. E., "Brief History of the Bozeman Fire Department, Dating From February 22, 1884 to February 22, 1909," (Bozeman: Gallatin County Historical Society, n.d.), p. 5.

[10] Thomas B. Quaw, in the *Belgrade Journal*, December 3, 1914.

[11] Ronald J. Iverson, *The Princess of the Prairie: A History of Belgrade, Montana* (Bozeman: N.p., 1965), p. 25.

[12] Iverson, p. 88.

[13] Iverson, p. 51.

[14] Iverson, pp. 52-53.

[15] Robert G. Athearn, *Westward the Briton* (Lincoln: University of Nebraska Press, 1953), p. 100.

[16] Isabelle Randall, *A Lady's Ranche Life in Montana* (London: W. H. Allen & Co., 1887), p. 12.

[17] Randall, p. 18.

[18] Randall, p. 19.

[19] Randall, p. 48.

[20] *Bozeman Avant Courier*, June 29, 1889.

[21] *Gallatin County Republican*, January 9, 1904.

[22] Edward B. Reynolds, "Montana Trader and His 'Ringer' Race Horse 'Take' Fox Hunting Riders of English Colony," *Philipsburg Mail*, October 7, 1933.

[23] *Rocky Mountain Husbandman*, August 26, 1886.

[24] John E. Mitchell and Richard H. Hart, "The Winter of 1886-1887 Ended the Era of the Open Range," *Montana Farmer-Stockman*, February 5, 1987.

[25] *Cheyenne Daily Sun*, December 8, 1887.

Chapter Eighteen

[1] *Bozeman Daily Chronicle*, August 10, 1954.

[2] *Bozeman Daily Chronicle*, September 14, 1887.

[3] *Bozeman Avant Courier*, May 22, 1890.

[4] John N. DeHaas and Bernice W. DeHaas, "Footlights and Fire Engines," *Montana, the Magazine of Western History* 16 (October 1967): 11.

[5] *Bozeman Avant Courier*, October 16, 1890.

[6] *Bozeman Avant Courier*, February 12, 1898.

[7] Charles Anceney III, *Charles Anceney and the Flying D Ranch* (Bozeman: Gallatin County Historical Society, 1986), p. 18.

[8] B. C. Forbes, "Anceney—Boss of Half-a-Million Acres," *Forbes Magazine* (September 1923).

[9] Entry for May 8, 1882, in the Charles D. Loughrey diaries, in the collections of the Gallatin County Historical Society, Bozeman, Montana.

[10] Loughrey diaries, February 27, 1887.

[11] Loughrey diaries, February 27, 1889.

[12] Loughrey diaries, August 13, 1889.

[13] Loughrey diaries, September 22, 1889.

Chapter Nineteen

[1] Thomas H. McKee, quoted in Merrill G. Burlingame, *Montana State University: A History* (Bozeman: Montana State University Office of Information, 1968), p. 12.

[2] Robert Rydell, Jeffrey Safford, and Pierce Mullen, *In The People's Interest* (Bozeman: Montana State University Foundation, 1992), p. 10.

[3] *Ibid.*

[4] Rydell *et al.*, p. 13.

[5] Michael Langohr, Sr., quoted in the *Bozeman Daily Chronicle*, December 27, 1970.

[6] *Bozeman Avant Courier*, July 30, 1892.

[7] Langohr, in the *Chronicle*.

[8] *Bozeman Avant Courier*, November 20, 1897.

[9] Merrill G. Burlingame, "Timberline—A Thriving Mining Town of 1880s," _Bozeman Daily Chronicle_, August 9, 1964.

[10] _Ibid._

[11] _Ibid._

Chapter Twenty

[1] AnnaBelle Phillips, supplement to the _High Country News_, August 2, 1978.

[2] _Bozeman Weekly Chronicle_, July 4, 1907.

[3] _Bozeman Weekly Chronicle_, August 8, 1907.

[4] _Bozeman Weekly Chronicle_, July 8, 1908.

[5] _Bozeman Weekly Chronicle_, July 30, 1908.

[6] Ira Swett, "Montana Trolleys," _Interurban Magazine_ 27 (Spring 1970): 27.

[7] Swett, p. 31.

[8] Don Baker, _The Montana Railroad: Alias the Jawbone_ (Boulder, Colo.: Fred Pruett Books, 1993), p. 53.

[9] Ivan Doig, _Heart Earth_ (New York: Macmillan Publishing Co., 1993), p. 102.

[10] Anita Petterson, note to Marguerite Fulker, May 1994, in the collections of the Gallatin County Historical Society, Bozeman, Montana.

[11] Christie family letters, David to Emma Christie, September 23, 1885, in the collections of the Gallatin County Historical Society, Bozeman, Montana.

[12] Lyle K. Williams, "Historically Speaking," pamphlet (Three Forks: January 1976), p. 34.

Chapter Twenty-one

[1] _Belgrade Journal_, August 11, 1910.

[2] _Gallatin Farmer and Stockman_, September 20, 1902.

[3] Herman Steen, _The O. W. Fisher Heritage_ (N.p.: Frank McCaffrey Publishers, 1961), p. 71.

[4] For a history of Belgrade, read Ron J. Iverson, _The Princess of the Prairie_ (Belgrade: N.p., 1965).

[5] Walter Cooper, "West Gallatin Northern Pacific Exploring Expedition," letter to daughter Mariam Bunker, October 10, 1940, in the McGill Collection, Merrill G. Burlingame Special Collections, Renne Library, Montana State University at Bozeman.

[6] Michael P. Malone, "The Gallatin Canyon and the Tides of History," _Montana, The Magazine of Western History_ 22 (summer 1973): 7.

[7] For a study of the Gallatin Canyon, see Janet Cronin and Dorothy Vick, _Montana's Gallatin Canyon_ (Missoula: Mountain Press Publishing Co., 1992).

Chapter Twenty-two

[1] Rick Boylan, "The Elegant Ellen," _Bozeman Daily Chronicle_, March 29, 1983.

[2] For a history of the Bozeman Opera House see Bernice W. DeHaas and John N. DeHaas, "Footlights and Fire Engines: The Story of Bozeman's Glorious Old Opera House-City Hall," _Montana, The Magazine of Western History_ 17 (October 1967): 28-43.

[3] Helen E. Fechter, "An Alien in Her Native Land," in _In Celebration of Our Past_ (Bozeman: Gallatin County Historical Society, 1991), p. 72.

[4] _Bozeman Daily Chronicle_, October 16, 1918.

[5] AnnaBelle Phillips, "First Roundup was in 1919," _Bozeman Daily Chronicle_, August 22, 1970.

[6] Berg Clark, Gallatin County Bicentennial Oral History Project, in the collections of the Gallatin County Historical Society, Bozeman, Montana.

[7] Della Doyle, Gallatin County Bicentennial Oral History Project.

[8] Merrill G. Burlingame, *A History of Montana State University* (Bozeman: MSU Office of Information, 1968), p. 37.

[9] Burlingame, *History of MSU*, p. 77.

Chapter Twenty-three

[1] *Bozeman Avant Courier*, April 5, 1883.

[2] Connie Staudohar, "Bozeman Women's Heritage Trail" (Bozeman: Connie Staudohar, 1994), p. 13.

[3] Bernice W. DeHaas and John N. DeHaas, "Footlights and Fire Engines" *Montana, The Magazine of Western History* 17 (October 1967): 28.

[4] *Bozeman Avant Courier*, August 16, 1883.

[5] *Bozeman Avant Courier*, April 20, 1884.

[6] *Bozeman Avant Courier*, January 3, 1884.

[7] *Bozeman Avant Courier*, October 3, 1905.

[8] *Republican Courier*, April 20, 1906.

[9] Cortlandt L. Freeman, "The Growing Up Years: The First 100 Years of Bozeman as an Incorporated City From 1883 to 1983" in *Bozeman, Montana* (Bozeman: Gallatin County Historical Society, 1988), p. 78.

[10] *Montana Taxpayer* 5 (March 1948): 4.

[11] K. Ross Toole, *Montana, An Uncommon Land* (Norman: University of Oklahoma Press, 1959), pp. 235-236.

[12] James R. MacDonald, *Bozeman's Historic Resources* (Bozeman: City-County Planning Board, August 10, 1954), p. 101.

[13] Merrill G. Burlingame, *Montana State University: A History* (Bozeman: Montana State University Office of Information, 1968), pp. 71-72.

[14] Burlingame, *Montana State University: A History*, p. 73.

[15] William Sharp, Jr., "The C.C.C. at Squaw Creek," manuscript at the Gallatin County Historical Society, Bozeman, Montana.

[16] *Bozeman Daily Chronicle*, October 24, 1936.

Chapter Twenty-four

[1] Tracy Ellig, "Karst Kamp Daredevils," *Bozeman Daily Chronicle*, January 5, 1995.

[2] *Ibid.*

[3] Kay Widmer, "Skiing—As I Remember It," paper presented to the Gallatin County Historical Society, Bozeman, Montana, p. 1.

[4] Widmer, p. 6.

[5] Widmer, p. 8.

[6] William Ennis to E. J. Owenhouse, letter dated July 23, 1891. In the collections of the Gallatin County Historical Society, Bozeman.

[7] Edmund Christopherson, *The Night the Mountain Fell* (West Yellowstone: Yellowstone Publications, 1960 and 1961), p. 5.

[8] William Merrick interview with author, March 6, 1995.

Chapter Twenty-five

[1] Jim DeWolf, "Bozeman Faces Tough Decisions on Growth," *Bozeman Daily Chronicle*, May 14, 1975.

[2] Mettler v. Ames Realty Company, *Montana Reports* 61 (1921): 152-71.

[3] *Rocky Mountain Husbandman*, January 29, 1885.

[4] Merrill G. Burlingame, "Joseph M. Lindley," in the collection of the Gallatin County Historical Society, Bozeman, Montana.

[5] Robert Rydell, Jeffrey Safford, and Pierce Mullen, *In the People's Interest* (Bozeman: Montana State University Foundation, 1992), p. 59.

[6] Rydell *et al.*, p. 61.

[7] "Extra: The Flood of Fallacy Dissected and Exposed," handbill in the collections of the Gallatin County Historical Society, Bozeman, Montana.

[8] Roland R. Renne, "The Future of the Land-Grant College," April 10, 1945, 81002/7, folder BO (242) University Archives, Renne Library, Montana State University at Bozeman.

[9] Interview with Richard Roeder, November 14, 1991, in Rydell *et al.*, p. 96.

[10] Robert T. Smith, "The Big Sky Development: A Lesson for the Future," *American West* 12 (September 1975): 46.

[11] Louise Keightley in the *Bozeman Daily Chronicle*, February 11, 1971.

[12] Smith, p. 62.

[13] *Ibid.*

[14] As quoted in Frank Browning, "Big Sky: Chet Huntley's New Home on the Range," *Ramparts* 10 (April 1972): 42.

[15] David Penwell, quoted in Eric Wiltse, "Big Sky, Montana: A Long Road to Success," *Bozeman Daily Chronicle*, October 13, 1981.

[16] *Ibid.*

[17] For a more detailed story of these events, read Janet Swenson, *Victims: The Kari Swenson Story* (Boulder: Pruett Publishing Co., 1989).

Chapter Twenty-six

[1] Quoted in Barbara Johnson Smith, "Southwestern Montana: Living Close to the Land," *Bozeman Daily Chronicle*, June 9, 1985.

[2] Dan O'Brian, "Montana's Cow Town With Charm," *New York Times*, May 9, 1993.

[3] Ray White, interviews with author, January 19 and April 13, 1995.

[4] Quoted in Jim Robbins, "Go West? Go Away, Say Folks in Montana," *Boston Globe*, December 22, 1993.

[5] William Kittredge, "The Last Safe Place," *Time*, September 6, 1993, p. 27.

[6] Montana Department of Revenue, Biennial Reports, as quoted in *Montana Business Quarterly* 33 (Spring 1995): graph, p. 29.

[7] Ivan Doig, *Heart Earth* (New York: The Macmillan Co., 1993), p. 102.

[8] *Pacific Daily News*, Guam, January 10, 1973, p. 25.

[9] Roxana Hegeman, "Big Changes in Small Towns," *Bozeman Daily Chronicle*, March 3, 1991.

BIBLIOGRAPHY

Unpublished Notes:

Alderson, William White. "Across the Plains to Montana in 1864 to Gallatin Valley, Montana, 1864-1879." Diary in the collections of the Gallatin County Historical Society, Bozeman, Montana.

Allen, J. I. Notes on expeditions of 1875, 1876, and 1877. In the collections of the Gallatin County Historical Society, Bozeman, Montana.

Bean, John Barker. "Adventure in Early Montana: A Reminiscence of John (Jack) Barker Bean." Manuscript in the collections of the Gallatin County Historical Society, Bozeman, Montana.

Benham, Bessie. Interview with William "Billy" Frazier, April 3 and 4, 1940. In the collections of the Gallatin County Historical Society, Bozeman, Montana.

Bennett, Marshall. "Benjamin F. Bembrick's Knowledge of the Death of John Bozeman." Paper in the Merrill G. Burlingame Special Collections, Renne Library, Montana State University at Bozeman.

Bozeman, John. Letters, 1866-1867. In the collections of the Gallatin County Historical Society, Bozeman, Montana.

Burlingame, Merrill G. Research notes and papers. In Merrill G. Burlingame Special Collections, Renne Library, Montana State University at Bozeman.

_____. "The Gallatin County Female Semainary, 1872-1878." Paper, April 1929. In the collections of the Gallatin County Historical Society, Bozeman, Montana.

_____. "The Un-natural History of Bozeman." Paper presented to the Quest for Knowledge Men's Club, Bozeman, Montana, November 18, 1975. In the collections of the Gallatin County Historical Society, Bozeman, Montana.

Carter, Cecilia. "The History of the Springhill Comunity." Paper, 1976, in the collections of the Gallatin County Historical Society, Bozeman, Montana.

Coffman, Laura. "Streets and Men." Paper in the collections of the Gallatin County Historical Society, Bozeman, Montana.

Cooper, Walter. Correspondence with daughter Marian Cooper Bunker. In the McGill Collection, Merrill G. Burlingame Special Collections, Renne Library, Montana State University at Bozeman.

Davis, Leslie B. "Archeology and Geology of the Schmitt Mine." Paper, 1982, in Merrill G. Burlingame Special Collections, Renne Library, Montana State University at Bozeman.

East Gallatin Claim Association. Minutes, August 9, 1864 to February 11, 1865. In collections of the Gallatin County Historical Society, Bozeman, Montana.

Fix, Philip Forsyth. "Structure of Gallatin Valley, Montana." Doctoral thesis, University of Colorado at Boulder, 1940.

Flanders, George W., Jr. "A History of the Flanders Sawmill." Paper in Merrill G. Burlingame Special Collections, Renne Library, Montana State University at Bozeman.

Fleming, Walter. "We Knew You Were Coming: A Native Perspective of European Settlement in North America." Paper presented to Montana Historical Society Annual Conference, Helena, Montana, October 25, 1991.

Fryslie, Norma C. "Historical Sketch of Early and Present Bozeman Banks." Paper, 1953, in collections of the Gallatin County Historical Society, Bozeman, Montana.

Ghent, W. J. "Biography of John Colter." Manuscript in the collections of the Gallatin County Historical Society, Bozeman, Montana.

Gourley, Jim. "The Story of a March: Gold Seekers Against Redskins; Bozeman to Wolf Mountains." Undated clipping in Rosa Beall scrapbook, Merrill G. Burlingame Special Collections, Renne Library, Montana State University at Bozeman.

Houston, Elizabeth Lina Alderson. "Early History of Methodist Episcopal Church." Paper, 1915, in the collections of the Gallatin County Historical Society, Bozeman, Montana.

Huttinga, Debbie. "From Slabtown to Gallatin Gateway." Manuscript, 1989, in the collections of the Gallatin County Historical Society, Bozeman, Montana.

Jones, Jefferson. "The Murder of John Bozeman?" Paper, Quest for Knowledge Men's Club, December 13, 1955. In the collections of the Gallatin County Historical Society, Bozeman, Montana.

Kenney, Joseph L., and Thomas Rhoten. Letters from the Gallatin, 1864. In Merrill G. Burlingame Special Collections, Renne Library, Montana State University at Bozeman.

Koch, Peter. Letter to Laurie Koch, November 8, 1871. In the collections of the Gallatin County Historical Society, Bozeman, Montana.

Lessley, W. W. "Adjudication of Water Rights in Gallatin County." Paper in Merrill G. Burlingame Special Collections, Renne Library, Montana State University at Bozeman.

Loughrey, Charles D. Diaries, 1882, 1887, 1889, 1893, 1896, and 1897. In the collections of the Gallatin County Historical Society, Bozeman, Montana.

McDonald, Rita. "Notes on the Three Forks Area, 1862-1869." Paper, 1955. In Merrill G. Burlingame Special Collections, Renne Library, Montana State University at Bozeman.

Merriam, Harold G. "Ethnic Settlement of Montana." Paper, July 9, 1942. In Merrill G. Burlingame Special Collections, Renne Library, Montana State University, Bozeman.

Mills, Mary Sales. "Zachariah Sales." Paper, 1939, in McGill Collection, Merrill G. Burlingame Special Collections, Renne Library, Montana State University at Bozeman.

Moser, C. E. "Brief History of the Bozeman Fire Department Dating from February 22, 1884 to February 22, 1909." Manuscript in the collections of the Gallatin County Historical Society, Bozeman, Montana.

Napton, Lewis Kyle. "Canyon and Valley: Preliminary Archeological Survey of the Gallatin Area." Master's thesis, University of Montana at Missoula, 1967.

Nowels, Edward L. "Old Trail Creek Track." Paper in collections of Gallatin County Historical Society, Bozeman, Montana.

Parker, John G. Letter to Robert G. Dunbar, May 2, 1979. In Merrill G. Burlingame Special Collections, Renne Library, Montana State University at Bozeman.

Parker, M. C. Letter to Robert G. Dunbar, June 11 and 13, 1979. In Merrill G. Burlingame Special Collections, Renne Library, Montana State University at Bozeman.

Purple, Edwin R. Diary. In Merrill G. Burlingame Special Collections, Renne Library, Montana State University at Bozeman.

Story, Thomas Byron. "The Death of John Bozeman," note to Merrill G. Burlingame, May 9, 1945. In collections of the Gallatin County Historical Society, Bozeman, Montana.

Tesmer, Curt, and Ted Gusey. "Bear Canyon History." Paper in the collections of the Gallatin County Historical Society, Bozeman, Montana.

Thane, James L., Jr. "Thomas Francis Meagher, The Acting One." Master's thesis, University of Montana at Missoula, 1967.

Tracy, Sarah J. Bessey. "The Brides of Pioneers." Speech, Bozeman, Montana, 1898. In the collections of the Gallatin County Historical Society, Bozeman, Montana.

Wessel, Veris A. "A Brief History of Bozeman Schools." Paper, 1963. In the collections of the Gallatin County Historical Society, Bozeman, Montana.

Widmer, Kay. "Skiing—As I Remember It." Manuscript in the collections of the Gallatin County Historical Society, Bozeman, Montana.

Willson, Fred Fielding. "Bozeman." Paper, Quest for Knowledge Men's Club, October 15, 1940. In the collections of the Gallatin County Historical Society, Bozeman, Montana.

Newspapers

Billings Gazette

Bozeman Avant Courier

Bozeman Daily Chronicle

Bozeman Times

Butte Miner

Gallatin County Republican

Gallatin County Tribune and Belgrade Journal

Great Falls Tribune

Helena Herald

Jefferson Valley News

Livingston Enterprise

Montana Farmer-Stockman

Montana Pick and Plow

Montana Post

New York Times

Philipsburg Mail

Three Forks Herald

Three Forks News

Books, Articles, and Pamphlets

A Goodly Heritage: A History of the Churchill and Amsterdam Area of Montana. Rev. ed. Churchill, Mont.: Churchill-Amsterdam Historical Society, 1989.

Alderson, William White. "Gold Camp Tubers." *Montana, The Magazine of Western History* 3 (autumn 1953): 46-49.

Alter, J. Cecil. *Jim Bridger*. Reprint (1925). Norman, Okla.: University of Oklahoma Press, 1962.

Anceney, Charles L., III. "The Anceneys of the Flying D Ranch." Pamphlet. Bozeman, Mont.: Gallatin County Historical Society, n.d.

Athearn, Robert G. "Early Territorial Montana: A Problem in Colonial Administration." *Montana, The Magazine of Western History* 1 (summer 1951): 15-21.

_____. *High Country Empire*. New York: McGraw-Hill, 1960.

_____. *Thomas Francis Meagher: An Irish Revolutionary in America*. Studies in History No. 1. Boulder: University of Colorado Press, 1949.

_____. *Westward the Briton*. Reprint (1953). Lincoln: University of Nebraska Press, 1962.

Baker, Don. *The Montana Railroad: Alias the Jawbone*. Boulder: Fred Pruett Books, 1990.

Baker, John David. "The West in 1876." *American West* 13 (July-August 1976): 35-38.

Bancroft, Hubert Howe. *Works*. Vol. 31, *History of Washington, Idaho and Montana*. San Francisco: History Company, 1890.

Barry, T. Neilson, "Lieutenant Jeremy Pinch." *Oregon Historical Quarterly* 38 (September 1937): 323-327.

Bates, Grace. *Gallatin County: Places and Things, Present and Past*. Rev. ed. Bozeman: Grace Bates, 1995.

Beal, Merrill D. *Story of Man in Yellowstone*. Rev. ed. Mammoth, Wyo.: Yellowstone Library & Museum Assoc., 1956.

Beall, Rosa Barker. "Bozeman's Early Schools." *Contributions to the Montana Historical Society*. Vol. 7. Helena: State Publishing Co., 1910, 304-11.

_____."Montana's Early History: A Pioneer Woman's Recollection of People and Events Connected with Montana's Early History." *Contributions to the Montana Historical Society*, Vol. 8. Helena: State Publishing Co., 1917, 295-303.

Berry, Don. *A Majority of Scoundrels*. New York: Harper & Bros., 1961.

Blevins, Winfred. *Dictionary of the American West*. New York: Facts on File, 1993.

Bonar, John A. "John Merin Bozeman." *Montana Magazine* 2 (winter 1971-1972): 42-43.

"Bozeman and Its Surroundings." *The Rockies Illustrated Magazine* 4 (September 1892).

Bozeman City Directory, 1892-1893. Bozeman: J. D. Radford & Co., 1892.

Bozeman City Directory, 1900 to present. Bozeman: R. L. Polk & Co.

Brackett, Albert G. "A Trip Through the Rocky Mountains." *Contributions to the Montana Historical Society*, Vol. 8. Helena: State Publishing Co., 1917, 329-344.

Bradbury, John. *Travels in the Interior of America*. Liverpool: Smith & Galway, 1817.

Bradley, James. "Lt. James Bradley's Journal." *Contributions to the Montana Historical Society*. Vol. 2. Helena: State Publishing Co., 1886, 140-154.

_____. "The Yellowstone Expedition of 1874." *Contributions to the Montana Historical Society*, Vol. 8. Helena: State Publishing Co., 1917, 104-126.

Brown, Dee. *The Fetterman Massacre* (formerly *Fort Phil Kearny: An American Saga*). Lincoln: University of Nebraska Press, 1971.

Brown, Mark H. *The Plainsmen of the Yellowstone*. New York: G. P. Putnam's Sons, 1961.

Bryan, William L., Jr. *Montana's Indians: Yesterday and Today*. Helena: Montana Magazine, Inc., 1985.

Burlingame, Merrill G. "The Andrew Jackson Doane Family." *Montana, The Magazine of Western History* 1 (winter 1951): 5-13.

_____. *Gallatin Century of Progress*. Bozeman: Gallatin County Centennial Publication, 1964.

_____. *Gallatin County's Heritage: A Report of Progress, 1805-1976*. Bozeman: Gallatin County Centennial Publication, 1978.

_____. *The Grand Avenue Christian Church*. Bozeman: Grand Avenue Christian Church, 1988.

_____. "The Influence of the Military in the Building of Montana." *Pacific Northwest Review* 29 (1938): 135-150.

_____. "John M. Bozeman, Montana Trailmaker." *Mississippi Valley Historical Review* 28 (March 1941): 541-568. Revised 1971, 1983, and reprinted by the Museum of the Rockies, Bozeman, Montana.

_____. "Law and Order in Gallatin County." Pamphlet, rev. ed. Bozeman: Gallatin County Historical Society, 1987

_____. *The Montana Frontier*. Helena: State Publishing Co., 1942.

_____. *Montana State University: A History*. Bozeman: Montana State University Office of Information, 1968.

_____. "Montana's Righteous Hangmen: A Reconsideration." *Montana, The Magazine of Western History* 28 (October 1978): 36-49.

Burlingame, Merrill, and K. Ross Toole, eds. *A History of Montana*. 3 vols. New York: Lewis Historical Publishing Co., 1957.

Butscher, L. C., ed. "An Account of Adventures in the Great American Desert by His Royal Highness, Duke Paul Wilhelm von Wurttenberg." *New Mexico Historical Review* 17 (1942).

Callaway, Llewellyn L. "Early Montana Masons." Pamphlet. Billings: N.p., 1951.

_____. *Montana's Righteous Hangmen*. Norman: University of Oklahoma Press, 1982.

Campbell, John Lyle. *Idaho: Six Months in the New Diggings: The Emigrant's Guide Overland*. New York: J. L. Campbell, 1864.

Cheney, Roberta Carkeek. *Names on the Face of Montana*. Missoula: Mountain Press Publishing Company, 1983.

Chittenden, Hiram Martin. *American Fur Trade of the Far West*. 2 vols. Reprint (1902, 1935). Stanford: Academic Reprints, 1954.

_____. *The Yellowstone National Park*. R. A. Bartlett, ed. Norman: University of Oklahoma Press, 1964.

Chittenden, Hiram, and A. T. Richardson, eds. *The Life, Letters and Travels of Father Pierre-Jean DeSmet, S.J., 1801-1873*. New York: Francis P. Harper, 1905.

Christopherson, Edmund. *The Night the Mountain Fell*. West Yellowstone: Yellowstone Publications, 1960.

City Plan for Bozeman, Montana. Denver: S. R. DeBoer & Co., 1958.

Clow, Bertha. "Foods of the Montana Pioneers." Pamphlet. Bozeman: Gallatin County Historical Society, 1988.

Cronin, Janet and Dorothy Vick. *Montana's Gallatin Canyon*. Missoula: Mountain Press Publishing Company, 1992.

Cushman, Dan. *The Great North Trail*. New York: McGraw-Hill, 1966.

Davis, Henry. "Wales to Montana: 1860s." Pamphlet. Bozeman: Gallatin County Historical Society.

Davison, Stanley R., and Dale Tash. "Confederate Backwash in Montana Territory." *Montana, The Magazine of Western History* 17 (autumn 1967): 50-58.

DeHaas, John N., and Bernice W. DeHaas. "Footlights and Fire Engines: The Story of Bozeman's Glorious Old Opera House-City Hall." *Montana, The Magazine of Western History* 17 (autumn 1967): 28-43.

Denning, Fran. *Growing Pains: Three Forks, Montana, 1908-1976*. Three Forks: N.p., 1975.

DeVoto, Bernard. *Across the Wide Missouri*. Boston: Houghton Mifflin Company, 1964.

_____. The Course of Empire. Boston: Houghton Mifflin Co., 1962.

DeYoung, William, and L. H. Smith. "Soil Survey of the Gallatin Valley, Montana." U.S. Department of Agriculture, Series 1931, No. 16. Washington, D.C.: Government Printing Office, 1936.

Dimsdale, Thomas J. *The Vigilantes of Montana*. Reprint (1866). Norman: University of Oklahoma Press, 1953.

Doig, Ivan. *Heart Earth*. New York: Macmillan, 1993.

Dunbar, Elizabeth. "Three Forks, the Gateway." Pamphlet. N.p., 1926.

Dunbar, Robert G. "The Adaptability of Water Law to the Aridity of the West." *Journal of the West* 24 (January 1985): 57-65.

_____. "Agriculture." In Merrill G. Burlingame and K. Ross Toole, *A History of Montana*. Vol. 1: 281-310. New York: Lewis Historical Publishing Co., 1957.

_____. "The Economic Development of the Gallatin Valley." *Pacific Northwest Quarterly* 47 (October 1956): 117-123.

_____. *Forging New Rights in Western Waters*. Lincoln: University of Nebraska Press, 1983.

_____. "The Search For a Stable Water Right in Montana." *Agricultural History* 28 (October 1954): 138-148.

Dunraven, Earl of. *The Great Divide: Travels in the Upper Yellowstone in the Summer of 1874*. London: Chatto & Windus, 1876.

Eagle, Sam P., Jr., and John Edwin. "West Yellowstone's 70th Anniversary, 1908-1978." Pamphlet. West Yellowstone: N.p., 1978.

Edsall, E. S.,ed. "The Gallatin Valley, Montana," *The Coast* 15 (June 1908): 6.

"Eighty Years . . . 1868-1948: St. James Episcopal Church." Pamphlet. Bozeman: St. James Episcopal Church, 1948.

Ellsworth W. H., ed. *Bozeman, Montana Illustrated: A History of the Gallatin Valley and the City of Bozeman*. Bozeman: Avant Courier Publishing Company, 1898.

Emery, Wesley P. "The Execution of Bill Hunter." In *Contributions to the Montana Historical Society*, Vol. 7. Helena: State Publishing Co., 1910, 167-174.

Ewers, John C. "The Story of the Blackfeet." Pamphlet. Haskell Institute, 1944.

Fechter, Helen E. "The Big Horn Gun." In *In Celebration of Our Past, 1993*. Bozeman: Gallatin County Historical Society, 1993.

_____. "The Chinese in Bozeman." In *In Celebration of Our Past, 1992*. Bozeman: Gallatin County Historical Society, 1992.

Ferris, Warren Angus. *Life in the Rocky Mountains*. Leroy R. Hafen, ed. Denver: Old West Publishing Company, 1983.

"First Presbyterian Church, Bozeman, Montana." Pamphlet. Bozeman: First Presbyterian Church, 1972.

Folsom, David E. "The Valley of the Upper Yellowstone." In *Contributions to the Montana Historical Society*, Vol. 5, pp. 356-369. Helena: State Publishing Co., 1904.

Forbes, B. C. "Anceney—Boss of Half-a-Million Acres." *Forbes Magazine* (September 1923): 642-644, 656-657, 661, 665.

Freeman, Cortlandt L. "The Growing Up Years: The First 100 Years of Bozeman as an Incorporated City from 1883-1983." In *Bozeman, Montana*. Bozeman: Gallatin County Historical Society, 1988.

Gallatin City: Book of Records for the Town of Gallatin and Surrounding Country. Book A. Dacotha Territory: N.p., 1862.

"Gallatin County Government." Pamphlet. Rev. ed. Bozeman: League of Women Voters, 1992.

Gallatin Pioneers: The First 50 Years, 1868-1918. Bozeman: N.p., 1984.

Garner, Anne. *Who's Who in the Bozeman Cemetery: A Guide to Historic Gravesites.* Bozeman: The Bozarts Press, 1987.

Garcia, Andrew. *Tough Trip Through Paradise.* Reprint (1967). Bennett H. Stein, ed. Sausalito, Calif.: Comstock Editions, Inc., 1981.

Ghent, W. J. "Jeremy Pinch Again." *Oregon Historical Quarterly* 40 (December 1939): 307-314.

Gillette, Warren. "The Quest of Warren Gillette," Brian Cockhill, ed. *Montana, The Magazine of Western History* 22 (summer 1972): 12-30.

Gilluly, Sam. *The Press Gang: A Century of Montana Newspapers, 1885-1985.* Helena: Montana Press Assoc., 1985.

Hafen, Leroy, ed. *Mountain Men and Fur Traders of the Far West.* Lincoln: University of Nebraska Press, 1982.

Haines, Aubrey L. "Lost in the Yellowstone." *Montana, The Magazine of Western History* 22 (summer 1972): 31-41.

_____. *The Yellowstone Story.* 2 vols. Boulder: University of Colorado Press, 1977.

Haines, Francis, Sr. "Red Men of the Plains, 1500-1870." *American West* 10 (July 1973): 32-37.

Hamilton, James McClellan. *From Wilderness to Statehood: A History of Montana.* Portland, Ore.: Binfords & Mort, 1957.

Hapner, Leora M. *As I Look Back.* Bozeman: Montana State College, 1960.

Harris, Burton. *John Colter: His Years in the Rockies.* Reprint (1952). Basin, Wyo.: Big Horn Books, 1977.

Headwaters Herald. Helena: State Publishing Company, n.d.

Headwaters Heritage History. Three Forks, Mont.: Three Forks Area Historical Society, 1983.

Hebard, Grace Raymond, and E. A. Brininstool. *The Bozeman Trail.* 2 vols. Reprint (1961). Lincoln: University of Nebraska Press, 1990.

Hedges, Cornelius. "Early Masonry in Montana." *Rocky Mountain Magazine* 1 (September 1900): 13-17.

Heitman, Francis B. *Historical Register and Dictionary of the U.S. Army.* Vol. 1. Washington, D.C.: Government Printing Office, 1903.

Heman, Howard W. "Water Rights Under the Law of Montana." *Montana Law Review* 10 (spring 1949): 13-34.

Hill, Burton S. "Bozeman and the Bozeman Trail." *Annals of Wyoming* 36 (October 1964): 205-233.

"Historical Map of Gallatin County." Billings: Montana Institute of the Arts, 1951.

Houston, Elizabeth Lina Alderson. *Early History of Gallatin County, Montana.* Bozeman: Sons and Daughters of the Pioneers of Gallatin County, 1933.

Howard, Joseph Kinsey. *Montana: High, Wide, and Handsome.* Reprint (1943). Lincoln: University of Nebraska Press, 1983.

Hutchins, James S. "Poison in the Pemmican." *Montana, The Magazine of Western History* 8 (summer 1958): 8-25.

"In the Egypt of America, Gallatin Valley." Pamphlet. Bozeman: N.p., 1905 and 1908.

"Irrigation of Montana." Pamphlet. N.p., n.d.

Iverson, Ronald J. *The Princess of the Prairie: A History of Belgrade, Montana.* Bozeman: N.p., 1965.

Jackson, Donald. *Among the Sleeping Giants.* Urbana: University of Illinois Press, 1987.

_____. "Call Him a Good Old Dog, But Don't Call Him Scannon." *We Proceeded On* 2 (August 1985).

_____, ed. *Letters of the Lewis and Clark Expedition With Related Documents, 1783-1854.* Urbana: University of Illinois Press, 1962.

Jackson, W. Turrentine. "The Creation of Yellowstone National Park." *Montana, The Magazine of Western History* 7 (July 1957): 36-51.

_____. "The Washburn Doane Expedition." *Montana, The Magazine of Western History* 7 (July 1957): 52-65.

James, Thomas. *Three Years Among the Indians and Mexicans.* Philadelphia and New York: J. B. Lippincott Co., 1962.

Johnson, Dorothy. *The Bloody Bozeman.* New York: McGraw-Hill, 1971.

_____. "The Patience of Frank Kirkaldie." *Montana, The Magazine of Western History* 21 (winter 1971): 12-27.

"Journals of Lewis and Clark at the Three Forks: Clark's Journey Across the Gallatin Valley, 1805-1806." McGill Museum Publication No. 3, 1964.

Kappler, Charles J. *Indian Affairs, Laws and Treaties*, Vol. 2, p. 736. Washington, D.C., Government Printing Office, 1904.

Kirkpatrick, James. "A Reminiscence of John Bozeman." *Frontier* 9 (May 1929) or in Paul C. Phillips, ed., *Historical Reprints, Sources of Northwest History.* Vol. 7, pp. 3-7. Missoula: University of Montana, n.d.

Koch, Peter. "Historical Sketch: Bozeman, Gallatin Valley and Bozeman Pass." *Contributions to the Montana Historical Society*, Vol. 2. Helena: State Publishing Company, 1896, 126-139.

_____. "Journal of Peter Koch, 1869 and 1870." *Frontier* 9 (January 1929).

Koury, Michael J. *Military Posts of Montana.* Bellevue, Nebr.: Old Army Press, 1970.

Kraenzel, Carl Frederick. *The Great Plains in Transition.* Norman: University of Oklahoma Press, 1955.

_____. "Montana's Population Changes, 1920 to 1950." Bulletin 520, July 1956. Agricultural Experiment Station, Montana State College, Bozeman, Montana.

Kubik, Barbara. "John Colter—One of Lewis and Clark's Men." *We Proceeded On* (May-June 1983): 10-15.

Lane, Harrison. "Custer's Massacre." Pamphlet. No. 7 in *Montana Heritage Series.* Helena: Montana Historical Society Press, 1955.

Langford, Nathaniel Pitt. *The Discovery of Yellowstone Park.* Reprint (1905). Lincoln: University of Nebraska Press, 1972.

_____. Preface, "The Folsom-Cook Exploration of the Upper Yellowstone in the Year 1869." In *Contributions to the Montana Historical Society*, Vol. 5. Helena: State Publishing Co., 1904, 349-355.

_____. *Vigilante Days and Ways.* Reprint (1893). Missoula: Montana State University Press, 1957.

_____. "The Wonders of the Yellowstone." Part 1. *Scribner's Monthly* 2 (May 1871): 1-17.

_____. "The Wonders of the Yellowstone." Part 2. *Scribner's Monthly* 2 (June 1871): 113-128.

Lavender, David. *The Way to the Western Sea.* New York: Harper & Row, 1988.

Leeson, Michael A., ed. *History of Montana, 1739-1885.* Chicago: Warner, Beers & Co., 1885.

Lindsley, Margaret Hawks. "Major Andrew Henry in Idaho." Pamphlet. N.p., 1985.

Malone, Michael P. "The Gallatin Canyon and the Tides of History." *Montana, The Magazine of Western History* 23 (summer 1973): 2-17.

Malone, Michael P., Richard B. Roeder, and William L. Lang. *Montana: A History of Two Centuries.* Rev. ed. Seattle: University of Washington Press, 1991.

Malouf, Carling I., and Stuart Conner, eds. "Symposium on Buffalo Jumps." *Montana Archeological Society, Memoir No. 1*, May 1962.

_____. "Missouri River Headwaters Archeology." *Archeology in Montana* 16 (January-April 1975).

Manhattan Area History. Manhattan, Mont.: Manhattan Area History Book Committee, 1986.

"Manhattan, Montana, and its Last Hundred Years." Pamphlet. Manhattan, Mont.: Manhattan Chamber of Commerce, 1968.

McClure, A. K. *Three Thousand Miles Through the Rocky Mountains.* Philadelphia: J. B. Lippincott & Co., 1869.

McDonald, James R. *Bozeman's Historic Resources.* Bozeman: City County Planning Board, 1984.

McDonald, Rita, and Merrill G. Burlingame. "Montana's First Commercial Coal Mine." *Pacific Northwest Quarterly* 47 (January 1956): 23-28.

McKelvey, S. D. *Botanical Explorations of the Trans-Mississippi West, 1790-1850.* Jamaica Plains, Mass.: Arnold Arboretum, Harvard University, 1955.

McKinnon, L. C. "Trail Blazing to Glory." *Real West* (December 1982).

Meredith, Emily R. Letter in *Frontier and Midland* 17 (summer 1937): historical section.

Michener, Thomas. "The South End of Gallatin County." *The Coast* 15 (June 1908): 431-433.

Mills, Edward Laird. *Plains, Peaks and Pioneers.* Portland, Ore.: Binfords & Mort, 1947.

Minor, Davis, Paul Bishop, and Kingston Heath, comps. *One-Room Schools of Gallatin County.* Bozeman: N.p., 1980.

Mitchell, John E. and Richard H. Hart. "The Winter of 1886-1887 Ended the Era of the Open Range." *Montana Farmer-Stockman* (February 1987).

The Montana Almanac. Missoula: University of Montana, 1957.

Morgan, Dale Lowell. *Jedediah Smith and the Opening of the West*. Lincoln: University of Nebraska Press, 1953.

_____. *The West of William H. Ashley*. Denver: Old West Publishing Co., 1964.

Murray, Robert A. *The Bozeman Trail: Highway of History*. Boulder, Colo.: Pruett Publishing Company, 1988.

Nealley, Edward B. "A Year in Montana." *Atlantic Monthly* 28 (August 1866): 236-250.

Niebel, Esther C. "A Century of Service: History of the First Methodist Church, 1866-1966 Bozeman, Montana." Pamphlet. Bozeman: First Methodist Church, 1966.

Niven, Francis. *Manhattan Omnibus: Stories of Historical Interest of Manhattan and Its Surrounding Communities*. Bozeman: F. Niven, 1989.

Osgood, Ernest Staples. "Clark on the Yellowstone, 1806." *Montana, The Magazine of Western History* 18 (summer 1968): 8.

_____. *The Day of the Cattleman*. Chicago: University of Chicago Press, 1929.

Pace, Dick. "William W. Alderson: The Editor Who Told it Like it Was," *Montana, The Magazine of Western History* 22 (winter 1972): 87-89.

Patten, George Y. "Water Rights in Montana." *Rocky Mountain Law Review* 23 (December 1950): 162-170.

Peale, A.C. *Geologic Atlas of the U.S., Three Forks Folio, Montana*. Washington, D.C.: U.S. Geological Survey, 1876.

Peavy, Linda, ed. *Canyon Cookery*. Bozeman: Bridger Canyon Women's Club, 1978.

Peavy, Linda, and Ursula Smith. *Women in Waiting in the Westward Movement*. Norman: University of Oklahoma Press, 1994.

Peltier, Jerome, ed. *Banditti of the Rocky Mountains*. Minneapolis: Ross & Haines, 1964.

Perry, Eugene S. *Montana and the Geologic Past*. N.p., 1962.

Phillips, Paul C. *The Fur Trade*. 2 vols. Norman: University of Oklahoma Press, 1961.

Porter, A. Hayden. "To God Be the Glory: History of the Dry Creek Bible Church." Pamphlet. Reprint (1959). N.p., 1986.

Progressive Men of Montana. Chicago: A. W. Bowen & Co., 1900.

Putnam, James Bruce. "The Evolution of a Frontier Town: Bozeman, Montana, and Its Search for Economic Stability, 1864-1877." Reprint (Masters thesis, Montana State University at Bozeman, 1973). In *Bozeman, Montana*. Bozeman: Gallatin County Historical Society, 1988.

Quivey, Addison M. "The Yellowstone Expedition of 1874." *Contributions to the Montana Historical Society*, Vol. 1, pp. 236-250. Helena: N.p., 1876.

Rackley, Barbara Fifer. "The Hard Winter of 1886-1887." *Montana, The Magazine of Western History* 21 (winter 1971): 50-59.

Randall, Lady Isabelle. *A Lady's Ranche Life in Montana*. London: W. H. Allen & Co., 1887.

Raynolds, W. F. *Report on the Exploration of the Yellowstone and Missouri Rivers in 1859-1860*. 40th Cong., 1st sess., ex. doc. no. 77.

Rich, Melinda M. "Speech, First Presbyterian Church Quarterly Centennial, 1872-1897." Pamphlet, ed. P. C. Waite and W. M. Cobleigh. Bozeman: Gallatin County Historical Society, n.d.

Richardson, Albert D. *Beyond the Mississippi*. Hartford: American Publishing Co., 1867.

Rickey, Don, Jr. "The Big Horn Gun." *Guns* (April 1966): 24-25; 49-50.

Roberts, Albert E. *Geology and Coal Resources of the Livingston Coal Field, Gallatin and Park Counties*. United States Geological Survey, Professional Paper 526-A. Washington, D.C.: Government Printing Office, 1966.

Roe, Frances. *Army Letters From an Officer's Wife*. New York: D. Appleton & Co., 1909.

Russell, Osborne. *Journal of a Trapper, 1834-1843*. Aubrey L. Haines, ed. Lincoln: University of Nebraska Press, 1955.

Rydell, Robert, Jeffrey Safford, and Pierce Mullen. *In the People's Interest*. Bozeman: Montana State University Foundation, 1992.

Sales, A. H. *Stock Brands of Gallatin County, Montana, 1910*. N.p., 1910.

Sanders, Helen Fitzgerald. *History of Montana*. 3 vols. New York: Lewis Historical Publishing Co., 1913.

Schulessler, Raymond. "The Horse and the Plains Indian." Pamphlet. N.p.: Northern Cheyenne Planning Committee, 1972.

Seibel, Dennis. *Fort Ellis, Montana Territory, 1867-1886*. Bozeman: Dennis Seibel, 1996.

Selemeier, Lewis W. "First Camera on the Yellowstone." *Montana, The Magazine of Western History* 22 (summer 1972): 42-53.

Simms, S. C. *Traditions of the Crow*. Chicago: Field Columbian Museum, Publication 85, Vol. 2, No. 6 (October 1903).

Skarsten, M. O. *George Drouillard*. Glendale: Arthur H., Clark Company, 1964.

Smith, Phyllis. "Learning About Mabel Cruikshank." In *In Celebration of Our Past, 1989*. Bozeman: Gallatin County Historical Society, 1989.

_____. "Charles D. Loughrey: Early Bozeman Photographer." In *In Celebration of Our Past, 1990*. Bozeman: Gallatin County Historical Society, 1990.

_____. "English Days in the Gallatin Valley." In *In Celebration of Our Past, 1991*. Bozeman: Gallatin County Historical Society, 1991.

_____. "Bozeman Names Have a History." Pamphlet. Bozeman: Gallatin County Historical Society, 1996.

Smits, David D. "The Frontier Army and the Destruction of the Buffalo, 1865-1883." *Western Historical Quarterly* 25 (autumn 1994): 313-338.

Snow, Richard F. "Town at Trail's End." *American Heritage* (July-August 1992): 26-28.

Sprague, Marshall. "The Dude From Limerick." *American West* 3 (fall 1966): 53-61, 92-94.

Staudohar, Connie. "Bozeman Women's Heritage Trail." Pamphlet. Bozeman: N.p., 1994.

Steen, Herman. *The O. W. Fisher Heritage*. N.p.: Frank McCaffrey Publishers, 1961.

Stegner, Wallace. *Wolf Willow*. Reprint. Lincoln: University of Nebraska Press, 1980.

Stevens, Aaron B. "Something Hidden Go and Find It." *American West* 13 (November-December 1976): 42-44.

Stevens, Isaac I. Narrative and Final Report of Exploration For a Route For a Pacific Railroad—Saint Paul to Puget Sound, 1855. Vol. 12, bk. 1, 36th Cong., 1st sess. Washington D.C.: Thomas H. Ford, 1860.

Stout, Tom. *Montana, Its Story and Biography*. 3 vols. Chicago and New York: American Historical Society, 1921.

Stuart, Granville. *Forty Years on the Frontier*. 2 vols. Paul C. Phillips, ed. Cleveland: Arthur H. Clark Co., 1925.

_____. "Montana As It Is." *Frontier* 12 (November 1931).

_____. "The Yellowstone Expedition of 1863." In *Contributions to the Montana Historical Society*. Vol. 1, pp. 187-188. Helena: N.p., 1876.

Stuart, John G., *et al. Belgrade, Montana, the First 100 Years*. Belgrade: N.p., 1936.

Sullivan, Noelle. "Lila Lee Rides into Town: Bozeman, Montana, and the Coming of the Movies." In *In Celebration of Our Past, 1991*. Bozeman: Gallatin County Historical Society, 1991.

Swartout, Robert R., Jr. "The Chinese Experience in Frontier Montana." In *Montana Heritage*. Helena: Montana Historical Society Press, 1992.

Swenson, Janet. *Victims: The Story of Kari Swenson*. Boulder, Colo.: Pruett Publishing Co., 1989.

Swett, Ira. "Montana Trolleys." *Interurban Magazine* 27 (spring 1970): 26-43.

Tessendorf, K. C. "Red Death on the Missouri." *American West* 14 (January-February 1977): 48-53.

Thane, James L., Jr. "The Myth of Confederate Sentiment in Montana." *Montana, The Magazine of Western History* 17 (April 1967): 14-19.

Thomas, Davis and Karin Ronnefeldt, eds. "Winter at Fort Clark," *American West* 14 (January-February 1977): 36.

Thompson, Larry S. *Montana's Explorers: The Pioneer Naturalists*. Helena: Montana Magazine Inc., 1985.

Thrapp, Dan L. *Vengeance! The Saga of Poor Tom Cover*. El Segundo, Calif.: Upton & Sons Publishers, 1989.

Thwaites, Reuben Gold. "Newly Discovered Personal Records of Lewis and Clark." *Scribner's Magazine* (June 1904).

_____, ed. *The Original Journals of the Lewis and Clark Expedition, 1804-1806*. 8 vols. New York: Dodd, Mead & Co., 1904.

Tkach, John R., ed. *Medicine in Bozeman, Montana*. Bozeman: N.p., 1983.

Todd, Bayard, and Erma Todd. "Salesville and the Todd Family." Pamphlet. N.p., 1984. In the collections of the Gallatin County Historical Society, Bozeman, Montana.

Toole, K. Ross. *Montana, An Uncommon Land.* Norman: University of Oklahoma Press, 1959.

Topping, Eugene S. *Chronicles of the Yellowstone.* Saint Paul: Pioneer Press Co., 1883.

Tracy, Sarah J. Bessey. *The Diary and Reminiscences of Mrs. William H. Tracy.* Bozeman: Gallatin County Historical Society, 1985.

Trail, E. B. "The Life and Adventures of John Colter." *Old Travois Trails* 2 (January-February 1942).

Tuttle, Daniel S. *Reminiscences of a Missionary Bishop.* New York: Thomas Whittaker, 1906.

Vichorek, Daniel N. *Montana's Homestead Era.* Helena: Montana Magazine, Inc., 1987.

Victor, Frances Fuller. *The River of the West: The Adventures of Joe Meek.* Missoula: Mountain Press Publishing Co., 1983.

Waldron, Ellis L. *Montana Politics Since 1864.* Missoula: University of Montana Press, 1958.

Walter, Dave. "The Baker Massacre." *Montana Magazine* (March-April 1987): 61-68.

Webb, Walter Prescott. *The Great Plains.* Boston: Ginn & Company, 1931.

Weibert, Don. *The 1874 Invasion of Montana: A Prelude to the Custer Disaster.* N.p.: Don Weibert, 1993.

Wessel, Thomas R. "Introduction." *Agricultural History* 51 (January 1977).

Whithorn, Doris. "Coal Mining in Park and Gallatin Counties." In *In Celebration of Our Past, 1989.* Bozeman: Gallatin County Historical Society, 1989.

_____. *Photo History of Livingston-Bozeman Coal Country.* Livingston: Park County News, n.d.

Whithorn, Doris, and Bill Whithorn. "Montana—In the Good Old Days." Pamphlet. Nos. 1 and 2. Livingston: Park County News, 1967.

Williams, Lyle K. "Historically Speaking: Stories of the Men and Women Who Explored and Settled the Missouri River Headwaters." Pamphlet. Bozeman: Gallatin County Historical Society, 1976.

Wilson, M. L. "Evolution of Montana Agriculture in Its Early Period." *Proceedings of the Mississippi Valley Historical Association* 9 (1917-1918): 429-435.

Wojtowicz, Richard. *From Fish Farming to Fisheries Science: The Evolution of the Bozeman Fish Technology Center, 1892-1992.* Bozeman: Gallatin County Historical Society, 1992.

Wolcott, Phyllis Davis. "The Saga of Doc Nelson." Pamphlet. Bozeman: Gallatin County Historical Society, n.d.

Word, Samuel. "Diary of Colonel Samuel Word, Trip Across the Plains Starting at St. Joe, Missouri, May 7, 1863 and Arriving at Virginia City, Montana, October 3, 1863." *Contributions to the Montana Historical Society*, Vol. 8, pp. 37-92. Helena: State Publishing Co., 1917.

Wormington, H. M. *Ancient Man in North America.* Denver: Denver Museum of Natural History, Popular Series No. 4, 4th ed., 1957.

Wunder, John R. "The Law and Chinese in Frontier Montana." *Montana, The Magazine of Western History* 30 (July 1980): 18-31.

Yeager, Hattie Korine. "Bountiful Bozeman." *Montana Magazine* 63 (January-February 1984).

A P P E N D I X

GAZETTEER OF GEOGRAPHICAL NAMES
IN THE GALLATIN AREA

Accola: Small settlement, railroad siding, and elevator on the Milwaukee Road branch line from Bozeman to Menard. Named for Louis Accola.

Aldridge: Mining camp near Corwin Springs, now in Park County.

Almart: Lodge with store and cafe in Gallatin Canyon run by Alma and Art Vandecar in the 1940s.

Amsterdam: Unincorporated town in the Holland Settlement south of Manhattan that developed along the Northern Pacific branch line to Anceney in 1911. Earlier called Walrath.

Anaconda Copper: Mining area and coking operation on Meadow Creek near Storrs, south of Chestnut.

Anceney: Southern terminus of Northern Pacific branch line from Manhattan; was shipping point of Flying D Ranch cattle. Named for Charles Anceney who orginally spelled his surname "Anxionnaz."

Antelope Country: Early name for area south of Manhattan. Also called Hillyside.

Antelope Gardens: A site near Sappington where Fred and Josie Norris raised vegetables for commercial market.

Arnold: Railroad siding between Amsterdam and Anceney. Named for George Arnold, who died tragically while driving a horse-drawn combine.

Atkins: Settlement north of Gallatin Gateway and south of Axtell Bridge. Named for Cary Atkins.

Baker: Settlement east of Maudlow and south of Josephine. Later called Highlands.

Baker's Island: Island in the Jefferson River near Three Forks.

Balmont: A stop on the Gallatin Valley Railroad south of Bozeman. Before 1915, it was called Ballantyne.

Ballantyne: Earlier name for Balmont. Named for Edson Ballantyne.

Bannack: First capital of Montana Territory located in Madison County. Capital moved to Virginia City in 1865.

Bangtail: Camp just over Gallatin County border in Park County, in the Bangtail range.

Basin: Settlement in Gallatin Canyon; also called Spanish Creek.

Battle Ridge: The divide on Bridger Canyon Road; water on the south flows toward the Gallatin River; water on the east flows to the Shields River. Site of 1871 Indian-white conflict.

Bear Gulch: Earlier name for Jardine, a settlement northeast of Gardiner in Park County.

Bear Trap: Narrow canyon through which the Madison River flows on its way to Three Forks.

Beckman Flat: Area in Gallatin Canyon south of Squaw Creek settled by the Beckman family.

Belden: Coal mining community near Storrs.

Belgrade: Founded in the 1880s by Thomas Quaw to serve the new Northern Pacific railroad. Named for Serbian investors in the line. Incorporated in 1907.

Benson's Landing: Ferry operation south of present Livingston in Park County. Named for Amos Benson.

Big Sky: Resort on the West Fork of the Gallatin River built by newscaster Chet Huntley and others. Earlier called Crail.

Black Bear: Snow measuring station south of West Yellowstone.

Black's Crossing: Stage stop at Madison River Junction in 1890s.

Blacktail Pass: South of Maudlow at 5,840 feet.

Blackwood: Railroad siding and stockyard on the Gallatin Valley Railroad near Gallatin Gateway. Named for Edward L. Blackwood.

Blueberry Hill: Landfill two miles north of Bozeman.

Bozeman: Town named for trailmaker and settler John Bozeman on August 9, 1864. Called Jacobs' Crossing for short time. Became second county seat in 1867.

Bozeman Hot Springs: Natural hot springs and spa west of Bozeman. Earlier called Matthews Hot Springs, after owner Jerry Matthews. Later called Ferris Hot Springs, after owner E. M. Ferris.

Bozeman Pass: 5,712-foot pass east of Bozeman. Earlier called Yellowstone Pass.

Brackett: Settlement near Clyde Park. Named for Colonel C. G. Brackett, who brought the Second Cavalry to Fort Ellis in 1869.

Brewer: Railroad stop and spring north of Bozeman. Named for Henry Brewer.

Bridger Bowl: Ski resort seventeen miles north of Bozeman in Bridger Canyon.

Bridger Canyon: Northeast of Bozeman. Named for mountain man and guide Jim Bridger.

Bridger Pass: On Bridger Canyon Road at 6,138 feet.

Bridgetown: Early name for Old Town (Three Forks).

Bridgeville: Early name for Old Town (Three Forks).

Brown Hollow: Camp south of Gallatin Gateway.

Brown's Camp: Settlement in Gallatin Canyon.

Buck's T-4: Camp and dude ranch in Gallatin Canyon established by Helen and Buck Knight in the 1940s.

Buell: Railroad siding between Manhattan and Amsterdam. Named for Buell Heeb. Also called Heeb.

Buffalo Orchard: Area one mile east of Manhattan near Dry Creek.

Busch: Railroad siding north of Wisner between Bozeman and Menard. Named for railroad man Paul Busch.

Buttleman's: Railroad siding north of Willow Creek.

Buttermilk: Camp near Hebgen Lake.

Cabin Creek: Area near Hebgen Lake damaged by 1959 earthquake.

Camp Baker: Military camp and sawmill in Bridger Canyon. Used by Fort Ellis soldiers in the 1860s.

Camp Clark: See Camp Creek.

Camp Creek: Stage and railroad stop on the Gallatin Valley Railroad. Also called Camp Clark.

Camp Elizabeth Meagher: 1867 military camp eight miles east of Bozeman.

Camp Fairy: Camp near Fairy Lake in the Bridger Range.

Camp Ida Thoroughman: 1867 military camp at the mouth of the Shields River, four miles northeast of the present Livingston.

Camp Waters: Area north of Porcupine Creek on east side of Gallatin Canyon.

Camp Wilson: Camp on Buffalo Horn Creek in Gallatin Canyon. Named for Sam Wilson.

Camona: Railroad siding on branch line from Bozeman to Menard. Named for woman who waved the trains through and who reportedly always wore a kimono.

Canyon: Settlement on Sixteenmile Creek north of Josephine.

Canyon House: Stage stop on site of what would become Logan.

Cardinal: Station and siding on Sixteenmile Creek, north of Three Forks.

Carpenter: Railroad siding between Logan and Three Forks. Named for potato grower William Carpenter.

Catron: Railroad siding near Bozeman on the Gallatin Valley Railroad.

Cedar View: Settlement eight miles northeast of Manhattan.

Cedarview (Cedar Knoll, Pine Butte): Settlement west of Bozeman.

Center Hill: Coal mining area three miles south of Bozeman Pass.

Central Park: Settlement with ford and tollgate east of Manhattan. First site: west side of Gallatin River, later known as Old Central Park. Settlement moved to east side of river and named Cockrell's Bridge. Later named Fly or Fly's Bridges after William Fly. Renamed Creamery. Later called Central Park.

Chapman: Depot on Gallatin Valley Railroad after Gilroy stop. Named for John Chapman.

Chestnut: Coal mining town east of Bozeman. Named for Colonel James C. Chesnut. Postal authorities added the extra "t."

Chico: Settlement and hot springs in Yellowstone Valley, now in Park County.

Chimney Rock: Settlement south of Chestnut with saloon and post office.

Chisholm: Camp in the Hyalite region; named for the Chisholm family.

Churchill: Settlement seven miles south of Manhattan. Earlier called Godrey and Rotterdam.

Cinnabar: Settlement in Park County near Chico.

Cinnamon: Camp on creek near peak of same name in Gallatin Canyon.

CCC Camp: A Civilian Conservation Corps camp on Squaw Creek on Gallatin Canyon in the 1930s.

Clarkston: Settlement north of Logan, named for Guy Clark. Earlier called Magpie and Evergreen.

Clyde Park (or Clydepark): Settlement near the Shields River that takes its name from Clydesdale horses. Earlier called Sunnyside. Now in Park County.

Cobb Hill: Area six miles west of Bozeman. Named for Cobb family.

Cobette: Railroad stop south of West Yellowstone on the Oregon Short Line Railroad.

Cockrell's Bridge: See Central Park.

Cokedale: Coal mining community, now in Park County, where decaying coke ovens can still be seen. William Willams built the first coke oven there in 1881. Earlier called Williams.

Cooperhill: Logging camp in Bear Canyon west of Bozeman. Named for Walter Cooper.

Corette: Railroad siding on the Oregon Short Line on the South Fork of the Madison River. Named for a railroad attorney.

Coulston: Coal mining settlement near Storrs.

Courts: Earlier name for Reese Creek settlement.

Cowans: Settlement near Belgrade.

Craig: Settlement on Sixteenmile Creek.

Crail: Earlier name for Big Sky.

Cramer: See Springhill.

Crane: Railroad stop north of Clarkston.

Creamery: See Central Park.

Curtis Grove: Area near Baker Creek on Amsterdam Road.

Davies Springs: Twin springs at the mouth of Bridger Canyon, one warm and one cold, owned by W. J. Davies and sold to the federal government for the first fish hatchery.

Deer Park: Railroad siding and depot on Sixteenmile Creek.

Delamator: Coal mining settlement near Storrs.

Diamond City: Gold mining camp during the 1860s east of Helena, first in Gallatin County, then in Meagher County, now in Broadwater County. Confederate soldiers found gold in paying quantities in nearby Confederate Gulch.

Dogtown: Settlement near Four Corners on Middle Creek. Named because of great number of dogs on that site. Also called Middle Creek and Middleton.

Dry Creek: Settlement north of Belgrade and east of Manhattan.

Dumphy: Stage stop at Hamilton, west of the Gallatin River and south of Manhattan.

Duncan: Settlement north of Manhattan. Named for Scott Duncan.

Durham: Small settlement north of Menard.

Durston: Settlement west of Bozeman. Named for John H. Durston.

Dwelle's: Stage stop near Grayling. Named after Harry Dwelle.

East Gallatin: Community north of the East Gallatin River.

Edilou: Railroad siding on Bozeman-Menard line. Named after children of C. L. Allen.

Eldredge or Eldridge: Logging settlement in Gallatin Canyon. Also called Tie Camp.

Electric: Mining camp in Park County. Earlier called Horr.

Elk Creek: Settlement between Anceney and the Madison River.

Emigrant: See Fridley.

Erlice: Railroad siding on Milwaukee Railroad. Named for daughter of Taylor Hamilton.

Evergreen: See Clarkston.

Farmington: C. P. Blakeley's ranch, south of Central Park, designated as the county seat by the 1866 Legislature, revoked in 1869.

Ferris Hot Springs: See Bozeman Hot Springs.

Flathead Pass: East of Menard at 6,915 feet.

Fleming: Settlement east of Josephine and Middle Fork Creek.

Fly: See Central Park.

Flying D Ranch: Large ranch south of Anceney. Once cattle and horses grazed there; now it is a bison ranch.

Fort Ellis: Military fort east of Bozeman which operated from 1867 to 1887. Named for Colonel Augustus Van Horne Ellis, a Union officer killed at Gettysburg.

Fort Martin: Area where Yellowstone National Park buses were housed behind Gallatin Gateway Inn.

Francis: Settlement north of Maudlow on Sixteenmile Creek. Named after rancher Dean Francis. Earlier called Josephine.

Fridley: Settlement in Yellowstone Valley (now Park County). Named for Franklin Frederick Fridley, early Bozeman merchant. Now called Emigrant.

Fuller: See Gilroy.

Gallatin City: Settlement first established on west side of Madison-Jefferson River in 1863. Named for Albert Gallatin, Secretary of the Treasury during presidency of Thomas Jefferson. Settlement moved to east side of river one year later. Was first county seat.

Gallatin Gateway: Earlier settlement at mouth of Gallatin Canyon called Salesville. The Milwaukee Railroad changed its name to present Gallatin Gateway in 1927.

Gallatin Post: Military station on Specimen Creek in Gallatin Canyon.

Gallatin Station: Railroad station near Gallatin City south of Trident.

Gallop: Community in the north Dry Creek area. Named after rancher James H. Gallop.

Garden Gulch: Horseshoe Hills community near Dunbar Springs. After the earthquake of 1925, the springs no longer provided enough water for agriculture and the settlement died.

Gardiner: Community at north entrance to Yellowstone National Park, now in Park County.

Garfield: Settlement in 1860s.

Gilroy: Settlement east of Bozeman Hot Springs. Earlier called Fuller.

Godfrey: See Churchill.

Gooch Hill: Settlement between Bozeman and Gallatin Gateway. Named after Ed Gooch.

Goodell: Railroad stop four miles west of Maudlow.

Gowan: Railroad siding northeast of Belgrade.

Gowan Grove: Recreation area northeast of Belgrade.

Grayling: Settlement north of West Yellowstone. Also called Basin-Grayling.

Green Hollow: Settlement south of Salesville in 1880s.

Greenwood: Railroad siding south of Belgrade.

Groves: Mining settlement near Storrs.

Hamilton: Stage stop southeast of Manhattan. Named for Ted Hamilton. Settlement moved closer to Northern Pacific Railroad in 1884 and renamed Moreland. Renamed again Manhattan in 1891.

Harrison: Madison County community. Named for rancher Henry C. Harrison.

Hatfield: Settlement south of Sixteen.

Havana or Havana Ridge: Gold and silver town between the Madison and Gallatin Rivers and between Cherry and Spanish Creeks.

Headwaters State Park: Located near the three forks of the Missouri River south of Trident. Founded by Clark M. Maudlin.

Heeb: Railroad siding between Manhattan and Amsterdam named for Buell Heeb. Also called Buell.

Helena: Third capital of Montana, established in 1875. One hundred-some miles northwest of Bozeman. See also Bannack and Virginia City.

Henderson: 1870s settlement named for postmaster Stokes Henderson, who served from July to November 1878.

Highlands: Settlement forty miles north of Bozeman. Earlier called Baker.

Hillman: Railroad stop on Bozeman-Menard line. Named for A. J. Hillman.

Hills: Original site of Holland Settlement.

Hillsdale: Settlement south of Menard.

Hillyside: Early name for bench area south of Manhattan and west of Amsterdam.

Hodgman: Settlement east of Salesville on South Cottonwood Creek.

Hoffman: Coal mining community eight miles south of Chestnut. Named after State Senator Charles Hoffman.

Holland (Holland Station): Depot west of Cameron Bridge.

Hood Creek: Camp on Hood Creek near Hyalite Reservoir.

Horr: Mining settlement north of Gardiner, now in Park County. Later called Electric.

Horseshoe Hills: A series of arid hills at the north of the valley, named for the curious horseshoe bends in the Missouri River to the immediate west.

Hunter Hot Springs: Hot springs and spa now in Park County developed by Dr. Andrew Jackson Hunter in 1878.

Hyde: Settlement south of Logan, occasionally called Hutchison.

Initial Point: Survey point to establish Principal Meridian and Principal Parallel in 1867, located four and one-half miles south and one mile west of Willow Creek.

Jacob's Crossing: Named as a settlement in the claim association minutes of August 9, 1864 after trailmaker John J. Jacobs, partner of John Bozeman. The city of Bozeman was also named at that meeting.

Josephine: Settlement east of Maudlow on Sixteenmile Creek. Named after member of railroad man J. A. Harlow's family. Called Francis after 1939.

Karst: Site of 1901 Cold Spring Resort in Gallatin Canyon, founded by Pete Karst. Later called Karst Kamp.

Kerns: Railroad siding near Bozeman on the Gallatin Valley Railroad.

Kirkwood: Resort on the north side of Hebgen Lake.

Lay Settlement: Area south and east of Salesville, settled by members of the Lay family in the 1880s.

Leader: Early name of town of Ringling northeast of Bozeman, now in Park County.

Little Bear: Community southeast of Gallatin Gateway.

Livingston: Park County town on the Yellowstone River originally in Gallatin County. Earlier called Clark.

Logan: Unincorporated railroad center named after Adeline Logan family in 1885. Earlier called Canyon House.

Lombard: Railroad town on east side of Missouri River north of Three Forks with hotel and stores. Named for G. A. Lombard in 1903.

Lower Bridger: Community in Bridger Canyon, five miles from Bozeman, with school and creamery.

Lower Madison: Community south of Logan.

Lux: Railroad siding north of Bozeman. Named for farmer John Lux.

Madison Buffalo Jump: A pishkun seven miles south of Logan where Indian hunters chased bison over the cliffs to their death.

Magpie: Early name for Clarkston.

Mammoth Hot Springs: Headquarters for Yellowstone National Park, five miles south of Gardiner.

Manhattan: A town named in 1891 by New York malting company investors. First community called Hamilton which was one mile southeast of present site. In 1883, the settlement moved closer to the railroad and renamed Moreland by British horse breeders.

Matthews Hot Springs: Jerry Matthews first owned this spa; E. M. Ferris bought it and renamed it; now it is Bozeman Hot Springs.

Maudlow: Railroad town on Sixteenmile Creek. Named for Maud Harlow, wife of railroad man R. A. Harlow. Supported school, shops, post office, and grain storage.

Maxey: Coal mining settlement on Trail Creek Road, now in Park County. Post office at Chimney Rock.

McLees: Railroad siding north of Central Park. Named for I. S. McLees.

McLeod: Settlement south of Big Timber, now in Sweet Grass County.

Meadow: Coal mining area.

Menard: Community north of Belgrade, named for Teleford Menard, terminus of Turkey Red Railroad. Had grain elevator, post office, and community center.

Mica: Camp on Mica Creek in Spanish Creek Primitive Area.

Middle Creek: 1869 community on creek of same name.

Middleton: See Middle Creek and Dogtown.

Miller: Coal mining community near Timberline.

Minden: Railroad siding on Sixteenmile Creek.

Minor: Settlement now called Tom Miner.

Moose: Camp at head of Moose Creek.

Moose Flat: Camp north of Karst Kamp.

Moreland: See Hamilton and Manhattan.

Mountainside: Settlement south and east of Chestnut on Turkey Trail Railroad.

Muffane: Loading area on Milwaukee Railroad south of Menard.

Muir: Settlement named for railroad tunnel contractor John Muir, which was on divide between Livingston and Bozeman.

Murphy: Mining town south of Chestnut.

Nathon (Naltron): Railroad station on Sixteenmile Creek.

Nelson Ford (Nelson's Crossing): Settlement south of Central Park, established by John N. Nelson in 1864.

Norris: Town now in Madison County. Named for rancher Alexander Norris about 1880.

No Thirty: Camp in coal mining area.

Old Canyon: Railroad station near Lombard.

Old Town: Settlement northeast of present Three Forks, incorporated in 1884.

Ophir: Settlement in Gallatin Canyon on Porcupine Creek, meaning "Valley of Gold." Also called Porcupine.

Painted Canyon: Settlement near Lombard.

Pass Creek: Settlement near Menhard, west of Flathead Pass.

Patterson: Depot and railroad siding south of Bozeman. Named for J. L. Patterson.

Paul: Railroad stop on Gallatin Valley Railroad. Named after hotel man Asher Paul.

Pease: Railroad siding south of Amsterdam.

Penwell Settlement: Community near Springhill.

Pine Butte: Settlement west of Bozeman. Also called Cedarview.

Pony: Madison County gold town in the Tobacco Root Mountains. Named for Tecumseh Smith, nicknamed "Pony" because of his small stature. Town earlier called Strawberry.

Porcupine: See Ophir.

Potter: Settlement south of Bozeman Hot Springs, northeast of Axtell Bridge.

Powers: Railroad siding on the Northern Pacific line. Named for Glen Powers.

Pray: Settlement now in Park County.

Primus: Settlement near Pony in Madison County.

Rea: Settlement west of Bozeman.

Reasville: Settlement on Cherry Creek. Named for George Rea.

Recap (Rekap): Railroad siding between Trident and Clarkston operating about 1912.

Red Bluff: Mining town east of Norris in Madison County.

Reese Creek: Agricultural settlement on Reese Creek, which supported a store, blacksmith shop, cheese factory, church, and school. Named after settler John E. Reese.

Ringling: Town north of Livingston in Meagher County, named for noted circus family. Also called Leader.

Riverside: Earlier name for West Yellowstone. Also called Yellowstone.

Riverside Station: Settlement four miles east of West Yellowstone in Yellowstone National Park. Also called Wonderland.

Rock Creek: Settlement in Park County. Also called Criswell.

Romola or Ramola: Post office fourteen miles west of Bozeman.

Ross: Coal mining settlement between Timberline and Bozeman Pass.

Rotterdam: See Churchill.

Salesville: Community at mouth of Gallatin Canyon. Named for settler Zachariah Sales. Earlier called Slabtown because of logging activity. Renamed Gallatin Gateway in 1927.

Sand Creek: Mining community near Sappington around 1900.

Sappington: Settlement near the western edge of Gallatin County. Named for Henry H. Sappington.

Sedan: Settlement east of Flathead Pass and north of Livingston with stores and a cheese factory.

Sexton: Settlement near Springhill. Named for William O. Sexton.

Shedd's (Shed's, Shedd's Bridges): Community surrounding toll bridge on Madison River. Named for James Shedd, builder of bridges.

Sixteen: Settlement with depot and store on Sixteenmile Creek.

Skull: 1912 settlement east of Lombard.

Smokey Hollow: Area south of Chestnut.

Spain: Railroad siding on Northern Pacific Railroad named for Spain family.

Spanish Creek: Settlement in Gallatin Canyon. Also called Basin.

Springdale: Settlement along the Yellowstone River now in Park County. Area where John Bozeman was murdered.

Springhill: Settlement north of Bozeman below Ross Peak. Water-powered industries included distilleries, a furniture factory, flour mills, sawmills, and a blacksmith shop. Earlier called Cramer.

Squaw Creek: Site of ranger station and CCC camp in Gallatin Canyon.

Storey: Railroad siding between Belgrade and Bozeman.

Storrey: Settlement southeast of Chestnut on Northern Pacific line.

Storrs: Coal mining community three miles south of Chestnut. Named for Lucius S. Storrs. Site of Anaconda Copper coking operation.

Strawberry: Early name for Pony.

Sturgis Ranch: Stage stop and post office near Willow Creek.

Summerset: Settlement with store south of Maudlow.

Sunnyside: Settlement with post office at mouth of Brackett Creek in Bridger Canyon.

Three Forks: Settlement incorporated December 1909. Received its post office from Old Town during the night in 1908. See also Old Town, Bridgeville, Bridgeton.

Tie Camp: Another name for Eldridge (or Eldredge) in Gallatin Canyon.

Timber: Railroad siding on the Oregon Short Line near the head of the South Fork of the Madison River.

Timberline: Coal community near Bozeman Pass, operated by the Northern Pacific for fuel.

Torbet: Railroad siding named for a local rancher between Busch and Hillman on the Turkey Red railroad to Menard.

Trident: Settlement near three forks of the Missouri River centered around cement industry. County's largest employer in 1910. Once contained fifty company houses, post office, and general store.

Upper Bridger: Community in Bridger Canyon centered around school.

Upper Ross: Coal mining settlement east of Bozeman near Timberline.

Vaters: Coal town with post office east of Chestnut.

Vincent: Railroad siding between Amsterdam and Anceney. Named for Webb Vincent.

Virginia City: Second capital of Montana from 1865 to 1875, located in Madison County.

Walrath: Railroad siding on site of future Amsterdam. Named for attorney and rancher Andrew Walrath.

West End: Railroad siding and depot east of Bozeman near Northern Pacfic tunnel.

West Gallatin: Depot and stockyard on west side of Gallatin River one mile from Shedd's Bridge.

Westlake: Railroad siding on Amsterdam-Anceney branch line.

West Yellowstone: Settlement once called Riverside and Yellowstone, grew to town at west entrance to Yellowstone National Park when Oregon Short Line Railroad was built from Idaho in 1908. Incorporated in 1966. Now year-round recreation area.

Whiskey Point: Settlement with saloon two miles south of Chestnut.

White Siding: Railroad stop three miles south of Manhattan.

Willow Creek: Once a railroad community with post office, hotel, and general stores. Nearby Willow Creek was called the Philosophy River by explorers Lewis and Clark. Earlier called Windville.

Wilsall: Community now in Park County. Named for Albert Culbertson's son Will and daughter-in-law Sally.

Wilson Creek: Settlement southeast of Gallatin Gateway.

Windville: Early name for Willow Creek.

Wisner: Railroad stop on Bozeman-Menard line.

Woodland: Coal mining settlement south of Bozeman Pass.

Wylie's Camp: Settlement on Spanish Creek where W. W. Wylie, sometime Bozeman Superintendent of Schools, kept horses used for Yellowstone National Park tourist stages.

Yellowstone: Early name for West Yellowstone. Also called Riverside.

Yellowstone Pass: Early name for Bozeman Pass.

Note: For a more extensive treatment of area names and information, see Grace Bates, *Gallatin County: Places and Things, Past and Present,* rev. ed. (Bozeman: Grace Bates, 1994).

INDEX